A Fire in Their Hearts

3-16-06

To Bob

With warm regards
and respect,

Best wishes
Tony

A Fire in Their Hearts

Yiddish Socialists in New York

Tony Michels

Harvard University Press

Cambridge, Massachusetts, and London, England   2005

Publication of this book has been aided by a grant
from the Koret Foundation.

Library of Congress Cataloging-in-Publication Data

Michels, Tony.
A fire in their hearts : Yiddish socialists in New York / Tony Michels.
   p. cm.
Includes bibliographical references and index.
ISBN 0-674-01913-X (alk. paper)
1. Jewish socialists—New York (State)—New York—History—19th century.
2. Jewish socialists—New York (State)—New York—History—20th century.
3. Immigrants—New York (State)—New York—Political activity.
4. Yiddish language—Social aspects—New York (State)—New York.
5. Jews, East European—New York (State)—New York—History.
6. Working class Jews—New York (State)—New York—History.
7. Labor movement—New York (State)—New York—History.
8. New York (N.Y.)—Ethnic relations   I. Title.
HX550.J4M53 2005
335'.0092'39240747—dc22   2005050263

Designed by Gwen Nefsky Frankfeldt

Acknowledgments

I am indebted to a long list of people who played an important role in the writing of this book. Ann Lane and Barbara Epstein of the University of California–Santa Cruz stimulated my curiosity in the troubled history of the American left and encouraged me to become a historian. As a graduate student at Stanford University, I was fortunate to be able to study the history of Jews, American workers, and socialist and nationalist movements with Arnold Eisen, Mark Mancall, Aron Rodrigue, Karen Sawislak, and Steve Zipperstein. I benefited tremendously from their broadmindedness, knowledge, and generosity. I am especially grateful to Mark Mancall for accepting me into Stanford's Jewish studies program against all good judgment. His wide-ranging intellect and indifference to academic pretensions never ceased to amaze and delight me. Further to my benefit, Steve Zipperstein mentored me with uncommon care from beginning to end. Steve's erudition and high standards have been ongoing sources of inspiration. He remains a valued advisor and friend. I am also indebted to my fellow graduate students with whom I spent countless hours talking, commiserating, joking, and reading one another's work. I continue to learn from and enjoy the camaraderie of Cecile Kuznitz, Michelle McClellan, Ken Moss, Steve Rappaport, Jon Schoenwald, Nina Spiegal, and Sarah Stein. I am thankful to Hanna Berman, my first Yiddish teacher, for her ongoing friendship and excellent cooking. Having mentioned Yiddish, I must convey my gratitude to Gele and Joshua Fishman, Dr. Mordkhe Schaechter, and Avrom Novershtern for deepening my knowledge of Yiddish, as well as my love and respect for the language and its literature. The assistance of librarians and archivists at Stanford University's Green Library, New York University's Tamiment Institute, and the YIVO Institute for Jewish Research enabled me to conduct much of the research for this book. I thus offer my heartfelt thanks to Zachary Baker, Leo Greenbaum, Roger Kohn, Heidi Lerner, and Sonia Moss. Jesse Cohen of YIVO's photo archive rescued me at two critical moments. I owe a special thanks to Zachary Schrag for donating a family portrait used in this book.

At the University of Wisconsin–Madison I've enjoyed unflagging support from my colleagues in the History Department and the Moss/ Weinstein Center for Jewish Studies. Rachel Brenner, Chuck Cohen, Bill Cronon, Stan Kutler, Florencia Mallon, the late Elaine Marks, David Mc-Donald, Bill Reese, Mary Lou Roberts, Richard Ross, Stan Schultz, Steve Stern, and Lee Wandel provided invaluable assistance, encouragement, and advice. Jeremi Suri graciously introduced me to my future editor, Kathleen McDermott. Fran Hirsch and Brett Sheehan closely read early drafts of chapters, but also gave much more; a brief acknowledgment cannot convey my appreciation to them. My cousin, colleague, and future collaborator Jonathan Pollack and I spent many interesting hours discussing music, television, and the less respectable aspects of American Jewish history. I am very thankful to Ellen Litman for commenting on the manuscript with extraordinary thoughtfulness at the eleventh hour. Thea Browder and Ereck Jarvis gave very helpful research and editorial assistance. Patrick Michelson provided able translations from the Russian press. I could not have asked for a better group of friends and colleagues with whom to discuss the difficulties of writing and, equally important, escape from those difficulties when needed. Hawley Fogg-Davis, Jim Feldman, Steve Fram, Chad Goldberg, Jon Ivri and Simone Schweber, Amaud Johnson and Cherene Sherrard Johnson, Carol Lee, Dave Leheny, Tamir Moustaffa, Amy Quan Berry, Jon Schofer, Shifra Sharlin, and Ethelene Whitmire lent a sympathetic ear on more occasions than I can recall and more, no doubt, than they would care to remember. The late Herbert Hill made a deep impression on me over the course of many conversations about Jewish history, socialism, and African American history. I regret that I did not finish this book in time for Herbert to see it in print. Finally, I want to thank my colleague and mentor David Sorkin, who helped me in more ways than I probably realize. I consistently relied on David for sound advice, creative ideas, and the confidence to keep going. I could not have completed the book without him.

Outside Madison, Hasia Diner's concern, expertise, and generosity helped me see this book into print. David Fishman and Eli Lederhendler offered several important suggestions when this project was in its early phase. They might not remember this by now, but their comments influenced portions of the book. I benefited from many stimulating discussions with Eric Goldstein and his thoughtful comments on parts of the manuscript. Alisa Braun, Libby Garland, Annie Polland, and Daniel Soyer generously shared their research with me and opened my eyes to new aspects of American Jewish history. Eddie Portnoy and I spent hours discussing the minutia of the Yiddish press, as well as the more obscure reaches of American popular culture. Jeannine King played an intimate part in this book from its inception. Ronit Lerer-Shpak helped me to understand Chaim Zhitlovsky from a new perspective. Linda Ellis offered her ingenuity at a particularly crucial moment and taught me a lesson in persistence. Paula Daccarett's intellectual integrity, passion for history, and friendship buoyed my spirits throughout. Ralph DiLeone and Mark Vederman consistently highlighted the humorous aspects of American Jewish history. Mitch Hart, Cecile Kuznitz, and Ken Moss gave valuable comments on the manuscript and true friendship. And, finally, there is Vikram Parekh, who, whether in Santa Cruz, Afghanistan, Jersey City, or Kashmir never failed to come up with unconventional insights into the modern Jewish experience, the meaning of diaspora, and the importance of style.

It has been a great pleasure to work with Kathleen McDermott and her staff at Harvard University Press. I'm honored and gratified that Kathleen perceived a potentially worthwhile book in what was originally a rough manuscript. I could not have asked for a more thoughtful, professional, and humane editor. I also want to extend my gratitude to Ann

Twombly for her patient care in copyediting the manuscript. Harvard's anonymous readers helped me to improve and refine the finished product; I thank them for their valuable suggestions. I would be remiss if I forgot to express my appreciation to the following institutions for funding the research and writing of this book during its various stages: the YIVO Institute for Jewish Research, the Koret Foundation, the Littauer Foundation, the Memorial Foundation for Jewish Culture, the National Foundation for Jewish Culture, and the Graduate School of the University of Wisconsin.

A group of old, dear friends lifted my morale during the physically and emotionally taxing period spent writing this book. They kept things in perspective the way only childhood friends can. For their lasting friendship and humor, I thank Marc Auger, Sara Bromberg, Chris Friederich, Keith Gill, Brian Gingerich, Stiv Guisinger, Stett Holbrook, Joey Huebner, Paul Largent, Nicky Miljevich, Sharon Mishler, Dave Nelson, Laura Rattner, Leticia Ruano, Rudy Ruano and Ann Krolczyk, Matt Walker and Erin Dunavin Walker, Mark and Marie Wightman, and Mike Young. More than once they wondered what the hell I've been doing all these years—now they know.

Finally, I want to thank my siblings, Dana, Debbie, and Andy, for their undying love and devotion, blessings I regard as irreplaceable. I'm grateful to my beloved niece Hannah Michels, who closely read and commented on the manuscript twice. And, above all, I owe a debt of gratitude that cannot possibly be repaid to my mother, Eleanore Michels. Her contributions defy description, so I dedicate my book to her with deep love and respect.

Contents

Illustrations

A Fire in Their Hearts

Introduction

Socialism in American Jewish History

In March 1895 Abraham Cahan sat down to mark the fifth anniversary of New York's popular socialist Yiddish weekly *Di arbeter tsaytung (The Workers' Newspaper)*. Cahan, the newspaper's editor, used the opportunity to congratulate the city's immigrant Jews on how far they had progressed since his arrival from Russia thirteen years earlier. Although more Jews than ever labored in sweatshops and dwelled in filthy tenements, Cahan was impressed by the cultural and political ferment happening on the Lower East Side, the city's main Jewish quarter. New York's poor *yidn*, Cahan was pleased to report, were trying to better themselves and society. They were reading, attending lectures, demonstrating, and joining organizations. Yesterday's greenhorns, it seemed to Cahan, were becoming new people: idealistic, worldly in outlook (if not experience), and confident in themselves:

> The little Jewish soul, which five years ago was shrunken and pressed down in the narrow confines of the old, moldy little Jewish world, is today as broad as the entire world. It used to be engraved in old, faint letters: "The little Jews are my people, the Land of Israel is my small sliver of a world, and the Five Books of Moses is my religion." But now honest, large, golden letters sparkle: "Humanity is my people, the wide world is my fatherland, and helping everyone to advance toward happiness is my religion!"

Cahan acknowledged that New York's "little Jews" still had a long road to travel, the process of self-transformation far from complete. But he applauded their improvement and expected more in the future.[1]

Cahan's comments might be dismissed as the sort of exaggeration typically heard on anniversaries and other celebrations. Socialists, in particular, rarely missed an opportunity to herald the workers' revolution and, in doing so, often presented future goals as current reality. Nonetheless, other contemporary observers, both inside and outside the immigrant Jewish community, reached similar conclusions. Two years before Cahan's anniversary article, the journalist Ida Van Etten wrote: "The Russian Jews are naturally radicals on all social questions. . . . Thousands of the disciples of Karl Marx may be found among the organized Jewish workingmen. Their intense desire to study and discuss social questions I have never seen equalled." Six years later James Reynolds of the University Settlement identified in Jews an "extremist idealism, with an utter disregard for the restraining power of circumstances and conditions." "The Jew," a 1918 letter to the *New Republic* stated, "has, of course, been always a radical leader." Some commentators, like Van Etten, viewed the affinity of Jews for radicalism as a sign of healthy idealism and intellectuality although others, like Reynolds, expressed ambivalence about this "oriental" trait. Still others were downright hostile. Taken together, these perceptions amounted to a new image of Jews— the Jew as radical—that took shape in the 1890s. It was a stereotype that would gain wide currency during the Progressive Era, turn into a serious liability during World War I and the postwar Red Scare, and remain with Jews (often to their detriment) into the 1960s.[2]

The stereotype of the radical Jew was fairly accurate, as stereotypes go. This does not mean, of course, that it fit precisely. Many opposed socialism as a grave threat to Jewish tradition or wanted simply to get by without thought of grand programs for social change. Nonetheless, a surprisingly high number of Yiddish-speaking Jews—especially young ones—took to radical ideas with alacrity. They built a powerful movement, typically called the Jewish labor movement, which was arguably the largest, most creative upsurge in American Jewish history. New York's first Yiddish-speaking socialist group appeared in 1885, and, within a decade, thousands of immigrant Jews joined socialist unions, political parties, and voluntary associations. Many thousands more read socialist newspapers and attended socialist lectures, parades, "excursions," balls, and other cultural events. The Jewish labor movement faced numerous setbacks, but its overall dimensions grew with each decade. By 1917 some 59,000 people nationwide belonged to the Arbeter Ring (Workmen's Circle) fraternal order and 250,000 to the United Hebrew Trades. ("Why, even the bank clerks of the Jewish east side are union members!" *Labor Age* magazine declared in 1922.)[3] Close to 200,000 people read the socialist daily *Forverts*, making it the most widely circulated foreign-language newspaper in the United States. Between 1914 and 1920 New York's predominantly Jewish voting districts elected ten state assemblymen, seven city councilmen, one municipal judge, and one congressman on the Socialist Party ticket. Although the Socialist Party would never again attain such victories at the polls, the Jewish labor movement remained strong for several more decades. No movement won more support or inspired greater enthusiasm among Jews during the four-decade era of mass immigration between the 1880s and 1920s.

At the dawn of the immigration period few individuals would have predicted the rise of a radical Jewish workers' movement. Contrary to an old misperception, eastern European Jews did not import a preexisting socialist tradition to the United States. As of the 1880s only a tiny number of Jews in the Russian Empire, where the bulk of eastern European Jews lived, knew anything about socialist ideas before coming to America. It is true that a steadily growing number of Russian-speaking Jewish intellectuals (or aspiring intellectuals) participated in one or another revolutionary organization during the 1870s and 1880s. They amounted to a small number overall, however. (Of the 226 members of Narodnaia Volia [People's Will], the leading Russian revolutionary organization, 17 were Jewish men and 7 were Jewish women in 1885.) A distinct movement of Yiddish-speaking Jewish workers did not come into existence until the mid-1890s and did not gain a mass following until early in the twentieth century, almost two decades after the Jewish labor movement arose in New York.[4] In other words, the 1918 letter to the *New Republic* was mistaken: "the Jew" had not always been a radical; the Jew had become a radical in New York and other American cities. Eastern European Jews knew this. Invariably, newcomers were amazed by the assertiveness of New York's Jewish population. After witnessing an 1894 parade, a correspondent for *Voskhod (Dawn)*, Russia's premier Jewish journal, reported: "It would have been necessary for you to see this 5,000-strong group of Jewish workers—actively and proudly marching through the city to the sounds of popular songs and carrying the fluttering banners of various labor unions—in order to understand just what this great mass, which has so quickly adapted to the conditions of life in America, is able to do."[5] As *Voskhod's* correspondent recognized, that 1894 parade reflected profound changes in how the "great mass" of Jews thought and behaved. Thousands of people, who knew nothing of Karl Marx or his ideas before stepping foot on the island of Manhattan, were soon marching and striking and educating themselves in his name. Why were they doing this? What "conditions of life in America" encouraged Jewish immigrants to become socialists? What did they see in socialism? And how did socialists shape what was fast becoming the world's largest Jewish "community," if such a term can be used to describe a population so new and unsettled? *Voskhod's* correspondent could not have known the answers to those questions, but he understood they would have to be found right there in New York City.

The origin of the Jewish labor movement can be traced to the convergence of two disparate immigrant groups in a single section of lower Manhattan. When large numbers of eastern European Jews started arriving on New York's Lower East Side, they discovered a thriving socialist labor movement among German (mostly non-Jewish) immigrants, who constituted the majority of the area's population into the 1880s. A number of Jews, mainly Russian-speaking intellectuals, started learning the German language so they could mix with their neighbors and read their publications. German socialists welcomed the "Russians" and encouraged them to organize Jewish workers into unions and socialist groups of their own. They provided financial assistance, publicity, organizational models, and ideological guidance. With their help, Russian Jews created their labor movement in a German image. They experienced an unusual kind of Americanization, one guided not by native-born elites but by a larger, already established immigrant group. Through socialism, Russian Jews did not become so much Americanized as German-Americanized.[6]

The German socialist influence led to a second interesting twist in the "Americanization" of immigrant Jews, particularly regarding the Yiddish language. To organize Jewish workers, Russian-speaking intellectuals needed to employ Yiddish, the spoken language of nearly all eastern European Jewish immigrants. But many of the intellectuals either did not know Yiddish or had rejected it years earlier as a marker of cultural backwardness. They had to learn or relearn the *zhargon,* or Jewish vernacular, thousands of miles from Europe's Yiddish-speaking heartland. This return to Yiddish was initially justified as a short-term concession necessary only until immigrants learned English. Yet the trend toward Yiddish gathered momentum as the number of immigrants increased. Over the next four decades, Russian-speaking intellectuals continued to adopt Yiddish so they could take part in the East Side's political and cultural activities. Some intellectuals even began to glorify the once-scorned *zhargon* as the authentic voice of "the folk masses." They advocated a full-blown cultural renaissance in Yiddish, which they hoped would serve indefinitely as the primary medium of Jewish culture in the United States. Although the movement was controversial, proponents of *yidishe kultur* helped animate the new socialist culture arising from the Jewish labor movement. From Russian to Yiddish via German: such was the circuitous path of Americanization on New York's Lower East Side.

Uncovering the New York roots of Yiddish-language socialism casts a new light on the immigrant Jewish experience. It shows that New York's immigrant Jewish community was not a mere replica of eastern European Jewry, or "shtetl in macrocosm," in the words of one historian.[7] Rather, New York served as a laboratory of political and cultural innovation that influenced eastern Europe in ways historians are just beginning to recognize. As Jonathan Frankel has shown, New Yorkers played a pivotal role in the emergence of the Jewish labor movement in Russia. Inspired by what was happening in New York and, on a much smaller

scale, London, a group of Vilnius revolutionaries decided to start organizing Jewish workers using Yiddish in 1893 with the understanding
that they could rely on assistance from abroad. New York and London
came to their aid with Yiddish newspapers, pamphlets, and other illegal materials. More Jewish socialist groups arose and, in 1897, united
to form an underground political party known as the Bund (General
Jewish Labor Union of Lithuania, Poland, and Russia).[8] By the time of
Russia's abortive 1905 revolution, the Bund had grown into a popular
movement with perhaps as many as thirty thousand members. Influence
then moved in a westward direction.

After 1905 thousands of Bundists and other revolutionaries (from socialist-Zionists to Bolsheviks) made their way to New York and infused
the existing Jewish labor movement with new energy and ideas. Party
emissaries came to raise money or seek refuge during difficult times.
Visiting dignitaries such as "the grandmother of the Russian revolution," Katerina Breshko-Breshkovskaia, and Israel's future prime minister David Ben-Gurion found warm welcomes from New York's immigrant Jews. Even die-hard opponents of independent Jewish political
movements, such as Leon Trotsky, could not resist the pull of New
York's Jewish labor movement. In early 1917 one could often see Trotsky
holding forth among immigrant Jews in Café Monopole on Ninth Street
or read his articles in the daily *Forverts* and monthly *Di tsukunft* (which
commissioned them and then translated them into Yiddish). Individuals moved back and forth across the Atlantic, publications circulated
from country to country, and organizations were transplanted overseas. Distinct Jewish labor movements, comprising various, often conflicting ideological tendencies, developed on both sides of the Atlantic,
but before World War I New York could be considered their unofficial
capital.[9]

By World War I at least one Yiddish-speaking socialist group existed
in practically every city around the globe where eastern European Jews
had migrated. Yet socialism's influence and appeal varied from city to
city, thriving in certain places but not others. The world's first Jewish socialist club was founded in London in 1876, but socialism remained
confined to a small East End subculture that had nearly petered out by

1914. The Bund achieved its greatest strength in the Pale of Settlement's northwestern region, not in the cities in the south. In the United States, Chicago was home to a large Jewish labor movement, but other midwestern industrial cities, such as Detroit and Pittsburgh, were not. And before World War I the Jewish labor movement achieved its greatest strength in New York. In no other city did Jewish socialists win more adherents or exert a greater influence on the larger society. How, then, did New York differ from other urban Jewish centers?[10]

The rise of socialism among Jews in America's largest metropolis can be attributed to a number of causes that alone were not exclusive to New York but that came together in a unique way. New York's polyglot immigrant character was one important factor. In more culturally homogeneous countries, such as England, labor leaders discouraged Jews and other foreign-speaking workers from establishing autonomous, ethnic-based unions and political organizations. Similarly, many Russian socialists insisted in the name of "proletarian internationalism" that all workers, regardless of national background, join a single, Russian-speaking party. The socialist movement in New York, however, presented a different model of internationalism that reflected the population's immigrant character. In a city where most workers were from someplace else, the main socialist political parties and union federations allowed them to form distinct linguistic subunits. Jews could maintain autonomous, Yiddish-speaking organizations yet still participate in larger, multiethnic structures, such as the Socialist Party or New York's Central Labor Union. Jewish socialists were also linked to comrades overseas through the Socialist International and, after 1919, the Communist International. Such wider affiliations tremendously strengthened the optimism and self-confidence of Jewish socialists. Having allies beyond the Yiddish-speaking world demonstrated to Jews that they were not alone in their struggles, that they were part of something momentous, and that ancient prejudices could be overcome.[11]

Of course, New York was not the only multilingual city in the United States or Europe. What set New York apart from, say, Chicago or Odessa was the enormous size of its Jewish working class. New York attracted far more Yiddish-speaking Jews than did any other city in the world because of an abundance of manufacturing jobs (particularly in the garment industry) and the United States' generally liberal immigration policies. The Russian Empire's two largest Jewish communities—Warsaw and Odessa—numbered 301,000 and 219,423, respectively, just prior to World War I. In England only about 48,000 Jews settled in London's East End, the chief European destination for Jewish emigrants until passage of the 1905 Aliens Act. And the United States' second most populous city, Chicago, was home to about 100,000 Jews in 1907.[12] Yiddish New York dwarfed them all. An estimated 1,400,000 Jews lived in New York in 1914, the majority of whom were working class and poor. Jews constituted nearly 28 percent, or a plurality, of the city's population. According to a 1916 survey, more than 50 percent of economically active Jews worked in factories, sweatshops, and tenement apartments: 300,000 in New York's booming garment industry and another 100,000 in construction, cigar manufacturing, food processing, printing, and smaller industries. A significant minority of Jews also eked out a living as peddlers, small storekeepers, and petty entrepreneurs, occupations that did not necessarily bring more income or security than did wage work. To be sure, ambitious and fortunate individuals could climb their way out of poverty. Almost all clothing manufacturers were immigrant Jews (first central European and, by 1900, mostly eastern European) who had spent some time at a sewing machine. Nonetheless, wage workers and the precariously self-employed constituted the bulk of New York Jewry prior to the 1920s.[13]

Accompanying the growth of New York's Jewish working class was a parallel rise in the magnitude and scope of class conflict. Immigrant Jews spent most of their time working long hours (as many as eighteen per day in certain occupations) in miserable conditions for low pay. Everyday pursuits—earning a living, managing a home—proved highly volatile as strikes, consumer boycotts, and demonstrations erupted time and again. Hardly a single family was left untouched. Sooner or later just about every individual walked a picket line, marched in a parade, protested some injustice, or knew someone who had. The era's first major strike wave hit the East Side in 1886 and shut down every branch of the garment industry. Larger strikes broke out in 1890–1891, 1893–1894, and 1899–1900 and culminated in the giant "uprisings" and "revolts" of 1909–1914. An untold number of smaller conflagrations occurred in between. Recurring struggles produced an atmosphere of rebellion on the Lower East Side (home to more than 540,000 Jews in 1910) and satellite Jewish neighborhoods in Harlem, Brooklyn, and the Bronx. During periods of unrest one could see astonishing sights rarely witnessed in *der alter heym* (the old country): peddlers demanding an end to the capitalist system; housewives rioting for affordable kosher meat; striking bakers smashing the office windows of an unsympathetic Yiddish newspaper; young seamstresses assaulting older men who crossed their picket line.[14] "Nowhere in the world," the American representative of the Group for the Emancipation of Labor (forerunner to the Russian Social Democratic Workers' Party) reported at the end of the century, "is it possible to observe the internal antagonisms of Jews in the struggle between the exploiters and the exploited classes as it is in New York."[15]

By contrast, the Jewish working class developed in Russia's Pale of Settlement and the Galician region of Austria-Hungary in a stunted fashion. The uneven pace of industrialization in those regions and discrimination against Jews excluded most of them from large, mechanized factories. Eastern European Jews were confined mainly to tiny workshops whose owners were almost as poor as their employees, and their strikes were typically small and ineffectual.[16] They were "childish struggles" "between the poverty-stricken and the indigent," as Avrom Lesin, a pioneer of the Jewish labor movement in Minsk, quipped in 1897.[17] But in the United States yesterday's pauperized artisans and small traders became transformed suddenly into a huge proletariat, concentrated specifically in cities that manufactured ready-to-wear clothes. Those included Baltimore, Chicago, Philadelphia, and, above all, New York. New York's garment industry was the largest in the United States and employed the highest number and proportion of Jews. Nowhere else did Jews predominate both as employers and employees. In Chicago's men's apparel industry, for example, Jewish workers ranked behind two other immigrant groups, Czechs and Poles. New York's garment industry also played a more strategic role than Chicago's in the local economy. In a city based on small-scale production of consumer goods, over 47 percent of New York's factories produced clothing and employed more than 46 percent of its industrial workforce in 1910. (By contrast, Chicago's garment industry, the second largest in the country, was overshadowed by heavy industries, such as steel and meatpacking, which employed very few Jews.) The high concentration of Jews in one of New York's leading industries gave the Jewish labor movement a firm economic base and an unusual degree of power. Predominantly Jewish unions, led by Jewish socialists, such as the International Ladies' Garment Workers' Union (ILGWU), were among the largest in New York. Through them New York's Jewish workers could shape the social, political, and cultural landscape to a degree Lesin's "poverty-stricken" and "indigent" Jews could only imagine.[18] From the margins of Europe Jews had moved to the very heart of the world's new economic colossus: "the capital of capitalism, the capital of the twentieth century and the capital of the world."[19]

In addition to New York's extraordinarily large and militant Jewish working class, an energetic community of radical intellectuals played a crucial role in the rise and development of the Jewish labor movement. These intellectuals did not constitute a uniform group, divided as they were by gender, age, ideology, and other differences. Nonetheless, New York's radical Jewish intelligentsia formed a distinct subcommunity among the larger Jewish population by virtue of their common background, sense of purpose, and social function. Most of the intellectuals were men and women who, as youths in Russia, had rebelled against religious tradition, achieved some level of secular education, and participated in, or at least sympathized with, one or another revolutionary party.[20] They possessed an acute awareness of themselves as historical actors, as if the fate of an entire people depended on what they said and did. This was not just the conceit of a self-appointed vanguard, but an urgent response to events that affected Jews on both sides of the Atlantic: strikes, pogroms, wars, and revolutions. In an era of mounting crises, radical intellectuals believed it their duty to provide leadership to "the masses," however defined. As the labor historian John Laslett writes, the "common bond" between Jewish intellectuals and Jewish workers was "in many ways unique throughout the American labor movement."

As organizers, lecturers, journalists, educators, popular poets, and fiction writers, radical intellectuals translated day-to-day travails into a broad ideological framework and institutional structure. In doing so, they gained a devoted following among poor immigrants whose lives had been upended by the Atlantic crossing and the hardships of everyday life. "How I envied those Russian intelligencia [*sic*]!" one immigrant man recalls. "They were always at the top of every social function, the attraction of every circle and the ideal of every girl's dreams." To a large extent, the existence of the Jewish labor movement can be credited to this "Russian intelligencia."[21]

In Russia intellectuals played a similarly important role in the formation of the Bund and other revolutionary parties, but they faced an array of obstacles absent in New York. Government repression was the most serious of them. During the party's early years, Bundists were forced to meet secretly in forests, private homes, and backrooms on the edge of town just so they could read pamphlets (mostly smuggled from abroad), sing songs, or hear speeches. The failed revolution of 1905 brought some liberalization, but the czarist autocracy foreclosed possibilities for gradual reform, which would eventually ruin the regime in 1917. In New York, by contrast, intellectuals could say and do pretty much whatever they wanted short of armed insurrection. While Bundists smuggled contraband and dodged the omnipresent threat of arrest, socialists in New York published mass circulation newspapers and organized huge demonstrations for all to see. Freedoms of speech and assembly provided space in which Jewish labor could develop into a mass movement, years before one emerged in Russia. Not until America's entry into World War I would Jewish socialists confront a less benign situation.

Russian Jewish radicals also had to contend with a generally traditional Jewish population. This is not to say that Russian Jews were somehow insulated from general trends toward urbanization, acculturation, and secularization.[22] The existence of the Bund itself testified to this. Still, the pace of change was much slower in Russia than in the United States. Legal restrictions, which tightened or loosened depending on the reigning czar, hindered integration of Jews into Russian society. Within Jewish communities, traditional elites (whose status was drawn from some combination of wealth, family pedigree, and religious learning) continued to govern many aspects of Jewish life, especially in small cities and towns. Rabbis and other religious leaders (such as Hassidic *rebbes*) proved adept at responding to new challenges from within and outside the Jewish community. In reaction to educational reforms initiated by *maskilim* (proponents of Hebrew enlightenment, or *Haskalah*) and the Russian government, rabbis reinvigorated yeshivas (rabbinical academies) with improved funding, more rigorous curricula, and an activist spirit. By World War I religious leaders had established political parties, complete with workers' subsections, to compete against secular-radical parties. Ironically, they utilized a quintessentially modern method of popular mobilization—the political party and its press—to defend religious tradition. In the process, Russia's traditional Jews transformed themselves into traditionalist or Orthodox Jews: self-conscious, assertive defenders of religious law and custom. Orthodox Jews entered the twentieth century far more vital than their opponents would have expected.[23]

In New York, however, Orthodox Judaism (in all its internal variations) fell into a state of permanent crisis. Eastern Europe's most religiously observant Jews generally did not journey to the United States, which they rejected as an "impure land" full of dangerous temptations and liberties. Most devoutly Orthodox Jews obeyed their rabbis' injunctions to remain at home, where they could lead a pious life in the accustomed manner.[24] Further to the detriment of Orthodox Judaism in the United States, most immigrants tended to be young and, therefore, less tied to the ways of their parents. About 70 percent of immigrant Jews were between the ages of fourteen and forty-four at the time they landed in the United States, and another 25 percent were under the age of fourteen.[25] In New York young people enjoyed considerable personal freedom. They were not answerable to communal bodies capable of punishing deviant behavior—those did not exist in New York. Furthermore, immigrant children were much less subject to parental control. The rupture of family units caused by movement overseas, long hours spent working outside the home, and New York's generally permissive atmosphere caused a generational conflict parents were destined to lose.

With traditional structures of authority absent or in disarray, young people could pursue all sorts of interests and curiosities. "I was young and I was free here," one immigrant woman recalls.[26] In the socialist movement, young Jews could educate themselves, take part in important debates, build organizations, and participate in the running of things. Socialism promised young people both self-improvement and collective fulfillment: a "better, more beautiful world" that they could help to create.

Orthodox Jews did come to New York and regrouped as best they could. They built synagogues, schools, yeshivas, rabbinical associations, and other religious institutions.[27] Certain rabbis, such as Tsvi Hirsh Masliansky, could draw as many as one thousand people to his Friday evening sermons. Still, Orthodox rabbis had forever lost their dominance. They had come to a country where the law of the land separated church from state, where democratic norms held that clergymen should answer to laity (not the reverse), and where organizational pluralism had replaced a centralized, theocratic community. Everything seemed to be working against New York's beleaguered traditionalists. The state of Judaism, according to the historian Jonathan Sarna, was one of "spiritual crisis." Only 12 percent of America's three million Jews belonged to synagogues as of 1916. Sabbath observance was appallingly lax. Even nominally Orthodox Jews often worked on Saturdays, allowed themselves the pleasure of attending the Yiddish theater, or in some way transgressed the Sabbath. And religious education remained in shambles. (Of the children old enough to attend elementary school, fewer than 25 percent received any formal Jewish schooling. For children of high school age, the figure was a mere 1 percent.) Surrounded by insurmountable obstacles, Orthodox rabbis and their followers viewed themselves as a saving remnant struggling to preserve the very existence of Judaism. They differed about how to do this, as Jeffrey Gurock, a leading historian of Orthodoxy, has shown. "Resisters" refused to compromise with American society while "accommodators" (such as Masliansky) were willing to modify certain aspects of Judaism without sacrificing its fundamentals. Differences notwithstanding, both kinds of Orthodox Jews adopted a basically defensive posture toward the larger society.

They defined their task as preserving what little they could within an inhospitable environment.[28]

The defensiveness of Orthodox rabbis was evident in the public arena, where they played a negligible role as an organized group. Instead of building a political party or popular movement, they formed narrowly based pressure groups to promote specific religious interests. The Jewish Sabbath Observers Association (later renamed the Jewish Sabbath Alliance) was among the first and most important. Founded in 1894 during a year of severe economic depression and labor conflict, the association's purpose was to persuade Jews to stop desecrating the Sabbath. The association called on employers to cease conducting business on Saturdays and union leaders to include this as a demand during contract negotiations. The association also lobbied politicians against blue laws and the practice of holding school and government examinations on Saturdays. Defenders of the Sabbath met with some success over the years, but their organization's very existence betrayed Orthodoxy's fundamental weakness. The fact that rabbis had to plead with ordinary folk, the *amkho*, to fulfill a primary religious obligation reflected a humiliating loss of status. Deprived of coercive power, rabbis could do little more than beseech an indifferent public to do what had previously been done unquestioningly.[29] Even the association's victories, most notably in limiting Christianity's presence in public schools, highlighted the marginal standing of Orthodox rabbis in New York: they won their victories on the same constitutional basis that undermined the power of rabbis in the first place. Orthodox Jews could protest the presence of Christianity in the public sphere, but they could do little to advance Judaism's position.[30]

While rabbis and their followers worried about the sorry state of religious observance, socialists effectively responded to the primary concerns of immigrants: economic survival and adaptation to their new home. Socialists, not Orthodox Jews, elected candidates to office, published the most popular Yiddish newspaper, and built powerful unions and other mass membership organizations. Of course, not all those who joined the ILGWU or read the *Forverts* (about one hundred thousand and two hundred thousand people, respectively, as of 1920) adhered strictly to a radical political program or necessarily viewed themselves as radicals. Avowed socialists were in the minority, but they were a large minority who gained the approval of huge numbers of people beyond their ranks, including observant Jews. When, for example, religious schoolteachers and kosher meat slaughterers organized themselves into unions (itself a telling development), they chose to affiliate with the socialist United Hebrew Trades.[31] No alternative to the UHT existed nor did Orthodox Jews ever bother to create one. Orthodox rabbis might have sympathized with the plight of labor, but they believed it more urgent to promote their particular brand of Judaism. They made an understandable choice, but by standing on the sidelines, rabbis abdicated their historic leadership role. They denounced socialists as heretics and schismatics, but, in truth, Orthodox Jews more closely resembled a sect. As one sympathetic historian of Orthodoxy acknowledges, "Their impact on larger, non-Orthodox trends within the Jewish community remained virtually nil."[32] The fall of rabbis and the rise of socialists represented nothing short of a revolution in Jewish culture and politics.

In sum, a number of elements combined to make the Jewish labor movement such a potent force in New York City. These included the rise of an enormous Jewish working class concentrated in an economically strategic industry, the frequency of class conflict, the early support from German socialists, the unchallenged leadership of radical intellectuals, the collapse of old elites, and a comparatively free environment for political and cultural activity before World War I. One or more of those elements could be found in other cities in the United States and Europe, but only in New York did they coalesce. Not until the interwar period would Jewish labor movements abroad begin to eclipse New York's. In independent Poland the Bund achieved great popularity in cities such as Warsaw and Lodz, where, on the eve of World War II, the party won more than half the Jewish vote in local elections. In the Soviet Union the government's Jewish commissariat conducted a total overhaul of Jewish society that alternately captivated and horrified Jews around the globe. And in British-ruled Palestine socialist-Zionists constructed a different kind of collectivist society, one built from the bottom up in Hebrew. Yet these developments were still a long time away when New York's first

Jewish socialist group appeared in 1885. The Jewish labor movement was then just emerging and, over the next three decades, it would find its most congenial home in New York City.[33]

One hundred twenty years have passed since the birth of the Jewish labor movement, yet specialists in American Jewish history have paid little attention to it. One would not have predicted this in the 1970s, when the field of American Jewish history began to come of age. Scholarly and popular interest in the subject then seemed to be growing. In 1976 alone two academic journals dedicated special issues to the Jewish labor movement. In a general survey of American Jews published two years earlier, Henry Feingold described the labor movement as "the principal institution developed by East European Jewry in America."[34] Outside Jewish studies, specialists in labor and women's history (who in the 1970s were busy redefining the entire field of U.S. history) also started to take notice. They perceived in strikes, such as the 1909 "Uprising of the 20,000," fascinating arenas in which to explore the interplay among gender, class, and, to a lesser extent, ethnic identities.[35] And, beyond the academy, several popular books brought the Jewish labor movement to the wide reading public. Most notable was Irving Howe's *World of Our Fathers* (1976). Howe's monumental elegy to immigrant Jews did not focus exclusively on socialism, but Howe placed it at the center of his story. The book met with phenomenal success. *World of Our Fathers* won the prestigious National Book Award and became a best-seller, the most widely read history of American Jews ever published.[36] Yet, for all the interest generated during the 1970s, American Jewish historians have generally ignored socialism and faulted Howe for paying too much attention to it. Apart from occasional articles or chapters in books, little new research has been published.[37]

The indifference of American Jewish historians to the Jewish labor movement and to socialism generally can be attributed to the main preoccupation that has guided research on American Jews over the last two decades. Directly or indirectly, most historians have focused on a core question: can Jews maintain a vibrant ethnic community in the United States while participating fully in the larger society? This is an old question that dates back to the nineteenth century. Those who raised it most urgently were rabbis, on the one hand, and, on the other, secular Jewish nationalists who feared that Jews could not survive as a cohesive group in a democratic, relatively open society like the United States. They predicted that as Jews moved further away from their European roots, they would become absorbed into the proverbial melting pot. Communal bonds and cultural distinctiveness would be sacrificed for material success and social acceptance. Such anxiety about assimilation has been voiced in each generation, but it has increased precipitously since the 1970s because of rising intermarriage rates between Jews and gentiles. At the end of the twentieth century a number of Jewish communal reports, sociological studies, and popular books warned that Jews might vanish as an ethnic group unless strong countermeasures (such as intensive religious education) are taken. By no means have all commentators over the past century adopted a pessimistic stance, but the issue of Jewish "survival" and "continuity" remains more of a concern than ever before.[38]

The view of American Jews as overly assimilated finds expression in the traditionally second-class status of American Jewish history within Jewish studies. European Jewish historians, particularly those working within an older nationalist framework, have long dismissed the cultural vitality of American Jews. It has seemed to them that American-born Jews, largely ignorant of Hebrew and Yiddish, have failed to produce a worthy, indigenous Jewish culture. In addition, Europeanists have tended to regard the United States as peripheral to the major events and movements of the modern era, such as emancipation, the *Haskalah*, Zionism, and the Holocaust. "I'll tell you all you need to know about American Jewish history," a distinguished scholar is quoted as saying, "the Jews came to America, they abandoned their faith, they began to live like *goyim* [gentiles], and after a generation or two they intermarried and disappeared." Such attitudes have diminished significantly in recent years owing, in part, to a broader reconsideration of nationalist historiography, but there still exists an "unarticulated bias," in Todd Endelman's words, that the American Jewish experience is "uninstructive or irrelevant or unchallenging."[39]

In the face of criticisms and doubts voiced inside and outside the academy, American Jewish historians have felt compelled to defend the cultural bona fides of the people they study and, by extension, their own scholarly legitimacy. Bolstered by broader trends in the study of immigration and ethnicity, most Jewish historians have stressed group persistence and cultural creativity.[40] Instead of assimilation, they have posited an ongoing process of ethnic reinvention, often called synthesis. According to this idea, Jews have not become progressively deracinated, but, on the contrary, have continuously redefined Jewish culture, community, and identity by weaving elements of European Jewish tradition with middle-class American culture. This fruitful interchange, according to the consensus, has differed across place and time, so that it is impossible to speak of a uniform Jewish culture in the United States. Nonetheless, the process of synthesis has been motivated by a common goal, identified by Jonathan Sarna as "the quest to be fully a Jew and fully an American, both at the same time."[41] Most recent scholarship is dedicated to showing the myriad ways in which Jews have succeeded in this supposedly shared quest.[42]

By stressing synthesis, rather than assimilation, historians have expanded the conceptual boundaries of American Jewish history, as well as influenced the study of Jews in post-emancipation European countries, such as England, France, and Germany. Instead of using any standard of authenticity, American Jewish historians have employed elastic conceptions of what it means to be Jewish in a society where boundaries of culture and community are porous. In Jenna Weissman Joselit's words, American Jewish culture is a "protean and malleable construct," continually changing in ways that are different from, but no less valid than, their European antecedents. Influenced strongly by post-1960s "new social history," American Jewish historians tend to disregard "cultural authorities" and "elites" in favor of ordinary men and women. If "the folk" has considered its hybrid American Jewish culture to be "meaningful," as Joselit writes, then so be it.[43] The attitudes of the people themselves should be the sole measure of what is or is not valid. Synthesis thus provides a framework for evaluating American Jewish life on its own terms, not those imposed from Europe.

Although populist in tone and expansive in scope, the scholarly consensus in American Jewish history has placed its own limitations on the field. All too easily the inclination to affirm American Jews has slipped into an uncritical triumphalism. Echoing American national mythology, historians describe the United States as a land of "wonders" and "golden cities" where Jews enjoy endless opportunities to succeed as they please. Over and over they tell of prosperous men and women who are proud to be Jews and proud to be Americans and who somehow manage to blend harmoniously these identities.[44] Historians write a lot about middle-class Jews—their neighborhoods, synagogues, habits of consumption, and so on—but mostly ignore the many Jews who never made it into the middle class or somehow fell from it. For that matter, rarely do historians write about what middle-class Jews actually did for a living, whether legal, illegal, or somewhere in between (as was often the case for Jews working, say, in the garment and entertainment industries). "Making it" seems to have been so easy.[45] American Jewish history has thus been turned into a celebration of winners for whom winning comes easily and without costs. Themes of loss, alienation, ambivalence, disappointment, and rebellion—all prominent in American Jewish fiction and autobiography (in Yiddish and English)—barely exist in the major works of American Jewish history. Subjects that might reveal a less-than-sanguine version of the past have been filtered out or relegated to the background. In the success story that American Jewish history has become, the radical experience has been made irrelevant.[46]

American Jewish historians have generally disregarded the Jewish labor movement as a short-lived, transitional phenomenon. Most believe that the movement functioned as an agent of Americanization that helped immigrants to adjust to the mainstream of "American labor and American life generally" before fading away. In an influential 1952 article Will Herberg formulated the classic version of the socialism-as-Americanization thesis. Herberg argued that the great achievement of socialists was that they led the "immigrant Jew turned proletarian" away from the radical fringe toward the liberal center through participation in electoral politics, the give-and-take of collective bargaining, and other democratic processes and institutions. "The excited election campaigns in the big Jewish centers, the great political rallies addressed by Jewish and non-Jewish Socialist spellbinders," Herberg wrote, "did more to integrate the Jewish worker into American political life than any number of civics classes or formal Americanization programs could possibly have done."[47] Sooner or later, according to Herberg, socialists relinquished their radical ambitions and satisfied themselves with reforming society incrementally. In doing so, they turned immigrant Jews into modern Americans. A decade later Moses Rischin articulated a more nuanced version of Herberg's thesis in his pioneering history of New York Jews, *The Promised City* (1962), and it remains the standard interpretation of the Jewish labor movement to the present day.[48] (Irving Howe is the one major exception.) Contemporary historians write knowing that American Jews have become the largest, most affluent, and most secure Jewish community in the modern era. In retrospect, who could deny that the Jewish labor movement amounted to a brief phase in the successful adjustment of Jews to American society?

Upon closer inspection, however, that judgment can be seen as both a condescending and inaccurate description of socialism and its legacy. It is condescending because it refuses to evaluate socialism on its own terms. Socialists viewed the United States not as a "golden land" of endless possibilities, but as a country deeply divided between its democratic promise and the reality of economic exploitation immigrants contended with every day. Socialists intended to build a new society, not adapt to the existing one. Some socialists believed American society could be remade through peaceful means; others expected violent revolution at some point in the future. Some dreamed of a "cooperative commonwealth," others of a "dictatorship of the proletariat." Yet all socialists (Marxian social democrats, anarchists, communists, and so on) agreed that capitalism needed to be replaced by a new social order freed from poverty and bigotry. By dismissing this goal as youthful excess bound to give way to "Americanization," Herberg and like-minded historians have refused to take socialism—its ideas and goals, successes and failures— seriously. They have flattened the radical Jewish experience into a larger story of harmonious interaction between Jews and American society.

Jews, however, did not travel a short, direct road from Yiddish-language socialism to English-language liberalism. An ongoing tug-of-war between radical ideals and practical necessities shaped the Jewish labor movement from its beginning. A flare-up of strikes, an economic downturn, or a revolution overseas often rekindled utopian aspirations left dormant in calmer years. On the other hand, a return to prosperity, a rise in anti-Semitism, or political repression frequently produced the opposite effect. Furthermore, the contest between radicalism and reform was not limited to Yiddish-speaking immigrants. Immigrants fashioned an enduring, if conflict-ridden, left-wing political culture, which they passed on to their children and grandchildren. For the better part of a century, from roughly the 1880s to the 1960s, radical movements and ideas played a major role in the lives of American Jews. Socialism was not a "one-generation phenomenon," as most historians would have it. It was a formative experience in the history of the world's largest Jewish community. This is likely to be missed if one limits the scope of American Jewish history to the search for "synthesis," an idea that automatically excludes Jews who had an ambivalent, tenuous, or even hostile relationship to things Jewish, as many radicals had (and continue to have). Scholars have not entertained the possibility that such uneasy Jews have played a central role in American Jewish history. (It is telling that when the journal *American Jewish History* asked historians in 1988 to name the country's "greatest" Jewish leaders, not a single participant in the symposium chose a labor or socialist leader.)[49] To do so would require rethinking the basic frame through which American Jewish historians have interpreted the past.

From the Jewish labor movement's beginning, socialists regarded questions of Jewish identity, culture, and community as problematic. Was it permissible to be both a Jew and a socialist? If so, how? Should Jewish socialists identify with the Jewish people or the workers of the world? Could they do both at the same time? Jewish socialists argued these and similar questions with an intensity perhaps difficult to fathom in the post-1960s era of ethnic celebration. They were not alone in trying to reconcile competing claims of Jewish group identity and wider spheres of community. *Maskilim,* Reform Jews, and Zionists, for example, tried to do the same. Indeed, the challenge of combining particularistic and universalistic political and cultural strategies has defined the modern Jewish experience (and, arguably, that of all minority groups) since the European Enlightenment.[50] Socialists, however, experienced the most difficulty in accommodating Jews to broader group identities and loyalties. Classical Marxism divided the world into two basic categories (proletariat and bourgeoisie) and deemed the Jewish people an anachronism. Whereas Reform Jews, Zionists, and *maskilim* asked, "How should we refashion Judaism and Jewish culture to fit the modern world?" socialists started with a prior question, "May we remain Jews in the modern world?" Given the terms established by Marxists, those who answered "yes" did so only with careful justification against strong criticism.[51] American Jewish historians might be inclined to dismiss socialist quandaries as limited to intellectual elites, not the bulk of ordinary men and women. Yet this was not so. In one form or another "the Jewish question" was debated in mass circulation newspapers and public venues involving the broad Yiddish-speaking public. It touched an array of issues from aid to pogrom victims to the question of Sabbath observance to the establishment of a Jewish homeland. Jewish socialists thus brought into particularly sharp focus the central problem faced by all Jews in the modern period, one that has yet to be resolved: how should Jews define themselves in relation to the larger society and community of nations in which they live?[52]

The early Jewish socialists, for the most part, advocated a certain kind of assimilation, which they called "internationalism." They envisioned a working-class melting pot into which Jews and other immigrants would rapidly assimilate. Although rarely did they specify what a universal, working-class culture might look like in the United States, the founders of the Jewish labor movement entertained few doubts about its inevitability. The major socialist thinkers prescribed such an outcome and the alliance with German socialists provided evidence that internationalism could work in practice. The early Jewish socialists viewed themselves not as building a new Jewish culture in Yiddish (they denied such a thing was possible) but as preparing the masses to transcend their own allegedly parochial culture. Their goal, in Abraham Cahan's words, was "to erase all boundaries between Jew and non-Jew in the labor world." "We are no patriots of a special 'Jewish labor movement,'" Cahan's colleague Louis Miller explained in 1892. "We would like the Jews to be members of the American unions."[53] And yet, in their efforts to organize and educate ("enlighten") immigrant Jews, socialists built—in spite of themselves—a distinct Jewish labor movement and a new kind of Yiddish culture that was secular, politically radical, and universalistic. Internationalist in principle but based in a particular minority group, the Jewish labor movement contained a basic contradiction that would never be resolved. The early Jewish socialists created a labor movement they hoped to dissolve eventually and a Yiddish culture they denied could exist. They assumed a dual challenge: to transform both immigrant Jews and American society so that they could dissolve into it on their own terms.

Not until the first decade of the twentieth century did a substantial number of socialists begin to change their thinking about Jews. A wave of anti-Jewish riots in Russia, starting with the Kishinev pogrom in 1903, caused a crisis of confidence among socialists. Horrifying news from across the Atlantic forced some socialists to reassess their previous understanding of internationalism. Debate began about whether socialists could legitimately affirm a sense of Jewish group solidarity, at least during times of emergency. Reinforcing this trend was an influx of revolutionaries, mainly from Russia, who advocated both Jewish nationalism and socialism, in one form or another. The leading theoretician was Chaim Zhitlovsky, who envisioned an all-encompassing civilization in the Yiddish language: a radical idea that elevated the Jewish vernacular to a national language of intellectual discourse and artistic creativity. From the early 1900s forward, other socialist Jewish nationalists elaborated (albeit in different ways) Zhitlovsky's idea of *yidishe kultur* and worked toward its implementation.

Proponents of *yidishe kultur* arrived in the United States when socialism in New York and across the country was about to enter its most spectacular period of growth. From 1909 to 1920 a series of momentous events occurred: the giant labor uprisings and revolts between 1909 and 1914, the Socialist Party's election victories between 1914 and 1920, and the nationwide wildcat strikes of 1919. The Russian revolution and the post–World War I insurrections in Germany and Hungary also made profound impressions. In and around 1917 it seemed that anything was possible, that dreams could soon be made into reality. In this hopeful climate many socialists concluded that they had it within their power to create a sophisticated, self-sustaining culture in the Yiddish language, which would be no less worthy than that produced in any of the major European languages. Many veteran Jewish socialists of the 1880s and 1890s dismissed this goal as hopelessly utopian. In a country where Jews faced no legal barriers to participation in the larger society, they maintained, the natural flow of life headed toward English. But Yiddish cultural nationalists viewed America differently. They saw an enormous and growing Yiddish-speaking population packed into densely populated neighborhoods, possibilities for free expression unknown in Russia, and an already flourishing Yiddish press, theater, and imaginative literature. Material conditions seemed to encourage the development of *yidishe kultur* rather than inhibit it. Yiddish cultural nationalists were not alone in their view that foreign-language cultures could thrive in the United States. During the same period a number of prominent, English-speaking intellectuals, such as Horace Kallen, Rabbi Judah Magnes, and Randolph Bourne (who was not Jewish), started arguing that the melting pot was inaccurate as a description of the United States and undemocratic as a prescriptive norm. In its place Kallen spoke of a "democracy of nationalities," Magnes of a "republic of nationalities," and Bourne of a "trans-national America." Their ideas were impelled, in no small measure, by the vibrant cultural life they saw being developed by New York's immigrant Jews.[54] In an America swelling with immigrants, Yiddish cultural nationalists had reason to believe their ideas accorded well with its emerging multicultural society.

But the proponents of *yidishe kultur* also faced major problems. They had to contend with opposition from other socialists in the Jewish labor movement, the pressures and allure of the larger, English-speaking society, and a shortage of resources necessary for a self-sustaining, wide-ranging culture in the Yiddish language. Nobody, not even Zhitlovsky, could keep from worrying about the future of Yiddish in the United States. The very conditions that stimulated the upsurge in socialism and

Yiddish cultural creativity could also serve to undermine both. As a Yiddish literary critic wrote in 1909, "When one ponders Jewish life on American soil and asks: what is actually happening here? A renaissance or an agonizing moment of death? . . . We see one big, silent, veiled question mark. . . . How can one prophesize about our future when the present is so unclear, so insubstantial, so uncrystallized, so full of contradictions and contrasts?"[55]

On whichever side Jewish socialists stood, all shared an optimistic belief that both Jews and their adopted country could be remade into something much better than they then were. The promise of renewal had been a cherished ideal in American society since before the War for Independence. Jewish socialists were intent on testing its limits.

CHAPTER 1

Coming to Shore

Russian Radicals Discover the Jewish Working Class
in New York

Eighteen eighty-six is not typically considered a turning point in American Jewish history, but it ought to be. That was the year of "the Great Upheaval," when class conflict in the United States reached an unprecedented high. Among the many people swept up in the unrest were New York's immigrant Jews. On the city's Lower East Side thousands of Yiddish-speaking Jews participated in strikes, marched for the eight-hour workday, and supported Henry George's bid for mayor on the United Labor Party ticket. Radical intellectuals organized workers into unions, published Yiddish newspapers, and formed political groups. Although a small number of radicals had, a year earlier, started to propagate socialism in Yiddish, not until 1886 did the idea take hold. "To even think of a Jewish labor movement [before 1886] was crazy," the anarchist leader Shoel Yanovsky would later recall. Yet the tumultuous events of 1886 changed Yanovsky's life permanently. From that point forward he would devote himself to organizing and educating the Jewish "masses," in Yiddish. Yanovsky was not alone. He joined dozens of other intellectuals in laying the foundation of the Jewish labor movement. How, within about a year, did that previously inconceivable idea become an urgent and in many cases lifelong pursuit?[1]

The answer to this question can be found in the journey of New York's Russian Jewish intellectuals who founded the Jewish labor movement during the second half of the 1880s.[2] The earliest arrivals came in

1882 as members of a short-lived emigration movement called Am Oylom (Eternal People, the title of an 1872 polemic by the Hebrew writer Perets Smolenskin). Formed in response to the infamous pogroms of 1881–1882, Am Oylom's roughly one thousand members left the Russian Empire with the intention of establishing agricultural communes in the western United States. Am Oylom quickly petered out, but Russian Jewish intellectuals continued to emigrate to New York (and, to a lesser extent, other American cities) throughout the 1880s. Young, politically radical, and Russian-speaking, these men and women formed a distinct subcommunity on the Lower East Side. Referred to as "the Russian Colony," this intellectual community initially viewed itself as an American outpost of the Russian revolutionary movement. Yet, over time, members of the Russian Colony took an interest in the social and political life of their new home, particularly in the economic plight and cultural "backwardness" of immigrant Jews. Former members of Am Oylom created the first Yiddish-speaking socialist group, the Yidisher Arbeter Fareyn (Jewish Workers' Association), in April 1885. A year later the Yidisher Arbeter Fareyn stood at the forefront of the Great Upheaval and formed the cornerstone of the newborn Jewish labor movement. Thus, in a remarkably brief period, a group of previously marginal Russian Jewish intellectuals emerged as leaders of New York's burgeoning Jewish working class.[3]

In key respects the Russian Colony's intellectuals were unprepared for their task. To begin with, many of them had been raised in acculturated, Russian-speaking households or had been placed in Russian schools at a young age. Many possessed a poor grasp of Yiddish or did not know the language at all when they arrived in New York. Those who could speak Yiddish often refused to do so, having rejected their mother tongue years earlier as part of an overall rebellion against Jewish tradition. Practically all Russian Jewish intellectuals regarded Yiddish not as a full-fledged language but as an uncivilized dialect; this was an attitude shared by most secularly educated Jews in the nineteenth century. Thus, a language divide—part involuntary, part self-imposed—separated the Russian Colony's intellectuals (who numbered perhaps one thousand by 1890) from the vast majority of Yiddish-speaking Jews. In addition, the

Russian Jewish intellectuals had no prior experience in organizing workers, let alone Yiddish-speaking ones. As students in Russia during the 1870s and 1880s, they had become enchanted by revolutionary ideas, yet few actually participated in the revolutionary movement. In most instances their revolutionary activity consisted of reading illegal journals and books, a dangerous practice in its own right but not one that provided practical experience in labor organizing. Furthermore, revolutionary ideas absorbed in Russia offered little guidance in the United States. The Russian Jewish intellectuals did not bring a coherent system of thought or program, but a revolutionary mood, characterized by Ezra Mendelsohn as "a desire for rapid change, an end to oppression, a love for the 'people,' a hatred for authority."[4] They found the stuff of American socialism—union meetings, election campaigns, lectures— altogether prosaic. They longed for the aura of heroism, self-sacrifice, and danger surrounding Russia's revolutionary populist groups, such as Narodnaia Volia (People's Will). Yet at the same time the Russian Jewish intellectuals knew that the conspiratorial and violent methods of Narodnaia Volia did not fit American realities. By the mid-1880s some of them decided to do the unexpected: despite their political inexperience and ignorance of or bias against Yiddish, they forged an alliance with Jewish workers. What caused this reversal?

In part the decision of Russian-speaking intellectuals to create a Yiddish-speaking socialist movement can be explained by material circumstances. In the factories and tenements of New York's Lower East Side, intellectuals encountered for the first time a large and growing Jewish proletariat. Many intellectuals were themselves compelled to join the ranks of the working class after landing in New York: not knowing English, they had little choice. Their "exposure to working conditions," Mendelsohn states, "made them more sensitive to the needs of the Jewish working class and presented to them the possibility of organizing this class into unions." This "discovery" of the Jewish working class, according to Mendelsohn, led directly to a distinct, Yiddish-speaking labor movement. It was certainly true that direct contact with the nascent Jewish working class affected the Russian Colony's intellectuals, but it should not be considered the "all-important" factor behind the intellectuals' decision to take up Yiddish and organize Jewish workers. After all, as Mendelsohn mentions, most intellectuals worked in factories only briefly before they resumed their studies and found employment elsewhere, often in professions such as dentistry, medicine, and law.[5] Having improved their own situations, the Russian Colony's intellectuals could have chosen any number of options. They could have left Yiddish-speaking workers behind and joined the general socialist movement, or they could have abandoned radicalism for mainstream politics, or they could have retreated from politics altogether. In fact, numerous individuals chose one or more of these options at some point in their lives. Yet many intellectuals embarked on a different path. "Instead of secluding themselves in an egotistic shell and directing all of their efforts towards attaining material wealth and an outstanding career," George Price, a former member of Am Oylom, wrote in 1893, "many of the members of the intelligentsia . . . have been working to improve the economic and spiritual status of the Jewish masses."[6] The decision by Russian-speaking intellectuals to organize Yiddish-speaking workers should be seen as one of several possibilities. The intellectuals who made that choice did so not only because of exposure to the Jewish working class, but also because they rethought what it meant to be radicals and intellectuals in the United States.

To understand why Russian-speaking intellectuals decided to build a Yiddish-speaking workers' movement, one must appreciate the influence of another immigrant group: German American socialists. While historians have acknowledged the role of Germans, they have yet to pay much attention to it. Instead, they tend to emphasize either a vague process of Americanization or, in a contrary vein, the persistent hold of Russian ideas, such as nihilism and revolutionary populism. According to Steven Cassedy, for example, Russian Jewish intellectuals "simply applied [Russian radical] ideologies to their new context—or they continued to apply them to the old context, because for many immigrants Russia remained the focus of all political activity."[7] Cassedy exaggerates the influence of Russian thinkers on Jewish intellectuals after they settled in New York. Most intellectuals did not remain wedded exclusively to Russian ideas or focus their energies primarily on their country of origin. In fact, they struggled intensely to adapt to their new surroundings, which included interacting with other immigrants, such as German Americans. From their early days in New York, Russian Jewish intellectuals developed close contacts with their German neighbors, acquiring from them new ideologies, organizational models, and practical assistance. In 1885 the German influence became evident when several former members of Am Oylom with close ties to German socialists established the Yidisher Arbeter Fareyn. Most of the Russian Colony's intellectuals were, at first, skeptical: bias against Yiddish was still strong, as was admiration for the Russian revolutionary tradition. Attitudes, however, would change significantly, if not completely, over the next year. The momentous struggles of 1886, as interpreted through German socialist ideologies, compelled a new perspective. An important minority of intellectuals ceased thinking of themselves as Russian revolutionaries in exile and assumed a new role as Yiddish-speaking leaders of New York's Jewish working class. The Jewish labor movement was born.

From Russia to the Russian Colony

The men and women who would later establish New York's Jewish labor movement entered the 1880s as students in Russia's expanding school system. They were part of a small but rapidly growing stratum of Jews enrolled in Russian crown schools, technical schools, gymnasia, and universities. (The number of Jewish men and women enrolled in Russian universities, for example, increased from 129 in 1864 to 556 in 1880 to 1,858 in 1886: 3.14 percent, 6.8 percent, and 14.3 percent of the respective totals.)[8] Some were from affluent families and had attended government-run schools from an early age. Such relatively privileged Jews enjoyed the best chance of reaching university, which was necessary to be considered a full-fledged intellectual. Many more Jewish students, however, were raised in religious homes and had a longer road to travel. On their own or with assistance from tutors, they struggled to learn Russian and other subjects needed to pass entrance exams. Sometimes parents supported their children's efforts, but often they did not. Many parents feared that Russian education would cause their boys and girls to stray too far from Judaism and the Jewish community. As it turned out, they had good cause for fear. Acquisition of secular knowledge frequently resulted in rebellion against religious observance, belief in God, parental authority, and communal allegiance. Many students physically removed themselves from established Jewish communities by moving to faraway cities, such as Moscow and St. Petersburg, from which all but a tiny minority of Jews were excluded by government decree. They changed their names, their manner of dress, their language, and their ways of thinking. "Like zealots of a new religion," recalls Gregory Weinstein, a gymnasium student from Vilnius and member of Am Oylom, "we discarded everything—valuable as well as valueless—of the old teachings."[9]

As the number of Jewish students increased, so too did their participation in the revolutionary movement. Although never a majority, Jewish students were disproportionately likely to sympathize with revolutionary ideas and participate in a revolutionary group.[10] For most students the process started by reading works of literature, literary criticism, and political thought. Nikolai Chernyshevsky's utopian novel, *What Is to Be Done?* (1863), made an especially strong impression. Although dreadful from an esthetic standpoint, *What Is to Be Done?* served as "the gospel for generations of secularized Russian revolutionaries," as Cassedy writes. The novel's idealized depiction of communal living, advocacy of women's liberation, and celebration of revolutionary heroism captivated idealistic Jewish students. In late-night discussions young men and women (in many cases with only one foot out of the shtetl) railed against conventional morality, extolled literary realism, and spoke of "serving the people," the long-suffering *narod,* or peasantry. They started to envision a "free Russia," which they would help to usher in not as despised Jews, but as heroic fighters against the autocracy. More than anything, they wanted to join the Russian intelligentsia: that "secular priesthood" devoted to solving humanity's "ultimate questions" through revolutionary change.[11] A minority of intrepid students actually became full-time revolutionaries. Their double rebellion against both Jewish tradition and the czar was dangerous, thrilling, and emotionally painful all at once. In many cases it resulted in severed family ties, expulsion from school, arrest, and worse. But in those risks, hundreds of Jewish students sought their personal liberation and that of Russia as a whole. At the dawn of the 1880s they looked forward to a bright future for themselves in their country of birth.[12]

Everything would change starting in March 1881.[13] In that month members of Narodnaia Volia assassinated Czar Alexander II, a forward-thinking autocrat who had emancipated the serfs and ameliorated the position of Jews in Russian society. Rumor circulated that Jews instigated the killing. Four weeks after the assassination a pogrom broke out in the Ukrainian city of Elisavetgrad (now Kirovograd). Over the next twelve months anti-Jewish riots spread across Ukraine and, sporadically, as far north as Poland. In 1881 alone an estimated twenty thousand Jews had their homes destroyed and about one hundred thousand suffered major property loss. By the spring of 1882 pogroms had struck more than two hundred Jewish communities, leaving an estimated sixty dead. Occasional violence continued into 1884. The government blamed Jews for incurring the wrath of the "native" population by exploiting them through usury and other "unproductive" occupations. In May 1882 Alexander's successor, Alexander III, tightened occupational and residential restrictions on Jews, and state-run educational institutions began implementing quotas limiting the number of male Jews that could enroll in state-run schools. The era of reform had suddenly and harshly come to an end.[14]

The pogroms had a devastating effect on Russia's Jewish students. Many of them had believed that education and revolution would lead to a better future for themselves and the Russian people. Yet the *narod* had turned against Jews in indiscriminate violence, for which the victims themselves were officially blamed. To make matters worse, leaders of Narodnaia Volia welcomed the pogroms as early stirrings of a larger revolt (though the party would reverse that decision in 1884) against the wealthy and the government.[15] Jewish students thus felt abandoned from all sides. "The indifference and even satisfaction evidenced by our former comrades toward Jewish anguish left us shaken by a storm of pity and sorrow and rebellion," Boris Bogen, a gymnasium student in

Moscow, would later write. Another Moscow student recorded his torment in a diary entry dated February 10, 1882:

> I have begun to be driven by a sharp, merciless question: "Who are you?" . . . I try to convince myself: "Do I really *have to be somebody?*" But I cannot get away from the question . . ." "Of course, I am a Russian," I reply and feel that it is not true. On what do I base that answer? Only on my *own* sympathies and dreams. But fool, don't you see that to your ardent love, they respond with insulting and cold contempt? . . . No, first of all and unwillingly I am a Jew. . . . [But] my Judaism does not give me any satisfaction. What, apart from memories, does it give me? With what can I fill my existence? . . . My God, why are we refused the love and sympathy of those around us?

Three months later George Price wrote in his diary:

> The Russian Jew who contributed to the welfare of his country as much if not more than the other inhabitants, the Russian Jew who had mastered the Russian language and had acquired the customs of the country which he considered his own . . . this Jew has to fear that in this so-called civilized land and in the nineteenth century, he will be attacked with impunity by drunkards and ignorant people. . . . Am I not despised? Am I not urged to leave? Do I not hear the word Zhid, constantly? Can I even think that someone considers me a human being capable of thinking and feeling like others? Do I not rise daily with fear lest the hungry mob attack me and rob me of my possessions and destroy everything that I have acquired with the sweat of my brow? Do I not pray that my sisters may escape the clutches of drunkards lest they be raped? Do I not pray that my parents be not killed trying to defend their children and that my brothers and sisters do not die of hunger and thirst?[16]

Jewish students had staked their identities and futures on what now seemed to be an illusion. They wanted to become Russians, but "authentic" Russians had violently rejected them. They idolized Narodnaia Volia, but its leaders sided with the anti-Jewish mob. They hoped for revolution, but the assassination of Alexander II invited greater repression. The situation called for drastic solutions.

Emulating student revolutionaries who in 1873–1874 had gone to live and agitate among the Russian peasantry, Jewish students embarked on a "going to the people" of their own. As Jonathan Frankel has shown, they underwent a collective change in consciousness practically overnight. All of a sudden, Russia's Jewish student youth started to view ordinary Jews differently, as a suffering *narod* in its own right, which deserved their attention no less than the peasantry. In a dramatic reversal, young men and women who had so recently rebelled against their parents and communities now declared solidarity with the Jewish people. They attended communal gatherings in synagogues, formed self-defense groups, and debated solutions to "the Jewish question." In Kiev, for example, 118 students, almost the entire Jewish student body of Kiev University, organized a demonstration with speeches in Russian and, remarkably, Yiddish. "The sufferings of people whom we had never known," Bogen writes, "whose beliefs and aspirations had become a matter of indifference to us, and whose Yiddish speech was an alien jargon to our Russian-trained ears, suddenly moved us as we had never been moved by the miseries of those oppressed masses which motivated our Socialistic endeavors." The idea of an organized mass emigration quickly took hold in towns and cities throughout the Pale of Settlement. "Suddenly," Abraham Cahan writes in his autobiography, "it became clear to many young intellectual Jews that Russia was not their homeland and that a true home must be found for Jews." The main question was where to find this true home. Students divided into two groups: those who favored Ottoman Palestine and those who favored the United States. The pro-Palestinian students formed the Bilu, the forerunner of the modern Zionist movement. Those who supported going to the United States, the larger number, joined Am Oylom. One group would pave the way to a Jewish homeland in Palestine; the other would create the Jewish labor movement in New York.[17]

Two men from Odessa, Monya Bokal and Moyshe Herder, had established Am Oylom in May 1881. Bokal and Herder were not Russian-educated intellectuals but self-taught *maskilim* who worked as teachers in local Jewish schools. Their followers initially included "simple folk"— shopkeepers, small traders, artisans, and tailors—but student radicals soon got involved and assumed leadership of the group (a source of some tension). Additional Am Oylom groups formed in other cities, such as Kiev and Vilnius. Some groups consisted exclusively of students, other were mixed. By the same token, Am Oylom members did not share identical goals. Some wanted only to become independent farmers in the United States, while others (especially the students) considered private property to be immoral and insisted on creating communes. "The first colonies," a memorandum from the Kiev Am Oylom stated, must be "based on cooperative principles, the only wise and suitable ones, especially in a new country." A number of Am Oylom members went so far as to propose the creation of an autonomous Jewish region or canton in the western United States, a kind of Jewish version of Utah. Whatever their differences, all members agreed that Jews must leave Russia to escape persecution and "rehabilitate" themselves physically and spiritually by working the land. (The idea of moral uplift through agricultural labor was widely shared among Jewish reformers and *maskilim* during the nineteenth century.) "Our motto," one member of Am Oylom wrote, "is return to agriculture, and our aim, the physical and spiritual rehabilitation of our people. In free America . . . we shall demonstrate to the world that we are capable of manual labor." Members of Am Oylom thus hoped to lead a full-scale exodus to the United States.[18]

Six or seven loosely affiliated Am Oylom groups, numbering roughly one thousand members, came to the United States in 1882. Their expectations soared high at the outset. Members of Cahan's group, for example, "imagined a wonderful communist life . . . without 'mine' and 'thine.'"[19] Yet by the time Am Oylom crossed the Atlantic, doubt had set in. Were agrarian communes viable? Could they really solve the problem of anti-Semitism? Were they effective instruments of social change? After much debate and soul-searching most Am Oylom groups disbanded. All told, the movement created just three colonies—one in Oregon and two in South Dakota—totaling ninety-two members. These would-be farmers possessed none of the skills needed to survive on the land in a far-flung region of a foreign country. Because of "lack of funds, lack of experience, and the frailties of human nature," all three colonies collapsed by 1887. Am Oylom utterly failed, but its members would go on to establish a much more successful movement of Jewish workers.[20]

Almost immediately after their arrival in New York, erstwhile members of Am Oylom attempted to find a new focus for their energies. In July 1882 a student from St. Petersburg, F. Mirovitsh, formed the Propaganda Association in response to a recent dockworkers' strike in which Jews were used as scabs. The Propaganda Association proposed to "raise the intellectual and moral level of American Jewish immigrants and clarify the position that they should occupy regarding the working class in the United States." It promised to publish pamphlets and a newspaper in "the Jewish dialect," and to hold regular lectures in Yiddish and Russian. Very little came of these plans, however. The Propaganda Association published nothing. It held only two Yiddish lectures by Abraham Cahan; the rest were held in Russian and, occasionally, German. "I did not understand clearly," Cahan later acknowledged, "what our practical work ought to be." The Propaganda Association disappeared less than two years after its founding.[21]

The Propaganda Association's demise reflected a collective malaise among members and former members of Am Oylom. They wanted to "serve the people," but no longer knew how to act on this desire. Who were "the people" and what could it mean to serve them in New York? Had the ideal of serving the people become irrelevant and, if so, what role was left for the revolutionary intellectual to play? Such questions tormented New York's Russian Jewish radicals during the early 1880s. "After the stormy revolutionary life in Russia and the disappointments in our ideals," Chaim Spivak writes in his 1910 memoir, "we, the first Russian immigrants, in our first years here in America were bereft— without a goal in life, without ideals—in a word, we felt like a teacher without pupils." "I began to wish earnestly," Cahan recalls, "for someone who would provide the answers to my perplexities. But for the first four or five years of my life in America I heard no answers only perplexities."[22] Contributing to the gloom and confusion was the need to earn a living. As students in Russia, members of Am Oylom had supported themselves mainly by tutoring other Jewish students, which they could not do in New York without knowing English. Lacking money and practical skills, the intellectuals could find work only in workshops and factories. Invariably, they found manual labor arduous and working conditions awful. "Not having a profession or a trade," recalls Yisroel Kopelov, "lonely, without friends and without help, every one of us had to lead a desperate struggle for a piece of dried bread. The permanent worry and concern for tomorrow literally sucked the marrow out from our bones." Thus, members of an elite stratum of Russian Jewish students found themselves working and living among poor, ordinary Jews in the slums of New York. This was a kind of "going to the people," but not as originally conceived and not at all welcomed.[23]

As a way of coping with their sense of displacement and material poverty, the former students turned inward. Before too long their sense of Jewish group solidarity dissipated and they reverted to a prior identity as Russian revolutionaries (or aspiring revolutionaries) now living in exile. After the Propaganda Association's demise, they created a number of debating and discussion societies that attempted to recreate the atmosphere of the Russian *kruzhok,* or revolutionary circle. In June 1884 Nikolai Aleinikov, the former leader of the Kiev Am Oylom, established the Russian Workingmen's Union, which, despite the implication, was not a labor organization of any kind. The union ran a library and held weekly Sunday lectures followed by freewheeling discussions.[24] In late 1884 Abraham Cahan and Mikhail Zametkin broke away to form a new group, the Russian Labor Lyceum. They intended to focus more on political action than on theoretical debate, but in fact the lyceum differed little from its predecessor. Both groups disappeared by the end of 1885, only to be replaced in late 1886 by the Russian Progressive Union. It, too, eventually dissolved. Similar Russian-speaking groups, consisting entirely of Jews, continued to form and disband through the 1890s. An 1896 play by Yankev Gordin, himself a Russian-speaking intellectual, satirized the inflated sense of mission and identification with the Russian revolutionary movement characteristic of New York's Russian Colony. Originally written and performed in Russian, Gordin's one-act play depicts a meeting of a fictitious group called the Russian American Union with Broad Ideals. In the middle of the meeting, a member delivers an absurdly bombastic speech putting forth his vision for the group:

> Our Russian union can become the spokesman for the interests of the Russian people, the bearer of the Russian intelligentsia's ideals, the factor behind productive events, the center of the Russian revolution, the mover of political reforms . . . the mighty dam against reactionary obscurantism, the thesis behind actions and the antithesis behind counter-actions, the school of radical worldviews, the clearing house of progressive thoughts, the unifying point between Siberia and America, and between Russia and Europe![25]

Gordin's readers were meant to understand that nothing would come of the Russian Union with Broad Ideals. It was doomed, just like previous groups with similarly ridiculous names: The Russian-American Unification Federation of Movers of Culture and Emancipation, The Russian Revolutionary League of Victorious Fighters, The Coalition of Russian-American Conventions of Fighters for Freedom, Equality, and Brotherliness, and the like. In real life, as in Gordin's satire, the myriad Russian-speaking groups achieved little in practical terms. They did, however, serve an important function by easing the prevailing sense of home-sickness and dislocation. In groups such as the Russian Workingmen's Union, like-minded men and women revived, as much as possible, the old esprit de corps and idealism of their student days. "There I transported myself," Shoel Yanovsky, who came to the United States in 1885, writes, "in my imagination, to earlier times in Russia, where I had such beautiful and wonderful dreams." For Yanovsky and his contemporaries, "beautiful and wonderful dreams" seemed hopeless in New York.[26]

Apart from the various Russian-speaking associations, the Russian Colony developed a social life in more informal settings. On warm evenings clusters of young intellectuals could be found on the Lower East Side's tenement rooftops. The future Socialist Party leader Morris Hillquit (who came to New York in 1886) used to gather with friends on the rooftop of a Cherry Street tenement, which he describes in the third person:

> They felt unhappy and forlorn in their workshops, but at night on the roofs they again lived in a congenial atmosphere. Once more they were students among students, forgetting the miseries of their hard and toil-some lives and enjoying the pleasures of freedom and companionship with

the abandon and enthusiasm of youth. . . . It was a slice of old Russian life that was thus transported to Cherry Street by the uprooted young immigrants. . . . Most of their evenings were spent in discussion. And what discussion! There was not a mooted question in science, philosophy, or politics that was not aired in the ardent, impassioned, and tumultuous debate. . . . It was amusing to hear these mild-mannered and soft-spoken boys and girls talk glibly about blowing up buildings and killing tyrants.[27]

Another popular meeting place was Avrom Netter's house on Suffolk Street. Netter, a venerable, fatherly figure who had discovered the Russian revolutionary movement by way of the *Haskalah*, opened his home to dozens of young radicals. One could always find in his basement an assortment of "socialists, anarchists, agnostics, atheists, and run-of-the-mill radicals" studying and debating "all scientific and social problems."[28] In the second half of the 1880s, cafés, such as Isidore Zaks's on Division Street, became popular places to congregate. In this Russian Jewish subculture—constituted by assorted Russian-speaking societies, cafés, tenement rooftops, and private homes—young men and women weathered their early, difficult years in New York. They fostered friendships, romances, and rivalries that would last for decades. Cahan met his wife, Anna, an occasional translator of Russian literature, during this period. So, too, did Mikhail Zametkin, whose wife, Adella, would become a prominent lecturer and organizer in the Socialist Labor Party. "I am sure," Chaim Spivak writes "that such intimate friendships rescued many from suicide."[29]

A strong feeling of nostalgia pervaded the Russian Colony during the 1880s. Safe from arrest and pogroms, intellectuals started to forget what impelled them to leave Russia in the first place. They longed for the heady atmosphere of their student days and, at the same time, felt a strong alienation from their new home. In their eyes American society appeared materialistic and "soulless." It seemed that Gilded Age Americans cared only about money, while idealistic young revolutionaries rotted away in Russian prisons. Reverence for Narodnaia Volia returned, even before the party's disavowal of the pogroms in 1884. The Russian Colony raised money for the party, continued to read its publications, and celebrated every March the assassination of Alexander II. Young

1. N. Kozlovsky, *Russian Jewish Workers on a Tenement Rooftop*. From
B. Vaynshteyn (Bernard Weinstein), *Bilder fun yidishn arbeter-lebn in
Amerike* (New York: Workmen's Circle, 1935), p. 28. Courtesy of the
Workmen's Circle.

parents named their newborns after revolutionary heroes, such as the czar's assassin, Andrei Zheliabov.[30] As far as the intellectuals were concerned, they were Russian revolutionaries in exile. In point of fact, few of them had actively participated in the revolutionary movement or possessed the requisite university degree to qualify as full-fledged intellectuals. But in a city with few ethnic Russians (intellectuals or otherwise), Jews could assert an identity that had been denied to them in Russia itself. Without anybody to tell them otherwise, they defined themselves as they pleased. They felt themselves to be Russian, in Hillquit's words, by virtue of their "education, culture and habits, in manner, spirit, and ideology."[31] Whereas Jews in Russia aspired to join the revolutionary intelligentsia, in New York they *were* the intelligentsia—bearers of Russian literature, language, and ideas, and the country's sacred revolutionary tradition.[32]

Yet Russian attachments notwithstanding, the intellectuals did not insulate themselves completely from the surrounding society. They read feverishly across the spectrum of late nineteenth-century progressive thought and flirted with an array of radicals and reformers. There was William Frey (Vladimir Geins), a charismatic, Russian-born nobleman, pacifist, and vegetarian who, for a brief period, joined Am Oylom's New Odessa commune in Oregon; Edward King, a Scottish-born labor reformer and positivist; and Felix Adler, the founder of Ethical Culture, a secular offshoot of Reform Judaism. Members of the Russian Colony embraced, debated, and discarded their ideas in rapid succession. They were eager, indeed desperate, to reorient themselves in New York, if they could only figure out how. Eventually, they did so by following the path of an older and larger community of immigrant radicals: the social democrats and anarchists of "Little Germany."[33]

From the Russian Colony to Little Germany

When Russian Jews started arriving on the Lower East Side, the area was known as *Kleindeutschland,* the heart of New York's German immigrant community. Almost 170,000 Germans, 60 percent of the area's total population, lived there. Although the influx of eastern European Jews would, in the following decade, displace the Germans, Little Germany was still very much alive in the 1880s. One needed only to wander north of Grand Street to discover neighborhoods dotted by German labor lyceums, assembly halls, clubs, and saloons. Russian Jewish intellectuals frequented those venues and, through them, found a way out of their isolation. Little Germany served as their gateway to America.

What was Little Germany's appeal? The East Side was also home to a significant Irish population, but Russian Jewish intellectuals did not develop close ties with that community. Memoirists, in fact, rarely mention the Irish presence. One obvious factor was language. A small number of intellectuals had studied German in school or were raised in German-speaking areas of the Russian Empire, such as Riga. Furthermore, those who had knowledge of Yiddish (a Germanic language) could acquire German without terrible difficulty. Some individuals even chose to learn German before English. In this regard, Yiddish—otherwise a source of embarrassment—could be considered an asset.

A second, more decisive factor had to do with the prominence of socialists in Little Germany. Many German immigrants had been members of Germany's Social Democratic Party, the largest socialist party in Europe. In New York and cities across the country, they honored their socialist legacy by building sturdy trade unions, an influential press, and a rich network of social, cultural, and athletic associations. German immigrants also dominated the Socialist Labor Party (SLP), the mainstay of American socialism between the 1870s and 1890s. ("One would have thought," Cahan would later write of the SLP, "that the Americans were the foreigners and the Germans the natives.") Little Germany's socialists greatly impressed their Russian Jewish neighbors. They boasted an intellectual and political pedigree that stretched back to Karl Marx himself and demonstrated how to adapt to the United States without forfeiting radical commitments. If any group seemed worthy of emulation, German socialists were it. They were "able, self-disciplined, progressive, and sympathetic."[34]

Compared to German American socialism, Irish labor must have seemed alien and uninviting. In addition to the language barrier, Irish workers were, in the main, more conservative than their German counterparts. They had strong ties to the Catholic Church and the Tammany Hall Democratic Party, which was synonymous with corruption in New York.[35] Even the radical strain in Irish labor was imbued with Catholicism, as well as Irish nationalism. For Irish radicals, the historian Eric Foner explains, Catholicism "was not merely a religion, but almost a badge of nationality and culture." Foner credits radical Irish Catholics, in alliance with native-born Protestants, with playing a vital role in social reform movements.[36] Yet Christianity could not have provided such common ground between Irish and Jewish radicals. Hostile to all forms of religion, particularly one so closely associated with anti-Jewish persecution in Europe, Russian Jewish intellectuals could not easily view Irish labor leaders as models. It is true that German socialists, like the Irish, highly valued their own culture (or aspects of it), sometimes to the point of seeming chauvinistic to outsiders.[37] However, German socialists spoke in the name of the "international proletariat," not a particular religion or nation. Theirs was a universalistic and secular ideology. By advocating a system of political thought not bound by ethno-cultural background, German socialists created a "neutral" sphere into which Russian Jews could and did integrate. German socialists, consequently, served as the midwives of the Jewish labor movement.

Several individuals played particularly important roles in welcoming Russian Jews to Little Germany. One figure was Justus Schwab, "a magnificent looking man with broad shoulders, great tawny beard, and massive head." Schwab, who immigrated to the United States as a boy after Germany's failed 1848 revolution, owned a famous saloon on First Street where radicals from around New York used to congregate. Advertised as "the gathering-place for all bold, joyful and freedom-loving spirits," Schwab's saloon was for Russian Jews a congenial environment in which to mix with writers, activists, and labor leaders. "One could always find at Schwab's," one Yiddish journalist recounts, "a society of highly intelligent people discussing art, literature, and social questions." Emma Goldman, the most famous individual to emerge from New York's Russian Colony, considered Schwab a "comrade, advisor, and friend of all."[38]

If Schwab's saloon was Little Germany's most popular meeting place, then its most influential leaders were Sergius Schewitsch and Johann Most. The son of a Latvian nobleman, Schewitsch was born in the Russian Empire but educated in Germany. During his years abroad he rose through the ranks of the Social Democratic Party and married the journalist and actress Helene von Donniges, best remembered in socialist history as the woman for whom the party leader Ferdinand Lassalle lost his life in a duel. Schewitsch and von Donniges moved to New York after Bismarck passed his infamous antisocialist laws in 1878. Handsome and worldly, Schewitsch "cut a dashing figure in New York socialist circles." He was a talented lecturer in several languages, coeditor of the respected daily *New Yorker Volkszeitung (New York People's Newspaper),* and a national leader of the SLP until he and von Donniges returned to his native Riga in 1891.[39]

Johann Most, like Schewitsch, had roots in German social democracy, but his political career moved in a different direction. After serving two terms as a Reichstag deputy, Most was forced to flee Germany for London in 1878, and he then moved to New York in December 1882. By the time he arrived Most and a vocal minority of SLP members had grown disenchanted with social democracy, which they came to believe was too moderate and ineffectual. Instead, they espoused "revolutionary socialism," known more commonly as anarchism, which was "anti-statist, anti-parliamentarian, and anti-reformist." Anarchists rejected the social democratic position that electoral politics and unions could pave the way for either a socialist revolution or a gradual transformation of capitalism. Most and his followers believed that only through armed struggle, including acts of terror ("propaganda by deed"), could workers liberate themselves from capitalism. As editor of the weekly *Die Freiheit (Freedom),* which was funded, in part, by Schwab, and founder of the International Working People's Association, Most would remain America's preeminent anarchist until his death in 1906.[40]

From the beginning Russian Jewish intellectuals developed a deep and abiding respect for Most and Schewitsch. They regularly attended their lectures, read their newspapers, and became personally acquainted. Because he could speak both German and Russian fluently, Schewitsch was especially well situated to serve as an intermediary between Little

2. Sergius Schewitsch, editor of the German-language socialist daily *New Yorker Volkszeitung*. From Abraham Cahan, *Bleter fun mayn lebn*, vol. 2 (New York: Forverts Association, 1926), p. 103.

Germany and the Russian Colony. As far back as July 1882 the Propaganda Association had invited Schewitsch to address its first meeting and, from that point forward, he often gave lectures to Russian Jewish audiences. In turn, Russian Jewish intellectuals frequented Schewitsch's German lectures, even before they achieved facility in the language. Without exception they praised Schewitsch as a "grand," "splendid," and "fiery" orator. "When Schewitch spoke," the future Yiddish poet Dovid Edelshtat wrote to his sister in 1887, "I felt tears streaming from my eyes."[41] Johann Most developed an equally devoted following. Although he lacked Schewitsch's polish and charm, Most was nonetheless a powerful and charismatic public speaker in his own right. His Jewish followers often likened him to a *rebbe*, the spiritual leader of Hassidic (pietistic) Jewish communities. "He possessed," Yisroel Kopelov would recall, "the same enthusiasm, the same devotion to his ideal and to his truth, and the same readiness to sacrifice himself for the ideal."[42]

Russian Jewish intellectuals displayed equal enthusiasm for German socialist newspapers. Despite sharp ideological differences between Most's

Die Freiheit and Schewitsch's *Volkszeitung,* Russian Jews devoured both newspapers.[43] At a time when no Russian-language newspaper was published in New York,[44] the *Volkszeitung* and *Die Freiheit* filled the void. Russian Jewish intellectuals turned to them for general information, instruction in anarchist and social democratic thought, and exposure to new branches of European literature. If they did not know German already, they learned as they went along. Eventually, some individuals became fluent enough to contribute articles to German newspapers and, in several cases, even serve as editors. Others raised money, sold subscriptions, and volunteered in the editorial offices. In Kopelov's estimation, *Die Freiheit* "had no equal perhaps in the entire history of the radical press." "For us," Cahan writes, the *Volkszeitung* "was a real treasure. . . . This newspaper was the reason some of us learned German even before we learned English. It played a major role in our intellectual development." Cahan did not exaggerate. The *Volkszeitung*'s 1888 series on African Americans, for example, so moved one Russian Jewish reader that he traveled to the South, just weeks after his arrival in the United States, to witness the plight of blacks firsthand. On the occasion of its fiftieth anniversary, the *Volkszeitung* accurately described itself as a "beacon for its Jewish brothers."[45]

The German-Jewish relationship begun in the early 1880s continued into the following decade. During the 1890s Yiddish-speaking Jews became Most's "principal constituency." "On corners around Hester Street and Grand," Most's biographer writes, "Most got on his soapbox, peppered his German with Yiddish, and demanded revolution of Jews who gathered around and peppered their Yiddish with German, and applauded." Johanna Greie, editor of the *Volkszeitung*'s women's page, frequently addressed Jewish women's groups. And Alexander Jonas, after Schewitsch the leading German socialist, spoke at just about every significant Jewish labor event. "Between Jonas and the Jews of the East Side," one union leader recalls, "was vast, mutual sympathy. . . . He was always with them [at] all their large and small strikes. At every mass meeting you heard his clear, hardy voice." The pioneering Yiddish writer Morris Vintshevsky penned a tribute to German American socialists following the 1914 election of Meyer London to Congress, the first Jewish socialist to represent the East Side. Vintshevsky described the encounter between "German and Jew" in the fashion of a Biblical narrative: "In the beginning there is heaven and earth. But in Heaven there is not yet light and on Earth chaos reigns, and darkness is in the abyss. And Marx comes and says: 'Let there be light!' And it becomes light. . . . And the German brings Marx's Torah, with the torch in his hand. But, in the beginning, nobody wants it. . . . Yisrolik [that is, the ordinary Jew] however snatches it up. 'We shall hear and we shall obey,' he cries out and takes hold of the German's teaching."

Although Vintshevsky did not immigrate to the United States until 1894, he had previously lived in Germany and associated with German socialists in London, so by the time he arrived in America, he already appreciated the German influence. (Vintshevsky would later publish a portion of his memoirs in the *Volkszeitung*.) In short, contacts initiated by a small number of intellectuals during the 1880s developed into a lasting relationship between two immigrant labor movements.[46]

It should be noted that few Russian Jewish intellectuals converted suddenly to a particular ideology. Typically, an individual spent months and even years sorting through social democracy and anarchism. Anarchism initially held the stronger allure. Its disdain for gradual solutions and celebration of revolutionary heroism appealed to those enamored of Narodnaia Volia. Social democracy expected revolution at some future date, but its emphasis on building trade unions and participation in the existing political system demanded a fundamental revision of attitudes and ideas. Day-to-day organizational work struck many members of the Russian Colony as depressingly mundane. In Russia one could be arrested just for distributing a pamphlet or attending a meeting, but in the United States freedoms of speech and assembly made such activities seem ordinary: "businesslike" was the word often used. "When we consider the holy images of the Russian revolutionaries," Dovid Edelshtat complained in 1890, "full of self-sacrifice and immortal courage, and then we consider those who, in America, bear the name revolutionaries, what a sad comparison it is." "What kind of socialism could it be without conspiracy?" the young Abraham Cahan wondered. "What good was the fruit if it wasn't forbidden?"[47] Yet in the second half of the 1880s,

Cahan sided with social democracy. Cahan acquired from Germans terms and concepts—a general framework—for understanding American society and how to change it. He came to view the organization of workers through political parties, unions, and newspapers as legitimate. If all that seemed boring at first, Cahan and his contemporaries changed their attitudes eventually. In an 1887 interview George Price, then head of the Socialist Labor Party's Buffalo branch and editor of the German-language *Buffaloer Arbeiterzeitung,* told a reporter, "When I was in Russia, I was a nihilist and advocated violence and did my share in the movement. But in this country under different conditions I regard it as madness and criminality to counsel violence in a place where men can speak and write and vote. . . . There it is right to rebel and use violence; here the ballot is every man's weapon."[48] After consistent contact with German social democrats, Cahan writes, "the dream of an instant earthly paradise dissolved. The *New Yorker Volkszeitung* and the German-language socialist meeting took its place."[49]

The first concrete sign that German social democracy had begun to take hold appeared in January 1885 with the creation of the Russian Jewish Workers' Association (RJWA).[50] Two brothers, Numia and Mitia Gretsh, founded the group to propagate social democracy in Yiddish. Both brothers had been active in Odessa's revolutionary circles before the pogroms, and Mitia, the elder of two, had been arrested in 1881 for attempting to organize a Jewish self-defense group. They came to America in 1882 with the Odessa Am Oylom, but instead of joining the group's New Odessa commune in Oregon, they remained in New York. The Gretsh brothers learned German as they became frequent visitors to Little Germany and, in 1884, joined the Socialist Labor Party. In January 1885 they established the RJWA with assistance from other ex–Am Oylom leaders. It is not clear if the Gretshes' German comrades persuaded them to found the RJWA or if they undertook this initiative on their own. Whatever the case, the Gretsh brothers had taken an important step. Through the RJWA they established the first institutional connection between German social democracy and Yiddish-speaking workers.[51]

A month later a second group was established with the specific goal of publishing a socialist newspaper in Yiddish. That group, called the Yiddish Newspaper Workers' Association, also had strong German connections. Its members were Austro-Hungarian Jews who had immigrated to the United States during the 1870s and become active in the German-speaking labor movement. Jacob Schoen was the key figure. A former rabbinical student from Hungary, Schoen immigrated to New York in 1879 and found work as a presser in a clothing factory. In the early 1880s he joined the SLP and the *Volkszeitung*'s board of directors. Having established himself in the German movement and being fluent in Yiddish, Schoen, along with his circle of Austro-Hungarian Jews, was well situated to bring German social democracy to Yiddish-speaking immigrants. RJWA's members did not know of Schoen's plan until they spotted an announcement in the *Volkszeitung,* which often printed reports of lectures, meetings, and other functions in the Russian Colony. The two groups decided to meet, and in April they merged to create the Yidisher Arbeter Fareyn. With endorsements from the United German Trades and the *Volkszeitung* (which printed a poem in its honor) the Yidisher Arbeter Fareyn made impressive strides during its first six months. It raised $250 toward the publication of a Yiddish newspaper, held a series of public lectures in Yiddish, and organized the first demonstration of Jewish workers in a Labor Day parade. By 1886 the Yidisher Arbeter Fareyn had recruited more than one hundred members, including both Russian-speaking intellectuals and Yiddish-speaking workers.[52]

The establishment of the Yidisher Arbeter Fareyn thus signaled an important turning point. It demonstrated a new willingness within the Russian Colony to organize Jewish workers using their mother tongue. By jettisoning the word "Russian" from its name, the Yidisher Arbeter Fareyn signaled its openness to all Yiddish-speaking Jews regardless of where they came from in Europe. This decision rested on a new perception of Jewish workers as political actors and a new self-definition of intellectuals as labor leaders. In 1885 this change in consciousness had only begun to achieve organizational form. In the following year, however, local and national events would produce a watershed: the birth of a full-fledged Yiddish-speaking workers' movement.

The Great Upheaval

The Yidisher Arbeter Fareyn established its presence on the East Side as the nationwide movement for the eight-hour workday gained momentum. In 1884 the Federation of Organized Trades and Labor Unions, precursor to the American Federation of Labor (AFL), resolved that "eight hours shall constitute a legal day's work from and after May 1, 1886." The resolution initially received little attention, but by late 1885 trade unions across the country had taken up the demand. By the following spring the eight-hour day became the rallying cry of a national movement that would culminate in huge strikes, boycotts, May Day demonstrations, and Chicago's Haymarket riot. In "a frenzied hatred of labor for capital," strikers advocated not only an eight-hour workday, but higher wages, control over production, and, in some cases, abolition of wage labor itself. During this "Great Upheaval," almost five hundred thousand workers participated in more than fourteen hundred strikes nationwide. Union membership swelled to almost one million.[53] In the electoral arena, independent labor parties formed in all but four states and won scores of victories in municipal and state elections. The struggles of 1886, won and lost, had lasting repercussions in the United States and affected countries as far away as England, Germany, and Russia.[54]

The Great Upheaval shook New York harder than most cities. According to the Bureau of Labor Statistics of New York State, at least 77,250 workers struck against 1,195 establishments between November 1885 and November 1886. During the same period 165 labor boycotts took place. New York's Central Labor Union (CLU) grew to 120 unions representing between 40,000 and 50,000 members, making it the largest citywide federation of unions in the country.[55] The CLU spearheaded Henry George's landmark mayoral campaign, to that point the "most hotly contested campaign in the city's annals."[56] Amid this ferment, Yiddish-speaking Jews entered the stage of New York's labor movement and city politics.

Thousands of Jewish men and women participated in the tumultuous events of 1886. Strikes by Jewish workers had taken place occasionally as far back as 1873, but the number and size of strikes in 1886 far and away surpassed their predecessors. Cloak makers, the largest segment of the garment industry, stood at the forefront. In March about 4,500 employees (most though not all of whom were Jews) from ten firms struck to demand an end to the contracting system, which was responsible for driving down wages, creating sweatshops, and encouraging homework in tenement apartments. The strike brought the cloak industry "almost to a standstill," according to the *New York Sun*.[57] By year's end, a total of 9,166 cloak makers and workers in other branches of the women's clothing industry went on strike. Jews had established themselves as a significant force in New York labor.[58]

The events of 1886 galvanized the Russian Colony. The remarkable sight of men and women across ethnic, craft, and political lines mobilizing behind shared goals persuaded many in the Russian Colony that they "now stood at the threshold of a genuinely revolutionary period." "We were convinced," Cahan recollects, "that our demands would increase until the point would be reached when the entire American working class would rise to the barricades for a decisive struggle." Yanovsky believed with "perfect faith" that it was "'the beginning of the end,' that the redemption of the working class was at the door." In his 1907 memoir Mikhail Zametkin describes the new sense of mission that swept through the Russian Colony:

> The people do not want to come to us, then we'll go to them. The people do not understand our language, then we will speak to them more plainly, more simply, so they'll understand. The people do not understand their own historical mission, then we'll show at least a small form of practical action. The people don't grasp the fundamental principles of socialism, then we will lead them to where it's not so deep. . . . The people don't yet understand their own interests as a proletariat, but they understand what benefits them as factory workers.[59]

After four years of searching, Zametkin had discovered a new purpose. What he and other intellectuals dismissed as prosaic months earlier now seemed the most important thing to do.

The Russian Colony's intellectuals threw themselves into the strike movement. Under the auspices of the Yidisher Arbeter Fareyn (JWA:

Jewish Workers' Association), they held biweekly "agitational" lectures, organized unions, formulated demands, and negotiated contracts. Inevitably, the JWA's leaders encountered problems: neither they nor the people whom they sought to organize had any appreciable experience in labor activism. Gregory Weinstein, a former member of Am Oylom and a leader in the Yidisher Arbeter Fareyn, complained of "very ignorant and undisciplined followers." "Many a time," he recounts, "we found it difficult to restrain [Jewish workers] from breaking into a strike before they were prepared to hold out to a finish." Weinstein was correct, no doubt, but it is also likely that Jewish workers voiced criticisms of their own. With little or no experience, both sides had to learn by trial and error.[60] Despite difficulties the JWA achieved significant results during the year. It organized a Jewish contingent in the Central Labor Union's May Day parade of twenty thousand people and established the Anti-Sweating League, which successfully lobbied the state legislature to regulate sweatshops. Most important, the JWA organized a total of fourteen unions, including Yiddish typographers, bakers, purse makers, cap makers, shirtmakers, cloak makers, and peddlers. "It is true that peddlers are no wage-earners," the peddlers' union explained, "but proletarians they are. The difference between a working-man and a peddler is that the working-man gets a starvation wage, while the peddler starves without a wage." Three hundred people attended the union's first meeting in late October. It is unknown how many people joined the JWA and its allied unions because of a lack of documentation, but the JWA clearly stood at the forefront of the Jewish strike movement. It brought institutional and ideological coherence to what otherwise might have been spontaneous and unfocused protest.[61]

The new alliance forged between intellectuals and workers—prompted by the Great Upheaval and legitimated by German social democracy—compelled a shift in language from Russian to Yiddish. Intellectuals recognized that if they wanted to reach Jewish workers, then they would have to speak their language. This was no easy matter. First, intellectuals had to overcome or, at least, suspend their deep-seated bias against Yiddish. At best they viewed Yiddish with condescending affection, at worst with outright derision. In the eyes of most intellectuals,

Yiddish—or *zhargon,* as they called it—reflected a constricted, culturally backward Jewish society.[62] They associated *zhargon* with the intimacies of family, the yap of the shtetl marketplace, and the rote learning of *kheyder.*[63] Consequently, those who knew Yiddish often hid this fact from their peers. Chaim Spivak, a friend of Cahan's since at least 1883, did not realize he could speak Yiddish fluently until three years later. Cahan regarded Russian as the language of his "intellectual self," an attitude shared by nearly all his peers.[64] For those accustomed to using Russian as the language of intellectual discourse, the idea of delivering a lecture or speech in Yiddish seemed strange and inappropriate. As Yanovsky recalls, "When it came to speaking in Yiddish—in my mother tongue—I felt an inconceivable nervousness."[65] In addition to their ambivalence toward Yiddish, intellectuals faced the practical problem of having to learn Yiddish from scratch or learn it in a new capacity—as a medium of political propaganda. The results were not always successful. The intellectuals sometimes borrowed German vocabulary to such an extent that ordinary immigrants could barely understand what they said. Still, these immediate shortcomings were of secondary importance to the larger phenomenon at work: a growing number of intellectuals were making an effort to speak Yiddish years after they left it behind in Russia.

The appearance of socialist Yiddish newspapers represented most concretely the intellectuals' new commitment to Yiddish. In May 1886 Cahan and Charles Raevsky (both active in the Yidisher Arbeter Fareyn) brought out the first socialist Yiddish newspaper, *Di naye tsayt (The New Era).* However, with just ten dollars in capital, the two men could not afford printing costs and *Di naye tsayt* folded after four issues.[66] Around the same time two textile workers donated their combined savings of eight hundred dollars to start a second, more successful Yiddish newspaper. Named *Di nyu-yorker yidishe folkstsaytung (The New York Jewish People's Newspaper)* after the German *New Yorker Volkszeitung* (but with the appropriate modification), the new Yiddish weekly appeared in late June. Its editors, Abba Braslavsky and Moyshe Mints, were leading members of the Yidisher Arbeter Fareyn. Under the motto "science, organization, freedom," they promised to "show the Jewish worker his cor-

3. Abraham Cahan in 1883, one year after his arrival in the United States. From Abraham Cahan, *Bleter fun mayn lebn*, vol. 2 (New York: Forverts Association, 1926), p. 111.

rect place in the family of workers of the entire world, his duty to his suffering brothers, to open his eyes to his economic situation, to enlighten and show him what kind of world he lives in, why he suffers, and how he can overcome it." Braslavsky and Mints maintained a generally social democratic orientation, but they did not enforce a single party line. They welcomed anarchists, "Palestinophiles" (Mints was a former member of Bilu), and others without a defined political orientation. Braslavsky and Mints also introduced a new level of professionalism in Yiddish journalism, then in its formative period. They kept the *Folkstsaytung* free of crooked columns, smeared print, outdated news items, and sensationalistic stories often found in contemporary Yiddish newspapers. By the standards of its time, the *Folkstsaytung* can be considered a success. It had a circulation of about fifteen hundred, with readers as far away as Burlington, Vermont, Lynn, Massachusetts, and Milwaukee, Wisconsin. The *Folkstsaytung* was not the most popular Yiddish newspaper (that honor went to the nominally Orthodox *Yidishes tageblat (Jewish Daily News)*, but it introduced socialism into the emerging Yiddish newspaper market.[67]

With the establishment of the Yidisher Arbeter Fareyn, its allied unions, and the *Folkstsaytung*, a distinct Jewish labor movement (identified as such in Yiddish as *di yidishe arbeter bavegung*) had come into existence. This development provoked opposition from preexisting elites who claimed to speak on behalf of the immigrant Jewish population but could not deny the new threat confronting them. Orthodox rabbis denounced the Jewish labor movement's leaders, without distinction, as "nihilists" and "anarchists" who promoted heretical ideas and undermined Jewish communal harmony. The Hungarian-born rabbi Moses Weinberger, for example, pilloried Braslavsky and Mints in a Hebrew booklet published in 1887:

> Their aim is to breathe fire into the hearts of Jewish workers who have heretofore shown exemplary tolerance; to arouse hatred and dissatisfaction among those laborers of our people who have always been peaceful, quiet, and satisfied; and to sow animosity and discord among the poor of the nation against the rich and the well-to-do. In general they want to provoke disputes between men and their brothers. They seek to widen intellectual cleavages, incite workers to war, put an end to peace and harmony, and open Jews' eyes to nihilism—one of the few forbidden teachings that up to now has not forged inroads into the Israelite camp.[68]

Kasriel Sarasohn, a rabbi and publisher of the *Yidishes tageblat* (which maintained a more flexible approach to Orthodox Judaism than Weinberger), attacked the Yidisher Arbeter Fareyn in similar terms. In response to a boycott against his newspaper organized by the Yidisher Arbeter Fareyn, Sarasohn denounced its leaders as "professional agitators" who "incite the Jewish workingmen to strikes, boycotts, and riots."[69] Whereas socialists sought to mobilize popular discontent, Sarasohn and Weinberger viewed it as harmful and wanted to mediate or stifle class conflict as much as possible. They accomplished little, however. They denounced socialist intellectuals for "inciting" Jewish workers but failed to offer a positive alternative. By standing on the sidelines, they left a power vacuum that the "nihilists" and "agitators" eagerly filled. Wealthy uptown Jewish communal leaders also proved to be impotent. They deemed the Yidisher Arbeter Fareyn—indeed any form of Jewish political organization—as separatist and un-American. Yet they did little more than complain, thus allowing the Russian Colony's intellectuals to emerge as a new source of leadership and authority.

The Yidisher Arbeter Fareyn reached the peak of its influence during Henry George's landmark mayoral campaign. The events leading up to the campaign began in early July 1886, when five leaders of a boycott against a German beer garden were sentenced to prison on charges of extortion. The Central Labor Union responded with a protest rally, and several days later it decided to field its own candidate for the upcoming mayoral election. In August the CLU formed the United Labor Party and nominated Henry George as its candidate. George, a newspaper editor, lecturer, and author of the famous tract *Progress and Poverty* (1879), was not a socialist, nor were the United Labor Party's mostly Irish American leaders. Rather, George was a pro-labor reformer who supported public works, the abolition of prison and tenement labor, and better sanitation laws. Above all, George advocated a single tax on undeveloped real estate in order to redistribute wealth. From the socialist perspective, George's single tax plan seemed all too limited, but the SLP and the German *Volkszeitung* nonetheless supported George in a broad, if shaky, coalition of "single taxers," "Greenbackers," trade unionists, and middle-class reformers.[70]

Following the lead of German socialists, the Yidisher Arbeter Fareyn and the *Folkstsaytung* also endorsed Henry George. For many of the East Side's Russian Jewish intellectuals, participation in an election campaign on behalf of a reformist candidate in a capitalist country was a hard compromise to make. Still, despite George's shortcomings—and the Yidisher Arbeter Fareyn's leaders vigorously pointed those out—the widespread public enthusiasm for George proved difficult to resist. Describing one of George's rallies, Mikhail Zametkin recalls, "It was a joy to stand at Union Square and see how union after union, just like true battalions of the revolution, came and marched by as if on battle maneuvers. . . . We knew that we were united and that the United Labor Party was a force."[71] The Yidisher Arbeter Fareyn created a special, eleven-member committee, led by Gregory Weinstein, to direct George's campaign in the East Side's Jewish neighborhoods. The committee coordinated its efforts with English- and German-speaking organizations, thus furthering ties between the Yidisher Arbeter Fareyn (and, by extension, Yiddish-speaking workers generally) and New York's larger labor movement. Weinstein's committee raised funds, registered voters, and organized campaign rallies.[72] At least three unions allied with the Yidisher Arbeter Fareyn organized their own George campaign committees. During October meetings and rallies occurred almost every night. The Union of Jewish Peddlers, for example, organized a rally on October 18 that was attended by some five hundred people. Reportedly more than two hundred people joined the Yidisher Arbeter Fareyn that night. Four days later the group organized a parade with speeches in Yiddish, German, and English. On October 28, five days before the election, a large audience packed Coburg Hall to hear speeches by Schewitsch and George himself. George depicted himself as "the American Moses," who would "lead the Jews from their present-day Egypt." Using such Biblical imagery to great effect, George inspired "the enthusiasm and interest of the ordinary worker, peddler, and storekeeper."[73]

George won 68,110 votes, which was the highest number received by any third-party candidate for New York City mayor in the nineteenth century. George placed ahead of the Republican candidate, Theodore Roosevelt, but he lost the election to Abram Hewitt, a reform Democrat backed by Tammany Hall. It is not clear how many Jews voted for George on election day, but he quite likely won a plurality, if not a majority, of votes in the East Side's heavily Jewish wards. Hewitt carried no Jewish ward. The *Folkstsaytung* mourned George's defeat, but it did not consider his campaign a failure.[74] According to the newspaper, George had "awakened the mute and beaten-down slaves, planted in their hearts a new hope, and a stronger belief in their future." In the *Folkstsaytung's* opinion, the Jewish proletariat now constituted a political force, which was an important first step in struggles to come.[75]

However, neither the *Folkstsaytung* nor the Yidisher Arbeter Fareyn spoke for the entire Russian Jewish intelligentsia, particularly for the portion that turned toward anarchism. As Johann Most taught them,

4. The popular lecturer and journalist Mikhail Zametkin in 1890. Courtesy of the YIVO Institute for Jewish Research. From Abraham Cahan, *Bleter fun mayn lebn,* vol. 2 (New York: Forverts Association, 1926), p. 439.

the Russian Colony's newborn anarchists denied that capitalism could be overturned through elections and unions. By the fall of 1886 Most and his followers found plenty of evidence for their position in repeated incidents of police brutality, the judiciary's antilabor bias, George's defeat, and, above all, Chicago's Haymarket affair. No other event provoked more outrage than Haymarket. The riot on May 4, the subsequent repression of Chicago's radicals, the frame-up of the city's anarchist leaders, and their execution in November 1887 seemed to confirm Most's contention that American democracy was a sham. To many of the Russian Colony's intellectuals, the events of 1886 revealed the United States to be no better than Russia. "This is the land of the much-praised freedom and equality?" Yanovsky and his friends asked themselves. "There is a right to strike . . . and yet [strikers] are treated as though they were wild animals! Indeed, it's better in a country like Russia where the workers at least know in advance that striking is forbidden."[76] The strategy put forward by Most was to preach revolution until a portion of the American working class was prepared to take action. He was convinced that an armed insurrection led by several hundred workers could easily overthrow the small bourgeoisie that ruled over the majority of American citizens. In one famous speech, which landed him in jail, Most demonstrated how to use a rifle and called on audience members to take up arms. None of Most's Russian Jewish followers actually stormed the barricades, but on October 6 (the evening of Yom Kippur, the holiest day on the Jewish religious calendar), a group of them founded the first Yiddish-speaking anarchist group, the Pioneers of Liberty (Pionere der Frayhayt). The group's immediate purpose was to raise public support for Chicago's imprisoned anarchists and counteract the influence of social democracy among Jewish workers. In future months the Pioneers attracted many prominent intellectuals, including Yanovsky, Dovid Edelshtat, Emma Goldman, and Annie Netter (Avrom Netter's daughter).[77] Thus, even as the Great Upheaval impelled the Russian Colony's intellectuals toward an alliance with Yiddish-speaking workers, it served to crystallize ideological differences among them. Anarchists and social democrats now formed distinct camps and differences between them would only worsen by the end of the 1880s.

With Henry George's November defeat, the Great Upheaval wound down in New York. Already by the summer of 1886 courts had ruled against the use of boycotts and employers had mounted an effective counterattack against strikers through the formation of manufacturers' associations. Concessions won in successful strikes—shorter hours, higher wages, and cleaner work conditions—proved fleeting. Clothing manufacturers reneged on agreements and newly established unions crumbled. The industry's seasonal cycles of production, intense competition between small firms, and chaotic subcontracting systems undermined the conditions needed for stable unions. For their part, Jewish workers quickly lost interest in maintaining their unions, which they considered nothing more than short-term weapons for winning strikes. "Our immigrant Jewish workers," one union leader later explained, "saw no difference between a union and a strike. . . . The finish of a strike, successful or unsuccessful, naturally meant the finish of the union." By the spring of 1887 all fourteen unions organized by the Yidisher Arbeter Fareyn had disappeared. In early July the Yidisher Arbeter Fareyn itself disbanded. Two and a half years later the *Folkstsaytung* published its last issue, falling victim to escalating partisan disputes.[78]

The collapse of the Jewish strike movement mirrored larger local and national trends. Across the country union membership plummeted and independent labor parties dissolved after 1886, though not without achieving some gains. In New York labor unity gave way to previous political, ethnic, and craft divisions. The United Labor Party's leaders expelled (with George's approval) the socialist element from its convention in August 1887, and its remaining leaders were co-opted into the Democratic Party. Meanwhile, the Central Labor Union splintered into three federations competing for dwindling memberships. The surviving unions moved in an increasingly conservative direction, which the rise of the American Federation of Labor beginning in December 1886 highlighted. Under the leadership of Samuel Gompers, himself a product of the German socialist milieu, the AFL and most of its affiliated unions renounced independent labor politics, socialist or otherwise. Gompers instead pursued a cautious strategy of organizing skilled workers and "scorned social reform for the here and now, and sought to better con-

ditions in the workplace within the framework of the existing order."
Even socialist-led German unions retreated "into organizing activities
that were more in compliance with pure and simple unionism."[79] By
1887 the Great Upheaval had come to an end.

Post-1886 Legacies

Short-term failures notwithstanding, the Great Upheaval amounted
to more than a momentary outburst of protest. Immediately afterward a
core group of intellectuals and newly radicalized workers started to rebuild the Jewish labor movement. In September 1887 former members
of the Yidisher Arbeter Fareyn established the first Yiddish-speaking
branch (Section 8) of the Socialist Labor Party. Within a decade the
party had twenty-five Yiddish branches across the country. In October 1888 Section 8 established the United Hebrew Trades (UHT)—
explicitly modeled after the United German Trades—for the purpose of
organizing Yiddish-speaking Jews in every branch of industry where
they worked.[80] And in March 1890, less than three months after the
Folkstsaytung's demise, social democrats launched a more successful
weekly, *Di arbeter tsaytung*, which paved the way for the wildly popular
daily *Forverts (Forward)* in 1897. Anarchists also made progress. By the
early 1890s they established branches of the Pioneers of Liberty in more
than six cities and published their own weekly organ, *Di fraye arbeter
shtime (The Free Voice of Labor)*. Within a decade of the Great Upheaval,
then, the Jewish labor movement developed into a popular, nationwide
movement.[81]

It is true that some individuals active during the Great Upheaval dis-
tanced themselves from the Jewish labor movement after 1886. Some
pursued professional careers or became active in German- or English-
speaking organizations. Numia Gretsh, for example, became more involved in the German movement and eventually became the SLP's national secretary (by then changing his last name to Rose). Yet, overall,
the number of Russian Jewish intellectuals who gravitated to the Jewish
labor movement increased over time. Some of the newly "Yiddishized"
intellectuals worked as full-time activists and writers; others combined

social activism with professional careers; and still others volunteered their free time sporadically. Whatever the case, more and more intellectuals chose to use Yiddish to organize and "enlighten" the immigrant masses. (According to my tally, at least sixty individuals contributed articles and literary works to the socialist Yiddish press between 1886 and 1900.) This contrasted with Russia, where Jewish intellectuals were still tied mainly to Hebrew or the Russian language. "In Russia," Boris Bogen wrote in an 1894 correspondence to *Voskhod*, "when the best people attempted in their time to educate their brethren in order to increase their intellectual and moral level, it never occurred to anyone that they had to use *zhargon* as a means to this goal."[82] Bogen somewhat overstated his point: individual *maskilim* had published Yiddish fiction, literary almanacs, and, with less success, newspapers as far back as the early 1860s. In addition, about the time *Voskhod* published Bogen's article, Jewish revolutionaries were taking initial steps toward propagating socialism in Yiddish, a fact Bogen could not have known.[83] But in New York the decision to use Yiddish, and to do so in multiple capacities, was a widespread phenomenon. Between the mid-1880s and 1900, a large number of intellectuals, based in a cluster of socialist organizations and newspapers, chose Yiddish as their primary medium of education, political mobilization, public discourse, and literary production. Nowhere else in the United States or Europe (including Warsaw) could one find such a developed, Yiddish-speaking intelligentsia at that time.[84]

Very few intellectuals, it must be added, considered Yiddish a value in its own right. They did not regard it as equal to major European languages, nor did they desire to create a distinctive, self-sustaining culture in Yiddish. (That idea, an outgrowth of Jewish nationalism, would not gain currency until after 1900.) Rather, socialist intellectuals justified Yiddish in utilitarian terms as the necessary medium to reach the largest number of Jewish workers. Thus, Charles Raevsky argued in an 1887 speech to the Russian Progressive Union, "The place of all Russian Jews is in the Yidisher Arbeter Fareyn, where everyone can be more useful with speeches and debates in the Yiddish language than with Russian lectures."[85] Intellectuals pointed out that they wanted immigrants to learn English as quickly as possible and expected Yiddish to disappear in the near future, within two or three decades. Their ultimate goal was to unite Jewish workers with workers of all backgrounds. According to this "internationalist" perspective, the Jewish labor movement would be a transitional phase; its purpose was to abolish itself.[86]

Yet even as socialists committed themselves in principle to assimilation, they immersed themselves in an autonomous, all-Jewish labor movement. In doing so, they developed a more positive attitude toward *zhargon*. In arguing for Yiddish's usefulness, the Jewish labor movement's early leaders often challenged negative perceptions of the language. Against skeptics and critics, they affirmed the capacity of Yiddish for intellectual and literary expression. In response to a Boston Reform rabbi who, in 1889, demeaned Yiddish as "a jargon . . . which only the *unintelligent* speak," the anarchist leader Michael Kohn wrote, "Our broad literature on socialism will serve as fair proof that we are able to express all we want in our Jewish tongue, or, as you prefer to call it, jargon."[87] The following year, Philip Krants, then the editor of the weekly *Di arbeter tsaytung*, published an appeal for Yiddish writers in *Znamia (Banner)*, New York's first Russian-language newspaper. Krants explained his own evolution toward Yiddish and assured *Znamia*'s readers, "There is nothing easier to do than speak in the Jewish vernacular once you've acquired the ability to write and know a particular vernacular style." He continued:

> Five years ago I too was unable to write a simple phrase in the Jewish dialect, but after several attempts I was already in a position to compose intelligible articles filled with extremely serious content. I know several other Yiddish [*zhargonnye*] journalists who previously never dreamed that they would be in their present occupation, but who now write about the most complex issues in a simple and comprehensible language for the Jewish masses. All it would take is a little bit of effort and patience to overcome these rather insignificant problems.[88]

Such statements reflected a significantly changed attitude toward Yiddish among Russian-speaking Jewish intellectuals. No longer did they automatically consider Yiddish loathsome or embarrassing. While most intellectuals continued to refer to Yiddish as *zhargon*, they used the term in a less pejorative way than before. (The word *zhargon* literally means "Jewish vernacular" or "dialect," not necessarily "jargon" in a negative sense.) Some individuals, like Kohn, were even prepared to underscore Yiddish's positive attributes. Increasingly, intellectuals adopted Yiddish without apology or defensiveness. By the end of the 1890s the precedent had been firmly established and the choice seemed obvious to more and more people.

It is safe to surmise that many intellectuals would have preferred to remain loyal to Russian if it were a viable option. This is evidenced by repeated efforts to form Russian-speaking organizations and publish Russian-language newspapers. In mid-1888, for example, former members of the Russian Progressive Union established a Russian-speaking branch (Section 17) of the SLP. Yet it disbanded sometime in the early 1890s. Likewise, between 1889 and 1899 Russian Jewish intellectuals published six Russian-language newspapers, all of which quickly went out of business owing to a shortage of readers. (Hebrew writers in New York also moved to Yiddish for similar reasons.)[89] *Znamia,* for example, survived less than twelve months and its editor, Louis Miller, subsequently switched to writing in Yiddish full-time. He also left the Russian-speaking Section 17 for the SLP's Yiddish-speaking branch. Other would-be Russian writers followed, Morris Hillquit, Yankev Gordin, Isaac Hourwich, and Louis Boudin among them. Miller would achieve prominence as a popular lecturer, newspaperman, and labor lawyer; Hillquit as an attorney and Socialist Party leader; Gordin as a celebrated playwright and lecturer; Hourwich as an economist, union leader, and writer; and Boudin as an expert on Marxian thought. (Boudin, Hillquit, and Hourwich would achieve recognition in the wider, English-speaking world as well.) Russian Jewish intellectuals understood that through Yiddish (and, in some cases, English) they could reach a large audience and perhaps earn a living. The failure of Russian newspapers coupled with the rise of the Yiddish socialist press, and the Jewish labor movement generally, presented its own compelling logic.[90]

While the trend toward Yiddish gained momentum at the end of the nineteenth century, it did not wholly negate prior Russian attachments. Intellectuals, by and large, still preferred to speak Russian among themselves. One could stroll down East Broadway, the hub of Jewish intellectual life on the Lower East Side, and hear the sound of Russian in and around its cafés. East Broadway was dubbed *"East Broadvayskaia Ulitsa"* for that reason. Furthermore, the Russian orientation of Jewish intellectuals no longer isolated them from the larger society. Knowledge of Russian politics and culture gave Jewish intellectuals special cachet within broader intellectual circles, especially during and after Russia's 1905 revolution. Greenwich Village intellectuals, for example, came to regard the Lower East Side with "new seriousness," as the historian Christine Stansell explains. They viewed the Lower East Side's Jewish intellectuals as representatives and interpreters of the Russian revolutionary movement at a time when it commanded international attention. If one wanted to learn the differences between Mensheviks and Bolsheviks, or meet emissaries from the Socialist Revolutionary Party, or discuss the works of Gogol, Tolstoy, or Chekhov, then the East Side was the best place to visit. By interacting with East Siders, Greenwich Village's affluent, native-born intellectuals moved from "the more staid realms of reform into a bohemia open to different sorts of radicalism."[91]

Russian-born Jews were not the only intellectuals to move toward Yiddish and the Jewish labor movement. Jewish intellectuals from different, non-Russian-speaking backgrounds followed a similar trajectory. The Romanian-born writer Konrad Bercovici, for example, "learned Yiddish rapidly" to participate "in the brouhaha of [public] discussions." "It was odd," Bercovici notes, "that the first language in which I learned to write in the United States should have been Yiddish, a language more alien to me than English was."[92] More surprising, American-educated, English-speaking Jews also found their way to Yiddish. Although much fewer in number than Russian-speaking Jewish intellectuals, they testified to the Jewish labor movement's attraction during the 1890s and 1900s. William Edlin, a graduate of Stanford University and a close associate of Jack London, was enticed to New York in 1896 by "stories of the great movement among Jews there." Edlin subsequently established himself as a socialist leader, journalist, and, in 1914, editor of the influential daily *Der tog (The Day)*.[93] Edlin was not unique. Other Americanized Jews were similarly drawn to the Jewish labor movement's "atmosphere of accomplishment," to quote *Forverts*'s manager, Adolph Held. Jewish intellectuals came from different backgrounds and countries, but their paths increasingly converged in New York's Jewish labor movement.[94]

The pull toward New York was felt overseas, as well. London's East End suffered a veritable brain drain during the late 1880s and 1890s as its foremost socialist writers, lecturers, and organizers relocated to New York. The 1894 departure of the poet, essayist, and lecturer Morris Vintshevsky, regarded on both sides of the Atlantic as the grandfather of Jewish socialism, signaled London's diminished status.[95] At the same time, émigrés from eastern Europe invariably chose New York over London as their preferred destination. In 1897, for example, the pioneer Jewish socialist and poet Avrom Lesin left Minsk for New York because he "was fed up with the minor disputes, and had heard rumors of the 30,000 organized Jewish workers—real factory workers [in New York]."[96] Lesin went on to play a major role in the development of Yiddish letters as editor of *Di tsukunft (The Future)*, the premier Yiddish magazine in America. Other important Russian Yiddish writers associated with the early socialist movement, including Dovid Pinsky, Yoel Entin, and B. Gorin, immigrated to New York around the same time.

The aftereffects of the Great Upheaval were not limited to the United States, as events in New York reverberated across the Atlantic. Even before the Great Upheaval subsided, news of what was happening in New York had reached Russia. In 1886 copies of the *Folkstsaytung* were shipped to the Pale of Settlement for distribution in Brest-Litovsk, Białystok, Vilnius, and Minsk. Authorities in St. Petersburg soon learned about the newspaper and banned it for "harmful" criticism of the government.[97] Nonetheless, Yiddish publications from abroad continued to find their way into Russia and eventually had an effect. Russian Jewish revolutionaries, Jonathan Frankel has shown, decided to propagate socialism in Yiddish by consciously following the example set by New York and London. Whereas in the 1880s and early 1890s revolutionaries exclusively conducted Russian-language "propaganda" for select groups of workers, in the 1890s they started to carry out Yiddish-language "agitation" for the masses. *In di gasn, tsu di masn* ("in the streets, to the masses") became the slogan. Social democrats in Vilnius were the first to embark on this path in 1893, but the idea soon caught on in other cities in the Pale's northwestern region and Congress Poland, or Russian Poland. Some Jewish socialist groups affiliated with the Polish Socialist Party (PPS); others united in 1897 to form the Bund, the first Jewish political party in Russia and a founder of the Russian Social Democratic Workers' Party in 1898.[98] As the future Menshevik leader Julius Martov explained, he and other Vilnius social democrats adopted their "new program" on the expectation that they could rely on Yiddish materials from abroad. Their expectation proved correct. During the 1890s and early 1900s socialists in New York and, to a lesser extent, London supplied a steady flow of illegal Yiddish publications. Between 1896 and 1899, for example, the Yiddish Socialist Post from America to Russia (formed to send literature to Russia) sent 6,066 copies of pamphlets to the Polish Socialist Party's Yiddish section. Both the PPS and the Bund also smuggled large quantities of *Di tsukunft* to educate workers about science, history, politics, and philosophy. ("It used to be a true holiday," one "underground fighter" from Minsk recalls, when copies of *Di tsukunft* arrived.) In addition, songs by New York's beloved "sweatshop poets," such as Dovid Edelshtat and Morris Vintshevsky, also became staples of socialist agitation.[99] Thus, in 1896 a group of Warsaw socialists could report that they distributed "the entire American socialist Yiddish literature, especially *Di tsukunft*."[100] Through the printed page, New Yorkers literally exported Yiddish-language socialism to the Russian Empire.

But the people affected most immediately by the Great Upheaval were its participants. The young men and women who founded the Jewish labor movement had lived in a near-constant state of crisis during the early 1880s. In Russia they had rebelled against their families and communities only to have their revolutionary dreams shattered by anti-Jewish violence and government reaction. In response to the pogroms, hundreds of young intellectuals journeyed to the United States with hopes of building utopian communes. They again suffered disappointment following the collapse of Am Oylom. Adrift in New York, Russian Jewish intellectuals searched for some way to reconcile revolutionary ideals with lived realities, eventually finding a new orientation in Little Germany. Under the influence of German immigrant socialists, Russian Jewish intellectuals decided to organize and educate Yiddish-speaking workers. It was a strange idea for people who previously could not or would not speak Yiddish and had no prior experience as labor organizers. Nonetheless, the Great Upheaval gave it a new urgency and thrust a previously marginal group of intellectuals to the forefront of this, the first major strike wave among Jewish workers. If the long-term implications of 1886 were not immediately clear, many intellectuals finished the year with a new sense of purpose. Speaking for many of his peers, Abraham Cahan would later recall, "My heart felt lighter. The fog was gone. I had come to shore."[101]

CHAPTER 2

Speaking to "Moyshe"

Socialists Create a Yiddish Public Culture

The Lower East Side in the 1890s looked very different from the way it had in the previous decade. Newcomers discovered a rapidly growing Jewish population—numbering nearly three hundred thousand by 1900—brimming with energy. In repeated labor conflicts, tens of thousands of people walked picket lines, demonstrated, and marched in parades. In especially volatile years, such as 1890 and 1894, strikes took place practically every week. On any weekend socialist intellectuals gave Yiddish lectures on myriad topics from science to literature to political theory. Dozens of workers' self-education societies, political clubs, and mutual aid societies sprang up. People who had never seen a Yiddish newspaper in Europe soon became devoted readers, looking to the press for guidance, information, and entertainment. Public squares, lyceums, clubhouses, and cafés were filled with men and women arguing issues of the day. The multitude of Yiddish speakers had transformed the East Side's social and cultural geography: Little Germany had given way to "the Jewish ghetto" with a spirit of its own.

In this dynamic setting, socialism gained a popular following among immigrant Jews. Between 1887 and 1897 Jews established five Yiddish-speaking branches of the Socialist Labor Party in New York City, four in neighboring New Jersey cities, and sixteen elsewhere in the United States. An undetermined number of Jews also joined the SLP's English-speaking branches, as well as German-, Polish-, Romanian-, and Russian-speaking branches. During elections Jewish neighborhoods on the Lower East Side and in Brooklyn formed "the backbone of SLP support."[1] The party's campaign rallies reportedly drew upward of ten thousand to fifteen thousand Jewish supporters, and its candidates received more than 30 percent of immigrant Jewish votes cast in the late 1890s. By then Jews had displaced Germans as the SLP's dominant group. "The shift from German hegemony to Jewish active participation," one historian writes, "is, in a way, the summary of the SLP's evolution during [1890–1896]."[2]

As impressive as the SLP's gains were, party membership and election results fail to capture socialism's broad appeal. Many men had not yet become citizens and women had not yet won the right to vote. Furthermore, only the most ideologically motivated individuals joined a political party like the SLP or the anarchist Pioneers of Liberty. One joined a party out of commitment to its ideas, not because it offered tangible benefits (as did trade unions and mutual aid societies). From the perspective of most poor immigrants, payment of monthly party dues was an additional expense they could ill afford. Unions attracted thousands more members than the SLP (thirteen thousand people joined unions affiliated with the pro-SLP United Hebrew Trades as of October 1890, compared to seventy who joined the SLP's main Yiddish branch), but they likewise provide too narrow a perspective on socialism's role in immigrant Jewish life. The so-called Jewish unions in the garment industry suffered chronic instability during the 1890s as membership rose and fell dramatically with each new round of strikes. Many individuals sympathetic to socialism joined a union during a strike, only to see it disintegrate after the unrest subsided. Conventional wisdom thus held that Jews made "good strikers, but bad trade unionists." It would take socialists another one to two decades to build powerful, stable unions and win elections to public office.

To appreciate socialism's influence during the 1890s, one must look beyond formal organizations into the wider public sphere, the social realm "in which something like a public opinion is formed."[3] A multiplicity of venues, from cafés to assembly halls to parks, constituted the

Yiddish-speaking public sphere. In those venues activists and intellectuals interacted with a broad section of the population. They articulated socialism not so much as a doctrine, but as "a whole climate of opinion that cemented, both socially and intellectually, a Jewish world in turmoil," to quote the historian Moses Rischin.[4]

Socialists shaped public opinion in three particularly important ways: through Yiddish lectures and speeches; through the Yiddish press and social activities associated with it; and through workers' education societies, which were intimately involved in the other two arenas. Thousands of men and women encountered socialism daily when they read a Yiddish newspaper, listened to a lecturer or soapbox preacher, attended a mass meeting, or took part in a "literary evening," "excursion," anniversary celebration, or fund-raiser. Large numbers of people lived socialism in the streets, parks, and halls of New York. They forged a new collective identity through socialism's idioms, ideas, and organizations.

Socialism held an especially strong attraction to young adults in their teens and twenties. Men and women in this numerically significant age cohort differed from other immigrants in ways often overlooked by historians who tend to lump all immigrants together as a single generation.[5] On the one hand, young adults were less Americanized than children who attended public schools, spoke English, and generally had brought over less "cultural baggage" from eastern Europe. On the other hand, these young adults, though still Yiddish-speaking, were not tied to the traditional ways of their parents. Samuel Chotzinoff, who, like his two sisters, became radicalized during the late 1890s and 1900s, provides a glimpse into this in-between generation of immigrants as he used to observe them in Rutgers Square:

> The majority of these young people were immigrants, and their language was still Yiddish, with an admixture of Russian, Polish, Romanian, German, and English words and phrases. They worked in dark, fetid sweatshops, in airless attics and cellars. They attended night schools and read liberal, socialist, or anarchist newspapers and magazines. Politically and ideologically they were at odds with their parents and grandparents, who leaned through habit and tradition toward conservatism and paternalism.

> In the minds of the older people, unionism or criticism of constituted authority and resistance to it invariably led to atheism, or at least to a slackness in the laws and traditions of religious orthodoxy.[6]

Chotzinoff, the son of a strict rabbi, goes too far in describing older immigrants as hidebound traditionalists. They too got caught up in the ferment of New York. Yet older immigrants often felt a disorientation and defensiveness that young people did not. Uninterested in observing Judaism's customs and laws, young adults eagerly welcomed change. Unencumbered by parental authority, they enjoyed enough personal freedom to pursue new curiosities. As one memoirist writes of the young anarchists he used to see around East Broadway, "Most of them were in their 'teens, newly arrived from the small towns and villages of Russia and Galicia and Poland, where they were compelled to follow small-town *derech eretz* (conventions) and the strict rules of Orthodoxy. Now they were behaving like young colts let out to pasture for the first time."[7] Yiddish socialism in the 1890s can be considered a youth movement at a time when young people set the tone for the larger immigrant population. As the Yiddish adage held, *"In Amerike, dertsyen di kinder di eltern"* (In America, the children raise their parents).

Most men and women did not preoccupy themselves with the fine points of socialist thought. What they valued most was socialism's broad message of dignity and hope for "a better, more beautiful world," a world where ideals of "freedom, equality, and brotherhood" would prevail. Socialists taught, in the words of one man, "how poverty can be eradicated, how every child can receive an education, how life can be made more beautiful and noble." "In the socialist movement," the union leader Joseph Schlossberg recalls, "you heard for the first time language which meant to us that we were regarded as human beings with human rights. That was the attraction for us in the socialist movement. That's how I entered it. And my interest in studying it intellectually came later."[8] In addition to its message of collective redemption, the socialist movement offered means for individual expression and self-improvement. Reading a newspaper, delivering a speech, or marching in a parade might seem ordinary from today's perspective, but young men and women from autocratic countries found such activities thrilling. In these and other ways, previously lower elements of Jewish society—youth, women, the unlearned, and the poor—discovered that they could educate themselves, take part in important debates, build their own institutions, and participate in the running of things. Young Jews embraced the socialist promise of a new world and the possibility that they could help create it.

Socialist Yiddish Lectures

On August 18, 1882, some one hundred people packed into a German saloon on Sixth Street to hear Abraham Cahan deliver a lecture on socialism, the first of its kind in Yiddish. Cahan was then a member of the Propaganda Association, the first radical club established by former members of Am Oylom. During the two months before August 18 the Propaganda Association had organized lectures in Russian and, occasionally, German. Recognizing that few immigrant Jews understood those languages, Cahan urged the Propaganda Association to switch to Yiddish. His associates laughed at the idea. Holding a lecture in *zhargon:* what could be more absurd? They agreed to go along with Cahan's suggestion, but "more in jest than in earnest." Cahan and Bernard Weinstein, a friend from the cigar factory where he worked, distributed leaflets around the East Side's Jewish quarter. When the evening of Cahan's lecture arrived, he spoke for two hours on "socialism and the teaching of Karl Marx," a subject he actually knew little about and the audience even less. Still, the lecture was a success. According to Weinstein, Cahan "lit a flame of inspiration and enthusiasm. It felt as if the blind could suddenly see, as if the dumb could suddenly speak, and as if the deaf could suddenly hear." Pleased with the response, Cahan soon gave a second lecture, in which he called on the overflow audience to march up Fifth Avenue with "irons and axes" and "take the palaces from the millionaires." Audience members applauded, asked questions, and went home.[9]

Despite Cahan's promising debut, he delivered no more lectures in Yiddish for the Propaganda Association. Like his contemporaries, Cahan remained wedded to Russian, the language of his "intellectual self." Speaking in Yiddish would not become widely accepted until the Great Upheaval, four years later. With the rise of the Jewish labor movement in 1886, what had been considered laughable came to be viewed as necessary. Every month hundreds or thousands of new immigrants landed in New York with no prior exposure to socialist ideas, formal secular education, or experience in labor organizations and political parties. The entire socialist project, as the intellectuals understood it, depended on altering how the Jewish masses thought and behaved. Intellectuals, as well as the more "conscious" workers, considered most immigrant Jews "ignorant," "totally uncultured," and possessing a "petit bourgeois" mentality produced by the long-standing involvement of eastern European Jews in commerce.[10] As one intellectual wrote in 1892, the "experience [of Jewish workers] in struggle is insignificant, the fighters themselves—still undeveloped." At the same time, intellectuals often praised Jews for expressing an above-average hunger for knowledge and inclination toward radical ideas. The intellectuals thus wanted to "enlighten" the masses, to teach socialism and general subjects, on the principle that workers needed to understand the world in order to change it. "We hold," the *Folkstsaytung* declared in June 1886, "that the uneducated state of the worker is one of the main things that embitters his life, makes him dispirited, pinches his neck, bends him to the ground, and does not let him raise his head." After the Great Upheaval, the movement's intellectuals were determined to raise the heads of Jewish workers. "Enlightenment," or *oyfklerung,* to use the Yiddish term, became something of a sacred mission.[11]

Whether a Jewish immigrant heard the word *oyfklerung* before leaving Europe, he or she certainly encountered it soon after arriving on the Lower East Side. Just about every forward-thinking person invoked it during a decade when to be a forward-thinking person meant to be, in some sense, a socialist. Although socialists rarely, if ever, explained in detail the meaning of *oyfklerung,* they proclaimed its importance at every turn: in lectures, articles, poems, and newspaper mastheads. In practice, *oyfklerung* meant spreading socialist ideas and secular education with special emphasis on *visnshaft* (the natural, physical, and social sciences) and, to a lesser extent, literature (mainly of the realist genre). As both process and goal, *oyfklerung* stressed individual betterment for the purpose of social change. Belief in self-improvement through education was not unique to Jewish socialists. A plethora of reform institutions in late nineteenth-century New York offered educational opportunities in English to working-class immigrants. Yet only socialists used the immigrants' mother tongue and in the service of a popular movement committed to remaking American society.[12]

It is tempting to connect the socialist idea of *oyfklerung* to the *Haskalah*, or Hebrew enlightenment.[13] To be sure, many of New York's early socialist intellectuals had come into contact with individuals, ideas, and institutions associated with the *Haskalah* in its various permutations. A very small number had even identified themselves as *maskilim* at an earlier point in their lives. (Morris Vintshevsky, for example, started off a *maskil* and Hebrew poet in the 1870s before switching to Yiddish and labor activism in the 1880s.) One can detect in both *oyfklerung* and *Haskalah* a similar belief, derived from the general European Enlightenment, in the redemptive capacity of secular knowledge. *Maskilim* and socialists alike insisted that Jews needed to overcome their backwardness through education.[14]

Even so, it would be misleading to consider Jewish socialism a radical offshoot or descendent of the *Haskalah*. New York's Jewish socialists rarely, if ever, claimed that legacy. On the contrary, they intentionally used the word *oyfklerung*, adapted from the German *Aufklärung*, rather than the Hebrew equivalent. The major intellectual influences on Jewish socialists in New York were such German thinkers as Karl Marx, Friedrich Engels, Ferdinand Lassalle, and Karl Liebknecht, not Russian *maskilim*, such as Isaac Ber Levinson, Y. L. Gordon, Shmuel Finn, and Perets Smolenskin. On rare occasions when socialists discussed the *Haskalah*, they usually criticized its valorization of the Hebrew language, respect for religious tradition, and moderate political orientation. In the eyes of socialists, the methods and goals of *maskilim* (which were actually more diverse than socialists seemed to recognize)[15] were elitist, ineffectual, and, in any case, out of place in New York, where few Jews could read Hebrew.[16] Finally, whereas *maskilim* wanted to create a new kind of Hebrew-based Jewish culture, most early socialists dismissed any form of Jewish identity and culture as irredeemably retrograde. The purpose of *oyfklerung* was to introduce Yiddish-speaking Jews to ideas and knowledge produced in other languages so they could ultimately transcend their own allegedly parochial culture. Socialists looked forward to a kind of working-class melting pot into which Jews and other immigrant groups would rapidly assimilate. They did not specify what a universalistic, working-class culture might look like, but Jewish socialists entertained few doubts about its inevitability. The Socialist Labor Party's multilingual structure, which united radicals from different backgrounds, provided evidence that "internationalism" could work in practice: the party could be seen as the kernel of the society to come. The task of Jewish socialists, Abraham Cahan pronounced in 1890, was "to erase all boundaries between Jew and non-Jew in the labor world." Very few of Cahan's comrades would disagree in the 1890s.[17]

How to begin? German American socialists had the benefit of an established socialist tradition from which they could draw. They brought to the United States "insurance and benefit societies, educational clubs and schools, singing and theater societies, typical forms of celebration and leisure, and a radical literary tradition," as the historian Hartmut Keil points out.[18] German American socialists also imported many publications from their homeland. In 1874, for example, German immigrants in Chicago could purchase seventeen labor newspapers published in Germany. Immigrant Jews, by contrast, had no socialist tradition to transplant. They would have to invent one, and do so in a language that was, for many socialist leaders, unfamiliar or considered unsuited to spreading *oyfklerung*.

Building the kinds of institutions German Americans took for granted required a lot of money, which the newly "Yiddishized" intellectuals did not have. Funds were especially tight during the early years of the Jewish labor movement. In the late 1880s Bernard Weinstein, then secretary of SLP Section 8, frequently had to borrow money from the party's German leadership just to rent halls for meetings. "The Germans," Weinstein recalls, "took to making wry faces when we used to request money for the hall. They, the German comrades, used to get a hall for free because they drank a lot of beer, but the Jewish comrades were meager beer drinkers. And anyway they did not have a nickel to spare for it."[19] It took the SLP's Jewish activists five years before they could establish a permanent headquarters in a rented, three-story house on Delancey Street in 1892. This, like each new project, required public fund-raisers, benefits, and appeals. Bringing socialism to Yiddish-speaking Jews would necessarily be a collective effort.[20]

Public lectures provided the cheapest, most direct way for socialists to get out their message. Every week, several times a week, the movement's intellectuals volunteered to speak on myriad topics: "Socialism and Religion," "The Development of Private Property," "The Necessity of Education," "Socialism from A to Z," "The Origin of Rights," "History as Science," "What Is Trade Unionism?" and many others. Education in Yiddish was generally unheard of in the late nineteenth century. The city's settlement houses and philanthropic institutions offered dozens of public lectures for immigrants, but in English, not Yiddish. The Educational Alliance, which wealthy uptown Jews generously funded, actually banned Yiddish, viewing it as an obstacle to Americanization. Not until 1899 would the alliance revise this policy, almost fifteen years behind the Jewish labor movement.[21]

It is impossible to know how many people attended socialist lectures. Newspaper reports sometimes gave numbers but, more typically, they used general terms like "well attended," "very well attended," and "packed." These descriptions could refer to audiences as small as two dozen or upward of five hundred, depending on the speaker, selected topic, and size of venue. What is known is that Yiddish lectures were highly popular pastimes, particularly among the young. Whereas older immigrants still enjoyed listening to an old-fashioned religious sermon, or *droshe,* on the Sabbath, young people flocked to hear intellectuals address some political, historical, cultural, or scientific topic. According to a 1913 Columbia University study, almost 32 percent of Russian Jewish men between the ages of seventeen and twenty-five attended at least one lecture per week; men between twenty-five and thirty-five followed close behind; and single men frequented lectures twice as often as their married counterparts. The Columbia study did not survey women, but evidence suggests little difference from men. Men and women alike regarded lectures as social events no less than educational opportunities. The Columbia study found that young Russian Jews were more likely to attend a lecture than a synagogue service, dance hall, saloon, card game, night school, and at least five other pastimes surveyed. No other immigrant group attended lectures in higher numbers.[22]

In all likelihood trained pedagogues would have found much to criticize in socialist Yiddish lectures. Lecturers had a tendency to address whatever subject interested them or they deemed important, with little concern for balance. "One can hear 2 lectures in the same night on Tolstoy and, in the course of entire years, not hear a single lecture on Newton," one lecturer wrote in a 1904 issue of the *Forverts*.[23] Furthermore, few lecturers could claim expertise in the subjects they addressed, including the most important one, socialism. Pressures of earning a living had prevented many of the East Side's Jewish intellectuals (Cahan, to name one) from completing their studies after they settled in the United States. Those who did save enough money to enroll in university gravitated, for practical reasons, to professions. A small elite earned advanced degrees in the humanities or sciences, but the most highly educated intellectuals rarely lectured in Yiddish. "Most of our lecturers," the writer Leon Kobrin later acknowledged, "perused a book, or sometimes a pamphlet, and then lectured on it to the broad public."[24]

Socialist Yiddish lectures often lacked depth, but audience members found them challenging anyway. Attendees often came to lectures tired after a long day's work, only to hear unfamiliar information in a foreign vocabulary. "Quite likely," notes Marcus Ravage, a devotee of socialist lectures, "most of us could not have passed an examination in any of the subjects we heard discussed." What inspired Ravage and others was a sense of personal elevation and intellectual discovery. In the lecture hall immigrants could temporarily escape from their squalid surroundings and hear captivating ideas of a better future. "There was a peculiar, intoxicating joy," Ravage continues, "in just sitting there and drinking in the words of the speakers which to us were echoes from a higher world than ours." "It was new to me," a tailor named Bernard Fenster recalls, "new words and a new way of thinking . . . and this breathed new life into me, a new desire to progress and to make myself into a *mentsh* [a decent, humane person]. I knew that I was not yet a *mentsh,* I was ignorant." For Ravage and Fenster, the specific information they heard mattered less than the general point: individuals could make themselves into better human beings—*mentshn*—as they struggled to improve society. "The strongest impression," Adolph Held recounts, "was the words . . . Freedom. Freedom. From poverty. From living this way on the East Side. From living ten in a room, from working in the shops."[25]

Erudition, in other words, did not necessarily make for successful lectures. The most popular and effective speakers possessed other important attributes: theatricality, charisma, mastery of colloquial Yiddish, and ability to simplify complicated ideas. Judged by these criteria, Cahan was considered the best lecturer among the East Side's Jewish intellectuals. During the 1890s Cahan attained unparalleled stature in New York Jewish life. He did not hold important administrative positions in any union or the Socialist Labor Party. Rather, Cahan's influence came through public speaking and journalism. He edited the weekly *Di arbeter tsaytung* between 1891 and 1897, and, after 1902, he molded the daily *Forverts* into the most popular Yiddish newspaper in the country. A highly talented journalist, Cahan was also a dynamic speaker who occupied center stage at countless public gatherings: rallies, parades, fundraisers, anniversaries, and other occasions. In the words of one colleague, Cahan was a "people's tribune."[26]

Written texts of Cahan's lectures (or any others) in the 1890s do not exist. Recollections and contemporary writings, however, provide some sense of what Cahan said and how he said it. The first quality that distinguished Cahan as an outstanding public speaker was his command of the Jewish vernacular. He eschewed the artificially Germanized Yiddish typical of late nineteenth-century journalists, creative writers, and stage actors. Instead, Cahan used a folksy *"yidishe yidish"* so that "even the most uneducated worker could understand it." He often substituted foreign political concepts with readily familiar religious terms. A boycott, Cahan would explain, was like a *kheyrem,* or writ of excommunication. He used to liken a union card to a *mezuze,* an amulet used to shield a home from evil spirits. In the words of one contemporary, Cahan spoke "to 'Moyshe' like a 'Moyshe,'" or as one common Jew to another. Ironically, many of Cahan's peers in the 1890s would, in later decades, criticize him for corrupting Yiddish with too many English words. Yet nobody would deny Cahan's early innovations in rendering socialism intelligible to the ordinary person.[27] Cahan often did that by casting socialism in spiritual terms. Cahan himself was an atheist, but he understood that socialism needed to inspire people the way religion had previously done. Disaffection from Judaism alone, Cahan believed, might actually cause harm if it was not replaced by another compelling worldview and set of practices. Was the saloon preferable to the synagogue? Was the profit motive less objectionable than a superstitious belief in God? Cahan did not think so. Socialism could fill the void left by religion if only presented properly. In a pamphlet written as a series of letters to a new immigrant, Cahan explained socialism as a form of spiritual salvation: "You will become a new person [in the socialist movement]. Life will become for you broader, richer, higher, and more beautiful. Well, the rich man has his worldly pleasures: he eats well, he goes to the theater, he travels in automobiles; he has his various delights. The worker does not have all this. For the worker the socialist ideal is a necessity. It sweetens his sad life. It gives him a spiritual pleasure which is higher than all."[28]

Cahan did not claim to be a great orator, that is, someone who spoke "in an exalted tone with considered and polished sentences." He was too excitable and undisciplined for that. "Imaginative power," not cogency, was Cahan's strongest attribute. Aiming to inspire listeners more than edify them, Cahan adopted the style of a traditional Jewish preacher or *magid*, illustrating his points with parables, jokes, and dramatic gestures. (For a time during the early 1890s Cahan even wrote a newspaper column under the pseudonym *Der proletarishker magid*, the proletarian preacher.) Cahan gave formal, didactic lectures, but his theatrical speeches won most acclaim.

One of Cahan's favorite speeches was a fictitious dialogue between a "greenhorn" and a more Americanized, "yellow" immigrant about the incompatibility of capitalism and political democracy. In this dialogue the older immigrant begins by teaching the newcomer the basics of

American government, but by the end the greenhorn winds up giving a lesson of his own. The dialogue begins with the Americanized immigrant explaining the difference between a republic and a monarchy. "A republic is a country without an emperor. All are equal citizens; they elect a president for a specific period of time, and afterward they elect others. The entire people are the boss over the government." To illustrate his point, the Americanized immigrant contrasts public buildings, such as the police department, city hall, and post office, with various private businesses: a department store, bank, machine shop, telegraph company, and so on. Still not sure of the difference, the greenhorn asks naively: "Are these businesses republics? Do they elect presidents? Do people have a say in how they're run?" The Americanized immigrant explains, to the dismay of his interlocutor, that the public does not democratically govern private businesses.

> Does that mean that Mr. Jones is an emperor over the machine shop which you showed me?
> I must admit that the answer is "yes."
> Does this mean that the factory is not a republic but a monarchy?
> I don't have any choice; I must answer "yes."

The dialogue continues in this fashion until the newcomer, now agitated, points out the inconsistency between a republican political system and an autocratic economic system.

> Let's see: how much time do your citizens spend in the post office? Perhaps several minutes each month. . . . And in your City Hall he probably spends even less time. But in Mr. Jones's factory he spends the entire day. And the same is true of the clerks who work in Mr. Wannamaker's store, right?
> Yes, but what do you want with this conclusion? . . . When he leaves the factory, he is in a democratic country.
> Yes, but for seven hours he sleeps and it doesn't matter if he dreams in a monarchy or a republic. And when there is no work, it doesn't matter when you're hungry if there's a president or a czar. When one does have work . . . there is only three or four hours when you live in a republic. . . . The worker spends his most important hours, therefore, without citizenship rights. So, why do you say today that your America is a republic?

By the end of the dialogue, the greenhorn has turned the tables. He understands better than his more assimilated acquaintance how the country has failed to live up to its democratic promise. The implication is clear: it is the task of outsiders, like those who sat in Cahan's audience, to redeem the United States.[29]

Contemporary and retrospective accounts testify to Cahan's tremendous popularity. Leon Kobrin, no friend of Cahan for most of his career, describes the excitement surrounding his 1892 visit to Philadelphia during a shirtmakers' strike. The union had invited Cahan to speak at a gathering in the local German Labor Lyceum, which Kobrin recounts in his memoirs.

> Impatience reminiscent of fanatical Hassidic Jews waiting for their *rebbe* could be felt in the hall. And then somebody appeared in the entrance of the hall . . . "Perhaps it's him." The impatience grows. The question "Will he come?" is heard more often and louder. One after the next someone leaves his seat, runs to the door, and looks outside. And suddenly a pair of girls with their cheeks aflame comes running in with a couple of other youngsters, breathless! "He's coming! He's here!" . . . The audience with burning faces sits turned around to the door. Awe looks out of their eyes, awe and inspiration. The women's eyes sparkle and adoration lights their smiling, feminine lips, which I have since seen so many times in the theater among women when their adored actor appears on the stage. Abraham Cahan has arrived. The audience welcomes him with stormy applause. It gets noisy with voices, hands, enthusiastic eyes, and surely—enthusiastic hearts. Because the movement was then still young, so was the audience's belief in the [socialist] ideal, and in their eyes, Cahan was its prophet.[30]

Kobrin uses three different comparisons to describe Cahan because the social type he represented—the Yiddish-speaking socialist intellectual—had no precedent in Jewish tradition. He was not really comparable to a *rebbe*, a prophet, or a stage actor, but he combined elements of each: he was a charismatic leader, a tribune for social justice, an entertainer, and indeed a celebrity. Whatever analogy one might use, there was no mistaking the adoration and respect young immigrants accorded him. Three years after the Philadelphia strike, Jacob Panken, New York's future socialist judge, saw Cahan speak at a May Day parade. "I felt that

[Cahan] spoke to me individually," Panken recalls. "It was heart to heart, man to man. . . . Cahan spoke to each individual. His words were soul stirring and the logic of his argument would not be denied." Cahan received comparable accolades during his first nationwide lecture tour, arranged by the SLP's Yiddish branches at the time of the terrible 1894 depression. In Cleveland, where no Yiddish party branch existed until his visit, nine hundred people reportedly turned out to see Cahan. In Chicago Cahan made "an impression that will never be forgotten." In St. Louis a standing room audience listened to Cahan "explain in plain Yiddish the main principles of socialism and [show] the causes of the current economic crisis." In Rochester the audience interrupted Cahan with "thunderous applause" and "resounding shouts of hurrah." Nobody drew a larger or more enthusiastic following than Cahan did.[31]

Cahan was not the only popular speaker among the East Side's socialist intellectuals. About two dozen individuals consistently attracted large audiences in cities from New York to Chicago and Boston to Baltimore. The most frequent and beloved lecturers after Cahan were Benyomen Faygnboym, Louis Miller, and Mikhail Zametkin. Much of what late nineteenth-century immigrants knew about socialism, and a good number of other subjects, came from the mouths and pens of these men. Activists referred to them as *gedoylim*, or great men, an honorific traditionally reserved for highly learned rabbis. Some individuals would cite other personal favorites, such as the anarchist leaders Moyshe Kats and Shoel Yanovsky or, later in the decade, the playwright Yankev Gordin and the poet Morris Vintshevsky. But Cahan, Faygnboym, Miller, and Zametkin were the four most prominent figures of the Jewish labor movement throughout the 1890s.

Other than Cahan, Zametkin had lived in New York the longest. He came to the United States with the Odessa Am Oylom in 1882 and had been a prominent figure in the Russian Colony from its beginning. During the Great Upheaval, Zametkin joined the Yidisher Arbeter Fareyn and had remained active in all branches of the movement ever since. Although a close colleague of Cahan's, Zametkin differed in his approach to socialist agitation. Whereas Cahan aimed to reach the greenest of greenhorns, Zametkin felt a greater affinity for "the more enlightened workers" who already had some experience in the movement. With them in mind, he crafted lectures with "perfect architecture" intended to educate listeners rather than entertain them. What Zametkin lacked in folksy color he made up for in radical zeal. He possessed an unshakable commitment to social democracy's fundamental belief: the importance of immediate struggles and small gains in the inevitable transformation of capitalism into socialism. Contemporaries praised Zametkin as a man of "great inspiration who had the ability to carry away great masses of people with him."[32]

Louis Miller arrived in New York four or five years after Zametkin, when the Jewish labor movement was in embryonic form. In 1880 the Vilnius native had evaded arrest and fled to Western Europe and then made his way to the United States in 1886 or 1887. During his early years in New York, Miller immersed himself in the Russian Colony and studied law at night. He joined various Russian-speaking clubs, helped to found the SLP's Russian-speaking section, and edited the city's first Russian newspaper (started by his late older brother, a former member of Am Oylom). By 1890 Miller had decided to learn Yiddish and urged other Russian-speaking intellectuals to do the same. He devoted his energies to Yiddish journalism and the SLP's Section 8. As a journalist, lecturer, and union lawyer, Miller took his place in the front ranks of the Jewish labor movement. He spoke with a "resounding, pleasant voice" and had a flare for the dramatic. He would work himself up until he grew red in the face and "prowl the stage like a lion in a cage."[33] A number of colleagues considered Miller their best public speaker, even better than Cahan. He spoke with equal passion yet greater precision.

The last of the Jewish labor movement's four major figures to arrive in New York was Benyomen Faygnboym. Faygnboym came from a background very different from that of Cahan, Miller, and Zametkin. He had not attended Russian-language schools, did not speak Russian, and possessed no direct ties to the Russian revolutionary tradition. Born into a poor Hassidic family in Warsaw, Faygnboym received a rigorous religious education and studied in a yeshiva until his early twenties. When he broke with religion he did so through the Hebrew writings of *maskilim*, not by way of the Russian intelligentsia. Faygnboym discovered socialism in Antwerp shortly after he emigrated from Poland in 1884. He later moved to London and became an expert union organizer, journalist, and pamphleteer. In mid-1891, at the age of thirty-one, Faygnboym relocated to New York. As an autodidact unable to speak Russian—the hallmark of one's status as an intellectual in the Russian Colony—Faygnboym never quite stood on an equal footing with his peers. His knowledge of Hebrew and Polish did not count for much. Nonetheless, the Yiddish-speaking public regarded Faygnboym as a speaker and journalist of the highest caliber.

Faygnboym used his fluency in Yiddish and Jewish religious texts to great effect. He could talk socialism as if sitting in the *beysmedresh*, the synagogue study hall. He quoted widely and freely from the Bible, Talmud, and midrashic sources. His mannerisms and sing-song cadence betrayed his years in the yeshiva, a cause of some self-consciousness for Faygnboym. (Once during a lecture he took offense at a questioner in the audience who appeared to be mocking his manner of speech when, in reality, the person was another ex–yeshiva *bokher,* or student.) Like many renegade yeshiva students of his generation, Faygnboym nurtured a fierce hostility to religion. He specialized in withering critiques and parodies of Judaism. He delighted in pointing out inconsistencies and contradictions in the Bible, ridiculed religious superstitions, and celebrated Jewish heretics such as Spinoza. In his unrelenting hostility to Judaism, Faygnboym more closely resembled anarchists than social democrats who adhered to the principle, established by Germany's Social Democratic Party in 1875, that religion was a "private matter" to be tolerated. Regardless of whether audience members agreed with Faygnboym's militant atheism, they flocked to hear him speak. He was one of the few intellectuals to receive payment for his lectures during the 1890s.[34]

Other intellectuals certainly made their mark. During the first half of the 1890s Morris Hillquit frequently lectured on behalf of the United Hebrew Trades and the SLP, but Hillquit failed to make the same impact as his colleagues. His demeanor was too stiff, his style too formal, his Yiddish too wooden. Hillquit felt little rapport with the Yiddish-speaking masses. As one contemporary put it, he impressed audience mem-

5. Benyomen Faygnboym, "the most pious Marxist," prays at the altar of Karl Marx. The caption reads: "Dedicated to the fanatical heretic, B. Faygnboym, who has destroyed all gods except his own god—Karl Marx." From *Der groyser kundes*, October 25, 1912.

bers but did not enchant them. In the following decade Hillquit would become well known outside the immigrant Jewish world as a prominent attorney and national leader of the Socialist Party. He would retain ties to the Jewish labor movement, but Hillquit's deep involvement in it during the late 1880s and early 1890s turned out to be a prelude to other things.

In addition to the prominent men, there existed a small but important cohort of women lecturers. Emma Goldman was the most famous of them. Before she achieved widespread renown in the United States, Goldman was a highly successful lecturer in Yiddish and would return to Jewish audiences throughout her life. Large crowds used to turn out to hear her speak on subjects such as birth control, anarchism, and the death penalty. Standing in Goldman's shadow, meanwhile, were a number of lesser-known but highly talented women. Hutchins Hapgood offers the following ambivalent portrait of the East Side's women intellectuals in his 1902 classic, *The Spirit of the Ghetto:*

> Emotionally strong and attached by Russian tradition to a rebellious doctrine, they are deeply unconventional in theory and sometimes in practice; altho the national morality of the Jewish race very definitely limits the extent to which they realize some of their ideas. The passionate feeling at the bottom of most of their "tendency" beliefs is that woman should stand on the same social basis as man, and should be weighed in the same scales. This ruling creed is held by all classes of the educated women of the Ghetto, from the poor sweatshop worker, who has recently felt the influence of Socialism, to the thoroughly trained "new woman" with her developed literary taste.[35]

Rarely, if ever, did these "strong," "unconventional" women occupy the highest positions of leadership, edit the major publications, or share top billing with men at mass meetings. Nonetheless, they achieved considerable prominence in women's socialist clubs that began appearing in the late 1880s. Within this separate women's sphere—distinct from but still closely connected through personal and organizational ties to the rest of the Jewish labor movement—women intellectuals exercised as much influence as the male *gedoylim*.

Mikhail Zametkin's wife, Adella Kean Zametkin, was one of those women. Born into a prosperous, educated (but still religious) family, Kean was privileged enough to have been given private lessons from a tutor at an early age. As a young woman she herself tutored poor girls, presaging her future activities in the United States. In 1888, at the age of twenty-five, Kean immigrated to New York, where she quickly gravitated to the socialist movement and met Zametkin, who had already established himself as a leader. In addition to her participation in the SLP, Kean Zametkin frequently lectured to women's groups and contributed to the leading socialist publications. In 1897 she helped found the daily *Forverts* and worked as it cashier. In later years Kean Zametkin wrote and lectured on nutrition, hygiene, birth control, child education, and other "women's issues." According to the *Forverts,* "She taught thousands of women simple things that are very necessary for the average working woman."[36]

Dr. Anna Amitin Ingerman can be considered the most extraordinary of the labor movement's women intellectuals. Born near the city of Gomel in White Russia in 1868, she was one of a growing number of women who attended gymnasium, the most prestigious form of secondary school in Russia. In the late 1880s Amitin moved to Berne, Switzerland, where she studied medicine and joined Georgy Plekhanov's Group for the Emancipation of Labor (GEL), the first organization of Russian Marxists. In this group she met her fellow medical student and future husband, Sergei Ingerman. The couple immigrated to the United States in the early 1890s, where they established the Russian Social Democratic Society for the purpose of raising funds for the GEL and, later, the Russian Social Democratic Workers' Party. For many decades the Ingermans served as ambassadors for the party's Menshevik wing. At the same time Anna Ingerman was very active in the local socialist movement. She was known for "her tireless service as lecturer and teacher for numerous Russian, German, Jewish, and American study circles, women's clubs, and workingmen's societies." With Adella Kean Zametkin and several other women, Ingerman helped found the Arbeterin Fareyn (Workingwomen's Society) in December 1893 and led four thousand Jewish women under its banner in the 1895 May Day parade. Ingerman also distinguished herself as an expert in Marxist theory. After her death in 1931 the *Forverts* praised Ingerman as one of the first women in New York to have mastered every volume of *Das Kapital*. The German *Volkszeitung* honored her as among the best "teachers of Marxism."[37]

Lecture halls and mass meetings were by no means the only place where immigrants heard socialist speeches. Every day (weather permitting) one could hear socialism preached on street corners and in parks dotting Jewish neighborhoods around New York. A focal point of activity was Rutgers Square, "a one block triangle situated at the junction of East Broadway, Canal, and Division Streets." Rutgers Square was a favorite place for young people to congregate, socialize, discuss, and debate. It "erupted 'Kultur' like an active volcano: religion and atheism, free love and vegetarianism, politics and ideologies." In the words of one former East Side resident, Rutgers Square "witnessed and harbored the emotions of its people who basked in their new freedoms to act and think as they pleased." In an unpublished autobiography, a man named Max Podell recounts visiting Rutgers Square as a favorite pastime. "All in all," Podell writes, "I was a typical East Side boarder, a proletariat [*sic*] and a socialist. I ate gefilte fish on Fridays, worked on Saturdays, went to the Jewish theaters on Sundays, and attended socialist meetings at Rutgers Square during the rest of the days."[38]

The atmosphere of Rutgers Square (and similar public places) differed from that of the lecture hall. It was more interactive, chaotic, and egalitarian. In open-air meetings one encountered a volley of soapbox oratory often delivered by teenagers just getting started in the labor movement. The best soapboxers did not dwell on a single point too long, but jumped from one idea to the next without spending more than a couple of minutes on each. The trick was to capture the attention of a transient crowd going about its daily business. That required both brevity and spontaneity. Crowd members did not necessarily wait to ask questions or state opinions: they might interject whenever they wanted and sometimes even take the stand themselves. Above all, soapboxers needed to convey a simple message: that socialism offered the solution to their problems. Adolph Held, who honed his talents as a street-corner agitator in a group called the Wendell Phillips Revolutionary Society, explained that the "general concept" was to give "a warm word . . . words of hope . . . so one isn't so sad and dry." Although young soapboxers like Held did not enjoy the same respect as *gedoylim,* the good ones made a strong impact nonetheless. An immigrant man who used to frequent "open air meetings" explained: "Almost every evening, after a hard day's work, Jewish workers used to stand around a truck and listen to the speakers who agitated for socialism and trade unionism. For a boy not yet 18 years old, as I was then [1900], this was practically a discovery, because not only was America a new country for me, but socialism, anarchism, and trade unionism were even newer. These things awakened my imagination and I began to swim in a beautiful, though unreal, world."[39]

After getting a taste of public speech during the famous bakers' strike of 1899–1900, the young Samuel Chotzinoff concluded that if he failed to become an actor he "would certainly devote [his] life to the cause of downtrodden labor and address crowds nightly in Rutgers Square and on the street corners of the East Side." As it turned out, Chotzinoff pursued a successful career in radio broadcasting, but for others, such as Held, Rutgers Square and the East Side's street corners served as training grounds for later careers as labor and socialist leaders.[40]

The attraction of young people to socialist lectures and outdoor meetings deeply troubled Orthodox Jews. They viewed socialist lectures as just more evidence of the abysmal state of Jewish observance in New York. "In the time when the heart of every right-thinking Jew ached . . . considering how corrupted and crippled Jewish education was," Rabbi Tsvi Hirsh Masliansky writes in his memoir, "he became even more incensed and agitated from hearing and seeing the various mass meetings for the youth in the large halls and on the street corners."[41] Although sympathetic to labor, Masliansky feared socialists were leading Jewish workers astray and undermining communal unity. The essence of what one needed to know about the rights of labor, as far as Masliansky was concerned, could be found in the Bible: "Our Jewish workingmen may be proud of our Torah and of our Religion, which are exceedingly considerate of them, and are much more solicitous for their welfare than are the so-called "friends of labor," who, without knowledge or understanding of Judaism's teachings in this regard, are casting slurs upon the To-rah and mock at the many thousand-years-old traditions of the Jew."[42]

Masliansky, probably more than any other Orthodox leader, enjoyed a popular following. Hundreds of people used to attend his Friday evening sermons. However, Masliansky appealed mostly to older, more religious Jews. Few young immigrants cared about the "corrupted and crippled state of Jewish education." They found socialist lectures much more appealing. Lectures provided opportunities for young people to mingle socially, obtain some education, and hear an inspiring message relevant to their lives in New York. In the eyes of young Jews, Masliansky's sermons might as well have been ancient relics. Socialism, on the other hand, promised a "better, more beautiful world" in the not-too-distant future. "The socialist speakers used to build new enchanted worlds for the workers," Max Pine, a knee pants maker turned union leader, writes. "They told how the workers of the whole world were rising to struggle against their enemies and that every strike, every conflict with capital, is of the greatest significance for the coming revolution, which will redeem humanity from economic slavery."[43] Socialists placed immigrants like Pine at the center of a grand drama: if they only took the initiative, they could change the world. Ordinary immigrants already knew something about initiative, having traveled across the globe in search of better fortunes. Socialists struck a chord because they articulated that preexisting impulse into a worldview that bestowed a larger meaning to individual lives. Personal hardships had worldwide historical significance, socialists told immigrant Jews. At the end of a lecture or speech, listeners knew that their journey across the Atlantic had not been in vain; their daily struggles would soon be rewarded.

The Socialist Yiddish Press and Its Readers

In December 1899 an eighteen-year-old man known to history only by his initials, A.G., arrived in New York from a town in Poland. One of the first things that struck A.G. about his new home was the prevalence of Yiddish newspapers. Like almost every other Jewish immigrant in the late nineteenth century, A.G. had never seen a Yiddish newspaper in the

old country. Government censors had permitted only one poorly circulated Yiddish weekly (*Dos yidishes folksblat,* 1881–1890) during A.G.'s
years in the Russian Empire.[44] In New York, however, he discovered a
thriving Yiddish press: "Here I first opened my eyes and saw new worlds.
Every day I noticed new things and my desire to know everything grew
every day. I began to read Yiddish newspapers, which for me was one of
the first American wonders. In Khmelnik and Kelts I didn't see such
things. . . . And here suddenly, Yiddish newspapers! . . . I used to read all
the newspapers that were then published. I couldn't satisfy myself."[45]

By the time of A.G.'s arrival, New York's Yiddish press was almost
three decades old. The first Yiddish newspaper appeared in 1870 and
five others soon followed. Although most early publications failed, the
quantity, diversity, and popularity of Yiddish newspapers grew dramatically over the next two decades. By 1894 one could choose from three
Yiddish dailies, in addition to numerous weeklies and monthlies. The
combined circulation of Yiddish dailies reached 66,000 in 1900, 120,000
in 1904, 500,000 in 1910, and 650,000 in 1917.[46] Whereas Yiddish lectures appealed mainly to young adults who could spare an hour or two
in the evening, people of all ages read Yiddish newspapers. They could
be purchased inexpensively and read in the home, or just about anyplace
else. Even the minority of Jews who were illiterate—primarily older
women who had come to the United States as adults—often listened to
newspapers read aloud by friends and relatives. "All you have to do,"
Voskhod reported in 1894, "is go down to the Jewish quarter and you
will hear sellers hawking Yiddish newspapers; you will see the newspapers being bought up; wherever you go [Jewish immigrants] are reading; [and] they discuss what is read."[47] During the 1890s New York was
home to the world's first popular Yiddish newspaper market.

A number of factors contributed to the development of the Yiddish
press. First, the tremendous growth of the immigrant Jewish population
created a critical mass of potential readers. Between the early 1870s and
1900 the number of Jews on the East Side alone climbed from about
15,000 to 290,000. A parallel increase in the number of businesses catering to Yiddish speakers supplied newspapers with needed advertising revenue. Furthermore, the advent of the Linotype machine and the

falling cost of newsprint enabled publishers to print more copies and reduce prices from six cents to one penny. And, above all, people increasingly wanted to read newspapers. Immigrants recognized that newspapers could help them both adapt to their new country and stay informed about *der alter heym*. Local events, such as strikes, and events abroad, such as wars and pogroms, played an especially important role in stimulating demand. "It has become a necessity to have a newspaper at home," Russia's first Yiddish daily, *Der fraynd (The Friend),* reported in 1904. "Newspapers have become the main intellectual food of the Jewish immigrant in America."[48]

To appreciate the significance of *Der fraynd*'s observation, it should be kept in mind that Yiddish newspapers did not simply report daily events; rather, they functioned in several capacities at once. Yiddish newspapers provided education to those who could not read English or attend school. Articles on subjects such as biology, hygiene, and American government filled the pages of the Yiddish press. Yiddish newspapers functioned, to quote Irving Howe, as both "kindergarten and university." Yiddish newspapers also served as the main venues for Yiddish fiction, poetry, and criticism. Yiddish writers, from the best to the worst, published most of their work on the pages of newspapers. And, finally, Yiddish newspapers functioned as "agents of acculturation," introducing and interpreting American society, politics, and culture for their readers. "The Yiddish press, particularly the Socialistic branch of it, is an educative element of great value in the Ghetto," Hutchins Hapgood observed in 1902. "It has helped essentially extend the intellectual horizon of the Jew beyond the boundaries of the Talmud, and has largely displaced the rabbi in the position of teacher of the people." Twenty years later the sociologist Robert Park would reach the same conclusion. "In the Yiddish press," Park wrote, "the foreign-language newspaper may be said to have achieved form. . . . No other foreign-language press has succeeded in reflecting so much of the intimate life of the people which it represents, or reacted so powerfully upon the opinion, thought, and aspiration of the public for which it exists." Immigrants and outsiders alike agreed that the "most important social factor in the Ghetto is the newspaper."[49]

At the time of the Great Upheaval in 1886, the publisher Kasriel Tsvi

Sarasohn dominated the Yiddish press. Sarasohn was an ordained rabbi and *maskil* from Lithuania who, in 1869 at the age of thirty-four, immigrated to the United States. Five years later he began publishing the weekly *Di yidishe gazetn (The Jewish Gazette)*, the only Yiddish newspaper of the 1870s to survive the decade. In 1885 Sarasohn started what would become the first Yiddish daily, the *Yidishes tageblat*. (The *Tageblat* published only four to five times per week until 1894, when it started to come out every day but Saturday.) Unlike socialist newspapers, which claimed to represent only the Jewish working class, Sarasohn's daily spoke in the name of the Jewish people as a whole. As Sarasohn's son and business partner wrote in 1894, the *Tageblat* "is not a newspaper of a class against a class, it is a newspaper for all Jews [*kol yisroel*]." Sarasohn attempted to achieve that goal by maintaining an uneasy balance between defending tradition and welcoming change. The *Tageblat* promoted religious Orthodoxy yet advocated a selective approach to Americanization. It denounced socialists for dividing the Jewish people, but expressed concern for the plight of "honest" workers. Sarasohn thus positioned himself as a defender of Jewish unity who stood above destructive partisan divisions. His strategy worked well. By the late 1890s the *Tageblat*'s circulation climbed to almost forty thousand while, along the way, Sarasohn purchased a number of competing Yiddish newspapers around the country. Sarasohn can be considered the Yiddish press's first "magnate."[50]

Socialists detested Sarasohn, as he did them. After the Great Upheaval, Sarasohn repeatedly accused socialists of corrupting otherwise pious immigrants, fomenting strife among Jews, and besmirching their reputation as law-abiding Americans. Socialists, for their part, rejected the idea of Jewish unity, or *kol yisroel*. In a society divided by irreconcilably hostile classes, they argued, Jewish unity was a chimera that served the interests of bosses. Socialists branded Sarasohn (fairly or not) a reactionary, hypocrite, liar, and thief who stole money from Jewish charities for his own gain. (The last accusation, leveled by Faygnboym in 1897, resulted in a successful libel suit against him.) Socialists fought a very difficult battle to dislodge Sarasohn from his preeminent position in the Yiddish newspaper market. During the late 1880s a total of five socialist or radically oriented newspapers failed because of lack of money, inexperience, or political infighting. The *Folkstsaytung* survived the longest, from June 1886 to December 1889, but most lasted just a few months. During the following decade, however, socialists mounted an effective challenge against Sarasohn.[51] In March 1890, amid the period's second major strike wave, a group of social democrats established *Di arbeter tsaytung*. The newspaper's popularity far surpassed its founders' expectations and paved the way for the world's first socialist Yiddish daily, *Dos abend blat (The Evening Sheet),* in 1894. Three years later a factional dispute gave rise to the *Forverts*, which would surpass the *Tageblat* as the most popular Yiddish newspaper on "the Jewish street." By World War I the *Forverts*'s circulation amounted to more than that of all its competitors combined. *Di arbeter tsaytung* thus marked an important turning point: the beginning of socialism's ascendancy in the burgeoning Yiddish newspaper market.[52]

Events leading up to *Di arbeter tsaytung* began with a historic showdown between social democrats and anarchists. In late 1889 the Pioneers of Liberty approached the SLP's Yiddish sections with the idea of publishing a bipartisan newspaper. The Pioneers had published a weekly organ, *Di varhayt (The Truth),* earlier in the year but could not manage to keep it afloat for more than four months. Recognizing that they lacked sufficient money and popular support to go it alone, the Pioneers hoped to form an alliance with the SLP's Yiddish sections. According to their proposal, both parties would exercise joint control over the newspaper through two editors, an idea based on the radical London Yiddish newspaper, *Arbeter fraynd (Workers' Friend).* It was an unlikely plan: ideological and tactical differences between anarchists and social democrats had worsened since the Great Upheaval. The only possibility for cooperation rested in a shared disenchantment with the *Folkstsaytung*. Anarchists resented the weekly's social democratic bias, and a growing number of SLP members had come to view the *Folkstsaytung* as too eclectic and unreliable. Critics wanted a party organ, not an independent ally. Could they achieve that goal by cooperating with anarchists?[53]

Social democrats responded to the Pioneers with mixed reactions. In cities such as Chicago, where relations with anarchists remained friendly, SLP members supported the initiative. In New York, however, escalating disagreements had sapped the goodwill necessary for a bipartisan enterprise. From the social democrats' perspective, the *Arbeter fraynd* hardly offered a desirable model. The newspaper was officially bipartisan, but its social democratic editor, Philip Krants, had recently resigned in protest of the growing control of anarchists over the newspaper. SLP members thus had reason to wonder whether the Pioneers genuinely sought cooperation or whether they aimed to use social democrats to further their own cause. The SLP's Yiddish-speaking sections agreed to participate in a national conference to discuss the matter, but they probably did so with the intention of forcing a test of strength instead of finding common ground.

Forty-seven delegates representing thirty-one organizations (party branches, trade unions, and political clubs) attended the conference, which convened on Christmas Day 1889. Bewildered reporters from English-language newspapers attempted to follow the proceedings as debate raged for seven days and nights. In the end social democrats, led by Morris Hillquit and Louis Miller, defeated the Pioneers' proposal by one vote. They bolted the conference on January 2 and reconvened elsewhere to plan a new newspaper, to be named *Di arbeter tsaytung*. Seven months later, the Pioneers started a rival weekly, *Di fraye arbeter shtime*. Thus, a conference intended to unify the two camps resulted in a bitter split that would permanently divide social democrats and anarchists.[54]

Di arbeter tsaytung's founders began by organizing themselves into a cooperative publishing association. Devised by German American socialists, publishing associations were meant to ensure that a newspaper would serve the interests of the movement as a whole rather than those of a private publisher or editor. A publishing association collectively owned and managed its own newspapers. Members of the Arbeter Tsaytung Publishing Association raised money, elected staff members, and volunteered their time in the editorial office. To join the Arbeter Tsaytung Publishing Association one had to be a member of the SLP or a trade union affiliated with the pro-SLP United Hebrew Trades before being elected by a majority vote.[55] The publishing association's executive committee included Cahan, Hillquit, Miller, and Weinstein. Between January and March they conducted a successful campaign to raise money for *Di arbeter tsaytung*. Most of the funds came from sympathetic trade unions and the general public. The United German Trades donated one thousand dollars and a benefit theater performance raised four hundred dollars. Within nine weeks the publishing association collected the considerable sum of two thousand dollars.[56]

The publishing association's second major task was hiring an editor. Cahan was undoubtedly the best-qualified person in New York, but the association instead offered the job to London's Philip Krants. New Yorkers knew and respected the thirty-four-year-old Krants from his articles in *Arbeter fraynd*, which he coedited between 1885 and 1889. Krants was said to be a dedicated party man and staunch foe of anarchism. Rumor had it that he often slept in his office at night and went hungry before accepting payment from the newspaper. A native Russian speaker, Krants could not match Cahan's mastery of *mame-loshn*, the immigrants' mother tongue. Nonetheless, Krants had learned to write a clear, straightforward Yiddish during his years in London.[57] By choosing Krants over Cahan, members of the publishing association let it be known that they did not regard intimacy with Yiddish and traditional Jewish culture as primary qualifications. On the contrary, Krants's credentials as a Russian intellectual made him the preferred choice. Krants's parents had sent him to Russian schools rather than give him a religious Jewish education. He graduated from the St. Petersburg Technical Institute, which, although not as prestigious as university, was still an impressive achievement. Cahan, by contrast, went only as far as the Vilnius Teacher Training Institute, a government-run middle school for Jews a notch or so below a gymnasium. Furthermore, whereas Cahan had merely admired the revolutionary movement from afar, Krants had actually been arrested in 1877 for his involvement in the revolutionary group Zemlia i Volia (Land and Freedom). Later, as a member of Narodnaia Volia, he had associated with the conspirators who assassinated Alexander II. Krants's Russian political pedigree and education carried a lot of weight in New York. Next to Krants, Cahan looked like a provincial. Cahan would replace Krants (who resigned from *Di arbeter tsaytung* for personal reasons) in the summer of 1891, but Krants would remain the leading editor in the socialist Yiddish press for the rest of the decade.[58]

Krants arrived in New York in early February and took quickly to his new home. New York's "expansive and grateful field of activity" greatly impressed him. Demonstrations, strikes, meetings: everything happened on a grand scale. London's East End must have seemed small and cramped by comparison. Members of the publishing association showed Krants around the Lower East Side and threw parties in his honor. Krants, in turn, impressed his new comrades as worldly and refined: a gentleman in a contentious, unpolished community of activist-intellectuals and workers. To be sure, he was not a man of the people. Krants felt uncomfortable on a picket line or in front of large audiences. He might have been mistaken as aloof or snobbish were it not for his pleasant and respectful demeanor. Krants regarded himself as a "socialist teacher with a pen in hand," which was precisely what the publishing association expected him to be.[59]

The first issue of *Di arbeter tsaytung* appeared on March 7. "Our general goal," Krants explained, "is the construction of a social order based on true freedom, equality, and brotherhood." *Di arbeter tsaytung* would "help the workers in their political and economic struggles against the capitalists at every step, and awaken in them a spirit of freedom, independence, and class-consciousness."[60] Accordingly, Krants placed primary emphasis on politics and education. A typical issue of *Di arbeter tsaytung* included news about labor and socialist movements in the United States and Europe, an essay on socialist thought or an aspect of revolutionary history, and a polemic, or *feuilleton*. *Di arbeter tsaytung* also maintained "a high order of literary excellence" throughout the decade. In addition to the beloved "sweatshop" poet Morris Rosenfeld and other local talents, the newspaper featured important European Yiddish writers, such as the "grandfather" of Yiddish fiction, Sh. Y. Abramovitsh and, later in the 1890s, Y. L. Perets and Dovid Pinsky. Works from other European authors regularly appeared in translation. From a literary standpoint, *Di arbeter tsaytung* surpassed every other Yiddish newspaper.[61]

Next to Krants, Cahan was *Di arbeter tsaytung*'s most frequent con-

6. Philip Krants, the leading socialist Yiddish editor in the 1890s. From Y. Sh. Herts, *Di yidishe sotsyalistishe bavegung in Amerike* (New York: Der Veker, 1954), p. 33.

tributor during its first year. The two men brought distinct, sometimes clashing approaches to their craft. Krants infused *Di arbeter tsaytung* with a seriousness of purpose. He believed that a socialist newspaper ought to promote "enlightenment and . . . socialist ideas at every opportunity."[62] Cahan, on the other hand, bent more willingly to popular tastes and gave *Di arbeter tsaytung* a folksy quality. His most distinctive contribution was the *"Sedre,"* or commentary on the weekly Torah portion. Under the guise of "The Proletarian Preacher," Cahan commented on current events in the style of an old-world *magid*. In the *"Sedre"* of March 14, 1890, for example, Cahan interprets the following passage from Exodus in light of a major cloak makers' strike then under way:

"Va-yakel Moyshe": Moses assembled the children of Israel and said to them, *"Sheyshes yomim tasu melokho,"* you shall not work for the bosses more than six days a week, the seventh day you shall rest. . . . But what is actually the case? The children of Israel work eighteen hours a day . . . and have no Sabbath and no Sunday off. Ay, you may ask, can't they die from exhaustion? Indeed, die they do. But there is one commandment they do fulfill: Moses tells them in today's *sedre* that on the seventh day they shall not light fire. This they observe an entire week: there is nothing to cook, thank God, and no fire to cook with.[63]

Krants appreciated the ironic humor of such passages but objected to some of Cahan's other articles. He regarded Cahan's series on African cannibalism (translated from *Scribner's*) as rank sensationalism. In turn, Cahan viewed Krants's style as "dry" and "scholarly."[64] Differences between the two men would eventually widen into an all-out struggle for control over the publishing association, but during *Di arbeter tsaytung's* first year Krants and Cahan managed to accommodate one another.

Di arbeter tsaytung won "instantaneous" and "fantastic" popular approval from immigrant readers. A week before its debut the SLP's *Workingman's Advocate* reported, "Subscriptions pour in from every town and village of the United States where the Jewish dialect can be heard."[65] *Di arbeter tsaytung's* premier issue sold out and, a month later, the newspaper expanded from four to eight pages. Estimates of its circulation ranged between six thousand and eight thousand copies, an impressive figure for that time. The actual number of readers, though, was certainly larger, since single copies typically passed from hand to hand and were read collectively in small groups.[66] The publishing association had not expected to reach such a large readership so quickly. "We were intoxicated from our success," Cahan recalls. "The masses clasped *Di arbeter tsaytung* to their hearts straight away. Every issue was awaited impatiently in the Jewish quarter."[67]

Good timing, as well as good journalism, contributed to *Di arbeter tsaytung's* success. In 1890 and 1891 Jewish workers from every branch of the garment industry (and smaller industries) launched general strikes on a scale that surpassed that of the Great Upheaval. An estimated nine thousand Jews marched in the 1890 May Day parade (the first one since 1886) and fifteen thousand in September's Labor Day parade. "Not a single week has passed," Krants noted in January 1891, "without a couple of small strikes."[68] In October 1890 the United Hebrew Trades boasted twenty-five unions representing thirteen thousand members, up from three unions with fewer than eighty members two years earlier. Furthermore, *Di arbeter tsaytung's* main writers—Cahan, Hillquit, Miller, and Zametkin—played a major role in the strike movement. They spoke at countless rallies and "did every trifle for the unions," as Weinstein recalls. They negotiated settlements, taught bookkeeping, and instructed members in parliamentary procedure. Max Pine, a twenty-four-year-old knee pants worker in 1890, recalls feeling "amazed by constantly seeing their names in *Di arbeter tsaytung* and on circulars, by how they spoke at several gatherings in a single evening, and my highest desire was to look at these wonderful men."[69] Amid the near-constant unrest, Pine and many others looked to *Di arbeter tsaytung* as their guide.

Di arbeter tsaytung's first anniversary celebration elicited a remarkable outpouring of enthusiasm. An estimated fourteen thousand people showed up at the celebration in Cooper Union, far more than its auditorium could contain. "At least ten thousand people were turned away who were unable to enter the hall," the *New York World* reported. Krants described the scene as "tragi-comic." Thousands of people crowded the streets around Cooper Union. Throngs of others climbed through windows and broke open doors. Union members waved banners and marched into the building with or without tickets. The choir struggled in vain to push through the pandemonium outside. Inside the building, audience members greeted Zametkin, the master of ceremonies, with thunderous applause. Hillquit, Krants, and Miller delivered speeches. Cahan read numerous greetings sent by socialist groups and unions around the country. Johanna Greie and Alexander Jonas spoke on behalf of German American socialists. The German Progressive Musicians' Union performed and Morris Rosenfeld recited poetry. Never before had so many people celebrated a Yiddish newspaper.[70]

The Pioneers of Liberty, meanwhile, struggled to keep *Di fraye arbeter shtime* alive. Appearing in July 1890, four months after *Di arbeter tsaytung*, the newspaper was beset by problems from the beginning. Whereas *Di arbeter tsaytung* received generous support from the United German Trades and other unions, the Pioneers had no larger institutional backing. The organization raised only five hundred dollars, one-fourth the sum collected by the Arbeter Tsaytung Publishing Association. To make matters worse, a typesetters' strike against *Di fraye arbeter shtime* prompted the United Hebrew Trades to wage a boycott of the newspaper. The Pioneers attempted and failed to create a rival federation, which left the UHT with a veritable monopoly over the trade union move-

7. An early issue of *Di arbeter tsaytung* announcing "The coming social storm." The illustration appears to be an adaptation of Eugène Delacroix's 1830 painting *Liberty Leading the People.* From *Di arbeter tsaytung,* April 18, 1890, p. 1.

ment. *Di fraye arbeter shtime* ceased publication in 1892 and, after a brief resuscitation, again in 1893. Not until 1899 would the weekly appear on a regular schedule. In the words of one contributor, "*Di fraye arbeter shtime*, in direct contrast to *Di arbeter tsaytung*, was born with bad luck."[71]

The nexus between labor activism and Yiddish journalism, first evident in the *Folkstsaytung* in 1886 and *Di arbeter tsaytung* in 1890, produced yet a third newspaper in 1894, during the largest strike wave of the decade. The publishing association seized the opportunity to publish the first socialist Yiddish daily ever, *Dos abend blat.* "Now we know positively," the association declared, "that we have the necessary ability, that we are surely in a position to realize honestly and correctly our duty as publisher of a true socialist workers' newspaper."[72] The publishing association appointed Krants editor of *Dos abend blat.* In early February 1895 Krants reported that *Dos abend blat* had thirty-six thousand "worker-readers," no doubt a higher figure than the number of copies circulated.[73] *Dos abend blat*'s popularity did not mean that tens of thousands of readers suddenly identified themselves as Marxists. The Yiddish readership did not divide neatly into ideological or political camps, as most people read more than one newspaper. It was not unusual to see people at socialist rallies with copies of the *Tageblat* in their back pockets or, conversely, religiously observant Jews reading *Dos abend blat.* Adolph Held's father, a storekeeper and religious Jew, read both *Tageblat* and *Dos abend blat.*[74] "Our newspaper," Krants informed a European contributor in December 1896, "is read by nonworkers and primarily by the nonintellectual public."[75] People read a given newspaper for any number of reasons: for its literary offerings, practical information, entertaining feuds between writers, and so on. Still, by reading *Dos abend blat,* tens of thousands of people demonstrated an openness to radical ideas. They showed a willingness to read an avowedly Marxist publication every day, regardless of whether they agreed with it. This alone was remarkable if we keep in mind that few readers had prior exposure to radical ideas or newspapers in eastern Europe. Within just four years, then, between the strike waves of 1890 and 1894, the publishing association established its position in the Yiddish newspaper market. *Dos abend blat* and *Di arbeter tsaytung* still trailed behind Sarasohn's *Tageblat* and *Yidishe gazetn,* but they forged a large and stable readership. They brought socialism into the very center of the Yiddish newspaper market.

The third and final turning point in the development of the socialist Yiddish press occurred in 1897. In January the publishing association suffered a bitter internal split that mirrored a larger rebellion within the Socialist Labor Party against the dictatorial leadership of Daniel De Leon and his controversial trade union strategies. At the same time an internal factional conflict that had been brewing for almost three years contributed to the publishing association's collapse. A self-defined opposition, led by Cahan, Miller, and Vintshevsky, claimed that a clique had taken over the association and stifled dissenting opinions. "Loyalists," led by Krants, Faygnboym, and others, responded that no such clique existed, just a group of highly motivated volunteers. They maintained that the opposition was actually motivated not by democratic concerns but by personal ambition. They charged Cahan and his allies with wanting nothing more than to wrest control of *Dos abend blat* from Krants, whose approach to journalism they disliked. Cahan and his allies, they asserted, had become influenced by Hearst- and Pulitzer-style "yellow journalism" and wanted to transform *Dos abend blat* accordingly. Loyalists cast Krants as the standard-bearer of European social democracy, while Cahan was made to represent the corrupting influence of American commerce.[76]

On January 7 a large minority of fifty-two members broke from the publishing association. Representing twenty-three union locals and socialist clubs, they formed the Forverts Association for the purpose of publishing a new Yiddish daily, to be named the *Forverts* (after the German Social Democratic Party's *Vorwärts*). Over the next four months the Forverts Association embarked on a flurry of activity to promote the new daily and raise funds. Cahan, Miller, Zametkin, and Vintshevsky went on speaking tours around the country. Supporters scraped together whatever money they could, in some cases pawning their pocket watches and wedding rings. One of the Forverts Association's more creative endeavors was the so-called spoken newspaper, an oral presentation of the newspaper-to-be in front of large audiences. Two spoken newspapers took place in February and March. At the first performance Miller read an editorial, Zametkin delivered a lesson in Marxist theory, Cahan (the selected editor) gave an overview of the week's main events and, as "the proletarian preacher," commented on the week's Torah portion, and Vintshevsky recited poetry and read a *feuilleton*. Others read polemics, union announcements, and letters. After three and a half months of preparations, the first issue of the *Forverts* debuted on April 22, 1897.[77]

During its early years the *Forverts* faced severe financial difficulties and internal instability. But in 1902, after a five-year hiatus spent working for English newspapers, Cahan returned as editor and steered the newspaper in a new direction. He fashioned the *Forverts* into a general-interest daily, not a party organ like *Di arbeter tsaytung* or *Dos abend blat* (which finally went under in 1902). Cahan's *Forverts* remained an outspoken socialist newspaper allied with Eugene Debs's recently established Socialist Party. But the daily permitted diversity of opinion and struck a popular, even sensationalistic tone. In this sense, the contest between Krants's social democratic rectitude and Cahan's social democratic yellow journalism—evident in the earliest days of *Di arbeter tsaytung*—concluded in Cahan's favor. To be sure, Cahan faced constant criticism from staff writers and members of the Forverts Association, yet challengers never succeeded in dislodging him. Under Cahan's editorship the *Forverts* became the most popular Yiddish daily, and among the most popular foreign-language newspapers, in the United States. Its peak circulation hovered around a quarter million in the 1920s, with annual profits as high as two hundred thousand dollars.[78]

The thousands of men and women who attended events such as the *Forverts*'s spoken newspapers participated in what could be called a socialist "newspaper culture" consisting of excursions, balls, literary evenings, and anniversary celebrations.[79] The purpose of these events, in many instances, was to raise money. During the early years socialist Yiddish newspapers rarely earned enough revenue to pay for themselves, even as subscriptions and sales steadily grew. If *Di arbeter tsaytung*, for example, needed money to purchase a Linotype machine or pay its office bills, its publishing association turned to the public for support.

Public fund-raisers also served to foster a strong sense of community among readers and an identification with "their" newspapers. Significantly, neither Kasriel Sarasohn nor other commercial Yiddish publishers created a similar newspaper culture. "Mass meetings, balls, concerts, and picnics were never held in honor of or as benefits for the *Tageblat*," Sarasohn's son and business partner acknowledged in 1894. That was because the *Tageblat* was a private business, not the voice of a social movement. The *Tageblat* belonged to the Sarasohn family, whereas socialist newspapers were owned by democratically run publishing associations representing popular organizations. Socialist newspapers thus cultivated a uniquely intimate relationship with their readers.[80]

A sampling of events provides a glimpse into socialist newspaper culture. Among the most common were so-called literary evenings that featured recitals or performances by well-known Yiddish poets, playwrights, or actors. At large events, such as anniversaries and conventions, musical performances often accompanied literary readings. In December 1895 Abraham Cahan presided over an elaborate "literary-dramatic-musical-entertainment evening" held in honor of the monthly *Di tsukunft* and the sixth national convention of the SLP's Yiddish sections, which published the journal. Prominent actors performed works by Sh. Y. Abramovitsh ("the greatest Yiddish writer in the world"), Y. L. Perets ("the second-greatest writer in *zhargon*"), Yankev Gordin ("author of the best Yiddish dramas"), and others. An orchestra and choir treated audience members to a "magnificent concert" accompanied by "stereo-opticon pictures" of famous operas. Thirty-one portraits of European and American revolutionary heroes adorned the stage and were decorated with "splendid electrical effects."[81] Both small, one-person recitals and elaborate programs exposed immigrants to higher forms of literature and the performing arts, which socialists considered important vehicles of enlightenment and uplifting forms of entertainment.

Weekend boat excursions were another important aspect of socialist newspaper culture. Probably inspired by the German *Volkszeitung*, which advertised its excursions in *Di arbeter tsaytung*, these outings enabled workers to escape the oppressive heat and grime of summertime New York for an enjoyable day in the outdoors. *Di arbeter tsaytung* held its first excursion in 1890 and continued the events until the publishing association's collapse in 1897. For its July 1895 excursion *Di arbeter tsaytung* rented two boats, with a capacity of two thousand people, for a sixteen-mile journey up the Hudson River to Rockside Park. Men and women spent the day picnicking, playing games, strolling, and listening to music provided by an orchestra—for the price of twenty-five cents per ticket. The entire trip lasted about twelve hours. Later in the decade the *Forverts* organized much larger excursions. For its first one in June 1898 the *Forverts* hired six ships with a total capacity of twelve thousand people. The newspaper raffled off twenty-five prizes, including a new set of furniture and a bicycle. Excursions, like literary evenings, usually took place on the Sabbath, a sign of the growing indifference to religion among young immigrants.[82]

The largest social occasion organized by socialist newspapers was the masquerade ball. These balls were among the oldest socialist rituals, dating back to the early 1880s. Clubs, party branches, and unions used to hold balls to celebrate their respective anniversaries, commemorate events of revolutionary history (such as the Paris Commune and the assassination of Alexander II), and raise money for a particular cause. Among the best-remembered (because most scandalous) balls were the Pioneers of Liberty's Yom Kippur balls. Scheduled on the holiest day of the religious calendar, when Jews were supposed to be in the synagogue fasting and atoning for their sins, the anarchist balls featured singing, dancing, a buffet, and speeches by the likes of Johann Most, Johanna Greie, and Shoel Yanovsky. (At one ball, Most pronounced that overfed capitalists ought to fast, not undernourished proletarians.) Despite fierce controversy, Yom Kippur balls continued until 1901, when anarchists no longer considered it wise or necessary to continue their antireligious struggle. By this time balls for all kinds of occasions had become a well-established tradition among immigrant Jews.[83]

The largest and most successful ball was, without question, the *Forverts*'s annual masquerade ball. A socialist club named Voice of Labor organized the first one on January 18, 1898, as a fund-raiser for the then-struggling daily. Organizers rented the Grand Central Palace on Forty-second Street, one of New York's largest venues, with a capacity of six thousand. Despite extremely cold weather on the night of the ball, a huge crowd of people journeyed from the Lower East Side, Harlem, and Brooklyn. Police estimated that ten thousand men and women showed up for the occasion, though the *Forverts* claimed more. The scene provided "a glimpse into what the people look like in a time of revolution," the newspaper reported. The streets were "black with people" who overwhelmed policemen and broke through the main door without tickets. Thousands of people were turned back, including the playwright Yankev Gordin, who was scheduled to speak. Those fortunate to gain entry into the building celebrated and danced until sunrise. This "masquerade ball revolution," the *Forverts* wrote hyperbolically, was something that "no Jew in America, no Jew anywhere, no worker, no socialist from any country, regardless of language, has seen until now." In a decade of large demonstrations, parades, and celebrations, the masquerade ball was among the largest.[84]

The masquerade ball was remarkable not only as a show of support for the *Forverts,* but as a collective assertion of identity. Significantly, Voice of Labor made no pretense to place the ball within or against Jewish tradition. Organizers did not schedule it to coincide with Hannukah or Purim, a festive holiday which Jews typically celebrated in costume. The masquerade ball made a statement that the *Forverts* itself was reason enough to celebrate, the socialist cause its own justification. If the ball's timing revealed an indifference to religion, the costumes worn by participants reflected something of their own changing self-perceptions. Many individuals wore explicitly political costumes affirming socialist ideals. One woman came dressed as an "angel of social democracy," another wore a dress made from copies of a socialist newspaper, and a third woman adorned her dress with "revolutionary pictures." (Unfortunately, the *Forverts* did not print any illustrations.) One man somehow came dressed as "capital, religion, and labor" and another as "capital and labor." Less abstract costumes depicted a "wounded striker" and an "evicted family," demonstrating injustices regularly endured or feared by immigrants. Other costumes portrayed familiar types from East Side street life, but without obvious political content: "a blind peddler selling pencils," "a mad man," and a "blind man with a harmonica."

Some people dressed up as particular Jewish types from Eastern Europe: *kheyder* students, a matzoh baker, and a greenhorn. Such costumes expressed differentiation rather than identification. They implied, "We are no longer they." The costumes represented the immigrants' eastern European past, not their American present or future.

Other costumes displayed a different kind of cultural difference, not between old-fashioned and modern Jews, but between Jews and gentiles: "a Long Island farmer," a gypsy, an Italian worker, and a Russian peasant. It is impossible to know why these costumes were chosen or how they were perceived. Were they meant as parody, admiration, a combination of the two, or something else? And finally there were miscellaneous costumes, such as the female acrobat, which did not seem to fit into any larger category. Judges evidently did not evaluate costumes by political criteria. They awarded a first prize of twenty-five dollars to the "madman," second place went to the "blind man with harmonica," and a woman dressed as the Statue of Liberty (a costume that affirmed American ideals of freedom if not the current reality) won third place. The masquerade ball raised upward of seventeen hundred dollars for the *Forverts.*[85]

To compensate the many people turned away on January 18, Voice of Labor organized a second ball three weeks later attended by twenty-five hundred to three thousand people. Other benefits for the *Forverts* took place in Boston, Philadelphia, and Hartford.[86] After its highly successful beginning, the *Forverts* masquerade ball continued as an annual event for the next fourteen years and occasionally after that until 1917. At their peak the masquerade balls were held in Madison Square Garden and attracted as many as twenty thousand people. By that time the *Forverts* could afford to donate the proceeds to other socialist newspapers and organizations.[87]

At the heart of socialist newspaper culture was the act of reading itself. The rapid growth in the number and popularity of Yiddish newspapers should not obscure the fact that most immigrants faced considerable difficulty in becoming readers. Few individuals could simply pick up a Yiddish newspaper and read. Most had to learn how to read. It is true that a relatively high rate of literacy characterized immigrant Jewry, particularly in comparison with non-Jewish immigrants from eastern Europe. Russia's 1897 census reported that 64–66 percent of male Jews and 32–37 percent of female Jews over the age of ten could read in some language.[88] But what did literacy actually mean? Most immigrants, male and female, possessed only rudimentary reading and writing skills. The principal educational institution in Jewish society was the *kheyder,* which taught little more than the Hebrew alphabet, prayers, and the Bible to boys under the age of thirteen. Girls sometimes attended *kheyder* with their brothers for the first two years and, in scattered instances, special *khedorim* for girls, but generally girls received instruction at home in reading and writing Yiddish. The privileged minority of Jewish boys and girls who attended a government school were taught to read and write in Russian, not Yiddish.[89] Consequently, as the economic historian Arcadius Kahan notes, "The typical product of such elementary traditional instruction, which was the entire instruction for the poor classes [of boys], was a person semi-literate even in his own language. The reading of Hebrew characters in the prayer book did not guarantee the ability to read newspapers, books, etc." In the words of one immigrant man, "It perhaps sounds strange; I could pray in Hebrew but I could not read a [Yiddish] newspaper."[90]

Apart from their limited education, a major problem confronting readers was the peculiar language of Yiddish newspapers. In the late nineteenth century most journalists wrote in a highly Germanized Yiddish that came to be known as *daytshmerish.* This artificial language (also used by Yiddish stage actors at the time) was characterized by a semi-German syntax, a preponderance of German vocabulary, and German-influenced orthography. The following passage, transliterated from an 1873 newspaper, provides a good illustration: "Den tsvekk farfolgt arme kinder hier in der untershtadt velkhe eyne farnakhlesigte ertsiung haben nikht nur im hebreishn und der ihnen nothigen landes shprakhe tsu unterrikhtn, zondern in demzelbn eynem entshprekhendem handverk tsu lehrnen tsu lassen damit zi zelben keyne lage ba dem pedeler oder betler tsu verden um ihr breyd tsu gevinnen benotigt zayn zollen."[91]

This convoluted sentence contains at least eighteen German words (adapted, of course, to the Yiddish alphabet's Hebrew characters), such as *arme* instead of *oreme* (poor), *hier* instead of *do* (here), and *farnakhlesigte* instead of *opgelozte* (neglected). Even words native to Yiddish are spelled so as to make them sound more like German: *shprakhe* rather than *sphrakh* (language), *haben* rather than *hoben* (to have), *nikht* rather than *nisht* or *nit* (not), and so on. Readers thus had to learn a kind of newspaper language that was very different from the Yiddish they spoke. A Chicago editor estimated that the *Tageblat*'s readers in the late 1880s understood as little as one-fourth of the newspaper's content. The Yiddish of Sarasohn's *Di yidishe gazetn* appalled a correspondent for *Voskhod* in 1886. "It would be much easier and less time-consuming for you to make sense of Egyptian hieroglyphics," he wrote, "than to understand this journal of 'literature.'"[92]

Yiddish newspapers employed *daytshmerish* for at least four reasons. First, a number of early editors and writers came from a region of Poland near the Prussian border where the German influence was strongly felt. They spoke a blend of German and Yiddish called *Kalvalier daytsh* and transferred it to the pages of American Yiddish newspapers. A second factor had to do with negative perceptions of Yiddish. Many pioneer Yiddish journalists were, ironically, *maskilim* and Hebraists who regarded Yiddish as a corrupted version of German. They incorporated as much German as possible with the goal of "purifying" and "elevating" the Jewish vernacular. Third, many writers, particularly in the socialist camp, did not know Yiddish very well early in their careers. Cahan described Louis Miller and Morris Hillquit, for example, as "inexperienced" and "barely Jewish" when they started writing for *Di arbeter tsaytung* in 1890.[93] Such writers borrowed from German to compensate for their limited vocabulary and poor grasp of idiomatic Yiddish. Finally, the absence of a Yiddish journalistic tradition induced further reliance on German. Yiddish newspapers were a recent invention and the Yiddish language did not yet possess a vocabulary to describe events, ideas, and institutions specific to the United States. Nor did there exist generally agreed-upon rules of spelling and grammar. In the absence of a standardized, literary Yiddish (this would not come into existence until the twentieth century), early Yiddish journalists borrowed from the

German American press. A host of factors thus gave rise to *daytshmerish* during the Yiddish press's formative period.[94]

The quality of Yiddish used in socialist newspapers, though often criticized as *daytshmerish*, was actually no worse, and usually better, than many *kol yisroel* newspapers. A number of socialist writers, in fact, helped to wean the Yiddish press away from *daytshmerish* in the late 1880s and 1890s. The *Folkstsaytung*'s editors, Abba Braslavsky and Moyshe Mints, intentionally wrote in a more colloquial Yiddish than was considered appropriate at the time. Alexander Harkavy, a member of the Pioneers of Liberty (though hardly an orthodox anarchist), published a series of instructional articles in 1887 and 1888 on how to write proper Yiddish. As editor of *Di arbeter tsaytung* and the *Forverts,* Abraham Cahan tutored colleagues in how to write "plain" Yiddish. Rather than resort to German, Cahan coined new terms that had an authentic Yiddish flavor. Some of them, *pasirung* (incident) for example, would become part of everyday vocabulary by the early twentieth century.[95]

Nonetheless, the ideological influence of German socialists contributed to the use of German vocabulary in socialist Yiddish newspapers. In addition to the standard German words used widely in the Yiddish press, socialist newspapers contained a plethora of terms related particularly to the socialist movement, such as *partei-tage* (party convention), *yares-fest* (anniversary celebration), *genosse* (comrade), and many others. Each of those three terms had a readily familiar Yiddish equivalent, but socialists rarely used them. They regarded a Yiddish word like *khaver* (comrade), which was derived from Hebrew, as too culturally specific, too Jewish, to be used in an avowedly secular and universalistic movement.[96] The German language, by contrast, enjoyed high status, both in the world of socialism and in European civilization generally. In addition to German, readers confronted a daunting array of foreign loan words and neologisms that proved difficult to pronounce, let alone understand. *Yunyon* (union), *sotsyalizm* (socialism), and *anarkhizm* (anarchism) were frequently mispronounced as *yunye, tsitsilizm,* and *arkhizm.* The uninitiated often mistook the abbreviated word for comrade, *gen. (genosse),* to mean a military general. ("Who knew there were so many Jewish war heroes in the United States?" more than one immigrant wondered.) Even the layout of the printed page could cause confusion. According to a 1904 article in Russia's *Der fraynd,* newcomers sometimes tried to read across the page rather than down each column.[97]

Leon Kobrin humorously describes his reaction to hearing a young woman read aloud from *Di fraye arbeter shtime* shortly after his arrival in the United States in 1892. Proud to show off her sophistication, Kobrin's friend proceeds blithely unaware that "every word which falls from her mouth is virtually a deformed corpse. I can see she does not even know that a merciless pogrom is taking place in her mouth against the words of *Di fraye arbeter shtime.*" Immigrants, like the young woman Kobrin mentions, often viewed newspapers as a kind of status symbol that demonstrated that one was informed and no longer a greenhorn. A man named Shloyme Geltner, for example, used to carry a newspaper in his back pocket for "decoration," long before he learned how to read. Even well-educated immigrants had trouble with Yiddish newspapers. Kobrin acknowledges that he, too, found it difficult to understand *Di fraye arbeter shtime.* Such words as "'palliative,' 'revolt,' 'exploiter' . . . I've never heard these words in *zhargon* . . . for me, a new America." In Russia, American Yiddish baffled Jewish revolutionaries who imported socialist publications from abroad. "I admit," an early leader of the Bund writes, "that the half-German, sawdust language from America . . . was unintelligible to us." In several instances the Bund felt compelled to rewrite pamphlets from New York before distributing them. Nobody had an easy time reading the early Yiddish press.[98] Yiddish newspapers required skill and perseverance. There was no such thing as a casual reader.

Immigrants overcame their reading difficulties, as they did so many other daily problems, by seeking help from friends and family. Reading a newspaper was as much a collective endeavor as an individual one. Immigrants read together in private homes, parks, cafés, and workplaces. Photographs from the period show groups of young men and women posing with their favorite newspaper. Although the overall level of comprehension was initially low, a stratum of more advanced readers eventually emerged. Not satisfied with newspapers, they formed self-education societies where they read and discussed journals, pamphlets, and

8. A group of friends and relatives in Syracuse, New York, pose with a copy of the *Forverts*, ca. 1910. Socialists often posed for photographs with their favorite newspapers. Photo courtesy of the Schrag family.

books. Encouraged and valorized by socialist intellectuals, these men and women represented a new type of person on the immigrant Jewish scene: the self-educated worker.

Workers' Self-Education Societies

In January 1894 a Brooklyn man named Hyman Goldstein placed an announcement in *Di arbeter tsaytung* addressed to "brother workers." "The winter with its long nights," the announcement read, "always raises the question among workers who do not want to waste their time with playing cards and other such crude things—how should we spend our free time?" Goldstein answered his question by calling on readers to join him in founding a "continuing education society" *(fortbildung fareyn)* that would "aim to have a reading room, arrange lectures, and so on." Goldstein offered to donate his personal library and urged all interested individuals to contact him.[99] It is not known whether Goldstein followed through with his proposal, but quite likely he did. By the mid-1890s education societies were springing up in Jewish neighborhoods around New York and other cities. Although these societies were devised originally by intellectuals, ordinary men and women quickly embraced the idea and established societies on their own initiative.[100] The number of education societies and their members cannot be determined. No organizational records have survived, if ever they were kept. Unpublished oral histories, memoirs, and newspaper announcements provide only scraps of information. Taken together, however, these skimpy sources provide a glimpse into an important phenomenon.

The Pioneers of Liberty can be credited with founding the first workers' education society. Members of the organization started the society in order to deepen their knowledge of anarchist thought while at the same time cultivating a second-tier leadership among workers. "Our intellectual forces," Shoel Yanovsky recalls, "were too small to bear the responsibility of anarchist propaganda among the Jewish public." To strengthen their forces, Yanovsky and several others formed the Workers' Continuing Education Society (Arbeter Fortbildung Fareyn) in 1888. The group held weekly readings dedicated to a specific social or political question. An individual would read from a Yiddish pamphlet or booklet, and a discussion would follow. The meetings were well attended, but men usually outnumbered women and participated more actively. The Pioneers remedied this imbalance by creating an all-women's education society. In this more congenial environment, young women let their "modesty [fall] by the wayside" and eventually assumed leadership of the group. The Pioneers established two more societies within the year, one for Yiddish speakers and another for aspiring English speakers.[101]

The Pioneers started a trend. Between 1888 and 1900 at least twenty-five societies for the purpose of "education" *(bildung)*, "continuing education" *(fortbildung)*, and "self-education" *(zelbst-bildung)*—the three terms were used interchangeably—existed in the New York City area. An unknown number of similar societies and informal reading circles existed but did not place announcements in Yiddish newspapers. In addition, there were at least fifty socialist clubs that functioned, in part, as education societies but without designating themselves as such. Sergei Ingerman thus observed at the end of the decade, "Societies for self-development, as well as societies that hold discussions and lectures, have grown like wildflowers."[102]

Education societies and related socialist clubs were among an array of voluntary associations joined by immigrant Jews in the late nineteenth century. The most common were *landsmanshaftn:* mutual aid societies formed by friends, acquaintances, and coworkers from the same town, city, or province in eastern Europe. In many cases *landsmanshaftn* functioned as synagogues and fraternal lodges. Tens of thousands of immigrants joined them between the Civil War and World War I.[103]

Socialist societies differed from *landsmanshaftn* in character and purpose. First, while some of them grew out of kinship ties, membership was based on shared ideals, not place of origin in the old country. Second, unlike most *landsmanshaftn,* socialist societies typically included both men and women. All-male and all-female societies also existed, but they seem to have been in the minority. Third, whereas *landsmanshaftn* often affirmed a Jewish identity, socialist societies rarely, if ever, did. Their names stressed universalistic ideals of class solidarity, social progress, and enlightenment, as opposed to identification with the Jewish people or Judaism. Groups had names such as the Proletariat Society, Young Education Society, Young Friends' Progressive Education Society, and Brotherliness Workers' Continuing Education Society (which, despite the implication, included both men and women). Other groups, such as the Karl Marx Association, Ferdinand Lassalle Continuing Education Society, Bakunin Group, and William Morris Club, paid homage to luminaries of European socialism. (Members might have also perceived Lassalle and Marx as Jews, but this cannot be known.) At the same time, socialist societies avoided identifying themselves as American. With the exception of the abolitionist Wendell Phillips, socialists rarely adopted American heroes as namesakes. This reflected a European (especially German and Russian) intellectual orientation rather than a particular animus toward the United States. Overall, the names of socialist societies projected the universalistic and radical ideals of their members.

Finally, socialist societies differed from *landsmanshaftn* in their emphasis on intellectual development. Even groups that did not include the word *bildung* in their names almost always engaged in some kind of educational activity. Societies sponsored countless lectures by leading intellectuals. In December 1893 alone Anna Ingerman lectured on "women in the past, present, and future" to the Workingwomen's Society (Arbeterin Fareyn); the anarchist leader Moyshe Kats spoke on "social progress" to the Bakunin Group; and Benyomen Faygnboym talked about "the meaning of Christmas" on behalf of the Young Education Aid Society. Eventually the number of socialist societies increased to the point that they competed with one another for the most popular speakers. In 1904 the *Forverts* complained of a lecture "bazaar" in which societies tried to outdo one another in order to attract the largest crowds.[104] Immigrants who wanted to become lecturers themselves or simply gain confidence to speak publicly joined speech and debate clubs. The purpose of the Workers' Education Group, for example, was to give "beginners, too embarrassed to open their mouths at a large gathering, the opportunity to discuss and educate themselves in the power of speech." In such "self-development clubs" workers discovered that they did not have to sit passively as audience members. They learned how to voice their opinions and that their opinions mattered.[105]

Reading and group discussion were central aspects of workers' self-education. What they read can be determined fairly easily because few options existed in the 1890s. *Di arbeter tsaytung* in its first year advertised all of six pamphlets on socialism. Probably not a single Yiddish book on science, history, or political thought was published in the United States until a socialist publisher named A. M. Evelenko established the International Library in 1899.[106] Most educational material was published in the Yiddish periodical press. During the 1890s socialists published a number of journals for the purpose of "enlightening" workers. The SLP's Yiddish sections issued *Di tsukunft* (1892–1897, 1902–present) and *Di naye tsayt* (*The New Era;* 1898–1899); the Pioneers of Liberty brought out *Di fraye gezelshaft* (*The Free Society;* 1895–1900, 1910); and Alexander Harkavy published *Der nayer gayst* (*The New Spirit;* 1897–1900) with support from a private backer. Of these journals, *Di tsukunft* enjoyed the largest readership and longest lifetime. Although it ceased publication in 1897 because of the split in the SLP, the Arbeter Ring fraternal order revived *Di tsukunft* in 1902. Over the following four decades *Di tsukunft* flourished as a journal of political opinion, arts, and literature, reaching a peak circulation of about twenty thousand during the 1920s. The journal continues to this day.[107]

Di tsukunft's watchword was *visnshaft:* the natural, physical, and social sciences. Social democrats, more than anarchists, invested *visnshaft* with great transformative power as "the helper of the proletariat and the best weapon in the struggle for a better future." This was, in large measure, due to the fact that social democrats considered Marxist thought to be a kind of objective science. "Socialism," the SLP's Yiddish sections declared in 1891, "not only is a science built on a sharp critique of the ruling social order, but touches all aspects of social life and almost all aspects of human knowledge."[108] Philip Krants, *Di tsukunft's* first editor, explained the purpose of the journal in 1892: "Not only do we want the Jewish worker to know how he is being robbed, economically oppressed, and politically swindled by the capitalist class, and what he should do to throw off the capitalist yoke, we also want him to *understand* fully how mankind arrived at its current stage, how it lived earlier, and how it has developed." *Di tsukunft's* front cover illustrates a combination of socialist and Enlightenment themes. On the left side stands a robed woman holding a torch and leaning on a tablet that states, in Yiddish, "Workers of the world, unite." At her feet lie scholarly books and an array of scientific tools. "Wisdom" and "labor conquers all" appear in Latin. A rising sun in the background, like the name of the journal itself, expresses confidence in a bright future built on scientific knowledge and socialism.[109]

Every number of *Di tsukunft* opened with a biographical sketch of a radical thinker or leader, including people who predated or stood outside the Marxian tradition. The remainder of the journal carried articles on political economy, philosophy, biology, zoology, anthropology, astronomy, pedagogy, physics, psychology, religion, and literature. Readers could select from among articles such as "The Rise of the Proletariat in America," "On the American Women's Movement," "God, Religion, and Morals," "Work and Leisure," "Crime and Criminals," and "The Development of Nations." *Di tsukunft* also published original works of Yiddish fiction and poetry, as well as translations from French, German, and Russian. Critics would later point out that *Di tsukunft*'s articles too frequently contained errors and oversimplifications. Nonetheless, socialists at the time justifiably regarded *Di tsukunft* as a significant achievement. Nowhere else could immigrants learn about a wide array of scientific subjects written in a relatively good Yiddish. "Who in earlier years would have thought it possible!" Abraham Cahan, *Di tsukunft*'s second editor, boasted in December 1897. "A pure, scientific journal for the simple folk, in the simple language of the folk. . . . This is an event one could be proud of even were it in a major language of one of the gentile nations, and it is only the labor movement's pride!" By its fifth anniversary, *Di tsukunft* had printed "2,100 pages of *visnshaft*."[110]

Di tsukunft's founders understood the journal as an experiment. Did enough "serious workers" exist to support such a "socialist scientific monthly"? That question was answered definitively during *Di tsukunft*'s first several months. The early issues quickly sold out and people came to *Di tsukunft*'s editorial office offering to pay high prices for remaining copies. A shortage of writers, not readers, was the problem. Owing to lack of material, *Di tsukunft* was forced to publish irregularly until 1895. By then its circulation reached about thirty-five hundred, with an actual readership of about ten thousand, according to one contemporary estimate.[111] Readers formed Tsukunft Clubs to discuss articles and raise money for the journal. Education societies and SLP branches also relied on *Di tsukunft* as their main source of reading material. *Di tsukunft*'s secretary, Isaac Ortman, received hundreds of enthusiastic letters. Quoting from two of them in the journal's twentieth-anniversary issue, Ortman writes: "We read 'Di tsukunft' and simply can't believe our own eyes! Is this possible that in the hated jargon, in the language of servant girls, such deep thoughts can be expressed plainly and simply so that the ignorant might be introduced to the highest science? This is the greatest undertaking you can set for yourselves. We will do everything in our power to help you in your noble work." A second letter quoted by Ortman reads: "'Di tsukunft' is the only ray of light in our lives. We gather in a hall in the evening and somebody reads the learned articles aloud and then we discuss them. The effect that 'Di tsukunft' has had on us is indescribable. Finally, we have the possibility to partake in forbidden fruit from the tree of knowledge."[112]

Similar praise for *Di tsukunft* came from unexpected sources. An editorial note in an 1894 issue of Sarasohn's *Di yidishe gazetn* hailed *Di tsukunft* as "the only purely scientific journal in simple Yiddish." *Di yidishe gazetn* encouraged "everyone who loves education itself and wants the poor Jewish people to become more educated [to] support [*Di tsukunft*] in its holy task by circulating it." Rabbi Tsvi Hirsh Masliansky, the most popular Orthodox rabbi in New York, used to read *Di tsukunft* regularly for its educational articles. Such approval indicated how far attitudes had changed in New York. In eastern Europe rabbis and their students could not have openly read, let alone promoted, a journal like *Di tsukunft*. They would have been ostracized by their peers and arrested by authorities. Those who wanted to read such a *treyf-posl* (forbidden book) did so only on the sly. Yet New York's guardians of Jewish tradition applauded *Di tsukunft*'s "holy task."[113]

Socialist societies did not limit themselves to self-education. Many of them were also activist organizations. The Workingwomen's Society provides an outstanding example of a group that combined self-education with social activism. Founded in December 1893, the Workingwomen's Society had as its main goals the organization of the "women's trades," achievement of "equal political rights," and "to struggle hand in hand with the male proletariat for the liberation of humanity without difference of sex." Reportedly five hundred to six hundred women (and a few men) attended the Workingwomen's Society's first meeting, led by Adella Zametkin and an unidentified German woman. The society held regular lectures, raised money for the publication of Yiddish pamphlets, and helped organize several unions. In November 1894 the Workingwomen's Society called a meeting to urge wives of striking cloak makers to support their husbands. "As everyone knows," the society complained, "wives can be the biggest enemies of strikers." Some five hundred women "swore to support the men and not allow them back to work until the bosses give in." The Workingwomen's Society led a women's division among the larger Jewish procession in annual May Day parades. After the 1894 parade, the largest to that date, *Di yidishe gazetn* praised the group's leader ("a tall, strong blonde woman, with yellow-brown hair and blue eyes") for its dignified conduct. The Workingwomen's Society and other women's socialist groups forged a tradition of Jewish women's activism that would become a powerful force in the Jewish labor movement over the decades.[114]

In a 1904 series on New York, Russia's Yiddish daily, *Der fraynd,* took note of the feverish intellectual activity among immigrant Jews. With amazement the newspaper reported how barely literate men and women had developed a passion for education and ideas. "Among the immigrants who have never read anything but a Yiddish newspaper or book you can find many who debate whether Lassalle's 'iron' law of wages remains ironclad or not, or whether Darwin's 'survival of the fittest' applies to human society or not, or . . . whether Tolstoy is a greater artist or thinker."[115] By then the intellectual avidity of immigrant Jews and its correlate, their political radicalism, had become a common theme in the Yiddish and English press. "Israel's intellectual hunger," Edward Steiner commented in 1902, "is as great as its proverbial greed for wealth."[116] Steiner's backhanded compliment presumed that "Israel's intellectual hunger" was a "natural" characteristic, but *Der fraynd*'s correspondent knew otherwise. He recognized that the countless hours spent listening to lectures, reading newspapers and journals, attending meetings, and engaging in discussions that arose out of New York's Jewish labor movement. It was the product of a new, secular, radical culture in Yiddish.

Witness to recurrent class conflict and inspired by a universalistic, egalitarian vision for the future, socialists in the 1890s created a Yiddish-speaking culture based on lectures, the press, education societies, and political organizations. In that culture, learning and politics mixed with

9. A socialist self-education society in Chicago. Courtesy of the YIVO Institute for Jewish Research.

leisure and recreation. In a single weekend one might attend a street-corner rally, a poetry reading, and a riverboat excursion. Immigrants struggled to read socialist newspapers and celebrated them with masquerade balls and concerts. Socialists understood those activities as elements of the larger project of enlightenment in which uneducated workers would be transformed into "conscious" agents of social change. New values, cultural practices, and leaders coalesced through the socialist movement. The authority and celebrity that masses of young men and women accorded to radical intellectuals, such as Abraham Cahan and Adella Zametkin, reflected the momentous changes under way. All the while, Orthodox rabbis and other "right-thinking Jews," to quote Tsvi Hirsh Masliansky, bemoaned the "corrupted and crippled" state of traditional Judaism. Their dismay can be taken as a measure of socialist success.

Yet a fundamental contradiction pulled at the heart of this new so-cialist culture. Even as socialists built an all-Jewish, Yiddish-speaking movement, they professed an opposite goal: dissolution of the Jewish la-bor movement and, indeed, the entirety of Jewish culture, community, and identity. "We are no patriots of a special 'Jewish workers' move-ment,'" Louis Miller stated in an 1892 issue of *Di tsukunft*. "We would like the Jews to be members of the American unions."[117] "We have a new Torah," writer Shmuel Peskin declared in *Di tsukunft* in 1897, "and new brothers, the proletariat of all countries. . . . And the more we help each other, the quicker the world will be rid of all its problems."[118] Like most nineteenth-century socialists, Miller, Peskin, and their comrades were convinced that Jews (and other minority peoples or nations) were fated to assimilate into the larger societies in which they lived—all the more rapidly in democratic and industrial countries like the United States. And, since most Jewish socialists in the 1890s firmly believed that revo-lution loomed on the horizon, they in no way doubted the inevitability of Jewish assimilation in the United States.[119] Socialists did not think of themselves as building a new, Yiddish culture: that term did not then ex-ist in the United States. As far as most socialists were concerned, all they were doing was promoting enlightenment and spreading socialism in the Yiddish language, which most immigrant Jews happened to speak.

The discrepancy between daily reality and future goals defined social-ist Yiddish culture. On the one hand, Jewish socialists embraced the ideal of "proletarian internationalism" and disavowed all forms of Jew-ish collective identity. On the other, they established more organiza-tions, a multifaceted press, a mass Yiddish readership, and new social bonds based officially on the principle of working-class solidarity. The tension inherent in the Jewish labor movement—its universalistic thrust versus its ethnic particularity—could not remain submerged indefi-nitely. Sooner or later it would have to be addressed. In the 1900s ques-tions about the relationship between Jews and socialism came to the fore. Pressed by events in Russia and the emergence of Jewish nationalist ideologies, socialists began to question previously accepted ideas about internationalism and the negation of Jewish identity. Was the idea of a "Jewish socialist" necessarily a contradiction in terms? Could one be both a good socialist and a proud Jew? Was it possible to fashion a permanent, secular culture in the Yiddish language? These and similar questions provoked near-constant debate during the first two decades of the twentieth century, as a new wave of immigrants endeavored to redefine the Jewish labor movement.

CHAPTER 3

The Politics of *Yidishe Kultur*

Chaim Zhitlovsky and the Challenge of Jewish
Nationalism

Dr. Chaim Zhitlovsky came to New York City in October 1904 as an emissary of the Party of Socialist Revolutionaries (PSR), a descendent of Narodnaia Volia. The PSR had recently garnered international attention for its assassination of the Russian interior minister Vyacheslav Plehve. The party sent Zhitlovsky, who authored the PSR's program, to accompany Katerina Breshko-Breshkovskaia on a fund-raising tour of the United States. The sixty-year-old Breshkovskaia was already a legend among Russian Jewish radicals in America. In 1874 she had been among the first revolutionaries to live and agitate among the peasantry, a crime for which she served two decades in Siberian exile. In Russia and abroad Breshkovskaia was known as Babushka, the grandmother of the Russian revolution. "We had no anxiety about her success with the Yiddish population—her fame guaranteed it," Emma Goldman writes in her autobiography.[1] Breshkovskaia's arrival certainly did generate enormous enthusiasm among Jews. A welcoming committee of prominent intellectuals organized a large public reception at Cooper Union and the *Forverts* published several biographical articles followed by twenty-four interviews. Outside the immigrant Jewish community, Breshkovskaia met with civic leaders, businessmen, and intellectuals in cities across the country. Settlement houses and professional associations courted her. Dozens of English-language newspapers and magazines published stories about her life. By the time Breshkovskaia departed in March 1905, she and Zhitlovsky had raised more than ten thousand dollars for the Socialist Revolutionaries, enough to purchase a boatload of weapons destined for Russia.[2]

Unlike Breshkovskaia, the thirty-nine-year-old Zhitlovsky was barely known in the United States before his arrival. A number of East Side socialists had met with him during trips to Europe and read his occasional articles in the *Forverts* or other publications.[3] Still, in no way could Zhitlovsky be considered famous.[4] That, however, would change within a matter of weeks. Through a series of much-discussed lectures, debates, and articles, Zhitlovsky established himself as a highly influential figure in Jewish public life nationwide and in Canada. In addition to representing the Socialist Revolutionaries, Zhitlovsky sparked something of a revolution in American Jewish life. During his roughly eighteen-month stay in the United States, followed by a permanent move in 1908, Zhitlovsky tirelessly promoted the idea of a Yiddish cultural renaissance and elevated it to the level of a popular cause. He provoked fierce opposition, but he also won many adherents and sympathizers. In a remarkably brief period, Zhitlovsky spearheaded a new movement on behalf of *yidishe kultur,* a concept few people had heard of before.[5]

As it happened, Zhitlovsky came to the United States at a particularly opportune time. During the previous year and a half, the brutal Kishinev pogrom of April 1903 had thrown immigrant Jewry into an uproar. As reports of horrifying slaughter reached the United States, the socialist belief in Jewish assimilation ("internationalism") now struck many individuals as naive, even indecent. Anarchists and Marxian social democrats alike began to wonder if anti-Semitism was more persistent than they had recognized. Previously staunch internationalists now questioned whether commitment to the workers of the world must contradict loyalty to the Jewish people. In the 1890s several individuals had expressed similar feelings of Jewish solidarity and pride, but with little practical results. However, the Kishinev pogrom (followed by the pogrom wave of 1905—1906) produced sustained and concrete efforts to synthesize socialism with Jewish nationalism. Zhitlovsky, who brought to the United States a fully articulated theory of Jewish nationalism, greatly contributed to those efforts. He provided answers to the quandaries Jewish socialists in the United States were just beginning to address.

While many people disagreed with Zhitlovsky, everybody listened to his ideas and felt compelled to respond positively or negatively. No longer could internationalism, as previously understood, be taken for granted.[6]

As a revolutionary intellectual, Zhitlovsky had had little contact with the Yiddish-speaking folk whose destiny he wanted to shape until he came to the United States in 1904. During the preceding sixteen years, Zhitlovsky had lived mainly in Switzerland, where, in cities such as Berne and Zurich, he attended university and associated mainly with

10. Chaim Zhitlovsky and his mother in Vitebsk, 1907. From *Zhitlovsky-zamlbukh* (Warsaw: Farlag Bzhoza, 1929), p. 65.

other students and political exiles. It is true that Zhitlovsky had exercised a seminal influence on Jewish political parties, such as the Bund, that emerged around the turn of the century. Nonetheless, Zhitlovsky lived far removed from major Jewish population centers. His initial visit and subsequent relocation to the United States thus presented a great opportunity. For the first time, Zhitlovsky could propagate his ideas directly to large numbers of Yiddish-speaking Jews. He could begin to put theory into practice.

Yet if the United States offered possibilities, it also presented serious challenges. Zhitlovsky originally formulated his ideas about Jewish nationalism with eastern European Jews in mind. His ideas applied well to countries where Yiddish-speaking Jews had existed for many centuries as a separate corporate entity, but could they be transferred to the United States? Could American Jews really be expected to organize themselves into a Yiddish-speaking national minority, a nation within a nation? Could they develop *yidishe kultur* in a country that expected all immigrants to assimilate into the proverbial melting pot? Zhitlovsky answered yes to those questions and set out to convince others that the future of American Jews would be built in Yiddish or not at all.

Zhitlovsky's "Progressive Jewish Nationalism"

By the time Zhitlovsky arrived with Breshkovskaia in the United States, he had spent the previous two decades developing a synthesis between Jewish nationalism and revolutionary socialism. He began his efforts as a young member of Narodnaia Volia during the mid-1880s and continued through the next decade in Switzerland. Though Zhitlovsky underwent important shifts in thinking, as Jonathan Frankel has shown, his basic theoretical project remained constant. He thus brought to the United States a developed theory of Jewish nationalism previously alien to the Jewish labor movement.[7]

During his early years in the United States, Zhitlovsky put forward four major ideas. First, socialist internationalism and Jewish nationalism complemented one another rather than conflicted. Second, Yiddish-speaking Jews constituted a nation bounded by a common language and culture. Third, Jewish intellectuals ought to spearhead the build-ing of *yidishe kultur*, that is, an all-encompassing, primarily secular civi-lization in Yiddish. Fourth, and finally, to succeed, Yiddish-speaking Jews required collective self-governance in the Diaspora and a terri-tory somewhere (though not necessarily in Palestine) for a Jewish home-land. These ideas—*yidishe kultur*, "autonomism," and "territorialism"—formed the core of what Zhitlovsky called "progressive Jewish national-ism."

Zhitlovsky based his theory of Jewish nationalism on a distinction be-tween two concepts: "internationalism" and "cosmopolitanism." He elab-orated this distinction in an 1899 treatise entitled "Socialism and the National Question," which originally appeared in the Viennese socialist journal *Deutsche Worte*.[8] Zhitlovsky defined cosmopolitanism as a uto-pian desire to amalgamate all nations into a universal, undifferentiated humanity. The problem with cosmopolitanism, Zhitlovsky wrote, is that it claims to stand for universalism, but, in practice, it mandates the as-similation of small, weak national groups into larger, more powerful ones. Cosmopolitanism was really national chauvinism disguised as uni-versalism.[9] Zhitlovsky maintained that nations (though not necessarily states) are a basic fact of human existence and will forever continue in some form. At the same time, though critical of "cosmopolitans," Zhitlovsky opposed national "separatists" who rejected any conception of common humanity and wanted to isolate their respective nations from others. He affirmed the idea of a "general human culture" (com-prising all branches of science, humanistic knowledge, and art), but he understood it as arising from ongoing exchanges between individual na-tions. The national and the universal depend on one another for mutual enrichment: individual nations contribute to general human culture and vice versa.[10] The true meaning of internationalism, Zhitlovsky ar-gued, is not the denial of national differences in the name of an abstract universalism (as both socialists and nationalists tended to believe), but the cultural development of individual nations in cooperation with oth-ers. Properly understood, Zhitlovsky concluded, internationalism insists not on assimilation but on "the right of peoples to self-determination" and "brotherhood between peoples."[11]

But what is a nation? Who counts as a national group? These questions provoked constant debate among European socialists well into the twentieth century. Zhitlovsky adopted a broad definition of nationality. In "Socialism and the National Question" he does not make nationality dependent on a common territory or political independence. Rather, he defines nationality as a cultural construct formed out of shared historical experience. Language, religion, literature, folkways, feelings of group solidarity, collective psychology, and any number of other elements constitute a nation's culture: "A nation is a group of people that in the course of many generations has explained for itself all cultural questions common to humanity, and has thereby explained some cultural questions differently from other groups of people . . . and therefore elaborated distinct national forms of creativity, a distinct 'national' intellectual/spiritual or physical type that passes from generation to generation." According to this definition, Zhitlovsky considered Jews a nationality, along with other peoples who did not possess their own states or even constitute the majority of a population in a given territory. A nation might require some form of governmental support or state-sanctioned autonomy, but it need not strive for political independence. The task of socialists, particularly those belonging to oppressed minority nations, is to develop their national cultures in an internationalist spirit. Socialists should regard the cause of "progressive nationalism," Zhitlovsky concluded, as of equal importance to the struggle against class exploitation and political autocracy.[12]

In 1899 few European socialists, Jewish or otherwise, shared Zhitlovsky's broad cultural definition of nationality. Most contemporary theoreticians considered territory to be a definitive aspect. The major exceptions could be found in the Austrian Social Democratic Party. Karl Renner, for example, put forward an analysis very similar to Zhitlovksy's in 1899 and, later that year, the Austrian Social Democrats officially adopted Renner's proposal to grant extraterritorial autonomy to the Hapsburg Empire's various intermingled peoples.[13] However, the party did not recognize Yiddish-speaking Jews (concentrated in the empire's Galician region) as a national minority, even though they would seem to qualify as such according to the adopted criteria. Otto Bauer, another authority on "the national question" and himself a Jew, believed that eastern European Jews formerly constituted a nation in the premodern period, but the development of capitalism functioned inexorably to assimilate them into larger, surrounding nations. Bauer's denial of national rights to Jews, as the historian Enzo Traverso notes, did not reflect extensive knowledge of eastern European Jewish life, but an "a priori negation of any potentiality for development of Yiddish culture." In other words, Bauer simply did not want to grant Jews recognition as a nation.[14] As of 1899, then, Zhitlovsky stood nearly alone among socialists in his advocacy of Jewish national rights in the countries in which they lived.

Zhitlovsky actually paid little attention to Jews in "Socialism and the National Question." It was not a programmatic article for Jews but a general theoretical argument about nationalism in anticipation of the Austrian Social Democratic Party's congress. Zhitlovsky nonetheless wrote "Socialism and the National Question" with Jews in mind and elsewhere applied its ideas to the Jewish case. Having established the compatibility between internationalism and nationalism, he could effectively argue against the mainstream socialist belief in Jewish assimilation as both positive and inevitable. In an article entitled "Jew and Man" *(Yid un mentsh),* for example, he challenged the idea that Jews must choose between their allegedly parochial group and the larger society in which they lived. Cosmopolitans and national separatists both believed, for different reasons, that membership in a larger community of people (the citizenry, the international proletariat, the nation) required Jews to abandon membership in the Jewish nation. Zhitlovsky, by contrast, collapsed the dichotomy between "Jew" and "Man," by which he meant the particular and the universal. The essence of universalism, according to Zhitlovsky, was humanism. To become a forward-thinking, enlightened man or woman, one needed to cultivate a desire for knowledge, a sense of justice, an appreciation of beauty, a respect for human dignity, and a love of others. Jews did not need to acquire these attributes through assimilation, Zhitlovsky maintained. They existed within Jewish culture no less than they did in any other culture. They could be found in various sources: the Bible, the Talmud (which, Zhitlovsky contended, contained a more progressive labor code than that of most industrial countries), medieval Jewish philosophy, and contemporary Hebrew and Yiddish literature. Zhitlovsky did not claim that all aspects of Jewish tradition were positive, but that Jewish civilization, as it had evolved over the course of centuries, contained progressive elements. By drawing inspiration from the best aspects of Jewish heritage, one could develop a stronger "national" Jewish identity and, through it, a stronger identification with humanity generally. Conversely, those who chose assimilation committed an act of self-denial by submitting to the dominant society and, in doing so, violated humanistic values. One need not choose between "Jew" and "Man"; they were thoroughly enmeshed. By becoming more humanistic, one would become more Jewish, and vice versa. Thus Zhitlovsky's famous dictum: *"Vos mer mentsh, alts mer yid un vos mer yid, alts mer mentsh."* ("The more human, all the more Jewish, and the more Jewish, all the more human.")[15]

Zhitlovsky was one of many Jewish thinkers—nationalist and not—who wanted somehow to reconstruct Jewish culture along modern, secular lines. What distinguished Zhitlovsky from his contemporaries in, say, the Zionist movement was his insistence on the Yiddish language as the instrument of Jewish national revival. For Zhitlovsky (following German romantics such as Johann Gottfried von Herder) the vitality of any nation rested in its culture, which, in turn, depended on a distinctive language.[16] Without their own national language, Zhitlovsky believed, Jews would be doomed to extinction, and that language had to be Yiddish, the spoken language of the vast majority of Jews around the world. Zhitlovsky did not altogether dismiss Hebrew (or other Jewish languages, such as Ladino, a Jewish-Spanish amalgam), but he did not believe it could serve as the language of Jewish national regeneration because too few individuals could speak or read it. Zhitlovsky considered efforts to revive Hebrew as a spoken language to be sheer fantasy. He called on Jews to maintain Yiddish, take pride in it, and use it to build a new civilization that merged the Judaic past with "general human culture."

Among the first times Zhitlovsky wrote of *yidishe kultur* was in an 1898 article entitled "Zionism or Socialism," which appeared in the

Bund's *Der yidisher arbeter (The Jewish Worker).* (Zhitlovsky was not a member of the Bund, but he exerted a seminal influence on party members in Switzerland.) Most of "Zionism or Socialism" is dedicated to showing up Zionism as a hopelessly fantastic project unable to meet the practical problems facing the Jewish working masses. Yet, in the article's final pages Zhitlovsky presented his vision of *yidishe kultur,* which could only have seemed eccentric to contemporaries. It is worth quoting the passage at length:

> We as Jews hope: First, that the Yiddish literature of the Jewish people . . . will continually grow and grow . . . and will attain the level of the finest European literature. We hope that the Yiddish language, which is to us as dear and holy as German is to the Germans, Russian to the Russians, and Hebrew to the old-fashioned Jews, will become all the richer in words and expressions. It is now still poor, hard, and brittle because the learned Jews, the educated, the poets, and the belletrists, write nothing in Yiddish. . . . And only when Yiddish literature becomes rich in books and in all branches of science will the new generation not have to look for knowledge among the foreign [non-Jewish] peoples. He will be able to cultivate his human feelings and free thoughts in his home, in his own language. This will bind him even more to his people. Everything he will achieve in art and science will be brought out in Yiddish, and Yiddish culture and Yiddish education will grow continuously and will become a formidable force that will bind together as one not only the educated people with the folk, but also all Jews from all countries. . . . We Jews will have our schools . . . our high schools and technical schools, even our own universities. If three million Swiss can support ten universities, then the eight and a half million Jews who speak Yiddish can surely maintain twenty-five. And in such a way Jews will become among the most educated of peoples.[17]

This passage must have astounded readers. The Yiddish institutions envisioned by Zhitlovsky barely existed at that time in the Russian Empire, where the Bund operated and most Yiddish speakers lived. In 1898 there were no secular Yiddish schools of any kind, let alone universities. The Yiddish theater and Yiddish press were outlawed. (*Der yidisher arbeter* was an underground publication smuggled from abroad.) Works of Yiddish fiction and poetry had appeared in growing numbers since the

1860s, but only since the mid-1880s had people conceived of a self-sustaining Yiddish literary tradition, an idea invented by above all, Sholem Aleichem. Nobody considered Yiddish "holy," contrary to Zhitlovsky's description. To average Jews Yiddish was simply the humble language they happened to speak; they regarded Hebrew as the holy tongue. To most Russian-speaking intellectuals Yiddish was just an unfortunate *zhargon*. The idea that a modern Jewish nation could be forged through Yiddish would have struck most people as ridiculous.[18]

The Bund as a whole did not share Zhitlovsky's cultural nationalism in 1898. The party's Warsaw section inserted a disclaimer in copies of *Der yidisher arbeter* and the party leadership deleted the final section on *yidishe kultur* when it reprinted "Zionism or Socialism" as a pamphlet. Nonetheless, Zhitlovsky helped to move the Bund in a nationalist direction, as Jonathan Frankel has shown, through his influence on figures in Switzerland who, in turn, played a particularly important role in formulating the Bund's national program in the 1901 and 1903 conventions.[19] In 1899 the Bund's program advocated only for civil and political rights for Russian Jews. Two years later the Bund made the important step of identifying Jews as a nation and, in 1903, adopted the demand of "national cultural autonomy" for Russian Jews. Newer Jewish political parties (some revolutionary, others influenced by the liberal nationalist historian Simon Dubnov) followed suit by adopting even broader definitions of autonomy than the Bund's. By World War I some form of national autonomy had become a basic demand of Russian Jews. Frankel provides a genealogy:

> Although Dubnov and Zhitlovsky were the first to advocate autonomism (or extra-territorial self-government), the Bund alone took it up at an early stage (in 1901) and thus lent it real weight. It was adopted in the years 1905–6 by nearly all the Jewish parties in Russia and in 1918 (as "national rights") by the leaders of American Jewry [on behalf of eastern European Jews]. Via this route it found its way in 1919–20 into the Paris Peace Treaties, which dealt with the newly independent states of non-Soviet eastern Europe. Jewish autonomism was explicitly rejected by the Bolshevik regime. However, the related concept also first (but not exclusively) developed by the Bund—a Jewish nationality expressing itself

through the Yiddish language and a secular proletarian Yiddish culture—was absorbed, albeit temporarily, into official Soviet thinking in the 1920s.[20]

Thus, as the first revolutionary proponent of Jewish autonomy, Zhitlovsky played a pivotal role in the development of modern Jewish politics. "Having made up his mind early," Frankel writes, "he could effectively urge others to take a clear stand on the basic issues."[21]

Several years after he published "Zionism or Socialism," Zhitlovsky changed his mind about the question of territory. Horrified by the 1903 Kishinev pogrom and encouraged by new political currents among young Russian Jewish radicals, Zhitlovsky came to believe that Eastern European Jews required both autonomy in the countries where they lived and a Jewish homeland somewhere abroad—a position he had adamantly rejected in 1898. In early 1904 he joined a group called Vozrozhdenie (Rebirth), which aimed for the creation of a "fighting national party" committed to both revolutionary struggle in Russia and the establishment of a "territorial center" for Jews outside Russia.[22] Two years later, while Zhitlovsky was in the United States, members of Vozrozhdenie formed the Jewish Socialist Workers' Party, commonly known by its Russian acronym, SERP. Several months after SERP's founding in April 1906, Zhitlovsky returned to Europe and became one of its leaders. SERP advocated the creation of an extraterritorial diet (or *seim*) for all Russian Jews that would oversee cultural and educational affairs, levy taxes, coordinate emigration to a future Jewish territory, administer public health, and govern other aspects of Jewish life. In its first year SERP was one of four Russian Jewish revolutionary parties, all of which advocated some combination of socialism and Jewish nationalism: the Bund (which claimed 33,000 members in 1906), the Zionist Socialist Workers' Party (27,000 members), the Jewish Social Democratic Workers' Party—Poale Tsion (17,000 members), and SERP (about 13,500 members).[23]

Zhitlovsky himself did not establish any political party, but his synthesis of socialism and Jewish nationalism influenced the new Jewish parties coming into existence. In the United States Zhitlovsky would encounter a different situation: an established Jewish labor movement, almost two decades old by the time he set sail for America, whose leaders had, until recently, opposed any form of Jewish nationalism. Could American Jewish socialists be persuaded to take up the cause of Yiddish in particular and progressive Jewish nationalism generally?

Zhitlovsky in America, 1904–1914

Zhitlovsky made his first major public appearance in New York on November 12, 1904, at a large reception honoring him and Breshkovskaia. The event, held in Cooper Union, attracted several thousand people, who welcomed the two "freedom fighters" with "love, enthusiasm, joy, and respect," as the *Forverts* reported.[24] Most of the audience turned out to see Breshkovskaia, not Zhitlovsky, who was then little known in New York. The Cooper Union event thus brought Zhitlovsky into the limelight. Several weeks later Zhitlovsky secured his reputation as a superb orator and serious thinker with a series of ten Russian-language lectures on Marxism. In his lectures Zhitlovsky criticized the Marxian theory of historical materialism for failing to appreciate the role of ideas in driving historical change. He maintained that ideas could alter the course of history and, therefore, socialists need not wait for society to reach a prescribed stage of development. Socialists could bring about revolution through the right ideas and initiative, which, in the Russian context, could legitimately include assassination and other acts of political violence. By emphasizing ideas and free will over social evolution, Zhitlovsky faulted Marxism for being insufficiently revolutionary, too restrained by circumstances. Many social democrats objected to his critique of Marxism (which resembled that of anarchists), but nobody failed to recognize Zhitlovsky's erudition and eloquence. "His beautiful and sonorous voice," the writer Yankev Milkh, an orthodox Marxist in 1904, would recall, "his great learning, his fine and tactful conduct on the platform and respect for opponents, placed him higher than all others." Another Marxist, Dovid Shub, regarded Zhitlovsky as the best lecturer he had ever seen.[25]

While Zhitlovsky's initial visibility was owed to his position in the So-

cialist Revolutionary party, his lectures on Yiddish and Jewish nationalism captured the most attention. He excited large numbers of people by
insisting that one could be both an internationalist and a nationalist; a
Jew and a modern, progressive person; a lover of Yiddish and of "general
human culture." Zhitlovsky was not the first socialist intellectual to
speak in favor of Yiddish. New York's socialist intellectuals had developed a more or less positive attitude toward Yiddish ever since they had
started using the language in the 1880s. In 1890, for example, Philip
Krants had assured readers of the Russian-language *Znamia* that, with
"a little bit of effort and patience," it was possible to write in Yiddish
about "the most complex issues in a simple and comprehensible language for the Jewish masses." Abraham Cahan went so far as to affirm
the existence of a distinct Yiddish literary tradition. "That the Jewish
'zhargon' has a literature—a small literature, a poor literature, but a literature nonetheless—there can be no doubt," Cahan informed readers
of *Di tsukunft* in 1896.[26] Almost all intellectuals in the 1880s and 1890s,
however, expected Yiddish to disappear before long. Krants believed that
the Yiddish press would die out in two to three decades. Cahan continually urged Jewish immigrants to learn English as quickly as possible. The
journalist Peter Viernik predicted in 1898 that Yiddish literature would
be "entirely done for" within fifteen years. It was one thing to have a
friendly attitude toward Yiddish or use it for pragmatic reasons, but
quite another to view it as the language of Jewish national revival.[27]

Zhitlovsky presented a new vision of Yiddish as the language of a
modern civilization just beginning to bloom. He identified some of the
building blocks already in place—such as the Yiddish press and a Yiddish imaginative literature—but Zhitlovsky also spoke of schools for
children, institutions of higher learning, and scholarly research in Yiddish. He looked forward to the day when *yidishe kultur* in all its variety would stand on a par with the best of European and American civilization. Chemists and mathematicians would publish breakthrough
discoveries in Yiddish scientific journals. Poets would see their works
translated into French and Italian, English and Russian. Bookstores and
libraries would stock Yiddish translations of the classics of philosophy,
history, and political theory. Zhitlovsky took for granted that immi-

grants and their children would learn English, but he did not think they should have to choose between their mother tongue and the language of their adopted country. He envisioned a Yiddish-language culture as developed, expansive, and appealing as the surrounding English-language culture. Zhitlovsky's optimism invigorated public discussion. "The city raged from his utterances," one memoirist recalls. "The Jewish youth was enchanted by his speaking and the man himself." According to Yisroel Kopelov, "Everywhere—in the cafés, restaurants, editorial rooms, meetings, and private houses where more or less intelligent people gathered—people constantly chatted, discussed, and debated the lectures and issues the lecturer [Zhitlovsky] raised." "To hear Zhitlovsky became almost a fashion," Leon Kobrin writes. "Even those who did not understand what he had to say ran to hear him. When he held a lecture in Russian you could find individuals in the packed hall who did not understand a single word of Russian." Practically overnight, Zhitlovsky caused a sensation.[28]

Had Zhitlovsky arrived just two years earlier he probably would have caused little fanfare, but events in Russia between 1903 and 1906 created a favorable climate for him in New York. The Kishinev pogrom, the assassination of Plehve by Socialist Revolutionaries, the Russo-Japanese War, the 1905 revolution, and the subsequent wave of pogroms served to focus attention on Russia (and therefore on political emissaries such as Zhitlovsky) and generate sympathy for Jewish nationalism. The arrival en masse of Russian Jewish nationalists from one or another political party further bolstered Zhitlovsky's standing. Thousands of Socialist Territorialists, socialist-Zionists, and Bundists made their way to the United States and transplanted their respective programs onto American soil. Zhitlovsky, in short, came to the United States at the right time. Many veteran "internationalists" were ready to hear what he had to say, and a new wave of left-wing Jewish nationalists enlarged his constituency.

In addition, Zhitlovsky's persona greatly enhanced his popular appeal. Who he was and how he presented himself created an aura of celebrity and lent credibility to his ideas. Zhitlovsky embodied the consummate intellectual. He was a leader of an important revolutionary party, held a doctorate of philosophy, and spoke flawless Russian without a Yiddish accent (not to mention his fluency in German and knowledge of Hebrew). Nobody in New York's Russian Colony surpassed Zhitlovsky's depth of learning, revolutionary credentials, and mastery of Russian all together. At the same time Zhitlovsky spoke a sophisticated, elegant Yiddish of a kind few had ever heard before. His Yiddish was learned but not stilted or *daytshmerish*, colloquial but not artificially folksy. Zhitlovsky's rich lexicon mixed Hebrew words and phrases, Russian and German scholarly terms, original aphorisms, and expressions from his hometown of Vitebsk. He could expound at an abstract level yet with logical precision. According to one linguist, Zhitlovsky mastered "the art of the long sentence" better than anyone else, save the classic Yiddish fiction writers Sh. Y. Abramovitsh and Sholem Aleichem.[29]

Furthermore, Zhitlovsky never hesitated to opt for Yiddish, even when the occasion seemed to call for Russian. At his Cooper Union debut, for example, Zhitlovsky made a bold statement by speaking in Yiddish while everyone else on the platform spoke in Russian, thereby implying the equal status of the two. Zhitlovsky's decision surprised everyone present, as Kopelov, an organizer of the event, recorded two decades later: "And here comes a man who speaks an excellent Russian (and it is said that he also knows other languages very well), a delegate of an authentic Russian party—by his side sits a pure-blooded Russian woman—and he begins to speak, like a Jewish preacher delivering a sermon, in Yiddish. Wonder of wonders."[30] Audience members marveled at the quality of Zhitlovsky's Yiddish. "Who would believe," somebody remarked to Kopelov, "that one could express such thoughts so beautifully and clearly [in Yiddish]."[31] In the eyes of his admirers, Zhitlovsky represented the ideal modern Jew: an intellectual equally at home in "general human culture" and in the world of Yiddish-speaking Jewry. He radiated a degree of European cultivation that people had previously associated with cultural assimilation. Intellectuals had thought that the more Russian or generally European one was, the less Jewish. Zhitlovsky confounded the association between cultivation and assimilation. He was a man of high learning and yet a Jewish nationalist who championed the lowly *zhargon*—in both Russian and Yiddish—as a language of civilized culture. Every time Zhitlovsky stood before an audience he embodied the very thing he preached. "You are, you know, the prototype," Kopelov would write to Zhitlovsky in 1913. "The personification of our people."[32]

Kopelov was one of many anarchists enthralled by Zhitlovsky. Anarchists already shared, more or less, the Socialist Revolutionary's philosophical-political outlook, and many had grown sympathetic to Jewish nationalism since the Kishinev pogrom. Predisposed to Zhitlovsky's way of thinking, much of the anarchist intelligentsia—Kopelov, Moyshe Kats, Yankev Merison, Hillel Zolotarov, and others—flocked to Zhitlovsky "like hasidim to a beloved rebbe."[33] They faithfully attended his lectures, oversaw his professional affairs, and collaborated on projects. In 1906, for example, Kats and Zolotarov joined Zhitlovsky in editing the Socialist Territorialist newspaper *Dos folk (The People)*. Two years later Merison and Kopelov helped Zhitlovsky launch the monthly journal *Dos naye lebn (The New Life)*. The contrast between the 1890s and the 1900s could not have been starker. In the 1890s anarchists held festive balls on Yom Kippur and championed assimilation. They were the staunchest of internationalists. In the 1900s, however, anarchists embraced Zhitlovsky's call for the national rebirth of the Jewish people.[34]

Social democrats also took to Zhitlovsky, albeit more gradually than anarchists because of disagreements about Marxism. Literary figures such as Leon Kobrin and Avrom Lesin were among the first. Both men had dissented from the prevailing "internationalism" of the 1890s, but without articulating a coherent alternative. Kobrin, for example, caused a furor in *Dos abend blat* with an 1898 story about a mother who regrets her decision to raise her son without a Jewish identity.[35] Lesin, who introduced themes of Jewish national heroism in Yiddish poetry, would later recall that he felt a "vague dream" in the 1890s that socialism and Jewish identity could somehow be reconciled, but did not yet know how to act on it.[36] Zhitlovsky galvanized Kobrin and Lesin, as he did many others. Before Zhitlovsky, they had felt a visceral sympathy with Jewish nationalism (at least in its Yiddishist form) but lacked a vocabulary and conceptual framework to express their feelings and notions. After Zhitlovsky's arrival, Kobrin and Lesin responded quickly to his mes-

11–13. Anarchist intellectuals such as Yisroel Kopelov, Moyshe Kats, and Hillel Zolotarov (clockwise from upper left) were among Chaim Zhitlovsky's strongest supporters. Eliyohu Tsherikover, ed., *Geshikhte fun der yidisher arbeter bavegung in di Fareynikte shtatn*, vol. 2 (New York: YIVO, 1945), p. 313.

sage. As early as December 1904 they and a number of other writers helped Zhitlovsky to establish a society for the promotion of the Yiddish language and literature, which was probably the first of its kind in New York. Named the Yidisher Literatur Fareyn (Yiddish Literary Association), the group formulated a highly ambitious program. The association proposed regular literary readings and debates; a Yiddish lending library; the publication of Yiddish literary anthologies, grammars, and philological studies; a nationwide federation of Yiddish literary clubs; and an international conference of Yiddish writers. While the Yidisher Literatur Fareyn fell far short of its goals, it nonetheless managed to assemble a small library, hold twice-monthly literary readings of "the best work by our best writers," and publish a Yiddish literary journal. Reportedly more than one hundred people joined the Yidisher Literatur Fareyn. It is not clear how long the association survived, but its very existence reflected a new attitude toward Yiddish prompted by Zhitlovsky during his early months in the United States.[37]

To be sure, Zhitlovsky met with strong opposition. Abraham Cahan and Shoel Yanovsky, editors of the *Forverts* and *Di fraye arbeter shtime,* respectively, rejected Zhitlovsky's Jewish nationalism. So, too, did America's leading anarchist, Emma Goldman. "He never tired urging upon me," Goldman writes of Zhitlovsky, "that as a Jewish daughter I should devote myself to the cause of the Jews." Goldman would have none of it, however, as long as "social injustice is not confined to my own race."[38] One of the most famous debates during Zhitlovsky's first visit to the United States took place between him and Yankev Gordin. In a sweeping overview of Jewish history from the Biblical period to the turn of the twentieth century, Gordin turned Zhitlovsky's logic on its head by claiming that "the highest ideals of the Jewish people were never national but international." Gordin predicted that Yiddish (which he regarded as a lower offshoot of German) and the Jewish people as a whole were destined to disappear in the United States. "Hundreds of thousands of Jewish children," he declared, "are lost forever to the Yiddish language and the Jewish people." Gordin regarded as a hopeful sign the fact that national identities were disappearing. "Everything that is great, noble, and exalted carries not a national but an international character," Gordin stated. "Our idea of the man of the future, may he be a Turk or a Russian, Jew or German, is a great, thinking person."[39] Gordin showed no familiarity with recent theoretical writings on nationalism and relied heavily on straw men, rhetorical questions, and sarcasm.[40] Still, Gordin expressed legitimate and widely shared skepticism about the possibility of Yiddish's survival in the United States. Could Jews—especially the

American-born—be expected to retain Yiddish? Was not the second generation drifting away permanently? How could Zhitlovsky overlook all that?

In fact, Zhitlovsky did not turn a blind eye to assimilation. He well understood the allure of American society, as well as pressures to conform. The regnant ethos of "successism," Zhitlovsky lamented, encouraged immigrants to pursue economic advancement at the expense of their own "national cultures." Still, Zhitlovsky denied the inevitability of assimilation. American society did not function as a melting pot nor should it, Zhitlovsky argued. Like later "cultural pluralists," such as Horace Kallen, Zhitlovsky viewed American society as a collection of national groups—a nation of nationalities—that had yet to achieve their full potential. In cities across the country Jews and other immigrant groups produced vital foreign-language (or "national") cultures in the forms of theater, literature, newspapers, voluntary associations, and on and on. Even while Zhitlovsky criticized institutions such as the Yiddish press for being overly commercial, he believed they provided building blocks for a higher-quality Yiddish-language culture in the future. Zhitlovsky thus believed immigrant Jewry stood at the crossroads between Yiddish cultural revival and assimilation. (He failed to consider the in-between possibility that Jews could exist as an English-speaking ethnic group. Like many nationalists, Zhitlovsky viewed assimilation in monolithic terms.) Neither outcome was preordained: with sufficient will people could steer developments one way or another. This optimistic belief in the power of free will linked Zhitlovsky's revolutionary socialism with his Yiddish cultural nationalism.[41]

Zhitlovsky assigned intellectuals, the natural "thinkers and leaders" of all nations, the primary role in building *yidishe kultur*. The problem was, according to Zhitlovsky, that Jews suffered from a crisis of intellectual leadership. Zhitlovsky frequently bemoaned the fact that intellectuals had abandoned the Yiddish-speaking folk in pursuit of knowledge in other languages. The basic problem, according to Zhitlovsky, was that the Yiddish language lacked the necessary resources (such as books and schools) to be able to retain the "best" and "greatest" minds of the Jewish people. True, the Jewish labor movement had drawn some intellectuals back to Yiddish, but with the utilitarian goal of "enlightening" Jewish workers and eventually escorting them away from their mother tongue. Zhitlovsky wanted to guide that trend in a different direction. He wished to build a capacious Yiddish-language culture that would lure estranged intellectuals back to Yiddish and, in doing so, cultivate new Yiddish-speaking intellectuals. A top priority for Zhitlovsky, then, was the creation of "a new Jewish intelligentsia" committed to revolutionary socialism and "Jewish national rebirth" through Yiddish. He endeavored to achieve that after his return to the United States in mid-1908 with his new monthly journal, *Dos naye lebn*.[42]

Dos naye lebn marked a departure in the Yiddish press. It was at once highbrow, radical, and nationalistic. Whereas *Di tsukunft*, the main socialist Yiddish journal of the 1890s, offered elementary education to workers, *Dos naye lebn* served "the educated public." Articles in *Di tsukunft* introduced readers to the basic ideas of Marx or Darwin, instructed them in how to read poetry, and explained the workings of human anatomy, but *Dos naye lebn* presumed its readers knew all that. It eschewed "popularizations" (general overviews) in favor of specialized works in philosophy, political theory, and history. Zhitlovsky published articles on subjects such as "materialism and dialectical logic," "social monism," and the economics of immigration. At the same time, *Dos naye lebn* differed from the new, purely literary journals (such as those associated with the group of writers known as Di Yunge, The Young Ones) that had simultaneously begun to appear in places such as New York and Vilnius (the short-lived *Di literarishe monatshriftn* [*The Literary Monthly*] being an example from the latter). Unlike those journals, *Dos naye lebn* did not separate literature from politics or espouse art for its own sake.[43] *Dos naye lebn* was decidedly a political journal of the Jewish nationalist left. It provided a forum for political analysis and debate of Jewish national issues on both sides of the Atlantic. And yet *Dos naye lebn* did not treat fiction and poetry as subordinate to or instruments of a political agenda. It affirmed the autonomy of literature and was open to literary experimentation. In its thematic scope and level of sophistication, *Dos naye lebn* encapsulated the kind of *yidishe kultur* Zhitlovsky wanted to see built on a large scale. It represented *yidishe kultur* in practice.

Zhitlovsky's critics scoffed at *Dos naye lebn*. What practical use could such a journal have? How many people would want to read it, let alone could understand it? In *Di tsukunft*, Abraham Cahan rebuked *Dos naye lebn* for catering to an "intellectual aristocracy." Cahan and his colleagues had dedicated themselves over the previous two decades to popularizing general knowledge in plain and simple Yiddish. Now here was Zhitlovsky, writing about arcane philosophical topics (what does "moral philosophy and the end goal" mean, anyway?) in a language "which, he imagines, to be geared to a Yiddish university." Cahan conceded Zhitlovsky's attributes as a great Yiddish stylist, but he faulted him for inventing a kind of Yiddish nobody spoke and few understood. According to Cahan, one should write in the simplest possible Yiddish for the least educated reader. He dismissed Zhitlovsky's desire to fashion Yiddish into a *kultur shprakh*, the cultivated language of a modern nation. Cahan loved the Yiddish language and literature, but he believed that Yiddish could never be more than a humble *folks shprakh*, the vernacular of a small, downtrodden people. According to Cahan, Zhitlovsky's dream of a Yiddish cultural renaissance had little relevance to the masses of people who actually spoke Yiddish. Cahan insisted that Jews did not want or need *yidishe kultur* and thus faulted Zhitlovsky for trying to create "a culture without a people." Instead of trying to build a high intellectual culture in Yiddish, Cahan advised Zhitlovsky to make himself useful by providing immigrants with practical information in Yiddish until they could learn English.[44]

Zhitlovsky agreed that intellectuals needed to popularize knowledge in an easily digestible style, but he reprimanded Cahan for doing a poor job of it. Zhitlovsky displayed little respect for Cahan's intellectual capacities and considered him ill qualified to speak on matters of education. In 1905 Zhitlovsky had trounced Cahan in a debate over the question "Is Marxism Scientific?" In that famous debate, which would be discussed for many decades to come, Zhitlovsky delivered a tour de force of French and German philosophy while Cahan failed to respond in any appreciable way. At the end Zhitlovsky finished with a simple but devastating rejoinder: "Comrade Cahan, you do not understand what we are dealing with here." Cahan, the leading figure of the Jewish labor movement, exited the hall humiliated, and thus began a bitter, lifelong rivalry. If Cahan viewed Zhitlovsky as an intellectual snob, then Zhitlovsky regarded Cahan as a faker, a would-be intellectual leading the Jewish people astray. Cahan spoke of popularization, but what he was really doing, according to Zhitlovsky, was contributing to the ignorance of the Jewish masses. All too often, he pointed out, the *Forverts* (and other Yiddish newspapers) printed gross factual errors. One article, for example, defined aluminum as a kind of clay. "To be able to popularize," Zhitlovsky admonished Cahan, "one must first know something."[45]

Zhitlovsky did not doubt the value of popularization; rather, he disagreed with Cahan about the purpose of intellectuals in the Jewish labor movement. According to Cahan, intellectuals should be, above all, popularizers who brought general knowledge to Yiddish speakers who had never had the benefit of formal schooling. Their goal should be the promotion of cultural assimilation through *oyfklerung,* or enlightenment. He did not want to train the Yiddish-speaking public to be able to read *Dos naye lebn,* but to start them on their way to the wide world of knowledge in English. From Cahan's perspective *Dos naye lebn* was useless. Zhitlovsky, by contrast, wanted to go beyond *oyfklerung* toward the building up of *yidishe kultur,* of which popularization was just one aspect. To meet that goal, intellectuals needed not only to popularize knowledge for the masses, but also to create a multifaceted Yiddish-language culture of their own. They needed to provide reading material for the most educated as well as the least. The purpose of *Dos naye lebn* was to cultivate a new sort of Yiddish-speaking intelligentsia, not to sequester themselves from the public, but to serve the masses more effectively by providing them with a Yiddish high culture that would stem assimilation. *Dos naye lebn* would help aspiring intellectuals to remain wedded to Yiddish so they would not have to stray to other languages. Thus, the question of popularization hinged on the more ideologically charged question of assimilation, a question that would continue to cause debate for years to come.

To be sure, *Dos naye lebn* was no mass circulation magazine, but it reached a larger readership than Cahan seemed to acknowledge. Within its first year *Dos naye lebn* grew from fifty to one thousand subscribers and an overall circulation of three thousand across the United States, Canada, and Europe.[46] *Dos naye lebn*'s readers were not confined to a narrow "intellectual aristocracy," as Cahan would have it, but included people from different walks of life: intellectuals and autodidacts, workers and businessmen, city dwellers and country residents, some of whom sent letters to Zhitlovsky in praise of *Dos naye lebn*. A farmworker in Concord, Massachusetts (who felt "a little like an intellectual inside"), registered approval of Zhitlovsky's proposal for the creation of a "people's bank." A fruit and vegetable wholesaler in Los Angeles promised to support *Dos naye lebn* to the best of his abilities. A correspondent in Chattanooga reported that Zhitlovsky's article "Jew and Man" "has taken our town by storm." In cities such as Atlanta, Chicago, Montreal, and Rochester readers formed *Dos naye lebn* Clubs to raise money and sell subscriptions. A cigar maker in Cleveland went door-to-door on behalf of *Dos naye lebn,* and in 1913 a Detroit man toured the upper Midwest raising funds. *Dos naye lebn*'s readership was fairly diverse and nothing if not devoted.[47]

Dos naye lebn survived a total of six years, which was one year longer than *Di tsukunft*'s first run in the 1890s. The journal did not go under because of a shortage of readers or funds, as might be expected. Its circulation actually rose over time and its financial situation had stabilized in its last year. Ironically, the blame for *Dos naye lebn*'s demise can be attributed to Zhitlovsky himself. In 1913 Zhitlovsky traveled to Europe and Palestine on an extended stay, leaving *Dos naye lebn* in the hands of Yankev Merison and Yisroel Kopelov. They and the rest of *Dos naye lebn*'s editorial committee grew increasingly frustrated with Zhitlovsky during his absence. More than once Zhitlovsky postponed his return to the United States without supplying a firm date. He submitted articles past deadline and, on one occasion, published a memoir in another journal without informing his colleagues in advance. Merison, a physician by profession, shouldered most of the editorial responsibilities until the burden became too great. He quit in the fall of 1914 and *Dos naye lebn* ceased publication (though it would be revived briefly after World War I).

Despite its relatively brief lifespan, *Dos naye lebn* made a discernable impact on the Yiddish cultural landscape. In cities across the country readers formed clubs for the purpose of promoting *yidishe kultur*. In Omaha, Nebraska, followers of Zhitlovsky established a Jewish National Radical Club to "spread Yiddish literature and art," "combat the slavish spirit of assimilation," and "revive the will and consciousness of Jewish liberation." The Yiddish Cultural Society of Waterbury, Connecticut, operated a Yiddish library and held lectures on Yiddish language and literature. On the Lower East Side the *Dos naye lebn* Education Group engaged in weekly discussions, debates, and lectures about Jewish and "general human themes."[48] In July 1911 thirty-one Yiddish journalists, essayists, and belletrists formed the Yidisher Literatn Klob (Yiddish Writers' Club). Members included William Edlin, Alexander Harkavy, Moyshe Kats, Leon Kobrin, Philip Krants, Avrom Lesin, Yankev Merison, Morris Vintshevsky, and Hillel Zolotarov. The group identified "the elevation of Yiddish literature in all its forms," "sociability," and "mutual aid" as its goals. The Yidisher Literatn Klob organized celebrations in honor of eminent writers and "literary evenings" with concerts, theatrical performances, and readings. It named Zhitlovsky its first president.[49]

In addition to Yiddish cultural clubs, Zhitlovsky and *Dos naye lebn* inspired a number of important publishing ventures. In 1913, for example, Yankev Merison founded the Kropotkin Literatur Gezelshaft (Kropotkin Literature Society), a cooperative publishing house that brought out classic works of European socialism in Yiddish translation. On the surface this enterprise would appear to have nothing to do with *yidishe kultur*. Its statutes stated no Jewish nationalist goals and it published no works about Jewish subjects. Yet Merison, like Zhitlovsky, viewed translation as crucial to the larger project of building *yidishe kultur* inasmuch as it enlarged the overall corpus of Yiddish literature (in addition to deepening the Yiddish reading public's knowledge of socialist thought). By contrast, someone like Cahan saw little value in translation (as distinct from popularization) on the grounds that the typical Yiddish reader had neither the free time nor the education to sit down with a volume by Kropotkin, Marx, or Lassalle, while those educated enough to understand them could just as well read the originals or translations in other languages. The Kropotkin Literatur Gezelshaft, during its eleven-year existence, published a total of eighteen titles, including Sidney and Beatrice Webb's *History of Trade Unionism*, Marx's *Das Kapital* (three volumes), Kropotkin's *Memoirs of a Revolutionist*, and the selected writings of Ferdinand Lassalle. At its peak in 1918 the society had four thousand members (mostly "ordinary workers"), who paid one dollar per year toward the cost of each volume. Merison himself translated most of the books, usually working late at night without financial reward. His translation of *Das Kapital* took two years to complete and was regarded by colleagues as a masterpiece. It sold four thousand copies in the United States, and a Warsaw firm published a second edition in 1936 for distribution in Poland and the Soviet Union. Merison's translation of Kropotkin's *Memoirs* sold seven thousand copies in three printings and another thousand in a fourth printing published by a commercial company. Until it fell victim to internal political disputes in 1924, the Kropotkin Literatur Gezelshaft published the largest number of high-quality Yiddish translations of political thought.[50]

The Chicago book publisher L. M. Shteyn provides another example of Zhitlovsky's influence on the Jewish intelligentsia. Before coming to the United States in 1908, Shteyn (then known as Liova Fradkin) had been a member of Vladimir Lenin's Iskra faction of the Russian Social Democratic Workers' Party. Upon settling in Chicago, Fradkin underwent a cultural and political conversion after encountering Zhitlovsky and *Dos naye lebn*. He and his circle of friends began studying the Yiddish language, reading Yiddish books, and attending Yiddish lectures. Eventually Liova Fradkin—the "devoted Russian speaker, the assimilationist, the true 'Fonia'"—changed his name to the more Yiddish-sounding L. M. Shteyn and became Chicago's leading Yiddish cultural activist. His home served as "the address for all sorts of cultural-social meetings where heady problems faced by radical-progressive Jewish Chicago were discussed." In the 1920s Shteyn helped to found the Sholem Aleichem Institute, Chicago's premier Yiddish cultural organization, and the city's secular Yiddish school movement. In 1926 he established the L. M. Shteyn Farlag, which, over the next twenty-three years, published no fewer than forty high-quality art and literary books, mostly in Yiddish or multilingual editions. His books were regarded as "a jewel in every intelligent Jewish home."[51]

In the periodical press, *Dos naye lebn* paved the way for a number of new magazines and journals committed to *yidishe kultur* or, at least, a higher sort of Yiddish journal. In early 1909 Yankev Milkh started *Di naye velt (The New World)*, a quarterly for the study of American society, politics, and institutions. Milkh did not profess any interest in building *yidishe kultur*, but his decision to create a journal for "the most intelligent readers" reflected *Dos naye lebn*'s influence and Milkh's growing sympathy for Zhitlovsky's Yiddish cultural nationalism. (Milkh would join the Yidisher Literatn Klob two years later.) Other publications expressed an explicit Yiddish cultural agenda. In 1911 the poet Avrom Reyzin launched *Dos naye land (The New Country)*, an "illustrated weekly of literature, art, criticism, and culture." In 1912 the playwright Dovid Pinsky (an associate of Zhitlovsky's since the late 1890s) and union leader Joseph Schlossberg founded *Di yidishe vokhnshrift (The Jewish Weekly)*, a magazine of Yiddish literature and Jewish "national and nationalist" issues. In January 1914 the well-known editor, essayist, and book publisher Karl Fornberg brought out the monthly *Literatur un lebn (Literature and Life)*, which combined Yiddish literature with discussion of "our Jewish national and cultural life." Through a unique arrangement with the Vilnius literary magazine *Di yidishe velt (The Jewish World)*, both journals appeared in tandem under a single cover. This two-in-one format made *Literatur un lebn* America's first truly transnational Yiddish journal.[52]

Few of the new journals managed to survive for any length of time. *Di naye velt* published only two or three issues. *Di yidishe vokhnshrift* and *Dos naye land* lasted only a matter of months. And *Literatur un lebn* went under after one and a half years. The particular circumstances surrounding the demise of each journal differed, but shortage of money no doubt played the major role in each. The rise and fall of so many journals in such a brief time reflected the difficulty of building *yidishe kultur* among a predominantly poor immigrant population. They reached too few readers to be able to survive from sales and advertising revenue alone, yet they lacked external support by wealthy patrons, which generally did not exist in the Yiddish-speaking world (with rare exceptions, such as L. M. Shteyn). *Dos naye lebn* lasted the longest because of Zhitlovsky's extraordinary prestige and ability to mobilize followers. The most successful publications were the ones sponsored by political parties or publishing associations, which could raise money from members, sympathetic organizations, and the public at large. *Di tsukunft*, the one Yiddish journal to thrive over time, enjoyed sponsorship by the Socialist Labor Party's Yiddish-speaking sections between 1892 and 1897, the Arbeter Ring fraternal order from 1902 to 1912, and, most important, the Forverts Association starting in 1913. Ironically, the Forverts Association not only kept *Di tsukunft* afloat, but also made it possible for the magazine—the model of socialist didacticism in the 1890s—to become a paragon of *yidishe kultur* in the years following *Dos naye lebn's* demise.

The Forverts Association assumed ownership of *Di tsukunft* in January 1913, after several years of poor relations between its newspaper and *Di tsukunft*. In those years *Di tsukunft* had published intermittent attacks on the *Forverts,* which the Forverts Association wanted to halt once and for all. Despite skepticism on the part of *Di tsukunft*'s editorial board, the financial incentives proved too compelling to ignore. With annual profits approaching fifty thousand dollars, the Forverts Association could afford both to publish *Di tsukunft* in a more attractive format and to pay regular salaries and honoraria.[53] The Forverts Association granted the new editor, Avrom Lesin, editorial independence, provided that he refrain from criticizing the *Forverts*. Lesin agreed and then transformed *Di tsukunft* into a lively magazine of contemporary politics, society, and culture. In addition to giving *Di tsukunft* a more topical focus, Lesin infused it with Jewish content. *Di tsukunft*'s three previous editors (Vintshevsky, Fornberg, and A. S. Zaks) had paid attention to Jewish concerns between 1907 and 1912, but Lesin went much further. He brought socialism and Jewish subjects together in equal amounts, so that the presumed dichotomy between the two seemed to dissolve. The Jewish labor movement's affairs received as much attention as labor and socialism generally. Articles on Yiddish theater, anti-Semitism in the public schools, and Jewish "salon women" in Berlin appeared alongside those on women's suffrage, lynching, and child labor law. Lesin also fashioned *Di tsukunft* into a first-class literary journal. Literature had always had some presence in *Di tsukunft*, but under Lesin every issue carried poetry, fiction, book reviews, and critical essays by the best writers. It was the most prestigious Yiddish literary forum in the United States and respected abroad.[54]

Di tsukunft's circulation soared after Lesin became editor. He attracted educated readers (students, professionals, and intellectuals) who might otherwise ignore *Di tsukunft* for English-language magazines such as *The Masses* or *International Socialist Review* (which a number of *Di tsukunft*'s writers, such as Louis Boudin and Yankev Milkh, wrote for). At the same time *Di tsukunft* appealed to a large number of "intelligent workers" who would have found *Dos naye lebn* too difficult and abstruse. By the end of 1913 *Di tsukunft* claimed a circulation of seventeen thousand, an increase of seven thousand from the previous year. The actual number of readers, according to Lesin, surpassed fifty thousand.[55]

On December 29, 1912, followers and admirers of Chaim Zhitlovsky filled Carnegie Hall to celebrate his twenty-fifth year as a "revolutionary national thinker and author." The "most intelligent portion of the Jewish youth in New York" assembled in the auditorium, reported the daily *Di varhayt* (*The Truth*, edited by Louis Miller), along with well-wishers from Newark, Paterson, Philadelphia, and other neighboring cities. Hundreds of people had to be turned away at the door. On the platform sat the likes of Moyshe Kats, Yisroel Kopelov, Dovid Pinsky, Yankev Merison, and his wife, the writer Dr. Katerina Merison. Morris Vintshevsky presided over the event. Representatives of the Socialist Revolutionaries, Poale Tsion, Socialist Territorialists, Arbeter Ring, and the cloak makers' union gave speeches. Kats read a stirring tribute from the Yidisher Literatn Klob. Zhitlovsky received a five-minute standing ovation when he rose to speak. The Yiddish actor Rudolph Shildkraut read a sketch dedicated to his *"rebbe,"* which was followed by a one-hour concert by the famous violinist Efrem Zimbalist. The evening ended with Yankev Merison reading a selection of greetings sent from around the world, including one by Sholem Aleichem, who praised Zhitlovsky

THE
 POLITICS
 OF

14. The cover of a 1919 issue of *Di tsukunft* honoring its editor, Avrom Lesin. Author's collection.

as "the first person to show the world that our mother tongue is a language in which one can speak with talent and passion . . . for an intelligent audience." Everyone in Carnegie Hall would have agreed with *Di varhayt*'s description of Zhitlovsky as "one of the greatest fighters for the Jewish people, for its national liberation, for its cultural development."[56]

Eight years after first arriving in the United States, Zhitlovsky had reshaped public opinion as much as a single individual could. In the 1890s almost nobody expected Yiddish to survive. Intellectuals used Yiddish for the utilitarian purpose of spreading *oyfklerung*, of exposing immigrant Jews to radicalism and general secular knowledge so they could leave the Jewish world behind. Zhitlovsky championed an altogether different idea, that of a Yiddish cultural renaissance led by socialist intellectuals. By argument and personal example he stimulated the creation of literary societies, periodicals, and book publishers dedicated to advancing *yidishe kultur*. "It is not given to many men to have influenced others so deeply in so short a time as Dr. Schitlovsky [*sic*]," the prominent American-born rabbi Judah Magnes wrote in June 1906. "Any one who has eyes to see can know of the great change Dr. Schitlovsky has brought about in the spiritual make-up of the community of Russian Jews in this country. His true Jewish heart, his inexorable logic, his artistic and dignified eloquence have carried conviction with them and have given a new Jewish color to the life especially of our radical Jews."[57] As a passionate believer in the power of ideas to change history Zhitlovsky brought *yidishe kultur* to the forefront of public discussion.

Bundists and the Politics of *Yidishe Kultur*

Conspicuously absent from Zhitlovsky's anniversary celebration was any representative of the Bund, the first and largest Jewish political party, which Zhitlovsky influenced during its formative period. Individual Bundists attended his celebration, but the Central Union of Bundist Organizations in the United States declined to send a representative because of unspecified ideological differences with Zhitlovsky. The differences did not need to be stated. The Bund was an orthodox Marxian party; Zhitlovsky was a Socialist Revolutionary and critic of Marxism. Zhitlovsky was a full-throated Jewish nationalist; the Bund retained reservations about Jewish nationalism even while it put forward a "Jewish national program" inspired in large measure by Zhitlovsky. Given its importance in Jewish politics, the Bund reflected both Zhitlovsky's influence and its limitations. By virtue of their large numbers and adherence to Marxism, the dominant ideology of the Jewish labor movement, the Bundists who came to America carried the idea of *yidishe kultur* into the very heart of the movement. They gave it real political weight by using *yidishe kultur* as a political slogan and seeking to restructure the entire Jewish labor movement around it. At the same time, Bundists spoke so vaguely about the idea of *yidishe kultur* that it was difficult to discern what exactly they meant by it. Even so, the notion of *yidishe kultur,* in whatever form, was controversial enough to divide mainstream socialists. Bundists faced their toughest battles not against Zhitlovsky but against the socialist old guard—figures such as Cahan, Benyomen Faygnboym, and Mikhail Zametkin—who themselves disagreed about Jewish identity (Cahan did not share Faygnboym's militant atheism and strict internationalism) but together viewed Bundists as a menace. The old guard wanted to contain Bundist proponents of *yidishe kultur* or, at least, persuade them to leave Jewish nationalism (however ambivalent) at Ellis Island.

During the 1900s, and especially after the abortive 1905 revolution, thousands of Bundists (along with many other Russian Jewish revolutionaries) immigrated to the United States. Most of them initially felt alienated from their new country. Having tasted the thrill of insurrection, the post-1905 émigrés found life in America "insignificant and prosaic."[58] "Everyone was so cold and lived only for oneself," Lena Vaynberger, a garment worker in Philadelphia, felt. "Even in the unions they were so businesslike, there was no friendship and connectedness between one another."[59] Chicago's *Di yidishe arbeter velt (The Jewish Labor World)* captured the mood of the post-1905 arrivals. "We have in America a strong socialist movement," the newspaper wrote in 1908, "yet our newly arrived Russian [Jewish] revolutionaries are disappointed; they do not find barricades, there aren't any street demonstrations, there isn't marching with red flags."[60] Consequently, most Bundists kept to themselves during their early years in the United States and remained absorbed by events in Russia. In most cities where they settled, Bundists formed clubs, mutual aid societies, and *landsmanshaftn* that merged political and regional loyalties. By 1906 fifty-two groups totaling three thousand members belonged to the Central Union of Bundist Organizations, which sent $11,500 to the Russian Bund in 1907 alone. Thousands more Bundists continued to immigrate to the United States up until World War I.

Bundists did not isolate themselves indefinitely. After the 1905 revolution subsided, Bundists focused their attentions on the United States and integrated into the existing Jewish labor movement at all levels. Bundist *landsmanshaftn* and mutual aid societies became installed as branches of the Arbeter Ring, and political clubs reconstituted themselves as Yiddish-speaking branches of the Socialist Party. Individual Bundists joined trade unions and contributed new energy and talent. Bundist intellectuals joined the staffs of the major Yiddish publications.[61] Still, even while Bundists integrated into the Jewish labor movement, they retained a collective identity through personal ties, organizational affiliations, and ideological affinities.

In America Bundists encountered a Jewish labor movement organized very differently from the Bund in Russia. As Jonathan Frankel points out, "politics dominated" in the Russian Bund, meaning that the party's central apparatus controlled the press, trade unions, and mutual aid organizations.[62] In the United States, by contrast, the Jewish labor movement took on a decentralized form. The Socialist Party's Yiddish-speaking branches, the *Forverts*, the United Hebrew Trades, and the Arbeter Ring existed independently of one another. Even worse, from the perspective of Bundists, the Socialist Party's Yiddish-speaking branches were the movement's weakest segment. Party branches were scattered around the country without a unifying structure and they had comparatively few members.[63] The *Forverts*, on the other hand, had grown into the movement's most powerful institution because of its high circulation (surpassing one hundred thousand by 1910) and annual profits. The Forverts Association functioned as the movement's "interlocking directorate": the one institution that brought together representatives of all the labor and socialist organizations under one roof.[64] The ten-story *Forverts* building on East Broadway—the tallest one on the Lower East Side—stood as a constant reminder of the *Forverts*'s preeminent position in the public life of immigrant Jews.

In addition to the Jewish labor movement's decentralized structure, Bundists objected to its prevailing "cosmopolitan" or antinationalist orientation. Although Zhitlovsky had done much to change attitudes, many socialists continued to oppose any hint of Jewish nationalism. This was especially true in the Socialist Party's Yiddish sections, where many activists and leaders still identified themselves as "Yiddish-speaking" (not Jewish) socialists. Bundists, like Zhitlovsky, opposed their dismissal of *yidishkeyt* (Jewishness) as irrelevant or harmful. According to Bundists, socialism ought to serve Jewish cultural and political goals. Socialism needed to be given a Jewish character, whatever that might be, not simply translated into Yiddish. Bundists, in other words, wanted to remake the Jewish labor movement in the Bund's image by making it more politically centralized and more culturally Jewish.

Bundists started their protracted campaign with a little organization named the Jewish Socialist Agitation Bureau. At no point in the two-decade history of the Jewish labor movement had an organization so innocuous caused so much controversy. The Jewish Socialist Agitation Bureau, during its seven-year lifetime between 1905 and 1912, accomplished very little. It published a number of pamphlets and sponsored occasional lecture tours, and that was about all. And yet the Agitation Bureau served as a lightning rod of debate about Jewish nationalism. Was a Jewish political organization like the Agitation Bureau legitimate, or did it encourage Jewish "separatism"? If legitimate, what purpose should it serve? Should the Agitation Bureau be a purely "technical" organization that propagated socialism in Yiddish, or should it be a "Jewish national" organization that represented Jewish political and cultural interests? Since 1899 Bundists in Europe had argued such questions among themselves and with the Russian Social Democratic Workers' Party.[65] Those debates were followed and commented on in New York, but the influx of Bundists transplanted European debates onto American soil with continued urgency. Between 1907 and 1912 contention over the Agitation Bureau fused politics and culture into a single set of issues with wider implications for the Jewish labor movement.[66]

The Jewish Socialist Agitation Bureau

When a Rochester tailor named Max Kaufman established the Jewish Socialist Agitation Bureau in 1905, he could not have anticipated the controversy it would soon provoke in the Jewish labor movement. Kaufman founded the Agitation Bureau to send prominent lecturers from New York City to the smaller Jewish communities upstate. Over the next two years the Agitation Bureau treated Jewish denizens of Buffalo, Rochester, and Syracuse to lectures by figures such as Isaac Hourwich, Meyer London, and Mikhail Zametkin.[67] Encouraged by his modest achievement, Kaufman proposed in January 1907 to create a national federation of Yiddish-speaking Socialist Party branches. Other immigrant groups, such as the Finns, had already created similar federations, so why shouldn't Jews do the same? The practical benefits seemed obvious. "With unified forces, we will be able to achieve much," Kaufman explained in the *Forverts*. "We will have more speakers, more literature, we will generally do more practical work for our movement."[68] Yet what Kaufman considered a matter of organizational efficiency, others considered a question of Jewish nationalism.

Kaufman's proposal met with swift opposition from the Jewish labor movement's old-guard leaders. Kaufman's critics accused him of trying to create a Jewish political party along the lines of the Bund. Critics conceded that Jewish political parties might be necessary in Russia, but not in the United States, where Jews enjoyed equal political and civil rights. "Here in America special Russian Jewish wounds do not exist," Zametkin wrote in *Tsayt-gayst (Spirit of the Time)*, a political weekly owned by the Forverts Association. "Thus, here in America there can be no place and no value for special Russian Jewish remedies."[69] According to Zametkin, Jewish workers and non-Jewish workers shared the same basic goal: the abolition of wage labor. For that reason, Jews must unify with non-Jews in the Socialist Party rather than isolate themselves in a separate Jewish political party. "Separatism in all its forms," Zametkin warned, "is a sickness that can and must be healed. The infected have only to be held in quarantine, the carriers only to be left outside the camp." Other writers in *Tsayt-gayst* agreed. "Let us remember once and for all," Herts Burgin wrote, "that our national [Jewish] feelings, traditions, customs, and so on have nothing to do with the political-economic struggle for the liberation of the working class from exploitation."[70] Burgin and Zametkin refrained from commenting on other immigrant groups, leaving open the question of whether they opposed all foreign-language federations or just a Jewish federation.

Contrary to what critics claimed, Kaufman did not advocate an independent Jewish political party or any form of Jewish nationalism. As he explained in *Tsayt-gayst*, Kaufman wanted merely to create an organization that could more effectively propagate socialism among Yiddish-speaking Jews around the United States—nothing more.[71] Kaufman's opponents, however, refused to be mollified. In their minds, to speak of a national federation of Jewish socialists was tantamount to calling for an independent Jewish political party, which, in turn, implied a Jewish nationalist agenda. Regardless of Kaufman's assurances, old-guard socialists like Zametkin associated the Agitation Bureau with the Bund. They feared that the Agitation Bureau would be used to pry Jewish nationalism into the mainstream of the Jewish labor movement. Though mistaken in regard to Kaufman, Zametkin's fears proved to be well founded. Kaufman himself had not been a member of the Bund, but former party members played a large role in the Agitation Bureau. Several Bundist clubs helped to found the Agitation Bureau in 1905 and, according to a 1909 estimate, individual Bundists constituted 80–90 percent of the Agitation Bureau's membership, a figure that may have been exaggerated but probably not wildly so.[72] With so many Bundists in the Agitation Bureau, critics reasonably suspected they would try to convert the organization into an American version of the Russian original. If that suspicion seemed unwarranted to Kaufman in 1907, it would prove accurate no more than two years later.

Despite criticism, the Agitation Bureau's executive committee went forward with Kaufman's proposal. In July it invited all Yiddish-speaking

15. Delegates to the Jewish Socialist Agitation Bureau's annual convention in Cleveland, September 1908. Courtesy of the YIVO Institute for Jewish Research.

Socialist Party branches in the United States to its September convention. Delegates from more than seven states voted to reconstitute the Agitation Bureau as a national organization affiliated with the Socialist Party. In a gesture of solidarity, the convention declared the *Forverts* and *Tsayt-gayst* its "official organs." Yet the Agitation Bureau received a none-too-friendly welcome in New York City. A consortium of Yiddish-speaking party branches in Brooklyn and Manhattan (totaling at least seven hundred members) voted against joining the Agitation Bureau.[73] The *Forverts* offered little support in the coming months, though it did not boycott the Agitation Bureau altogether. In effect, the Agitation Bureau was "left outside the camp"; Zametkin's prediction in the pages of *Tsayt-gayst* had come true.

Debate over the Agitation Bureau took a new turn in the fall of 1908. By then a number of important Bundist leaders had arrived in the United States and gravitated to the Agitation Bureau. The newcomers were, on the whole, substantially younger (by ten to fifteen years), more radical, and more sympathetic to Jewish nationalism than Zametkin and his cohort. Two figures especially stood out: Ben-Tsien Hofman, known generally by his pseudonym, Tsivion, and A. S. Zaks. Both men came to the United States with impressive credentials. Zaks, a former rabbinical student, joined the Russian Jewish labor movement in 1895 at the age of seventeen. Arrested twice in 1901 for revolutionary activities, Zaks meanwhile developed an expertise in political economy, nationalism, and natural science. While studying agronomy in Berlin, Zaks published a number of well-received articles in *Tsayt-gayst, Di tsukunft,* and the *Forverts.* His talent for writing about serious subjects in an accessible Yiddish greatly impressed Abraham Cahan, who urged Zaks in 1906 to "Write! Write! Write!" for the *Forverts.*[74] In 1907 *Di tsukunft* invited Zaks to serve as its science editor. Zaks immigrated to the United States in the summer of 1908, but after a brief stay in New York he moved to Chicago to edit a new weekly newspaper, *Di yidishe arbeter velt.*[75]

Tsivion arrived in the United States several months after Zaks. By that point the thirty-four-year-old rabbinical-student-turned-revolutionary had been active in the Russian Jewish labor movement for almost half his life. Tsivion had participated in workers' educational "circles" in Lithuania during the early 1890s and joined the Bund in 1898 or 1899 while a student in Riga's polytechnic institute. In the spring of 1900 an underground courier gave Tsivion the sixth issue of *Der yidisher arbeter* (the Bund's organ from Switzerland), which contained Chaim Zhitlovsky's seminal article, "Zionism or Socialism." Zhitlovsky's rousing call for a Yiddish cultural renaissance made a strong impact on Tsivion, who already had Jewish nationalist leanings. He subsequently devoted much attention to nationalism generally and Jewish nationalism in particular in his writings. As a student in Berne, Switzerland, in 1900 Tsivion participated in Bundist student organizations and wrote for Bundist publications, as well as for the *Forverts* and *Di tsukunft*. Tsivion returned to Riga in 1903 and continued his political activities in the Bund. He wrote and circulated revolutionary proclamations, led demonstrations, and smuggled illegal literature from abroad, which resulted in his (second) arrest in 1904. The 1905 revolution brought Tsivion to Vilnius, where he edited the Bund's first Yiddish daily, *Der veker (The Awakener)*, until the government shut it down after about a month. Tsivion returned to Switzerland in 1906 and received a doctorate in natural science. In the fall of 1908 Tsivion immigrated to the United States and joined the staff of the *Forverts* as an editorial writer. His pithy and humorous style made him one of the most popular Yiddish columnists in the United States.[76]

Tsivion and Zaks were on friendly terms with the *Forverts* when they arrived in the United States in 1908, but relations deteriorated quickly. Zaks arrived in Chicago at a time when the Agitation Bureau's supporters were becoming increasingly upset with the *Forverts* for failing to offer money and publicity. (The Agitation Bureau relocated to Chicago after its September 1908 convention to be close to *Di yidishe arbeter velt* and the Socialist Party's national office.) Some critics attributed this indifference to regional snobbery: New York's inability to take smaller communities ("the country") seriously.[77] Others attributed it to fear of competition or a desire on the part of the *Forverts* to dominate the Jewish labor movement.[78] As editor of *Di yidishe arbeter velt*, Zaks joined the controversy. He published numerous letters, articles, and editorials criticizing the *Forverts* for "suppressing" the Agitation Bureau and *Di yidishe arbeter velt*. In December Zaks threatened an all-out conflict. "We are not looking to enflame, to make feuds in the movement," he stated in an editorial, "but if it comes to a conflict it will surely not be the guilt of the comrades from the country and their organ *Di yidishe arbeter velt*."[79] The *Forverts* responded with contempt. The Agitation Bureau, it stated, deserved no more than the little attention given to it. Why should the *Forverts* promote a puny, inconsequential organization like the Agitation Bureau? If anyone was to blame for the Agitation Bureau's poor situation it was Kaufman himself, "who is not even capable of writing down a single, printable line, as everyone who receives his rambling reports [*megiles*] knows." Kaufman and the Agitation Bureau's supporters should get their own house in order, the *Forverts* advised, instead of heaping abuse on others.[80]

Tensions came to a head in early 1909. On February 20 Cahan fired one of his news writers, Dr. Elizvit, apparently without explanation. Four of Elizvit's colleagues, including Tsivion, took his case to the *Forverts*'s management. They submitted a statement demanding Elizvit's reinstatement, higher pay for writers, and better treatment by the *Forverts*'s manager, who allegedly insulted writers and forced them to do extra work. Cahan promptly fired Tsivion and the other news writers. A protest movement against the *Forverts* quickly took shape. Writers such as Avrom Lesin and Avrom Reyzin demanded the reinstatement of the fired writers or they would cease contributing to the *Forverts*. A committee of twenty prominent intellectuals, including William Edlin, Karl Fornberg, Moyshe Kats, Yankev Milkh, and Joseph Schlossberg, issued a resolution promising moral and financial support to the fired *Forverts* writers. In early March reportedly two thousand people attended a rally in Clinton Hall to support the fired writers, the first of several mass meetings on the Lower East Side and Brooklyn. In the coming months public fund-raisers and theater benefits took place in Baltimore, Boston, Bridgeport, Buffalo, Philadelphia, Pittsburgh, Providence, and Syracuse. One hundred and two "progressive" organizations, mostly branches of the Arbeter Ring, formed the Forverts Arbitration Convention to persuade the *Forverts* to settle the conflict. (Some Jewish labor organizations, however, such as the cap makers' union, sided with the *Forverts*.) As of mid-May, the "writers' strike" remained unresolved.[81]

Meanwhile, Tsivion and Zaks issued scathing critiques of Cahan. They argued that Cahan had turned the *Forverts* into a "vulgar" newspaper for the sake of high profits and circulation. They faulted Cahan for printing sensationalistic news stories, human-interest features (exemplified by the famous *Bintl briv* advice column), and melodramatic potboilers known as *shund*. "The higher [the *Forverts*'s] circulation, the lower it stooped to the rabble [and] the more its socialism became watered down," Tsivion wrote in a June issue of *Di yidishe arbeter velt*. "Better a good, pure socialist newspaper with 20,000 readers, than a bad, impure socialist newspaper with 100,000 readers."[82] A good socialist newspaper, Tsivion admonished, ought to "serve as a guide and flag-bearer" by raising "high and proud the social-democratic banner of our proletarian class struggle."[83] Zaks not only criticized Cahan personally, but also identified a deeper structural problem in the Jewish labor movement: the absence of a strong political party that could exercise control over the *Forverts*. While the Forverts Association was supposed to oversee the newspaper, it in fact granted Cahan almost total independence as long as the *Forverts*'s circulation continued to rise. Freed from the responsibilities incumbent upon a party organ, Zaks argued, Cahan could mistreat his writers and neglect the Agitation Bureau (or any organization he deemed unworthy) with impunity. "An 'association press,'" Zaks wrote, "regardless of how honestly and seriously the members of the association wish to serve our ideals, always stands in danger of being a private venture. . . . As soon as the party's interests come into conflict with private interests . . . the general interests are sacrificed for the interests of a few individuals."[84] The socialist movement thus needed "a *party* press . . . controlled by party members to whom the press must be accountable and responsible."[85]

Zaks and Tsivion wanted to place the *Forverts* under party control, not because they wanted to impose a single perspective on the newspaper, but because they wanted to shield the *Forverts* from the allegedly corrupting influence of America's Yiddish newspaper market. In Russia the Bund's newspapers did not compete in a commercial market, which

16. A. S. Zaks (second row, center) with members of a self-education group in Chicago. Courtesy of the YIVO Institute for Jewish Research.

came into existence only after 1905.[86] Censorship forced party publications to circulate underground, mainly among participants in the revolutionary movement. Party leaders determined editorial content according to political imperatives, not commercial interests or financial gain. In the United States, however, newspapers answered to public opinion. Profit, not politics, governed. The *Forverts* competed with newspapers of all ideological persuasions in the "lively, heated, somewhat hoarse shout of the marketplace," to quote the Bundist leader Yankev Salutsky.[87] Tsivion and Zaks wanted to protect the *Forverts*'s socialist integrity against the logic of the commercial market. They wanted to subsume the *Forverts* under a political authority, such as the Agitation Bureau. In effect, Tsivion and Zaks advocated nothing less than a rebellion against the Jewish labor movement's established leadership, which was based in the *Forverts* and its publishing association.

It became clear in the summer of 1909 that Tsivion and Zaks had carried their attack on the *Forverts* too far. Even allies such as Morris Vintshevsky reprimanded them for overstepping their bounds. "Reorganizing the movement," Vintshevsky cautioned in *Di tsukunft*, "is the task of New York."[88] In September, during the Agitation Bureau's annual convention in Philadelphia, a delegation from New York moved to put down the incipient rebellion once and for all. As a first line of offense, New York delegates, including Cahan himself, proposed disbanding the Agitation Bureau completely.[89] After that failed, the New Yorkers proposed an alternative. Cahan promised to fund the Agitation Bureau if it would relocate to New York City, under the *Forverts*'s watchful eye. Though this was a clear attempt to co-opt the Agitation Bureau, members could not resist the offer, given the organization's precarious financial situation. (At the time the Agitation Bureau had less than one thousand dollars in its treasury.)[90] After much debate, the New Yorkers prevailed.[91] Abraham Shiplacoff, the future New York State assemblyman, was selected to replace Kaufman[92] and the legendary Bundist leader Baruch Charney Vladeck ("The Young Lassalle"), was chosen to be the new field organizer.[93] After the Philadelphia convention, New York continued its counterattack. Although the details are unclear, it seems that a number of intellectuals threatened to boycott *Di yidishe arbeter velt* unless Zaks resigned.[94] In the end an arrangement was brokered in which Zaks assumed the editorship of *Di tsukunft* while *Di tsukunft*'s editor at the time, Karl Fornberg, replaced Zaks at *Di yidishe arbeter velt*. Although a strong supporter of the Bund and critic of the *Forverts,* Fornberg had no interest in playing the role of insurgent. Thus, by relocating the Agitation Bureau to New York City and ousting Zaks from *Di yidishe arbeter velt,* Cahan and his allies effectively prevented a potential rebellion. In 1912 the Forverts Association would take over *Di tsukunft,* thus neutralizing another source of opposition.

The Agitation Bureau's move to New York brought few of the promised benefits. Between its 1909 convention and the following one in May 1911, the Agitation Bureau was practically moribund. Apart from a lecture tour by Vladeck and the publication of a couple of pamphlets, the Agitation Bureau accomplished nothing. Shiplacoff admitted that "so little has been done it saps any desire to write a report." Vintshevsky declared the Agitation Bureau "three-fourths dead." *Di yidishe arbeter velt* noted wryly that the Agitation Bureau existed only "as long as [Shiplacoff] writes letters."[95] Meanwhile, other segments of the Jewish labor movement grew dramatically. In November 1909 the famous general strike of shirtwaist makers, known as the "Uprising of 20,000," broke out. The uprising led to the "Great Revolt" of 60,000 cloak makers in the summer of 1910 and other massive strikes over the next five years. At the end of the strike wave, the needle trades emerged as one of the most highly organized industries in the United States.[96] The Arbeter Ring fraternal order also enjoyed substantial growth as its membership increased from about 14,000 in 1907 to almost 39,000 in 1910.[97] And, as always, the *Forverts*'s circulation rose with each passing year. Only the Agitation Bureau failed to progress. In May 1912 Shakhne Epshteyn, a former leader of the Central Union of Bundist Organizations, lamented, "We have a mighty Yiddish socialist press, we possess the largest Jewish labor mutual aid order [the Arbeter Ring] in the world, there exist among us innumerable socialist-revolutionary organizations and *landsmanshaftn*, but we do not have a single satisfactory Jewish socialist structure."[98]

For Bundists the question of how to create a "satisfactory Jewish socialist structure" was of utmost importance. To them it was only right and natural that a strong political organization should lead the Jewish labor movement. To do so, the Bundists argued, the Agitation Bureau must garner a mass following, which it could do only by redefining its purpose. Instead of being a "technical" organization that merely propagated socialism in the Yiddish language, the Agitation Bureau needed to address the full range of issues related to immigrant Jewish life. Tsivion stated the rationale:

> Jewish life daily calls forth questions on which we ought to adopt positions, not only as private persons, but as socialists, as party members. But where is the institution, where is the authority, which would work out tactics, show the correct path, and say what is necessary when it is needed and when it is demanded? A socialist party cannot and must not limit itself to official political life. Socialism is also the *Shulhan Arukh* [the authoritative medieval codification of Jewish law] of social life in its entirety."[99]

Zaks put forward a similar perspective. He believed the Agitation Bureau must "devote itself to special Jewish proletarian questions, to the economic as well as the general cultural condition of the broad Jewish masses [*folks-shikhtn*]."[100] Vintshevsky went so far as to suggest the Agitation Bureau should model itself after the Bund and adopt its name. The starting point, many Bundists agreed, should be the formulation of a "Jewish national program" that would articulate a set of goals for Jewish workers in the United States. Contrary to what "internationalists" like Zametkin claimed, Bundists maintained that Jewish workers, even in the United States, had special Jewish "national" interests in addition to general working-class interests. The Agitation Bureau needed to address those interests in order to become relevant. The Agitation Bureau needed to be, in Epshteyn's words, an "independent national organization with a central apparatus and a clear position on the Jewish Question."[101] That was precisely what Zametkin and other writers for *Tsaytgayst* had warned against back in 1907.[102]

But what could a "Jewish national program" possibly mean in the United States? How might one define the Jewish Question in a country where Jews enjoyed full civil and political rights? Bundists readily acknowledged that the Jewish Question in the United States had nothing to do with obtaining rights of any kind, let alone "national cultural autonomy." "To be sure," Epshteyn wrote in 1912, "we should not and cannot posit any political demands for the Jewish proletariat, as the Bund does in Russia, because we live in entirely different conditions, in free conditions of a democratic republic."[103] For Epshteyn and other Bundists, the Jewish Question was primarily a matter of culture, that is, how to develop a secular Yiddish culture of the kind first proposed by Zhitlovsky. "The national question in the United States," Epshteyn stated, "is no more than a cultural problem; but as a cultural problem the Jewish Question has lost none of its significance."[104] "For the time being," Tsivion concurred, "there can be no talk about a Jewish national question as a national political problem in America, but it can exist in part as a problem of culture."[105] Tsivion and Epshteyn, in other words, discarded the goal of Jewish communal autonomy while preserving the idea of Jewish "national culture." They wanted the Agitation Bureau to formulate a program that would place the development of *yidishe kultur* at its center. By doing so, Bundists believed, the Agitation Bureau would become more successful in spreading socialism and gaining members.

Old-guard internationalists condemned the idea of a Jewish national program just as they did the idea of *yidishe kultur* itself. They insisted that Jews in the United States had no particular Jewish interests, cultural, political, or otherwise. In Benyomen Faygnboym's words, Bundists had fallen under the spell of "nationalist opium."[106] Jewish issues of any kind had no business being mixed into the socialist movement. Jewish culture was a matter of private concern. If socialists wanted to maintain or celebrate Yiddish, they were free to do so as individuals, but they had no business bringing Jewish cultural issues into the political realm. The fact that Jewish workers speak Yiddish, Faygnboym argued, is the only thing that differentiates them from other workers, but the Jewish labor movement has already accounted for that difference. Finally, Faygnboym and like-minded socialists criticized the Bundists for being hopelessly vague about their goals. What did they want to achieve that was not already being done? "What *yidishkeyt* do they want?" Faygnboym demanded to know. "Yiddish newspapers? We have them. Yiddish lecturers? We have them. The party branches connected to a nationwide organization? We have it. Development of Yiddish literature? Our newspapers and journals do it. . . . My dear, what do you actually want?"[107] As long as Jews enjoyed the right to speak Yiddish, as long as the government did not suppress Yiddish culture, there was nothing more for socialists to do. Faygnboym made a valid point. Bundists constantly invoked the need for *yidishe kultur* and a Jewish national program, but they never themselves specified what they wanted to achieve in concrete terms. Whereas Zhitlovsky articulated his ideas at length, Bundists left theirs vague. What should the content of *yidishe kultur* be? Was there room for Hebrew? Were religious holidays, albeit in secularized form, permissible? Which kinds of institutions needed to be built? None of the Bundists addressed such questions, at least not in connection with the Agitation Bureau.

The unwillingness of Bundists to engage seriously the idea of a Jewish national program, even as they continually stressed its importance, reflected the ideological dilemmas they faced as orthodox Marxists. Since the Bund's beginning in Europe, party members had tried to steer a narrow course between affirmation of Jewish national identity and rejection of Jewish nationalism, which orthodox Marxism regarded as impermissible. To help navigate that dilemma, party theoreticians developed the doctrine of "neutralism." Neutralism held that Jews existed as a Yiddish-speaking nation in the present, but might or might not continue to exist as such in the future. Acknowledgment of the Jewish nation as it then existed was a necessary concession to reality, but advocacy of Jewish national survival (as Zhitlovsky did) was impermissible because it suggested a subjective desire to see Jews survive as a nation. "To be national," wrote a Bundist leader in 1904, "is to possess national self-consciousness—i.e., the recognition that certain individuals belong to my nation, and that my nation is no better or no worse . . . than all other nations."[108] On the other hand, nationalists, according to Tsivion, strove for the "maintenance" and "purity of [their] nation in order to protect it from assimilation."[109] Tsivion disavowed any subjective desire to see Yiddish and the Jewish people survive. Instead, he tried to show how allegedly objective social conditions worked to maintain Yiddish. (This approach differed from Zhitlovsky's; as a philosophical idealist, he stressed free will over the determinacy of social forces.) Tsivion outlined six factors that contributed to the survival of Yiddish and the cultural cohesiveness of immigrant Jews: densely populated Jewish neighborhoods, particular economic niches occupied by Jews, social distance between Jews and non-Jews, a common culture, trans-Atlantic contacts with eastern European Jews, and a subjective desire for group preservation (which many Jews felt regardless of whether Marxists approved). Neutralism thus rested on a fine distinction, not always tenable in practice, between recognition of the existing Jewish nation and advocacy of Jewish nationalism. Bundists labeled the former position "national" and the latter position "nationalistic."[110]

Though tortured in its subtlety (and eventually dropped by the Bund), the national-nationalist distinction served the useful polemical function of responding to those who demanded Jewish assimilation from an orthodox Marxian position. It allowed Bundists to turn the tables on the self-styled internationalists by accusing them of utopianism in their desire to force Jewish assimilation on "the natural course of life."[111] Echoing Zhitlovsky, Tsivion drew a distinction between "true" internationalism and "utopian" cosmopolitanism:

> Nowhere has socialism been so confused with cosmopolitanism than by Jewish socialists in America. Cosmopolitanism, which predicts the melding together of all the various nations into a single humanity, has found among Jewish socialists everywhere a warm welcome, and even more so by Jewish socialists in America. . . . Nations will not exist; the existence of individual nations is a reactionary phenomenon, a holdover from the old, decrepit conditions which are maintained and supported only by the capitalist social order—this is cosmopolitanism's main teaching. . . . Yes, the "Yiddish-speaking" socialist, this is a genuine American creature, like the type of "freethinker" who belongs to no nation. The American Jewish "freethinker" is that privileged person free of all obligations because of the one great sacrifice he has offered to mankind by eating pork sausage on buttered bread on Yom Kippur.[112]

To label oneself a "Yiddish-speaking" socialist rather than a Jewish one, to treat as irrelevant Jewish identity, culture, and nationality, was sheer folly. According to Tsivion and like-minded Bundists, a Jewish nation existed in the United States and socialists had to formulate their strategies accordingly. They needed to refashion the Agitation Bureau into a "Jewish national" organization that engaged Jewish cultural and communal issues. Yet Tsivion and others failed to explain how to do that. Because of ideological defensiveness, they devoted little attention to the subject of *yidishe kultur* and instead spent considerable energy demonstrating how "objective" social conditions worked to maintain Yiddish. If this approach prevented Bundists from engaging in a forthright discussion of *yidishe kultur*, it enabled them to capture the rhetorical high ground in debates over the Agitation Bureau. Bundists thus adopted Zhitlovsky's idea of *yidishe kultur*, divorced it as much as possible from Jewish nationalism, and brought it into the mainstream of the Jewish labor movement by attaching it to the Agitation Bureau.

The Jewish Socialist Federation

The debate over the Agitation Bureau continued unabated until 1912 and might have done so indefinitely were it not for an important external development. In May 1912 the Socialist Party adopted a new policy that allowed foreign-language federations to join the party as autonomous subsections. The main impetus for this change came from the Finnish Socialist Federation. Founded in 1904, this organization arranged with the Socialist Party in 1906 to establish a National Translator's Office financed by the federation's monthly dues. The arrangement established an official tie to the Socialist Party, but it did not entitle the Finnish Socialist Federation's members to participate in party affairs as full-fledged members. If one wanted to be a member of both the Finnish Socialist Federation and the Socialist Party, then one had to pay dues to each. In 1910 the Socialist Party amended its constitution to allow other foreign-language federations (Italian, Bohemian, South Slavic, Polish, Scandinavian, Hungarian) to follow the Finnish example and install translators in the Socialist Party's national office. Two year later the Socialist Party took the final step of granting foreign-language federations the status of autonomous subsections.[113] Under the new policy, a person who joined a federation automatically became a full-fledged member of the Socialist Party. This change in policy brought an influx of 20,000 new members into the Socialist Party in 1912. By 1919 foreign-language federations represented 53 percent of the party's some 120,000 members.[114]

Within the Jewish labor movement, the Socialist Party's new policy tilted the balance of power in favor of Bundists. It gave them legitimacy to establish a broadly focused Yiddish-language federation of the kind they had been advocating since 1908. The irony of the situation could not have escaped them. In 1903 the Bund had broken from the Russian Social Democratic Workers' Party (which it helped to establish in 1898) because the party refused to accept its autonomy. In the United States, however, the opposite occurred. The Jewish labor movement's leaders were the ones who opposed an autonomous Jewish federation, whereas the Socialist Party approved. Consequently, old-guard socialists, such as

Faygnboym and Zametkin, could no longer claim the Bundists were out of step with American conditions. The Socialist Party had determined otherwise.

Members of the Agitation Bureau immediately seized the new opportunity. In late May delegates to the Agitation Bureau's convention in Paterson, New Jersey, voted unanimously to join the Socialist Party as its official Yiddish-speaking subsection, renamed the Jewish Socialist Federation (JSF).[115] The establishment of the JSF stimulated a flurry of grassroots activity. Within one year the JSF's membership grew from 700 in twenty-four branches to roughly 2,000 in sixty-eight branches.[116] By 1915 the JSF had become the Socialist Party's third-largest foreign-language federation with 2,787 members.[117] (The Finnish and German federations had roughly 12,000 and 9,000 members, respectively.)[118] Membership would peak after the Russian revolution at about 8,000, with perhaps another 4,000 behind in their dues at any given time. JSF branches could be found in cities as far removed as Jacksonville, Florida, and Birmingham, Alabama.[119] In New York City alone there were twelve branches totaling roughly 3,000 members.[120] The JSF's influence was greater than its numbers would suggest because of the prominence of its leaders and the active role of its members in all segments of the Jewish labor movement. An estimated one-third of all delegates to the Arbeter Ring's 1914 convention, for example, were members of the JSF. The JSF's Philadelphia branch, which numbered about 300 members, served as the center of power in the city's Jewish labor movement.[121]

The JSF functioned as the American equivalent to the Bund. Bundists and their allies constituted the bulk of the JSF's membership and the entire National Executive Committee.[122] Bundist intellectuals, such as Epshteyn, Tsivion, Vladeck, Zaks, and later Max Goldfarb, A. Litvak, and Moyshe Olgin, were among the JSF's leaders and main writers for its weekly newspaper, *Di naye velt (The New World)*. Arguably the single most important figure in the JSF was Yankev Salutsky, its national secretary between 1912 and 1917 and editor of *Di naye velt*. Before immigrating to the United States in 1909, Salutsky had been a member of the Bund for seven years.[123] Facing a potential two-year prison sentence after his third arrest, Salutsky fled to Paris and then to New York. In addition to studying law and political economy at Columbia University, Salutsky became active in the Agitation Bureau and the Arbeter Ring. Although he had no prior experience as a Yiddish journalist, Salutsky soon became a recognized figure in the Yiddish press.[124] He was not considered a great orator, but his peers regarded him as a highly intelligent, capable leader.[125] According to one Harlem activist, members of the JSF treated Salutsky with "much respect and love."[126]

At the local level the JSF's branches conducted wide and varied activities. The Harlem branch, for example, was founded in 1912 by 35 members and grew to some 200 within two years (and to 390 members in 1918). Eight committees conducted the branch's day-to-day activities. The Women's Voting Rights Committee, for example, promoted the cause of suffrage among Jewish women in Harlem. (Women made up 30 percent of the branch's members in 1914.) The Naturalization Committee assisted 300 JSF members and "sympathizers" in becoming citizens during its first two years. The Educational Committee organized lectures, debates, discussions, and readings at the branch's club room on East 104th Street. At the committee's request, the Rand School of Social Science gave courses to branch members, for a small fee, on socialism, general history, "how to become a citizen," and English.[127] The committee also invited prominent intellectuals, such as Max Goldfarb, Tsivion, Zaks, and even Zametkin, to lecture on socialism and contemporary issues. The JSF's downtown branch, located on East Broadway, conducted a similarly broad range of activities. It held regular "open air" meetings around the East Side. During the winter of 1913–1914 it organized a course of twelve lectures on socialism by Louis Boudin, perhaps America's foremost authority on Marxism. The JSF's national leaders also gave regular lectures to the branch. Both the Harlem and downtown branches were very active in the trade union movement. During a large tailors' strike in 1912, for example, the Harlem branch's Trade-Union Committee ran a free kitchen for strikers and delivered food to the homes of those who felt ashamed to eat at the kitchen. In 1913 the branch raised money for the striking textile workers of Paterson, and members volunteered to take in children of strikers. (In 1914, 80 percent of the branch's membership belonged to a union.) In 1912 alone the

17. A meeting of Jewish Socialist Federation leaders in 1917. Sitting, right to left: Moyshe Terman, Hannah Salutsky, A. Litvak, Morris Vintshevsky, Max Goldfarb, Tsivion. Standing, right to left: Yankev Salutsky, Moyshe Olgin, Baruch Charney Vladeck, Dr. Frank Rozenblat, Shakhne Epshteyn. Uncredited photo from Tsivion's *Far 50 yor* (New York: Elias Laub Publishing Co., 1948) p. 247.

downtown branch helped to organize strikes by restaurant waiters, furriers, and tailors. Finally, both branches organized social events, such as concerts, picnics, balls, and excursions.[128] The JSF's national office published many pamphlets and books; a yearbook about developments in the labor movement, Yiddish culture, and Jewish communal politics; a workers' library; a weekly newspaper; and in 1918 an imprint that brought out Karl Marx's collected works in Yiddish.[129]

Still, the JSF failed to realize the Bundists' two major goals: a Jewish national program and the centralization of the Jewish labor movement under its auspices. At the 1912 Paterson convention, Bundists wanted the JSF's constitution to recognize the salience of "specific Jewish conditions" that would justify involvement in Jewish communal and cultural affairs. That seemingly harmless phrase fell far short of the kind of full-fledged "Jewish national program" that Bundists had advocated in previous years. Nonetheless, it aroused fierce opposition from Benyo-men Faygnboym and old-guard socialists who perceived any mention of Jewish conditions or interests as unwarranted. Shakhne Epshteyn responded on behalf of the Paterson convention's constitutional committee. He maintained, as he had over the preceding three years, that Jewish workers must have a political organization that attended to their cultural interests. "We must," Epshteyn said, "become an important factor in the development of our [Yiddish] culture, we must become its main bearer, which protects it from all attacks, from all obstacles."[130] In the end, however, delegates decided by a two-vote majority to omit the reference to "special Jewish conditions." Karl Fornberg, editor of *Di yidishe arbeter velt,* was one delegate who voted against the passage because he found it too vague to be of value, especially given the risk of alienating Faygnboym and his colleagues at the *Forverts.* A year later, delegates to the JSF's 1913 convention succeeded in passing a resolution referring to the "customs, psychology, and living conditions" of the Jewish working class, which proved to be the closest thing to a Jewish national program Bundists could achieve, given the ideological and political constraints within which they operated. Eventually even the most nationalistic members of JSF, such as Tsivion, gave up the idea. As Tsivion wrote in 1917:

> The Jewish Socialist Federation in America learned from the Bund that the socialist movement among the Jews in America should be adjusted to the Jewish street not only in language, but also to the living conditions, both economic and cultural [*gaystike*], of the Jewish people. But the Jewish Socialist Federation could not take from the Bund in Russia the most important Jewish point of its program, Jewish national cultural autonomy, which actually made the Bund what it is. It could not take possession of it because in America at this point there exists no national question.[131]

Bundists also failed to centralize the Jewish labor movement under the JSF's leadership. They made a bold attempt in 1917 during a convention of the National Workmen's Committee on Jewish Rights in the Belligerent Lands (NWC). The NWC's origins were in the American Jewish Congress movement launched by Zionist parties in 1914 to aid the war-torn Jewish population of eastern Europe.[132] Determined to prevent Zionists from taking the lead in rallying popular support, the Jewish Socialist Federation established the NWC in 1915 as a socialist alternative to the Jewish Congress movement. The NWC aimed to "mobilize both the international socialist movement and American public opinion at large" on behalf of east European Jewry. In this endeavor the JSF won support from the Forverts Association, the United Hebrew Trades, and the Arbeter Ring, which were naturally suspicious of collaborating with Zionists and nonsocialist forces in the Jewish community. At the NWC's February convention in 1917, the JSF took advantage of their leading position in the organization to propose transforming the NWC from a temporary body charged with responding to the European crisis into a permanent organization unifying the movement's main branches (a "permanent, organic union of all those Jewish labor organizations which stand for the class struggle in all its forms," in *Di naye velt*'s words).[133]

Initially it appeared that the JSF would succeed. A majority of the convention's delegates voted to maintain the NWC indefinitely, a decision *Di naye velt* praised as the "most important step as far as principles are concerned in the thirty years the [Jewish labor movement] had existed." A minority of delegates, led by Max Pine, president of the United Hebrew Trades, however, bolted the convention in protest. (Relations between the JSF and the UHT had been rather cool since 1913, when the UHT did not invite the JSF to its twenty-fifth anniversary celebration.) Unwilling to cede so much authority to the JSF, Pine and his allies insisted that the NWC remain an ad hoc body. This touched off a showdown between the old guard and the JSF's leaders, described by Epshteyn as a clash between generations and ideologies:

> Two trends fought each other—one the obsolete trend which is afraid of every new wind, of every new reform because these could—heaven forbid!—tear the rudder of power from its hands; and the other, the trend which seeks ever new ways in order to introduce more system, more life into the movement. . . . To the old trend belonged the out-dated elements who cannot see further than their noses and look upon everything with suspicion; to the new trend belong the intellectual elements, the more pro-

gressive and far-seeing. . . . And the victory went to the new trend not the old. . . . From [Max Pine's] hysterical shouting that we want to break the labor movement . . . one saw plainly that he had no concept of what the entire question is about. . . . Comrade Goldfarb is right when he said that we are ready to measure forces. . . . Those who do not reckon with the spirit of the times must leave the stage: that is the law of life.[134]

Yet Epshteyn's declaration of victory was premature. Though the JSF won a majority vote at the February NWC convention, its leaders failed to shore up sufficient political support to implement the convention's resolution. Aside from the fact that Epshteyn's uncompromising rhetoric offended many veterans, the plan seemed too audacious to the established leadership. Consequently, the executive committees of the United Hebrew Trades and the Arbeter Ring adopted resolutions opposing the permanent maintenance of the NWC. The matter was taken before the Forverts Association, which voted against the JSF. This was a major defeat for the JSF, and its aftereffects would be felt for years. Zhitlovsky and the Bundists succeeded in introducing new ideas about *yidishe kultur* and organizations intended to advance it, but, in doing so, they engendered a deep divide within the Jewish labor movement over the question of Jewish nationalism.

CHAPTER 4

Purely Secular, Thoroughly Jewish

The Arbeter Ring and Yiddish Education

In October 1918 a leading activist in the Arbeter Ring, Yankev Levin, published a brief article called *"Di veltlekhe yidishkeyt"* (Secular Jewishness) in the fraternal order's monthly magazine. Levin stated that a robust, multifaceted culture, at once "purely secular" and "thoroughly Jewish," had come into existence in the United States. He listed its components: political parties, union locals, mutual aid societies, literary clubs, dramatic clubs, choirs, and even chess clubs—all in Yiddish. The Yiddish press, Yiddish lectures, Yiddish literature, and Yiddish theater provided the "spiritual food" of this secular Jewish culture. Yiddish-language schools for children, or *folks-shuln,* served to transmit this culture to the next generation. This was secular *yidishkeyt*—much like what Zhitlovsky called *yidishe kultur*—and, as of 1918, it had reached its highest stage of development in the United States among working-class Jews. "This is the first time," Levin wrote, "that the Jews have built up a secular society which can develop in contact with modern, secular humanity." Notably, Levin did not justify the existence of this secular Jewish culture or ask whether it could or should persist in the future, as a like-minded socialist would have had to do in previous decades. He simply presented secular *yidishkeyt* as an established fact.[1]

Much of what Levin called secular *yidishkeyt* was developed by the Arbeter Ring. Founded in 1892 as a local mutual aid society and reorganized in 1900 as a nationwide fraternal order, the Arbeter Ring was the

Jewish labor movement's first stable mass membership organization. From 3 branches with 469 members in 1900, the Arbeter Ring grew to 38,886 members in 435 branches in 134 cities by 1910. Twelve years later 85,000 people in 750 branches across the country and in Canada (and eventually in London and Paris, as well) had joined the Arbeter Ring. The fraternal order offered an array of benefits to members several decades before the American welfare state came into existence. In addition to affordable health insurance, the Arbeter Ring in 1910 opened a sanitarium for members suffering from tuberculosis. In 1913 it established a Cemetery Department as an alternative to the *khevre kadishe*, or religious burial society, which traditionally oversaw burial of the dead. In 1919 it established a medical department with twenty-three doctors, which in 1922 was expanded into a full-fledged medical and dental center. In 1929 it created a Social Service Department that handled charitable services. By then the Arbeter Ring had paid $175 million dollars in death benefits to members since its founding in 1900. As of its twentieth anniversary, the Arbeter Ring's assets totaled more than $1,500,000.[2]

The Arbeter Ring was not the only or the largest Jewish fraternal order. The Independent Order of Brith Abraham, for example, founded by German and Hungarian Jews in 1887, boasted 210,000 members by the First World War. The Arbeter Ring, however, was the first politically radical fraternal order. The Arbeter Ring's radicalism differentiated it from other fraternal orders in several respects: it was avowedly secular (though Orthodox Jews were allowed to join), it admitted women as full-fledged members (rather than assigning them to ladies' auxiliaries), and, most important here, it devoted great attention to education and culture.[3] In 1910 the Arbeter Ring established an Education Committee to oversee the educational and cultural development of its members, six years before major unions, such as the ILGWU and Amalgamated Clothing Workers of America, established their more well-known workers' education programs (which placed the needle trade unions at the forefront of workers' education in the United States).[4] The Arbeter Ring's Education Committee organized myriad educational and cultural projects, including lecture tours, Yiddish schools, book publishing, choral and theater groups, and so on. More than any other organization, the

Arbeter Ring fostered the new secular *yidishkeyt* and the contradictions contained therein.

"The Mightiest Fortress": A Brief History of the Arbeter Ring

The men who founded the Arbeter Ring were not prominent intellectuals or leaders in the Jewish labor movement. They were shop workers who, with few exceptions, had recently discovered socialism in New York. The group's outstanding figure was a forty-one-year-old cap maker named Moyshe Goldraykh, the oldest, most worldly, and most experienced of the Arbeter Ring's founders. Goldraykh had immigrated to New York by an unusually circuitous route. Born in Poland, Goldraykh and his father fled to France in 1863 after the abortive Polish uprising against Russia. Seven years later the younger Goldraykh volunteered to fight in the Franco-Prussian War and, in 1871, participated in the Paris Commune. Goldraykh subsequently moved to England and Australia before settling in New York, where he became active in the cap makers' union. In early 1892 two cloak makers, Sam Grinberg and Harry Lasker, approached Goldraykh with the idea of establishing a mutual aid society. Their initiative was not wholly original. By then immigrant Jews had formed dozens of mutual aid societies, mainly in the form of *landsmanshaftn*. Grinberg and Lasker themselves had been members of a mutual aid society called the International Sick Fund, which was modeled after a similar German socialist *verein*. Yet Grinberg and Lasker felt uncomfortable in a group dominated by *gedoylim*, or big-name socialists. Seeking a more congenial environment, the two cloak makers decided to organize their own mutual aid society by and for workers. Goldraykh, Grinberg, Lasker, and several others met in Grinberg's apartment on Essex Street to make plans. They appointed Goldraykh chairman and on April 4, 1892, established the Arbeter Ring.[5]

The Arbeter Ring's founders did not intend to create an ordinary mutual aid society focused only on satisfying the financial needs of its members. They possessed a broader vision derived from the socialist ideal of *oyfklerung*. Grinberg, Lasker, Goldraykh, and their associates wanted the Arbeter Ring to promote self-education and contribute to larger struggles for a just society. "Our idea was not only to look after a sick man with a dollar a week," one member recalls. "Our aim was a much higher, deeper, and broader one . . . a more beautiful world with a better society, a society where people would be secure in their lives, not only after death, but cared for in life." Toward that goal, the Arbeter Ring placed *oyfklerung* at the center of its endeavors. Its 1893 constitution stipulated that some kind of educational meeting must take place twice every month. Members adhered to this rule by holding biweekly discussions and lectures, which were open to the public and drew as many as two hundred people at a time. In addition, the Arbeter Ring organized picnics, nature outings, Sunday dinners (sometimes followed by informal dances), and theater benefits. This combination of mutual aid, socialist education, and recreation proved highly attractive. By early 1896, 350 people had joined the Arbeter Ring. Two years later a second branch formed in Harlem, to be followed in 1899 by a third branch in Brooklyn. Of the dozens of socialist societies and clubs that arose during the 1890s, the Arbeter Ring was among the largest.[6]

Not everybody in the Jewish labor movement, however, welcomed the Arbeter Ring during its early years. Young, unmarried people felt little personal need for a mutual aid society. Hard-core political activists regarded the Arbeter Ring as a distraction from the main task at hand: advancement of the class struggle. Many socialists during the 1890s believed that capitalism stood on its last legs. In the near future, they predicted, American society would be freed from poverty and the Arbeter Ring would be rendered obsolete. It was more important to agitate for revolution than to join a group that merely helped people to cope with capitalism. The United Hebrew Trades went so far as to accuse the Arbeter Ring of undermining the trade union movement.[7]

Despite such indifference and occasional hostility, the Arbeter Ring steadily gained members. A crucial turning point occurred in September 1900, when a special conference was called to transform the Arbeter Ring into a nationwide fraternal order, headquartered in New York but comprising branches across the United States. Delegates based their decision on the time-honored socialist principle of strength through unity: individual mutual aid societies could become more financially secure by banding together into a large organization. By doing so, expenses would be shared by many rather than a few. Other socialist societies had attempted to unify during the 1890s, but the Arbeter Ring was the first to succeed.

Reconstituted as a national order, the Arbeter Ring invited Benyomen Faygnboym to be its first general secretary. (His acceptance signaled the Arbeter Ring's improved status within the Jewish labor movement.) In March 1901 Faygnboym publicly appealed to individuals and socialist groups to join the Arbeter Ring. To qualify, he explained, a branch must have a minimum of fifteen members and pay a deposit of three dollars per member. Prospective members did not need to adhere to any particular school of socialist thought. Faygnboym made clear that they must only sympathize with general socialist ideals of "freedom of thought and aspiration, workers' solidarity, and faithfulness to the interests of their class and its struggle against oppression and exploitation." Technically, this differed little from past policy: the Arbeter Ring had always defined itself as nonpartisan. According to its 1893 constitution, "Each person [between the ages of twenty and forty-five] may be accepted as a member of this society with no distinction based on religion, origin, sex, or conviction" as long as he or she possessed a "good moral character" and was in good physical and mental health.[8] Nonetheless, in practice, the pre-1900 Arbeter Ring expected members to be dedicated radicals of some kind. Thus, one candidate was rejected because he had allowed a copy of the conservative *Yidishes tageblat* into his home. Another person was denied admission for not knowing the name of Joseph Barondess, the popular leader of the cloak makers' union. (The applicant's ignorance was presumed to reflect "reactionary tendencies.")[9]

Faygnboym's 1901 appeal, therefore, signaled a departure. He welcomed not only anarchists and social democrats, but also independent radicals and even "progressive Zionists." Equally remarkable, especially coming from the pen of a fiery "internationalist" and atheist like Faygnboym, was the Arbeter Ring's conciliatory position toward religion: "Every member or branch may have whatever religious or philosophical conviction he [*sic*] wants. They may be pious Jews, pious Christians, freethinkers, atheists—as long as they do not wish to make use of the organization for their personal convictions, as long as they respect freedom of thought, and do not endeavor to harm the fighting working class, they are welcome as friends and members." The new "spirit of tolerance" expressed by Faygnboym can be attributed to an overall weakening of factional conflicts since the collapse of the Socialist Labor Party in 1897. After a decade of near-constant fighting between and among anarchists and social democrats, the Arbeter Ring's leaders were determined to steer the organization away from the debilitating factional quarrels of the recent past.[10]

While few people objected to the Arbeter Ring's political neutrality, its position of religious tolerance caused considerable debate. In September 1904 Leo Rozentsvayg, the Arbeter Ring's second general secretary, took a strong antireligious stand. In the anarchist weekly *Di fraye arbeter shtime*, he criticized not only Orthodox Jews but also "half-religious" Jews who attended synagogue only on major holidays, such as Rosh Hashana and Yom Kippur. He denounced such "Yom Kippur Jews" as "traitors" and encouraged them to reconsider their membership in the Arbeter Ring. "He who believes [in God]," Rozentsvayg declared, "is either a fool or a swindler." As the historian Annie Polland has shown, Rozentsvayg's article prompted a two-month-long debate in the *Forverts* involving nearly eighty readers from as far away as Alabama, 36 percent of whom agreed with Rozentsvayg that too many religious Jews could threaten the Arbeter Ring's socialist character. "If members of the Arbeter Ring want to go to synagogues," a Newark woman wrote, "we will have darkness instead of light. Instead of thinking men, we will have stupid men and instead of hoping that we will be freed from slavery, we will be enslaved even more." A Brooklyn man warned that religious Jews should be restricted, lest "believers become the majority, then they will teach us a severe lesson." The majority of respondents, however, favored religious tolerance if only to propagate socialism more effectively. "Imagine that [Eugene] Debs would announce that votes for him should come only from those people who do not believe in God, and that he does not want any votes from those who do believe," wrote one man. "I am afraid that then we would have no votes to count after the election." Other letter writers pointed out that belief in God did not necessarily

18. Arbeter Ring, souvenir journal, 1904. The banner reads, "We struggle against sickness, premature death, and capitalism." Courtesy of the YIVO Institute for Jewish Research.

diminish a person's commitment to socialism. They cited examples of fellow Arbeter Ring members who attended synagogue regularly yet were still active in the Socialist Party. While the *Forverts* debate revealed considerable hostility toward religion among Arbeter Ring members, in the end the organization's admissions policy remained unchanged.[11]

Unlike other Jewish fraternal orders, the Arbeter Ring admitted women as full-fledged members. By 1906, 2,543 of 7,969 members were women.[12] Though generally absent from the national leadership, women played an active role in local branches, most obviously in the "women's clubs," which started forming in early 1901. In February 1904 Arbeter Ring Branch 1 officially endorsed such clubs as a way of recruiting women into the organization and promoting women's equality generally. "Our members as progressive men," Branch 1 announced, "must once and for all understand that one part of humanity cannot be liberated and the other part left enslaved." Branch 1 requested that all male members of the Arbeter Ring remain at home with their children one night a week to allow their wives to attend club meetings.[13] The Arbeter Ring's women's clubs attracted mainly married women who had quit the paid workforce (and therefore could not join unions), but who still wanted to participate in the Jewish labor movement. Women's clubs prided themselves on freeing housewives from "the kitchen and routine of children" so they could partake in "the joy of social activism and self-education." The goal, as Fanny Katsman of Branch 498 explained, was "to take the woman out of her daily life and enrich her spiritual condition by social activism." Writing in 1919, an Illinois man paid tribute to one of his branch's dedicated women activists: "If you see someone running around with circulars from the Arbeter Ring, the Socialist Party branch, the ladies' auxiliary, or the People's Relief Committee; if someone earlier sold you a ticket to a concert and now wants to sell you a ticket to another undertaking, you don't need to think and ask, 'Who is this?' It is she." In 1929 the women's clubs formed a national federation to coordinate work and raise the status of women, who had yet to achieve full equality with men in the Arbeter Ring.[14]

The Arbeter Ring's decision to reconstitute itself as a nationwide order with flexible admissions requirements proved effective. In the weeks and months following its September 1900 conference, socialist groups of various kinds—mutual aid societies, self-education societies, political clubs, and the like—started joining the Arbeter Ring. On September 12 Brooklyn's International Workers' Benevolent Society was installed as Branch 4. Two months later Voice of Labor (initiator of the *Forverts* masquerade ball) became Branch 5. In January 1901 the Minsker Society established Branch 6. In West Hoboken, New Jersey, the Young Men's Aid Society founded Branch 7, making it the first Arbeter Ring branch outside New York. Many others followed.[15] During the decade the sharpest rise in membership occurred between 1907 and 1910, with more than nineteen thousand people joining in 1909 alone. That was due, in part, to the economic depression of 1907 to 1909, which compelled people to seek a modicum of financial security in mutual aid societies. The Arbeter Ring's growth was also due to the general surge in Jewish immigration after 1903, including the arrival en masse of Russian Jewish revolutionaries.[16] Thousands of Bundists and, to a lesser extent, Socialist Territorialists and socialist-Zionists formed Arbeter Ring branches.[17]

The Arbeter Ring's rapid growth during its first decade inevitably led to greater diversity in membership. No longer was every member a convinced socialist (of whatever persuasion) or even a wageworker. Small businessmen, clerks, self-employed craftsmen, and professionals could be found in the Arbeter Ring's ranks. The so-called country branches located in towns and small cities tended to have relatively few proletarians. Branch 208, in New Brunswick, New Jersey, provides an example. Its ten charter members included a "shop girl," a junk peddler, a grocer, a grocery clerk, a Rutgers University student, two milkmen, two painters, a carpenter, and a factory worker. Branches in large cities usually had a higher proportion of working-class members, but even they were not exclusively proletarian in composition. In 1913 New York's Branch 75 had 147 wageworkers. The remaining 51 members included 31 storekeepers, 4 artists, 3 salesmen, 2 journalists, 2 musicians, a druggist, a dentist, and a lawyer.[18]

By the same token, not everybody who joined the Arbeter Ring was a wholehearted radical. As already discussed, a significant number of religious and "half-religious" Jews joined the Arbeter Ring. In Johnstown, Pennsylvania, for example, the local Arbeter Ring held its meetings in an Orthodox synagogue to which every member belonged.[19] A participant in the 1904 *Forverts* debate on religion noted that his Brooklyn branch included ten "freethinkers" and twenty-five "believers." Another New Yorker reported that twenty-five of thirty-five fellow members attended synagogue on Rosh Hashana and Yom Kippur. While some such "half-enlightened" immigrants identified themselves as radicals, others did not. What they appreciated in the Arbeter Ring was its generally progressive outlook. They enjoyed "a fresher atmosphere than what one finds in synagogues or in other lodges," as Baruch Charney Vladeck, who traveled extensively across the United States in 1909, observed.[20]

Still, while a cross section of immigrant Jews joined the Arbeter Ring, radicals formed the bulk of its membership and all of its leadership. Across the country, Arbeter Ring branches participated in countless strikes and election campaigns for Socialist Party candidates. They raised tens of thousands of dollars for socialist publications, political parties in the United States and abroad, and myriad causes within and beyond the Yiddish-speaking world. Accounts kept between 1900 and 1925 reveal the Arbeter Ring's generosity. Branches 1 through 10, for example, donated a total of $4,108 to strikers, $2,497 to the Socialist Party, $1,100 to the Bund, $3,000 to other Russian revolutionary parties (this from Branch 10 alone), $7,960 to pogrom and war victims in Russia, $1,113 to the Hebrew Immigrant Aid Society, and $19,182 to other institutions. This represented just a small fraction of all moneys donated by Arbeter Ring members during that twenty-five-year period. In addition to local branches, the national office also gave money to organizations such as the Socialist Party–affiliated Rand School of Social Science and *The Messenger,* edited by the African American union leader A. Philip Randolph. In Avrom Lesin's words, the Arbeter Ring was "a practical school, where the worker learns to value the importance of solidarity and the importance of enlightenment, where he learns to know and to respect the unions of workers, as well as the party of the workers."[21]

Thus, ten years after its founding as a national order, members had good reason to feel proud of the Arbeter Ring. It may not have been the most prestigious organization in the Jewish labor movement. (The major leaders and intellectuals continued to earn their reputations in the Yiddish press, at the lectern, and on the picket line.) Nonetheless, between 1900 and 1910 the Arbeter Ring boasted a far greater membership—four times that of the United Hebrew Trades in 1909—than any other organization in the Jewish labor movement. "It is," A. S. Zaks wrote in 1910, "the mightiest fortress, which defends and protects all of our socialist conquests, and its anniversary means a victory for the idea of freedom and its movement forward."[22] In 1911 the socialist-Zionist leader Nachman Syrkin crowned the Arbeter Ring "the greatest Jewish socialist organization in the world."[23]

The Education Committee

Even as members celebrated the Arbeter Ring's tenth anniversary, many expressed concern about its educational work—the "soul" of the organization. To be sure, nobody accused the Arbeter Ring of neglecting the sacred task of enlightenment. Members established libraries, financed journals such as *Di tsukunft*, founded socialist Sunday schools for children, and, above all, organized lectures (363 of them in 1908 alone).[24] Still, many intellectuals and rank-and-file activists believed that much more should be accomplished, and more efficiently.

To begin with, the financial burden of education fell almost entirely on individual branches. According to an official report, the cost of lectures nearly doubled between 1909 and 1910, presumably owing to increased demand. A veteran lecturer such as Shoel Yanovsky charged only three dollars per lecture in or around 1906. Four years later a relative newcomer like Moyshe Terman (a Bundist who arrived in 1908) received eight to ten dollars per lecture.[25] Country branches paid the highest amounts for lectures because of their distance from major Jewish centers, where most intellectuals lived. Branches in outlying areas typically paid between thirty and thirty-five dollars per lecture, of which an estimated 60 percent went to travel expenses. The high cost of lectures and other financial obligations prevented many small branches from holding lectures. Even some large branches in New York City did not, for one reason or another, do so on a regular basis. Another problem was the uneven quality of lectures. Some were too sophisticated, others too rudimentary. In order to draw the largest possible crowd, some branches were known to hire speakers who merely entertained audiences with jokes. A branch in Pennsylvania was said to have invited an Orthodox rabbi to speak about the Talmud. Thus, Tsivion remarked in 1910 that the "lecture system has absolutely no system."[26]

Tsivion's complaint reflected a growing consensus in the Arbeter Ring. Increasingly, activists and intellectuals decried the "disorder" of the lecture "system." Many people concluded that the solution was a national committee that would coordinate lectures and perhaps develop new educational and cultural programs. The Arbeter Ring had made several steps in that direction during the first decade of the 1900s. The conventions of 1904 and 1907 twice approved the idea of a national education committee but, for some reason, failed to implement their resolutions.[27] Then, in January 1908, the newly established New York State Committee announced it would oversee education for the entire state. Over the next two years the committee organized seventy-eight lectures, mostly in New York City, and four socialist Sunday schools. Although the State Committee fell short of its mandate, its efforts encouraged those who wanted to create an education committee at the national level.[28] In May 1910 delegates to the national convention voted to establish the Educational Committee (EC) with a modest budget of two thousand dollars, or about five cents per member. (The convention also allocated ten thousand dollars for a monthly journal, Der fraynd [The Friend].) For the first time since the beginning of the Jewish labor movement, socialists possessed an institutional mechanism responsible for education on a national basis.[29]

The question of what exactly the EC should do caused constant debate. Should the committee simply increase the quantity of lectures or embark on new projects? Should it provide elementary education to the masses or also try to satisfy the intellectual needs of better-educated members? Should the EC encourage Americanization or build yidishe kultur? On several occasions the committee queried intellectuals and rank-and-file members, but an organization as ideologically diverse as the Arbeter Ring could not possibly reach full agreement. A loose coalition known as Di Yunge (The Young Ones, not to be confused with the poets known by the same name) favored an expansive approach to education and *yidishe kultur*. They advocated greater funding for the EC, a wide array of educational and cultural programs, and Yiddish schools for children. Those identified with Di Yunge (mostly Bundists, Socialist Territorialists, and socialist-Zionists) came into conflict with the Arbeter Ring's established leadership, labeled Di Alte (The Old-Timers). While members of Di Alte—many of whom were not actually old—did not object to education per se, they viewed the Arbeter Ring primarily as a "benefit society" that provided insurance and health services (such as the Arbeter Ring sanitarium).[30] Di Alte wanted the EC to do little more than assist educational work already undertaken by local branches. On several occasions they proposed to reduce the EC's budget to a paltry three hundred dollars or abolish it altogether. Di Yunge failed to gain control over the Arbeter Ring (except during the administrative year 1915–1916), but they held sway within the EC and succeeded in strengthening its position within the Arbeter Ring as a whole. Future conventions increased the EC's budget (to five thousand dollars by 1918), granted money for the publication of Yiddish books, and levied a special tax for Yiddish children's schools. Although supporters of the EC rightly complained that increases in the budget failed to keep pace with the Arbeter Ring's growing membership, the committee nonetheless received enough money to expand its educational and cultural programs over the years. Furthermore, the EC, in cooperation with grassroots activists, established local educational committees in at least thirteen cities across the United States. The establishment of the Educational Committee in 1910 thus inaugurated a second important turning point in the Arbeter Ring after its reorganization as a national order in 1900.[31]

During its first three years, the EC concentrated on increasing the quantity and quality of lectures. Between October 1911 and May 1912 the EC organized lecture tours by Mikhail Zametkin, Nachman Syrkin, Yankev Salutsky, and Baruch Charney Vladeck that covered the expanse of the United States and parts of Canada. All told, some twenty thousand people attended 220 lectures in sixty towns and cities.[32] In 1912 the

19. Souvenir journal celebrating the Arbeter Ring's tenth anniversary as a national fraternal order in 1910. The caption reads, "Unification." From *Der Arbeter Ring zamlbukh* (New York: Arbeter Ring, 1910), p. 1.

EC planned its most ambitious project to date: a twelve-part lecture series that promised to cover nothing less than "the development of the world and humanity" in all their "diversity and color."[33] Organized by Moyshe Terman, the series featured some of the most accomplished intellectuals in the Jewish labor movement. The roster included the Marxist scholar Louis Boudin, the expert translator Yankev Merison, and Nachman Syrkin, a major theoretician of socialist-Zionism and the author of two doctoral dissertations, on epistemology and historical philosophy. Terman invited each lecturer to survey one of the following fields: anthropology, astronomy, biology, cultural history, economic history, "esthetic culture," geology, intellectual culture, law, psychology, religion, and sociology. Lecturers were expected to introduce each field's fundamental ideas and trace their development over time. A. S. Zaks, for example, reviewed theories of biological evolution from Aristotle to Darwin. Boudin explored the relationship between "morality and rights" in different epochs. Terman covered the historical evolution of major religions. Never before had such a comprehensive series of lectures been attempted in Yiddish.

The "world and humanity" series took place five times between November 1912 and February 1913 in the Lower East Side, Harlem, Williamsburg, Brownsville (in Brooklyn), and the Bronx. A remarkable 15,499 people (of the Arbeter Ring's roughly 18,000 members in New York City) attended the series. On the East Side, an average of 726 people turned out every night.[34] The enthusiastic response convinced the EC to publish the lectures in book form as *Di velt un di mentsheyt (The World and Humanity)*. The EC sent letters to all 516 branches of the Arbeter Ring offering a 50 percent discount of one dollar per copy. By mid-July the EC had received 3,603 orders, and 700 more followed over the next four months. Several branches ordered as many as fifty books at a time. Advance orders provided enough money to publish six thousand copies of *Di velt un di mentsheyt*, one thousand more than initially planned.[35] The book appeared in December 1913 and sold out in a matter of months. The Arbeter Ring's organ, *Der fraynd*, reported in May that a Warsaw firm had purchased the rights to a second edition.[36]

Di velt un di mentsheyt can be regarded as a landmark in Yiddish book publishing. Since the 1880s a shortage of "scientific literature" in Yiddish had plagued socialists. Very few works of popular *visnshaft* existed because of the high cost of book publishing and a dearth of qualified (and willing) authors. The publisher A. M. Evelenko had brought out a handful of booklets on chemistry, astronomy, mechanics, and nature between 1899 and 1910. Evelenko went out of business sometime around 1911, however, after being publicly exposed as a spy for the Russian secret police.[37] *Di velt un di mentsheyt* thus filled a sorely felt lacuna. In terms of the amount and range of material covered, *Di velt un di mentsheyt* surpassed every previous Yiddish book. According to Philip Krants, it signaled "a new beginning in our Yiddish literature in America."[38]

Thousands of immigrant Jews evidently wanted to read *Di velt un di mentsheyt*, but how many could actually comprehend the book? In a review published in the *Forverts*, the veteran journalist M. Baranov claimed that only 20 percent of the Arbeter Ring's members could understand *Di velt un di mentsheyt*. The entire project, he stated, was overblown and ill conceived. The language was too difficult, the amount of information overwhelming, and the subjects poorly chosen. The Jewish working masses had no need for complicated discourses on esthetic culture or astronomy, Baranov wrote. They needed accessible lectures on practical subjects: American history, civics, hygiene, and child rearing. The Arbeter Ring's members had been tricked. The Educational Committee had promised them a useful scientific book and instead sold them "a lemon." Baranov recommended that in the future the EC "create enlightenment, not for a couple thousand members, but for all forty-five thousand."[39]

Abraham Cahan agreed with Baranov, but he invited readers to voice their opinions. In a symposium between February and April 1914, members of the Arbeter Ring weighed in on both sides. (It is impossible to know specific numbers because many microfilmed pages of the *Forverts* are illegible.) An anonymous member from Brooklyn complained that he expected to read about "important topics in an easy, simple, clear Yiddish," but he instead encountered so many difficult words and ideas that he put aside *Di velt un di mentsheyt* after an hour. Sam

Tsukerman of Pittsburgh was sure that 95 percent of his fellow branch members could not understand *Di velt un di mentsheyt*. And Shabse Bulgatsh, a past president of the Arbeter Ring, demanded that the EC use its money for "elementary education and not for difficult scientific books." Critics acknowledged that *Di velt un di mentsheyt* might benefit members who had formal schooling but added that those individuals could find better books in English or other languages. If one could understand a book like *Di velt un di mentsheyt*, Cahan stated, then one did not need it in Yiddish.[40]

Supporters of *Di velt un di mentsheyt* conceded the book was challenging but denied it was overly difficult. In one man's words, "My brain is already somewhat sharpened [from past religious study] and it is not very difficult for me to understand the book; and when something is hard for me to understand, it brings me more pleasure and benefit." Others argued that less-educated Jewish workers already had plenty of easy reading material, such as the *Forverts*'s own column on elementary science, whereas few Yiddish books existed for more advanced readers. A Providence man urged the Arbeter Ring to publish books for the most as well as the least educated members.[41] Terman criticized Baranov for failing to view the Arbeter Ring as a "living body" in which members acquired more education over time. Even if just a minority of members could read or understand *Di velt un di mentsheyt*, others would follow. Terman posited that those who did read the book would later discuss what they had learned with friends, family members, and coworkers. Those conversations would contribute to the general intellectual atmosphere in which ideas and terms circulated and affected public opinion. Terman thus expected that *Di velt un di mentsheyt* and similar books would gradually raise the intellectual level of the Jewish working class.[42]

On the surface, debate over *Di velt un di mentsheyt* hinged on the question of popularization: how to make scholarly knowledge available to the Yiddish-speaking masses. This question had to do with practical issues, such as vocabulary and writing style. Yet on a deeper level the question of popularization intersected with the debate over the future of Yiddish in the United States, raised initially by Zhitlovsky's journal *Dos naye lebn.* Critics such as Baranov and Cahan opposed *Di velt un di mentsheyt* not only because they believed it too difficult for "the average Jewish worker," but also because they wanted immigrant Jews to leave Yiddish behind as quickly as possible. According to Baranov and Cahan, popular education in Yiddish should serve as a gateway to linguistic and cultural assimilation. If workers wanted to progress beyond "the ABCs," then they should do so in English rather than in Yiddish. By contrast, Terman and other EC members (such as Zhitlovsky) wanted to foster intellectual development in Yiddish to the greatest extent possible. Although Terman did not justify *Di velt un di mentsheyt* as a contribution to *yidishe kultur,* his approach to popular education presumed the permanence, or at least long-term existence, of the Yiddish language. To be sure, attitudes about popularization did not corresponded precisely to those about Yiddish. Krants, for one, praised *Di velt un di mentsheyt* but saw no future for Yiddish in America. Nonetheless, the two issues could not be disentangled. The question of what to write about and how overlapped with the question of whether Yiddish could or should survive.

Criticism of *Di velt un di mentsheyt* notwithstanding, the book's financial success convinced many people that the Arbeter Ring should continue to publish books. Delegates to the 1914 national convention allocated a special book fund of two thousand dollars to the Educational Committee (and increased the EC's annual budget to three thousand dollars). The following year the EC published a two-volume history of the Americas by Philip Krants and began a series called the *Arbeter Ring Bibliotek (The Workmen's Circle Library).*[43] Over the next decade the series published twenty-one books on the natural and social sciences with a total press run of two hundred thousand copies.[44] Four of five titles went into second printings in 1917 alone. A. S. Zaks's three-volume textbook on political economy eventually went into five printings in the United States and was reprinted in both Poland and the Soviet Union.[45] In addition to its own publications, the EC distributed works by local and European authors. The EC published more "scientific literature" in Yiddish and at lower prices than commercial publishers, which lacked the ready-made infrastructure provided by the Arbeter Ring: a mass membership organization that funded, advertised (through *Der fraynd*), and distributed its books nationwide.[46]

As the debate surrounding *Di velt un di mentsheyt* demonstrated, illiteracy was a sensitive issue in the Arbeter Ring. Whereas many members admitted they could not understand a difficult book like *Di velt un di mentsheyt*, few regarded themselves as illiterate and took offense at any suggestion otherwise. During the 1913 national convention, for example, Zhitlovsky caused a furor when he mentioned in passing that 40 percent of the Arbeter Ring's members were illiterate. Zhitlovsky later confessed that he had made the remark carelessly and the figure of 40 percent (an unofficial estimate by one of the Arbeter Ring's national leaders) was probably inflated.[47] Sensitivities about illiteracy, as revealed by the Zhitlovsky flap, reflected an idealized view of learning absorbed from two main sources: traditional eastern European Jewish society (which accorded most prestige to religious scholars) and, more immediately, the Jewish labor movement (which valorized socialist intellectuals). Even though rabbinic authority had largely waned in immigrant Jewish life, the socialist ideal of enlightenment held wide currency. Illiteracy could only be cause for embarrassment in a social movement led by intellectuals who placed supreme value on *oyfklerung*.

With the uproar over "the 40 percent" in mind, the EC took care not to offend popular sensibilities in its educational programs. In 1914 it announced plans to create an "ABC School" *(Alef-beys shul)* to teach elementary reading, writing, and arithmetic. Anticipating resistance, the EC explained that poor people should not blame themselves for their lack of formal schooling or consider themselves unintelligent because of it. Intelligence and ignorance, the EC explained in *Der fraynd*, should not be confused with one another:

> The intelligence of our members is very high. Intelligence, however, does not express itself in writing, but in thinking, in feelings, and in convictions. In this regard, no other Jewish fraternal order can compare with our Arbeter Ring, where our members think and feel much more so than the members of other fraternal orders. But because our fraternal order is a

workers' order, there are many [members] who have not had, unfortunately, the opportunity in their childhood years to attend school. A proletarian child must in the earliest of youth worry about daily livelihood and has no time and no patience to devote himself to learning and writing.[48]

Despite such encouragement, few Arbeter Ring members enrolled in the ABC School. Only thirty students showed up for the first evening of classes, and most dropped out after several weeks. The teacher, S. Yellin, reported that fourteen of nineteen students quit one of his classes after learning how to sign their names in English. (Yellin did not indicate the age or sex of his students.) Several students continued until they learned how to count and write a brief letter in Yiddish for the sake of corresponding with relatives overseas. The remaining few students attended irregularly or quit out of embarrassment. Yellin offered to give them private lessons so their peers would not find out, but the students refused.[49]

On the other end of the spectrum, the EC devised several programs to train a cadre of worker-intellectuals who would, ideally, carry out educational work on their own. In 1914 the EC formed a Speakers' Club to prepare "capable and intelligent young people" to lead formal discussion groups. The club's roughly thirty members developed a menu of five topics, each divided into several subtopics, on contemporary issues such as "The IWW and the American Federation of Labor," "The Socialist Press and the Labor Movement," "Does the Yiddish Language Have a Future?" and "The Education Question and the Arbeter Ring." A total of eighty-two discussion groups operated in New York City alone. A step above the Speakers' Club were the EC's "study classes" for the purpose of instructing activists in how to give formal lectures. Students could take classes on "scientific socialism," physiology, physics, and trade unionism. Finally, and least successfully, the EC began a People's University in late 1916. The EC initially offered eleven courses, but taught only five because of low enrollment (political economy, civics, Jewish history, history of Yiddish literature, and the Yiddish language). Of the five, only one course, Zaks's on political economy, was completed. Evidently, the People's University was too advanced, time-consuming (courses met one night a week), or expensive (one dollar per course) for most Arbeter Ring members.[50]

The ABC School, on the one hand, and the "study classes," Speakers' Club, and People's University, on the other, appealed to the least and most educated (or most motivated) members, respectively. The vast majority of Arbeter Ring members satisfied their desire for education through public lectures, the mainstay of the EC's adult educational programs. Tens of thousands of people attended the Arbeter Ring's lectures every year. They were much improved over the socialist lectures of the 1890s. First, the EC offered a much wider selection of topics than had been available two decades earlier. In addition to old standards such as socialism, science, and world history, immigrants could now hear frequent lectures on literature, theater, and art. In 1913, for example, cultural topics accounted for about one-third of the EC's lectures. "Ibsen's Contribution to Women's Liberation" (William Edlin), "Culture and the Working Class" (Moyshe Terman), and "Ancient Greek Drama" (Yoel Entin) were among the titles. Significantly, lectures on Jewish subjects also made their way into the Arbeter Ring's roster. In the 1890s socialists all but ignored Jewish subjects, except to criticize Jewish religion and Jewish nationalism. That changed with the ideological shift toward Jewish nationalism after the turn of the century. The EC offered many lectures on Jewish history, religion, literature, nationalism, and contemporary politics. "The History of Jews in Spain" (Sh. Zetser), "The Bible, Not as Religion but as Literature" (Nachman Syrkin), "Socialism and Jewish Identity" (Tsivion), "The Development of Modern Yiddish Literature" (Shakhne Epshteyn), and "The Yiddish Theater" (Entin) were among the choices in 1913.[51]

The overall quality of socialist lectures had also improved greatly by the 1910s. In terms of language, the intellectuals now spoke a less Germanized, more authentic Yiddish than they had in the late nineteenth century. After two decades of experience, intellectuals had figured out how to express themselves without having to borrow from German. The new respect for Yiddish encouraged by Zhitlovsky and his followers was another factor. And, finally, the content of socialist lectures was much better by this time. The early intellectuals often possessed only a general familiarity with their subjects, but after furthering their own educations, they spoke with greater knowledge, sometimes even expertise. In addition, the more recent post-1905 intellectuals were, on the whole, better educated than their predecessors. Many of them came to the United States with university degrees and, in some cases, doctorates. (Zhitlovsky and Syrkin were the outstanding examples.) Many older socialists faulted these "professors" for speaking over the heads of "the broad masses," as the debate surrounding *Di velt un di mentsheyt* illustrated. They may have been correct, but that did not prevent large numbers of people from attending the EC's lectures.

A high point for the Education Committee was its brief collaboration with the New York City Board of Education. In 1915 Joseph Leipziger, director of the board's Adult Lecture Series, invited the EC to participate in a Yiddish lecture series under his bureau's auspices. The Adult Lecture Series had offered lectures in Yiddish since 1903 with great success. (During its peak year of 1914–1915, 90,028 people attended the board's Yiddish lectures.)[52] The board's lectures, however, differed significantly from the Arbeter Ring's. The board stressed health, hygiene, and "basic precepts and principles of American democratic government," to quote the historian Stephen Brumberg. Titles included "Why Is Our Country So Great?" "Moulding the Nation," "America's Greatest Literary Lights," and "Contagious Diseases." The Arbeter Ring's lectures, by contrast, addressed a wider array of topics (including Jewish ones), had a more international focus, and were often critical of the United States. The EC agreed to collaborate with the board, on the condition that it be permitted to select its lecturers and topics. After prolonged negotiations, Leipziger agreed. The Board of Education also agreed to provide space in public schools free of charge and distribute the Arbeter Ring's announcements in public libraries, which immigrant Jews patronized in high numbers.[53]

The series consisted of forty lectures in 1916–1917, twenty-eight by the Arbeter Ring and twelve by the Board of Education. The Arbeter Ring's lectures included topics such as "Revolution in Mexico" (Hillel Rogoff), "Of What Does Human Happiness Consist?" (Edlin), "Zionist

Hopes and the War" (Tsivion), "Women Yesterday and Today" (Zaks), "Trade-Unionism" (M. Smirnov), "The Main Characteristics of Modern European Drama" (Zolotarov), "The War and Jewish Immigration" (M. Regalsky), "New Trends in American Democracy" (Prof. Isaac Hourwich), and "Child Labor in America" (F. Gelibter). The EC did not indicate how many people attended, but it stated that the number was "much, much greater" than it would have been without the Board of Education's support. The EC considered the board's support to be of "great moral significance," but several of the Arbeter Ring's National Executive Committee objected. They argued that it was inappropriate for a socialist organization to cooperate with the government and forced the EC (then chaired by Shakhne Epshteyn) to withdraw from the arrangement after the first lecture season ended in 1917. Leipziger died that same year and the board's Adult Lecture Series slid into decline.[54]

In addition to lectures, the EC branched out into an array of cultural programs, particularly art, music, and theater. Socialists regarded the visual and performing arts not as upper-class luxuries, but as crucial to the intellectual and moral development of workers. A 1915 article in *Di tsukunft*, for example, explained that art could help to stimulate the imaginations and creative talents of Jewish workers, thereby helping them to struggle for "a better, more beautiful world." It called on the Arbeter Ring and all Jewish socialist organizations to cultivate an appreciation for art among Jewish workers.[55] Itsik Pirozhnikov, director of the Arbeter Ring's choir (founded in 1914), made a more general argument about the importance of esthetics for Jews. A formally trained musician from Warsaw, Pirozhnikov argued in *Der fraynd* that Jews had historically ignored esthetics because of a preoccupation with religious study and rituals. The consequences of esthetic neglect, according to Pirozhnikov, were everywhere: in the poor manners of immigrant Jews, the absence of decorations in Jewish homes, and the filthy streets of ghetto neighborhoods. (Significantly, Pirozhnikov did not consider the Yiddish language to be ugly, as had so many Jewish reformers since the beginning of the *Haskalah*.) By calling attention to the unseemly side of Jewish life, Pirozhnikov intended not to demean immigrant Jews, but to help them to become "modern," "civilized" people and contribute to the development of *yidishe kultur*.[56] The extent to which others in the Arbeter Ring shared Pirozhnikov's views is not known. But the fact that *Der fraynd* printed his article without rebuttal suggests his ideas met with at least some approval.

The EC did not apply rigid criteria to its cultural programs. The general standpoint of most socialists seems to have been that art ought to be ennobling and intellectually stimulating, as well as enjoyable. Programs exposed Arbeter Ring members to various forms of art, music, and theater: popular and elite, Jewish and non-Jewish, modern and ancient, radical and apolitical. The first and among the most successful were the EC's guided tours of New York City museums, called *shpatsirungen* (strolls). A Bronx activist who went by the last name of Liberty seems to have initiated the first *shpatsir* in December 1913. At Liberty's request, the EC arranged a tour of the Museum of Natural History that attracted some three hundred people. Over the next year the EC organized ten tours of the Metropolitan Museum of Art, the Brooklyn Museum of Art, and other New York City museums. The well-known art critic and illustrator Saul Raskin led most of the *shpatsirungen* and drew as many as four to five hundred people. In his tours Raskin would give a brief historical overview of each exhibit, highlight the major artists and their works, and draw comparisons between them. A man who heard Raskin speak in Philadelphia left convinced that "even" workers were "capable of enjoying art" and would do well "to spend a couple of hours in an art gallery."[57] For their part, museum administrators gladly accommodated the EC's tours. They kept their museums open at special times and set aside rooms for lectures, free of charge. The sight of hundreds of working-class Jews listening to lectures—in Yiddish, no less—on classical Roman sculpture or Italian Renaissance painting made a strong impression. "The managers and employees in the museums gazed with astonishment," Zelig Shereshevsky, the EC's secretary in 1914 and a women's clothing worker by trade, recalls. "They had never seen such a thing."[58] Later *shpatsirungen* took Arbeter Ring members to botanical gardens, zoos, and science museums.

While *shpatsirungen* introduced Arbeter Ring members to European high culture, the Arbeter Ring choir reflected the Jewish working-class experience. Under Pirozhnikov's direction, the choir sang mostly Yiddish folk and labor songs. Pirozhnikov also composed most of the music and occasionally wrote lyrics.[59] More than one hundred men and women had joined the Arbeter Ring choir by 1918. In addition to concerts organized by the Arbeter Ring, the choir performed at balls, anniversaries, and conventions connected to the Jewish labor movement. In 1919, for example, the choir performed at Carnegie Hall in honor of Morris Vintshevsky's sixtieth birthday. Pirozhnikov also trained quartets and soloists to perform at smaller events held by individual Arbeter Ring branches.[60] In a very different vein, the EC formed a forty-piece mandolin orchestra in 1918, which performed music by classical composers such as Tchaikovsky, Schubert, and Rimsky-Korsakov. The mandolin orchestra and the choir often performed at the same events.[61]

The Arbeter Ring's amateur theater group, the Fraye Yidishe Folksbine (Free Yiddish People's Theater), was one of the EC's most celebrated cultural projects. The Fraye Yidishe Folksbine grew out of an amateur Yiddish theater group named (in English) the Hebrew Dramatic League. A student of painting and sculpture at Cooper Union named Benyomen Kremer founded the Hebrew Dramatic League in 1907. In contrast to the formulaic (though wildly popular) melodramas and comedies known as *shund* that dominated the commercial Yiddish theater, the Hebrew Dramatic League produced only works of literary merit. (It claimed to be the first Yiddish theater group in the United States to perform a work by Sholem Aleichem.) Several other amateur groups committed to a "better Yiddish theater" merged into the Hebrew Dramatic League between 1910 and 1914.[62] Impressed by its productions, the EC invited the Hebrew Dramatic League to join the Arbeter Ring. It agreed only after long internal discussions and assurances from the EC that it would retain artistic control over its productions. In February 1915 the Hebrew Dramatic League changed its name to the Fraye Yidishe Folksbine, Branch 555 of the Arbeter Ring.

During its first year the Folksbine performed eight different one-act plays and eighty-six literary readings for Arbeter Ring branches.[63] But the Folksbine really established its presence on the Yiddish theater scene with its 1916 debut at the Neighborhood Playhouse. Two wealthy American Jews, Alice and Irene Lewisohn (relatives of the writer Ludwig

Lewisohn), started the Neighborhood Playhouse to bring affordable ballets, concerts, and plays to the residents of the Lower East Side. The Folksbine petitioned the Lewisohn sisters to use the Neighborhood Playhouse, but they flatly refused on the ground that Yiddish impeded the Americanization of immigrant Jews. Representatives of the EC persisted, explaining to "the non-Jewish Jewish women" that high-quality plays existed in Yiddish and were worthy of being performed at the Neighborhood Playhouse. After months of correspondence and meetings, the Lewisohn sisters relented. They granted permission on the condition that the Folksbine give a satisfactory performance of a play in its entirety accompanied by an English translation of the text. The Folksbine selected a play by Perets Hirshbeyn, and the Lewisohns were sufficiently impressed to allow the play to run thrice weekly for four weeks.

The Folksbine's first production was a "moral and financial success," and it secured a place for the Folksbine at the Neighborhood Playhouse in subsequent years. The Folksbine's plays enjoyed both financial success and critical acclaim. Theatergoers lined up for hours to purchase tickets to the Folksbine's production of Hirshbeyn's *Grine felder (Green Fields)*, a pastoral of rural Lithuanian Jewish life that had not yet been performed in the United States. The poet Menakhem Boreysho wrote, "They surprise you with their acting with their honest portrayals, but more than that. . . . You see the hard work in everyone's acting, the serious and sincere attitude, you see the love, which one expects from such a brilliant and pulsating work."[64] The Folksbine extended its run of *Grine felder* from two to four weeks at the Neighborhood Playhouse and performed it over fifty times in New York and elsewhere. Though it never displaced *shund* from the Yiddish theater, the Folksbine helped to pave the way for professional "art theaters" that came into being after World War I.[65]

"Our Hope, Our Future"

Starting in 1906, Arbeter Ring members in New York City and across the country began establishing socialist schools for children. This grassroots movement reflected deeply ambivalent feelings about American public education. On the one hand, Jewish socialists greatly admired the availability of free education in the United States. Having come from despotic countries such as Russia, where the government treated education as a privilege and restricted the number of Jewish students in state-run institutions, most Jewish socialists could not help being impressed by the inclusiveness of the American school system. On the other hand, Jewish socialists eyed public schools with deep suspicion. Public schools, in their view, served to perpetuate the existing capitalist order by inculcating students with values of individualism, competitiveness, national chauvinism, and militarism. "The public school is the strongest factor in maintaining the political power [of the capitalist system]," the Arbeter Ring's general secretary, Y. Vayntroyb, stated in 1909, "and it is therefore necessary to establish other schools, which will weaken the influence which the public schools have on the young minds." "The capitalist schools," Chicago's *Di yidishe arbeter velt* stated in 1911, "take our children . . . [who] emerge from the great capitalist, patriotic melting pot with certain dogmas . . . about the goodness, holiness, and greatness of today's order." As an "anti-toxin" to the "reactionary" influence of public schools on their children, Arbeter Ring members established socialist Sunday schools to encourage freedom of expression, creativity, and critical thought.[66]

Harlem's Branch 2 founded the first socialist Sunday school on November 10, 1906. Named the Children's Educational Circle, it began with forty-two students and four teachers. Between 1907 and 1910 branches in Harlem, the Lower East Side, Brooklyn, and the Bronx created eight similar schools, and the Arbeter Ring's New York State Committee assisted in the creation of an additional four. Although several schools closed or merged with others, the overall number of students increased. By 1910 fifty-two Arbeter Ring branches operated ten Sunday schools attended by about fifteen hundred pupils. (Several Socialist Party branches with non-Jewish members opened Sunday schools shortly after the Arbeter Ring did, but they received only reluctant support from the party and disappeared by 1920.) "There are easily a thousand children in these schools," the *New York Times* warned in 1910, "children who will, beyond peradventure, grow up to be Alexander Berkmanns and Emma Goldmans, with perhaps a Ferrer or a Tolstoy appearing."[67] Although the *New York Times* identified the Arbeter Ring's Sunday schools as anarchistic (implying they were guilty of rearing future bomb-throwers and assassins), in fact, most of them were oriented toward the Socialist Party, which opposed acts of political terror. (The exception was the Francisco Ferrer Sunday School, named after the famous Spanish anarchist and educator, located on Avenue A.) Nonetheless, the *New York Times* correctly noted that a rising number of Jewish parents wanted their children to receive a socialist education.

The curricula of the Sunday schools differed from one to the next, but they generally focused on history, political economy, biographies of famous revolutionaries and social reformers, contemporary social issues and politics, and natural science. The Arbeter Ring's Second Street School (attended by 120 to 150 students in 1911), for example, taught topics such as "Should Children Follow Their Parents?" "Tolstoy: His Life and Activity," "Reciprocity," "War and the Military," "The Modern School," and "The Earth and Its Elements." Other schools included lessons on the Mexican revolution, taxes and the state, social classes and class conflict, Darwin's theory of evolution, and the recent Triangle Shirtwaist fire. Singing, dancing, and poetry also played an important role in classes for young children.[68] Outside the classroom, students engaged in a number of extracurricular activities. In 1910, for example, 350 children participated in a "June Walk" to the Bronx's Claremont Park. Dressed in red sashes and red and white caps, they sang songs (a brass band also played) and carried banners with inscriptions such as "A Rebel Is No Coward," "The World Is My Country," "We Want Play, Not Work," "Labor Creates All Wealth, Who Gets It?" "A Wrong to One Is a Wrong to All," "Workers of the World Unite," and "Five Million Child Slaves in the Land of the Free." Older Sunday school students published *Young Socialist Magazine,* a twelve- to sixteen-page monthly that featured essays, short stories, and poems, such as "Socialist Mother Goose" ("Hickory, dickory, dock! Oh, girl, look up at the clock! And you strike, too; we'll see you through, For shorter day and better pay! And no hickory, dickory, dock!").[69]

The Arbeter Ring's Sunday schools faced hardships from the outset. First, the schools lacked competent teachers. Although plenty of men and women (the latter in higher numbers) volunteered with "vim and enthusiasm," few had received pedagogical training or knew what to do inside the classroom. Two schools closed after nearly all their teachers quit in frustration. "The students did not want to listen, did not want to show respect, and the teachers stopped coming," Konrad Bercovici, a Sunday school teacher himself, wrote in 1911.[70] The pro-socialist Rand School of Social Science helped to remedy the situation by offering courses, starting in 1908, on pedagogy and curriculum development, but it took several years for the number of teachers to stabilize. A dearth of instructional materials posed a second problem. No socialist curriculum for children existed when the first Arbeter Ring school opened in 1906. Teachers had to improvise, with varying degrees of success. Two professionally trained (non-Jewish) teachers in Arbeter Ring schools, Bertha Mailey and Bertha Matthews Fraser, eventually developed a coherent curriculum meant for all socialist Sunday schools in the United States (including those unrelated to the Arbeter Ring). Starting in 1910, they published a series of articles in the Socialist Party daily, *New York Call*, on pedagogy; Fraser later published a three-hundred-page book entitled *Outlines of Lessons for Socialist Schools for Children*. The lessons covered subjects such as the earth's natural resources, differences between the working and "idle" classes, the unequal distribution of wealth, and the socialist "remedy" for existing inequities.[71] The Arbeter Ring's Sunday schools adopted some of Fraser's lessons. Bercovici, for example, praised the lesson on the earth's resources as especially useful in explaining to city-raised children how food is grown. (Bercovici once asked a twelve-year-old boy where potatoes come from, to which he innocently replied, "From the grocery." When asked where the grocer gets his potatoes, the student answered, "From the wholesaler.") Still, despite efforts by Fraser and Mailey, the Arbeter Ring Sunday schools failed to develop a unified curriculum.[72]

In addition to internal problems, the Sunday schools faced mounting criticism from Arbeter Ring members who objected to the absence of Jewish content in the curricula. Not a single Sunday school taught subjects pertaining to Jews or used Yiddish as the language of instruction. Critics of the Sunday schools (mostly Bundists, Socialist Territorialists, and socialist-Zionists) argued for a new kind of school that would teach Jewish subjects in Yiddish. Proponents of Yiddish schools sparked a highly charged, protracted debate that brought into focus the central cultural question of the Jewish labor movement: should socialists work to dissolve all forms of Jewish culture and group loyalty or fashion a new kind of Jewish culture and community consonant with socialism? No issue proved more controversial in the Arbeter Ring during the 1910s.

The idea of Yiddish-language socialist schools originated with Chaim Zhitlovsky. In his seminal 1898 article, "Zionism or Socialism," Zhitlovsky proposed a Yiddish-language educational system that would extend from primary school to university.[73] Little became of Zhitlovsky's idea on either side of the Atlantic over the next decade. Upon his return to the United States in 1908, however, Zhitlovsky spearheaded a campaign to create Yiddish schools that would teach an array of Jewish subjects—literature, history, religion—from a secular, socialist standpoint. Zhitlovsky and other proponents of Yiddish schools not only objected to the "reactionary" political influence of public schools, but also blamed them for alienating English-speaking children from their Yiddish-speaking parents. They criticized public schools for "denationalizing" Jewish children, that is, divorcing them from Yiddish and their Jewish cultural heritage generally. In the words of Yoel Entin, a leading advocate of Yiddish schools and member of the socialist-Zionist party Poale Tsion, "The public school . . . must in fact be considered as a detrimental force, as it strives to Americanize the children by denationalizing them, thus digging deeper the chasm between the parents and their children." "The American public school—which strives to transform the children of immigrant nationalities into a formless porridge—is bankrupt," the Bundist A. Litvin argued.[74] Despite differences of opinion on other matters, Entin, Litvin, and other activists believed that the more familiar children became with the European Jewish past, the present Yiddish cultural renaissance, and the social struggles of the immigrant Jewish masses, the more sympathetic they would become to socialism.[75]

Yiddish schools would thus instill a Yiddish-based Jewish identity and a socialist identity at one and the same time. In the words of the poet Arn Glants-Leyeles, a school activist affiliated with the Socialist Territorialist Party:

> The child needs to know the language of his parents and the majority of the Jews. Through Yiddish he learns to know his parents and the masses of the people, their ideals and strivings in the present and their traditions in the past. But the children of socialist parents are [currently] far from the ideals of their parents; the father is [considered] a "greenhorn," and his socialist ideals are but one aspect of his greenness. The children do not know their parents' language, their world, their aims, and their thoughts. Yiddish, therefore, leads the child to his father and his folk, and to the progressive ideas of Jewish democracy and socialism.[76]

Similarly, Tsivion argued that the Yiddish language provided a crucial link between socialism and Jewish national consciousness:

> But we want the new generation also to know Yiddish so that they will not be a limb torn away from the Jewish people, so there will not be such a deep abyss separating the old from the young. . . . In short, we want the young generation to be not only ordinary socialists, but Jewish socialists. And the Yiddish language is one of the most important conditions of being a Jewish socialist. I would say that I am more optimistic that children who receive a Jewish education will be socialists compared to those who will receive only an American education. Until now, Jewish education has produced more socialists than American education, simply because those children who received a purely American education become estranged from the Jewish masses, from Christians, and from themselves as well.[77]

By promoting Yiddish as a link between parents and children, socialists like Tsivion played a dual role as both conservationists and radicals: they hoped to preserve something of the past even as they put forward a radical vision of the future. It was a difficult role to play. Advocates of Yiddish schools had once rebelled against their own upbringing, but, as parents themselves, they faced the problem of cultural transmission to their American-born or -raised children. They wanted to prevent their children from rejecting them, yet they also wanted their children to embrace the wider world beyond immigrant Jewish neighborhoods. Could they transmit their socialist Yiddish culture—still in its formative stage—to the next generation? Yiddish schools would be the test. For those who believed in the possibility of socialist Yiddish culture, Yiddish-language schools were "our hope, our future."

The Yiddish school movement began inauspiciously. In 1908 a man named Chaim Goldblum, apparently a Socialist Territorialist, started the first secular, Yiddish-language school for children in the Brownsville section of Brooklyn. Together with two other teachers, Goldblum devised a curriculum consisting of the Yiddish language, Jewish history, folk music, and Hebrew. Within two weeks, the school had twenty students, but it soon faced opposition from Orthodox Jews, who circulated a rumor that the school was actually a clandestine Christian mission. A number of parents were dismayed to discover an absence of religious content in the school and removed their children. Within a matter of weeks, attendance dwindled. At one point somebody threw a rock through a school window, wounding one of the teachers and frightening the remaining students away. Several subsequent attempts elsewhere in New York City also failed.[78]

Yiddish schools became viable only after they received organizational backing. Notably, this first came not from the Arbeter Ring, but from the Yidisher Natsyonaler Arbeter Farband (National Jewish Workers Alliance), the fraternal order affiliated with Poale Tsion. In October 1910 Poale Tsion passed a resolution introduced by Zhitlovsky (who along with many other Socialist Territorialists had joined Poale Tsion in 1909) in favor of what became known as National Radical Schools. After the resolution passed, the Yidisher Natsyonaler Arbeter Farband, referred to most commonly as the Farband, passed a similar resolution endorsing Yiddish schools. A school board decided in November that the curriculum would include Yiddish, Jewish history, Hebrew (taught in Yiddish), the Bible, Jewish religious history, and socialism. On December 10 the Farband opened the first National Radical School, located on the Lower East Side. The school faced significant financial difficulties, but by the second year the number of students reached almost one hundred. National Radical Schools opened in Chicago, Detroit, Montreal, and no fewer than five other cities by 1913. More than four thousand children studied in thirty-five to forty National Radical Schools or similar schools with designations such as "Free," "Modern," "Yiddish," and "Folk." Activists and teachers in these new Yiddish schools belonged to different political parties and disagreed over matters of curriculum. The status of Hebrew, for example, caused great disagreement. As early as 1913 some Socialist Territorialists, the party most closely associated with Zhitlovsky, started forming schools that came to be known as Sholem Aleichem *shuln,* which placed greater emphasis on Yiddish over Hebrew. Still, the Farband's National Radical Schools were important as the originator of socialist Yiddish schools in the United States.[79]

The Farband's decision to establish Yiddish schools gave impetus to a campaign for similar schools within the Arbeter Ring. Although Arbeter Ring members had proposed Yiddish schools in 1910, if not sooner, it took several years for the campaign to gain ground because of internal opposition from "internationalists." Zhitlovsky, who was a member of the Arbeter Ring and the Farband, was the foremost spokesman for Yiddish schools. He found his staunchest supporters among the Arbeter Ring's Socialist Territorialists and socialist-Zionists, who, for whatever reason, chose not to join the Farband. A much larger number of Bundists also embraced the idea of Yiddish schools (though not necessarily for the same reasons advanced by Zhitlovsky and his supporters). There were also Arbeter Ring members who did not belong to one of the Jewish political parties originating in eastern Europe, but who joined the cause for Yiddish schools nonetheless. Together, these different elements formed the amorphous grouping known as Di Yunge, which, among other things, put forward Yiddish schools as one of their chief goals. By 1914 Di Yunge's campaign had reached a high pitch, with rallies held several times a month. They tapped into a growing concern that, if the Arbeter Ring failed to establish Yiddish schools, members would send their children to ideologically objectionable Farband or Sholem Aleichem schools or, still worse, Orthodox Talmud Torahs, for lack of a better alternative.[80]

Yet opposition to Yiddish schools proved fierce, among both intellectuals, such as Abraham Cahan, Benyomen Faygnboym, Philip Krants, and Mikhail Zametkin, and rank-and-file members. Some critics considered it deluded to think that Yiddish schools could counteract the dominant (and positive) trend toward cultural assimilation. They argued that children were growing up fluent in English, just as they should. Others argued against Yiddish schools on practical grounds, asserting that the language of instruction should be English because that was the language that children understood best. A third position, which was not necessarily exclusive of the other two, held that Yiddish schools by definition constituted a form of Jewish group separatism that deviated from the norm of socialist internationalism.[81] Opponents of Yiddish schools were strong enough to prevent the issue from even being debated at national conventions until 1915. In that year the Education Committee introduced a mild resolution stating that the Arbeter Ring should "devote attention to the education of the young generation through free socialist Sunday schools, Yiddish and English, for children." (This was a watered-down version of an earlier recommendation by the Education Committee in favor specifically of Yiddish language schools.) The resolution was defeated by a vote of fifty-two to thirty-five.[82]

Despite opposition, proponents of Yiddish schools grew in strength from year to year. At the local level, some branches actually created their own Yiddish schools without approval or support from the national office. Between 1911 and 1916 Yiddish schools sprung up in Rock Island, Illinois, Paterson, New Jersey, Waterbury, Connecticut, Gloversville, New York, Toronto, and Winnipeg. In other cases members of the Arbeter Ring became active in existing Farband schools or cooperated with Socialist Territorialists in establishing politically nonpartisan schools.[83] Also, activists in several Jewish Socialist Federation branches (who, in most cases, were members of the Arbeter Ring, as well) started Yiddish schools. In 1915 the federation's Harlem branch, for example, founded a Yiddish Sunday school, and, in that same year, the federation's national convention declared it permissible for local branches to establish Yiddish schools, not for reasons of Jewish nationalism, but to "educate our children in a socialist spirit."[84] All this signaled a growing momentum in favor of Yiddish schools within the Arbeter Ring and the Jewish la-

20. A class in the first Arbeter Ring high school, Harlem, 1921. Courtesy of the YIVO Institute for Jewish Research.

bor movement generally. In 1916 the Arbeter Ring's national convention voted fifty-five to forty-three "to teach Yiddish to the children of Arbeter Ring members," but it provided no money for schools. The following year, the convention allocated one thousand dollars for the establishment of a pilot school in New York City. In 1918 delegates voted in favor of a special school tax, the amount of which (one or two cents) was to be determined by a national referendum. A majority of 2,186 to 1,974 voted for a two-cent school tax, thus providing Yiddish schools with a small but steady budget.[85] A pedagogical council decided that the Arbeter Ring's schools should "teach the children to read, write, and speak Yiddish well and acquaint [the children] with the life of the workers and the Jewish masses in America and elsewhere . . . with the history of the Jewish people and with highlights of the struggle for freedom in world history." The council also decided that "certain Jewish and general holidays, workers' holidays, and general freedom celebrations should be observed."

In the wake of the Arbeter Ring's decision, activists toured the United States encouraging local branches to form Yiddish schools, and *Der fraynd* published articles instructing members how to do so.[86] Two years later, no fewer than twenty-nine Yiddish schools existed across the United States. There were six schools in New York City alone by 1921, and twelve by 1924.[87] The Harlem Arbeter Ring school, founded in November 1918, was the organization's premier Yiddish school in New York. The school consisted of several components. Its first and largest component was the *folks-shul*, or elementary school for children under the age of twelve. It began with 208 students and grew to 294 by January 1920.[88] A year later, the Harlem Arbeter Ring school opened a *mitlshul*, or high school, for students between the ages of twelve and eighteen. The Harlem Arbeter Ring school also ran an art school and music school under the direction of two European-trained musicians, Madam Hanina Yaffa and Y. Vardi Rozenbaum. (Both had taught in Jerusalem for eight years before moving to New York.) And, finally, the Harlem Arbeter Ring school ran a teachers' training course conducted by intellectuals such as Dr. Avrom Kaspe, Tsivion, A. S. Zaks, Hillel Rogoff, and the literary critic and scholar Shmuel Niger. The training course offered classes on the history of the labor movement, political economy, natural science, pedagogy, psychology, history of revolutionary movements, American history and civics, English, Yiddish literature, Yiddish grammar, Jewish history, Hebrew, and other subjects. The course helped to correct the problem of lack of preparation faced earlier by the Arbeter Ring's Sunday schools.[89]

The head teacher and leading figure in the Harlem Arbeter Ring school was Yankev Levin. A graduate of Columbia University's Teachers' College, Levin authored the school's textbooks (used generally in the Arbeter Ring's Yiddish schools) and defined its mission.[90] Levin developed a curriculum that stressed Yiddish fluency. He intended students to become fully literate in Yiddish, not only so that they could communicate better with their parents and relatives, but also so that they themselves could contribute to the creation of *yidishe kultur* "as a high culture of a Jewish working people." At the same time Levin attached supreme importance to the task of cultivating character in the school's students. According to Levin, the school needed to foster a spirit of *mentshlekhkeyt*—civility and humanity—as a counterweight to what he viewed as the coarseness of New York street culture and narrowness of public schools. At the Harlem Arbeter Ring school, Levin boasted, a "refined" atmosphere prevailed. Intellectual and artistic pursuits took priority over sports. Fighting and swearing were prohibited. Mutuality and cooperation triumphed over individualism and selfishness. (The American notion of "mind[ing] your own business," Levin explained, had no place in the school.) Through *yidishe kultur, mentshlekhkeyt,* and socialism, the Harlem Arbeter Ring school would give birth to "a new generation with higher ideals, more refined thoughts, and a higher intelligence."[91]

The Harlem school's curriculum consisted of Yiddish language (reading, writing, diction), Yiddish literature, Jewish history, cultural history, "heroes" of freedom movements and science, song (folk and classical), dance (folk and classical), and group discussions about current events. The school also ran a "story hour" every afternoon for neighborhood children who were not enrolled in the school. The high school taught some of the same subjects as the lower classes (Yiddish language and literature, for example) but included additional classes in political economy, the Bible, Hebrew, stenography, and typewriting.[92] Students in the *folks-shul* and *mitlshul* could choose from eight clubs that engaged in a wide range of activities. They produced Yiddish plays, organized memorials for Yiddish writers, attended concerts, frequented the acclaimed Yiddish Art Theater on the Lower East Side, published Yiddish newspapers and journals, and organized discussions on contemporary issues. Students also helped to raise funds for Yiddish schools in Lithuania and Poland and collected Yiddish books for Soviet Russia. Mothers formed a club to help the school "morally and financially" and organized lectures for parents on hygiene, education, and other subjects.

Because of its size and Levin's indefatigable efforts, the Harlem school served as a model for other Yiddish Schools. The administration decided to open another school in Harlem. By 1924 two schools opened on the Lower East Side, five in Brooklyn, and one in the Bronx.[93] The schools created a summer camp called *Kinderland*, a "children's republic," where boys and girls could lead a "normal life" in a "healthy place" with fresh air, plenty of rest, and good food. At that point between 4,500 and 5,000 students attended sixty-five Arbeter Ring Yiddish schools nationwide.[94] Still, the Arbeter Ring schools faced problems. During the Harlem school's first five years, 1,327 students registered, but a significant portion dropped out for a variety of reasons, such as lack of time or money. Of the boys who quit, 30 percent did so because their parents wanted to give them some religious education, probably to prepare them for a bar mitzvah. But ultimately the biggest problem was the end of open immigration to the United States. In 1921 and 1924, Congress passed legislation that all but halted immigration from Europe, especially from its eastern and southern portions. With the end of mass immigration, the number of Yiddish-speaking Jews inexorably declined. Although 75,000 children had attended Arbeter Ring schools by 1934, the prospect of raising a second generation of American-born Jews fluent in Yiddish grew ever more elusive. Proponents of Yiddish schools thought otherwise in 1918, when the Arbeter Ring finally committed itself to the establishment of Yiddish schools. Optimism ran high when, in those days following the Russian revolution, many socialists believed they could achieve anything. That optimism would be tested in the years following World War I.[95]

CHAPTER 5

"We Sought a Home for Our Souls"

The Communist Gamble

Nineteen-seventeen was a momentous year for immigrant Jews. On March 15 word arrived that Czar Nicholas had abdicated his throne in the face of strikes, riots, mutinous soldiers, and a defiant Duma. Finally, the Russian autocracy had been toppled. Yiddish headlines declared: "A New Light Rises over Russia. Nicolai Arrested" *(Forverts);* "The Czar behind Iron Bars" *(Di varhayt);* "Russia Frees Itself from the Czar!" *(Der tog);* "Nicolai Renounces Throne! Revolution Wins in Russia after a Three-Day Battle" *(Der morgn zhurnal);* and "Czar Arrested" *(Tageblat).* The revolution elicited a joyous outpouring from immigrant Jews. On March 20 an estimated fifteen thousand people attended a mass meeting in Madison Square Garden organized by the *Forverts,* Arbeter Ring, United Hebrew Trades, Jewish Socialist Federation, Central Union of Bundist Organizations in the United States, Socialist Party, and Russian Social Democratic Federation. Later in the evening Leon Trotsky addressed a large rally in Harlem's Lenox Casino while demonstrations took place in the streets and parks of the Lower East Side. The *New York Tribune* described the heady, postrevolution atmosphere:

> The East Side was dazed at first. Slowly the importance of the news became clearer. And then occurred unusual scenes. Men embraced one another in the streets. Women cried and laughed for happiness. Thousands gathered in Seward Park, to read the bulletins of the Yiddish dailies. . . . In the cafés,

toasts were drunk to the members of the Duma. . . . In the cafés and the synagogues, on street corners and in their homes, the Jews of the city showed what the fall of the Czar meant to them. It was a personal victory for them.

Jews from all walks of life felt as if they were "facing a miracle."[1]

The March revolution initiated a small exodus of socialists from the United States. The *Forverts*'s labor editor and the Jewish Socialist Federation leader, Max Goldfarb, left for Russia in 1917, only to emerge several years later as a Red Army general. On a single day in June a departing ship carried Shakhne Epshteyn, Moyshe Terman, A. Litvak, the Marxist Zionist theoretician Ber Borokhov, the future historian of Jewish socialism Eliyohu Tsherikover, and other intellectuals and activists representing the gamut of Jewish political parties. The future Soviet leaders Trotsky and Nicolai Bukharin also left New York for Russia in early 1917.[2] "Life is strange: my body is in America," Baruch Charney Vladeck wrote. "My heart and head and soul and life are in that great wonderful land, which was so cursed and which is now so blessed, the land of my youth and my revived dreams—Russia." Vladeck remained in New York, but the March revolution lured more than 850 Jews and 7,557 Russian nationals (which probably included numerous Jews who chose not to identify themselves as such) back to Russia.[3]

The vast majority of Jewish socialists, of course, stayed in New York, but they had cause to celebrate their own victories in 1917. In the November elections the city's main Jewish precincts elected seven aldermen, ten state assemblymen, and a municipal judge on the Socialist Party ticket. (A year earlier, East Side voters had sent Meyer London to Congress for a second term.)[4] In the weeks and months leading up to the election, hundreds upon hundreds of open-air meetings, rallies, demonstrations, and debates took place in working-class Jewish neighborhoods. In October thousands of schoolchildren in Jewish neighborhoods launched a "full-scale revolt" against the mayor's attempt to implement the Gary Plan, a controversial program that included a lengthened school day, shop work for students, and a twofold increase in the number of students in selected schools (without a commensurate increase in teachers).[5] In Harlem the Socialist Party's "housewife section" conducted rent strikes that "made life miserable for the landlords who jacked up the rents during the war-created housing shortage." On any given evening crowds of people would gather in "Trotsky Square" on 110th Street and Fifth Avenue or stroll up and down Madison, Lenox, and Fifth Avenues listening to Socialist Party speakers stationed every few blocks. "These were indeed exciting times, unforgettable and delirious nights," August Claessens, Harlem's German American Socialist assemblyman recalls. "Harlem was ablaze with hope of victory and great enthusiasm." After the November election victories, the beloved poet Morris Rosenfeld congratulated New York's Jewish working class in verse: *"Du host gevunen, du host endlekh zikh aleyn gefunen"* ("You have finally won, you have finally come into your own").[6]

Then, on November 8, the Bolshevik party seized power. Many socialists initially expressed doubts about the new government. Maybe the Bolsheviks had acted too hastily? Were Lenin's dictatorial methods really necessary? But Jewish socialists (and, to some extent, Jewish public opinion generally) grew more pro-Soviet into 1918 and 1919. The civil war, the mass slaughter of Jews by czarist forces, and the release of pent-up utopian aspirations drew all but a few die-hard opponents closer to Moscow. "We have criticized them," Abraham Cahan wrote of the Bolsheviks, "some of their utterances often irritate us; but who can help rejoicing in their triumph? Who can help going into ecstasy over the Socialist spirit with which they have enthroned the country, which they now rule?"[7] By 1919 Cahan refused to allow criticism of the Soviet Union in the *Forverts.* That same year insurrections broke out in Germany and Hungary, where a Jew stood at the helm of a short-lived revolutionary government. In the United States massive labor conflict swept across the country. Workers actually took over Seattle during a general strike.[8] As the decade drew to a close, it seemed to many Jewish socialists (which is to say many New York Jews) that they stood at the dawn of a new era. Revolution had come to Russia, Germany, and Hungary, and who was to say the United States wouldn't be next? Anything seemed possible.

Yet ominous developments cast a shadow over the optimism of 1917.

In April America's entry into World War I touched off a period of repression, anti-Semitism, and nativism. Congress passed the Espionage Act in 1917 and the Sedition Act in 1918; in March 1919 the New York state legislature created the so-called Lusk Committee to investigate the "scope, tendencies and ramifications" of "seditious activities" in the state; later in the year Attorney General A. Mitchell Palmer launched the anti-Communist raids that bore his name.[9] All those actions came bearing down on the Jewish labor movement. The postmaster general threatened to revoke the *Forverts*'s second-class mailing privileges because of its antiwar stand, a move that would have bankrupted the newspaper (as it did many others across the United States) were it not for the intercession of Louis Marshall, the head of the American Jewish Committee. The Lusk Committee continued to monitor the *Forverts* and spy on radical Jewish organizations. "These damned kikes," an agent reported in October 1918, "have a stranglehold and I feel I must work not only night but day and night to help kill this movement now and quick."[10] In 1919 police on the Lower East Side arrested a young anarchist named Mollie Steimer and four men for distributing leaflets protesting the American invasion of Siberia. One man was beaten by the police and left for dead in prison. Steimer and the others were released in 1920 on the provision they leave the country for Russia at their own expense. In 1919 the Arbeter Ring felt compelled to suspend its national lecture tours because of the climate of fear and repression. In one of the most egregious incidents of the period, members of the New York State Assembly expelled five Socialist Party assemblymen (three of them Jews) in March 1920 on charges of disloyalty. Pro-Soviet pamphlets by Tsivion and the *Forverts* writer Hillel Rogoff were used as evidence against them. When voters returned the Socialists to office, the State Assembly again expelled them. Meanwhile, Henry Ford's *Dearborn Independent* informed several hundred thousand readers that Jews had masterminded the Bolshevik revolution as part of a larger plot against the Western world. Immigrant Jews were now widely seen as subversives.[11]

Within this atmosphere of revolutionary excitement on the one hand and government repression on the other, a small but significant number of Jewish radicals turned to Communism. The Jewish Communist movement arose out of a welter of factional struggles and debates that might seem, eight decades later, far removed from the day-to-day lives of most Jewish immigrants. The people involved were relatively few and they spoke in a hopelessly arcane political vocabulary about events in a distant country. Yet these same people and disputes laid the foundation for what would become, during the 1920s, a popular movement that would affect the future of Jews and radicals in the United States for the next three decades. The locus of conflict was the Jewish Socialist Federation. In 1919 a self-defined Left Wing faction emerged in the JSF, as it did in the Socialist Party as a whole. Members of the Left Wing argued that the Bolshevik seizure of power marked the beginning of a period of worldwide revolution. They believed socialists needed to adopt the ideas and methods of Russian Bolsheviks and prepare for an imminent seizure of power in the United States. Although the Left Wing was few in number at first, more Jewish socialists, including those initially hostile to the Bolsheviks, turned to Communism over the next several years. From the perspective of Communist Party leaders, the success of Communism in the United States depended on Jews. Despite the Red Scare, the Jewish labor movement was larger than ever and remained radical in orientation. If Communists failed to make inroads into the Jewish labor movement, party leaders believed, they risked isolation in American society. They communicated this to Moscow and enlisted Soviet support. In December 1921 Communists gained a foothold through a merger with the Jewish Socialist Federation (which had moved leftward since 1919) and the publication of a daily newspaper called *Di frayhayt* (*Freedom*) in April 1922. Yet, though party leaders considered Jews crucial to the success of Communism, they refused to allow Jews (or any ethnic subgroup) the same degree of autonomy they had enjoyed in the Socialist Party. The status of Jews thereby became a source of great controversy in the early Communist movement.

The emergence of a Jewish Communist movement brought debates about Jewish nationalism and internationalism into sharp focus once again. Some viewed Communism as a vehicle with which to transcend, once and for all, Jewish and all other national identities. They infused the old idea of internationalism with a new degree of militancy. Yet others viewed the Communist movement as a way to bring together two long hoped-for goals: social revolution and a Yiddish cultural renaissance. They wagered that a break from the Jewish labor mainstream and an alliance with the nascent Communist movement could reinvigorate Yiddish culture and the Jewish labor movement. It was a gamble many would soon regret.

The Beginning of Jewish Communism

Sometime in January 1919 five members of the Jewish Socialist Federation's downtown branch, all in their twenties, met in a basement restaurant on the Lower East Side to figure out how they might enact the Bolshevik revolution on American soil. They decided to form a faction called the Left Wing of the Jewish Socialist Federation and brought out a newspaper with an appropriately militant name, *Der kamf (The Struggle)*. Left-Wingers entertained only a vague idea of what they should fight for, but they were young and impatient and demanded revolution—now. A small but growing number of JSF activists had similar feelings and formed allied Left Wing factions elsewhere in New York City, Boston, Chicago, Detroit, New Haven, Philadelphia, and other cities. In the coming months the Left Wing would wreak havoc in the JSF.[12]

The JSF's Left Wing emerged as part of a larger trend in the Socialist Party. During the first half of 1919 self-defined Left Wing factions were on the rise in other foreign-language federations and Socialist Party branches across the country. The ideological roots of the Socialist Party's Left Wing dated back to 1915, but not until early 1919 did it coalesce as an oppositional movement. The impetus was provided by the Soviet government's decision to establish the Third (or Communist) International. On January 24 the Third International's executive committee issued a call to socialists everywhere to take power "at once" and establish a "dictatorship of the proletariat." To achieve that goal, the Third International instructed its supporters abroad to split their respective socialist parties by "separating out the revolutionary elements, in a pitiless criticism of its leaders and in systematically dividing its adherents."[13] The Third International's appeal struck an especially strong chord within the Socialist Party's foreign-language federations, which totaled fifty-seven thousand people, or 53 percent of the party's membership. By April the Left Wing gained control of the Hungarian, Lithuanian, Latvian, Polish, Russian, South Slavic, and Ukrainian federations, in addition to Socialist Party locals in ten cities and three boroughs in New York.[14] Responding to the Third International's appeal, the Left Wing waged a bitter war against so-called centrists and right-wingers. The line dividing American Socialists, unlike that in most European socialist parties, was not between supporters and opponents of the war (the Socialist Party came out resolutely against America's entry), nor was it between supporters and opponents of the Bolshevik revolution (most Socialists endorsed the Soviet government). The Left Wing's rationale for splitting the party was that by doing so it would free itself from unnecessary constraints, a first step toward establishing a dictatorship of the proletariat in the United States. On the basis of the Third International's pronouncements and with massive strikes under way in 1919, Left-Wingers believed that the United States verged "on revolutionary action," as John Dos Passos would later write.[15]

The Left Wing gained much ground during the first half of 1919. In the Socialist Party's spring elections, Left-Wingers won twelve of fifteen seats on the party's National Executive Committee. For the centrist and right wing leaders to accept the election results would mean allowing the Socialist Party's destruction or its conversion "into an effigy of the Russian original." In late May, for better or worse, the party's acting National Executive Committee decided to nullify the election results. It also suspended the seven rebellious foreign-language federations and expelled the entire party organization of Michigan, which had amended its constitution in such a way as to align itself with the Left Wing. All told, seventy thousand members, mostly in the foreign-language federations, were expelled or suspended from the Socialist Party. In September, after a flurry of debates, meetings, and conventions, the Left Wing established two parties: the Communist Party and the Communist Labor Party. The Socialist Party was left in shambles.[16]

In the beginning the Jewish Socialist Federation's Left Wing expressed no interest in breaking from the Socialist Party. "We are not seeking a split in the party," *Der kamf*'s program stated on February 16. "We publish this paper with the most peaceful of intentions."[17] But attitudes quickly changed as the Jewish left oriented itself toward the Socialist Party's larger Left Wing. In addition to developing contacts with opposition leaders, Jewish Left-Wingers began studying Vladimir Lenin's *State and Revolution* and adopted its doctrine of dictatorship of the proletariat as the blueprint for social revolution in the United States. "I started reading and all the complex problems suddenly became beautifully clear," a leader of the JSF's Left Wing later wrote. "I read the book until I knew it by heart, and joined the Left Wing. From there it was only a step to Communism."[18] By April Left-Wingers were condemning the JSF leadership, calling for the ouster of *Di naye velt*'s editor, Yankev Salutsky, opposing Meyer London's reelection bid for Congress, and agitating for a revolutionary alternative to the Socialist Party. Along the way, the Left Wing turned JSF locals into battlegrounds, paralyzing all other activity at a high point in the organization's membership. At the JSF's national convention in late May, the Left Wing fully intended to provoke a split. Left Wing delegates introduced two resolutions: one calling for an immediate break from the Socialist Party and the other endorsing proletarian dictatorship as a goal. Both were defeated.[19]

Unlike most other foreign-language federations, the majority of the JSF's membership and the entire national leadership opposed the Left Wing. The majority shared the Left Wing's enthusiasm for the Bolshevik revolution and wanted the Socialist Party to move in a more radical direction, but they rejected the Left Wing's efforts to imitate the Bolsheviks in the here and now. Most JSF members did not believe in the immediate prospect of social revolution, were willing to work within the existing political system, and wanted to remain part of the Socialist Party, whatever its flaws. "We are interested," Salutsky editorialized in *Di naye velt*, "that the party should be left wing . . . should think and conduct itself in a revolutionary manner, in the socialist and Marxian sense of the word. But the organization of a 'Left Wing' into a clique, which uses the methods of a clique, will be of no use to the stated goal."[20] In a more strongly worded denunciation in the *Forverts*, Moyshe Olgin wrote: "The young men of this group live in a little world created in their own imagination where everything is as they like it to be. The workers are united, class-conscious, organized, and armed. Only one thing remains to be done: begin the final conflict."[21] Tsivion, who initially sympathized with the Left Wing, concluded in the May 30 issue of *Di naye velt* that "the main task of the Jewish Socialist Federation at its national convention in Boston should be . . . to detach the ultra–left wing [*oysgelinktn fligl*], if it wants to continue to exist." The JSF's National Executive introduced a resolution stipulating, among other things, that all individuals who affiliated with the Left Wing would "be expelled automatically from the Jewish Socialist Federation." The resolution passed by a vote of seventy-four to thirty-eight, with seventeen abstentions. The Left Wing immediately withdrew from the JSF and, three months later, joined the Communist Party.[22]

How was the JSF able to withstand its Left Wing? Several historians have attributed this to the leadership's radical orientation, which, they say, stole the Left Wing's revolutionary thunder. By staking out a position to the left of the Socialist Party's leadership, the JSF's leadership "siphoned off accumulated impatience among the rank and file."[23] This explanation holds true to some extent but is inadequate by itself. After all, leaders of other foreign-language federations, such as the Russian and Latvian federations, were also very radical, but this did not prevent their own Left Wings from taking over. Indeed, leaders such as Nicholas Hourwich (Isaac Hourwich's son) of the Russian federation spearheaded the Left Wing. The relevant question, then, is not why the JSF's leadership effectively contained its Left Wing, but why the Left Wing had little appeal to the majority of its members and leaders in the first place?

The answer can be found, in part, in the JSF's strong attachments to the Socialist Party. Comparison with the Russian federation, a Left Wing stronghold, is instructive. Whereas the JSF had roots in the Socialist Party going back to the Jewish Socialist Agitation Bureau in 1905, the Russian federation did not come into existence until 1915. Almost 80 percent of the Russian federation's 3,985 members joined between March 1918 and March 1919. For example, Gregory Weinstein, the editor of the federation's *Novi Mir*, was disqualified from serving on the

Socialist Party's New York State Committee in January 1918 because he had been a party member for less than two years. In the following year, Weinstein would become "the most arrogant and vociferous force within the Left Wing," according to the historian Theodore Draper.[24] In contrast with the Russian federation, the JSF's membership had grown steadily from the outset, so that by 1919 the organization had developed a cadre of veteran activists and leaders deeply rooted in the Socialist Party. To name several examples: Morris Vintshevsky had been a founding member of the party in 1901; Tsivion and Salutsky joined no later than 1910; and Olgin joined shortly after his immigration to the United States in 1914. Likewise, the oldest and largest foreign-language body in the Socialist Party—the Finnish Socialist Federation—resisted the Left Wing in 1919.[25]

The second reason for the Jewish Socialist Federation's loyalty to the Socialist Party had to do with the political culture of the Bund, in which most JSF members had come of age. More than any other revolutionary party in Russia, the Bund emphasized internal unity. From its birth in 1897 until the Russian civil war of 1919, the Bund suffered not a single split.[26] Such unity was exceptional in the context of east European revolutionary politics. In 1893, for example, Polish socialists divided into two parties, the Polish Social Democratic Party and the Polish Socialist Party, which itself split in 1906. In 1903 Menshevik and Bolshevik factions formed within the Russian Social Democratic Workers' Party, just five years after the party's founding. And Poale Tsion produced two off-shoots between 1905 and 1906.[27] As Jonathan Frankel observes, the Bund was like "a close-knit family where emotional loyalties outweigh antagonistic beliefs." For the sake of unity, Bundists invested "enormous efforts" in "patching over, playing down, and even denying the existence of dispute and disagreement."[28] Having absorbed an ethos of unity at an early age, most members of the JSF recoiled from the Left Wing in 1919.

Four months after the Left Wing broke from the Jewish Socialist Federation in May 1919, its members convened in Philadelphia and voted to join the Communist Party as its official Yiddish-language section. (A small breakaway group joined the Communist Labor Party, which would later merge with the Communist Party under pressure from Moscow.) Renamed the Jewish Communist Federation, it claimed 1,000 members in forty-five branches of a total 27,341 Communist Party members. The Jewish Communist Federation led a precarious existence from the start. Between November 1919 and January 1920 federal agents twice raided the federation's national office, confiscating Yiddish translations of Lenin, Trotsky, and the *Communist Manifesto*. *Der kamf* ceased publication in January and three subsequent Communist Yiddish newspapers failed over the next eight months. By February the Jewish Communist Federation had gone underground with the rest of the party. Its second convention, held secretly in June, reported a "great shortage in intellectual forces" and "material means." The federation's membership had shrunk to 374 in twelve branches and included few individuals of high standing in the Jewish labor movement.[29] Its national secretary was a little-known thirty-year-old named Alexander Bittelman. A former JSF activist in Harlem, Bittelman first achieved some recognition as the editor of *Der kamf* in the spring of 1919. As he himself later acknowledged, Bittelman brought no practical experience to the job, let alone journalistic talent. He was, according to one contemporary, "neither a forceful speaker nor a lucid writer." That someone as unimpressive as Bittelman could have been chosen to edit *Der kamf* and lead the Jewish Communist Federation reflected poorly on the organization's resources.[30]

In addition to political repression, the early Jewish Communists suffered from their own sectarianism. In language reminiscent of (though more strident than) the old "Yiddish-speaking" socialists of the 1890s and 1900s, the Jewish Communist Federation disavowed any and all Jewish communal ties or interests. Its program pledged only "to propagandize Communist ideas in the Yiddish language."[31] "The Jewish workers of America," the federation declared in June 1920, "must begin to consider all their interests—economic, political, and national—from only one standpoint: from the standpoint of social revolution."[32] On that basis, the Jewish Communist Federation refused to participate in any of the broad-based relief efforts on behalf of Russian Jews, at a time when they were being subjected to the largest slaughter hitherto known in modern Jewish history.[33] The federation's slogan, "The salvation of the Jewish people lies in the victory of international Communism,"[34] isolated Jewish Communists from the very masses they claimed to lead.

Not until the summer of 1921 did the Jewish Communist Federation's situation begin to improve. The Red Scare had subsided by then, giving Communists more latitude. Furthermore, under strong pressure from Moscow, the Communist Party and the United Communist Party (formerly the Communist Labor Party) merged, thereby healing a two-year-old rift. For the first time Communists were unified in a single political party—the Communist Party of America—with ten to twelve thousand members.[35] A third important development was the return of Shakhne Epshteyn to the United States. Epshteyn had traveled to Russia in June 1917 and, though initially opposed to the Bolshevik government, joined the Communist Party several years later. He edited various Russian and Yiddish publications, directed the government-run Yiddish publishing house, and was a leader in the Communist Party's Jewish Section, or Yevsekstia.[36] In June or July the Third International assigned Epshteyn to do "party work" in America, with the particular mission of organizing a new Yiddish newspaper.[37] Using the pseudonym Yoysef Berson, Epshteyn established the weekly Der emes (The Truth), named after the Russian Communist Party's Yiddish daily. An experienced newspaperman and essayist widely recognized among immigrant Jews, Epshteyn brought some flair and professionalism to Der emes, which he managed to bring out on a regular weekly schedule. Thus, with assistance from Moscow, the Jewish Communist movement finally started to coalesce in the summer of 1921.[38]

Inching toward Moscow

While the Jewish Communists' situation began to improve in mid-1921, the Jewish Socialist Federation faced an impending crisis. During the two years since its May 1919 convention, the JSF had degenerated into continual infighting over the question of whether to remain in the Socialist Party. Most JSF members still dismissed the Communist Party as hopelessly sectarian, ineffectual, and intoxicated by revolutionary

21. The Jewish Socialist Federation leader Yankev Salutsky, later known in the English-speaking world as J. B. S. Hardman. Uncredited photo from Y. Sh. Herts, *Di yidishe sotsyalistishe bavegung in Amerike* (New York: Der Veker, 1954), p. 64.

fantasies. They recognized that the United States stood far from the threshold of class war. Yet JSF members grew increasingly impatient with the Socialist Party. The JSF's trajectory can be traced through Yankev Salutsky, *Di naye velt*'s editor and the single most important figure in the JSF. Between 1919 and 1921 Salutsky fought a two-front battle. On the one hand, he argued against leaving the Socialist Party, insisting that it could be pushed in a more radical direction. On the other hand, Salutsky grew more and more critical of the Socialist Party for not adopting a sufficiently revolutionary program. Following the party's May 1920 convention, Salutsky faulted leaders such as Morris Hillquit for placing too much faith in political elections at the expense of political protest. Salutsky was especially critical of the Socialist Party for not responding forcefully enough to the expulsion of five of its members from the New York State Assembly just a few months earlier. The party, according to Salutsky, needed to endorse alternative forms of democracy, such as soviets or workers' councils. Salutsky also called on the Socialist Party to join the Third International, which he viewed not as an instrument of Moscow but as an alliance of Communist and non-Communist revolutionary parties. Salutsky, in other words, wanted the impossible: a party at once revolutionary and pragmatic, pro-Soviet and attuned to American conditions. His desire, born of the revolutionary events of 1917–1919, was widely shared in the Jewish Socialist Federation. Yet by 1921 the prospects for a revolutionary but non-Communist party had grown remote. The postwar strikes had subsided and the insurrections in Europe had been crushed. Still, with the Jewish Communist Federation pulling to the left, Salutsky grew all the more adamant.[39]

In May 1921 Salutsky, Olgin, and a group of like-minded radicals formed the Committee for the Third International. Their purpose was to persuade the Socialist Party to join the Third International immediately and unconditionally. The Socialist Party had, in fact, applied for membership in early 1920, but the Third International responded by denouncing the party as a traitor to the working class. Now the party again declared itself willing to join the Third International, provided that Moscow permit its organizational independence and not require adoption of the principle of dictatorship of the proletariat, conditions that the Third International would not accept. Salutsky, who had reservations about joining the Third International in 1919, was prepared to accept Moscow's terms in 1921. He viewed the Committee for the Third International as a last-ditch effort to win over the Socialist Party at its June convention. The convention, however, voted against unconditional affiliation. Consequently, Salutsky, the JSF's National Executive Committee, and the Committee for the Third International decided the time had come to quit the Socialist Party.

The JSF decided to put the question to a vote during a special convention in September. By then the JSF was a shell of its former self, with a membership of one thousand or fewer, but its prospective divorce from the Socialist Party had serious implications for the Jewish labor movement as a whole.[40] Though much weakened, the JSF was still an important part of the Jewish labor movement. Tsivion, for example, was a very popular writer for the *Forverts* and a leader in the Arbeter Ring; Salutsky was the educational director of the Amalgamated Clothing Workers of America and editor of its weekly newspaper; and Olgin was a prominent *Forverts* writer. The JSF's impending break from the Socialist Party could reverberate into a rebellion against the established leadership of the major Jewish socialist organizations. The Arbeter Ring, the United Hebrew Trades, and the Forverts (which in 1921 were more powerful than ever) could all be affected. The Forverts Association called a meeting of its roughly three hundred members in August and, with representatives of all the major organizations present, threatened to do everything possible to punish the JSF if it went ahead with the split.[41] This was not the first time the Jewish Socialist Federation had found itself at odds with the *Forverts* and the old guard of the Jewish labor movement. The Jewish Socialist Federation had grown out of a conflict with the old guard and had confronted it numerous times since 1912 (most seriously in its bid to seize control of the National Workmen's Committee in early 1917). In the eyes of the Jewish Socialist Federation's leaders, the old guard was once again trying to suppress the organization. As *Di naye velt* editorialized: "Actually, it is an old story. The *Forverts,* as an institution, as a distinct, organized group in American socialism, has fought against the Federation since its birth. . . . The founding of the Federation itself was a conscious act of rebellion of the Jewish workers against the hegemony of the *Forverts* machine. . . . That the Federation never let itself be controlled by the *Forverts* and its flag bearers certainly did not help the Federation curry favor with the paper."[42] A second editorial stated:

> The Jewish Socialist Federation was created in a labor movement that raised great unions, strong, rich and radical. But the wanton, disorderly world of the labor movement failed to turn the unions into a single base of support for the Socialist Party [that is, its official Yiddish-language section, the Jewish Socialist Federation], but a place where the word party was either foreign or scorned. The Federation raised the banner of close cooperation between the Party and the unions, cooperation with mutual responsibility and ideological influence. The Federation wanted union members to be socialists in the unions and the socialists in the Party to be fighters for the unions.[43]

Thus, as the JSF's September convention drew near, the old conflict between the JSF and the *Forverts* assumed renewed urgency. In the past conflict could be contained because of the JSF's privileged status as the

Socialist Party's official Yiddish-language section. But the situation had drastically changed since 1919. America's would-be Bolsheviks had torn apart the Socialist Party and pulled the JSF leftward. For the first time the JSF now threatened to break ranks from the rest of the Jewish labor movement.

The outcome of the JSF's convention, which opened on September 3 in the *Forverts* building, was a foregone conclusion.[44] The JSF's National Executive Committee and most of the intellectuals—Salutsky, Tsivion, Olgin, Lilliput (the pen name of Gavriel Kretshmar), A. S. Zaks, Pesakh Novik, and Morris Vintshevsky—wanted to break from the Socialist Party.[45] Avrom Lesin and Baruch Charney Vladeck were the only two intellectuals who sided with the Socialist Party. (Although Lesin supported the Soviet government with his "entire heart," he considered the JSF's militancy irresponsible during a time of growing conservativism and anti-Semitism. A "communist East Side," he cautioned, "when America is so far from even socialism, when America is so far from even liberalism, is as bad an idea as a Jewish commissar in the Ukraine [where an anti-Semitic bloodbath had recently been perpetrated by pro-czarist forces during the civil war].")[46] Representatives of the Arbeter Ring, the *Forverts,* and the unions—the so-called official socialists—also opposed splitting. On September 4, after hours of stormy debate, delegates voted forty-one to thirty-three in favor of leaving the Socialist Party. The final decision was met "with silence, without applause." JSF members had been bound together by strong personal and organizational ties that had, in many cases, originated in the Bund two decades earlier. The organization was like a "family," to quote one Harlem activist, and the divorce was painful for both sides. The minority left the convention and established a new organization, the Jewish Socialist Farband.[47] The majority regrouped to plan their next move.[48]

In a postconvention manifesto the Jewish Socialist Federation's executive committee explained its decision and appealed to Jewish workers to

---

22. "How do you mix the contents of these two pots together and come out with one dish?" The Jewish Socialist Federation ponders how to create a more radical Socialist Party. From *Der groyser kundes,* July 2, 1920.

join its cause. The Bolshevik revolution, the manifesto stated, had ushered in a new era that put social revolution within reach in the United States and around the world. The Socialist Party, however, had failed to grasp this new reality and therefore abdicated its role as the leader of the class-conscious proletariat. It had become a party of "bourgeois sympathizers and half-socialist petty-bourgeois elements."[49] Furthermore, the JSF's manifesto accused the Socialist Party of corrupting the Jewish labor movement "with a feeling of dullness, cowardice, indifference to political problems, irresponsibility, political ignorance, and political disorganization."[50] At the same time, the JSF criticized the Communist Party for believing that it could "*immediately* call upon the masses to revolt" and "capture power." The JSF thus confronted a twofold problem. On one side stood the Socialist Party's "meaningless socialism" and on the other side stood the Communist Party's "make-believe, revolutionary conspiratorialism" that had "no place in life." As an alternative to both parties, the JSF wanted to help build a "broad mass proletarian party" that would uphold revolutionary principles without losing touch with reality.[51]

Yet, in fact, the Jewish Socialist Federation possessed few options. After the convention, the Forverts Association fired every writer who sided with the JSF (Moyshe Olgin, Tsivion, Pesakh Novik, Lilliput, and, for about two months, Hillel Rogoff) and evicted the JSF from its building. In one stroke, the JSF was practically cast out of the Jewish labor movement.[52] The JSF had nowhere to go. Two months earlier, Salutsky had explored the possibility of a merger with the Communist Party if it would agree to become an aboveground organization. The party, however, flatly refused. In a letter dated August 1, 1921, the party's general secretary, Ludwig Katterfeld, informed Salutsky that the JSF would have to accept the existence and primacy of the underground Communist Party as a precondition to a merger. "The underground organization," he wrote, "is absolutely necessary for the performance of revolutionary, communist work in this country." Katterfeld conceded that "an open organization" could be established at a future date, but it would have to be controlled by the underground party. "A failure to recognize this cardinal point of the power of the underground organization," he wrote, "would be a failure to recognize the fundamental principles in a communist organization and would indicate a serious flaw in the understanding of the nature of the communist movement."[53] As disenchanted as Salutsky had become with the Socialist Party by 1921, he could not accept a secretive, underground organization like the Communist Party. "Can the Federation go with the Communist Party?" Salutsky asked in the September 2 issue of *Di naye velt.* The "answer, at least in the meanwhile, is negative."[54] The Communists ridiculed the JSF's neutrality. "The Federation," Shakhne Epshteyn wrote in *Der emes,* "has put itself on a false path, on the path of wavering, neither here nor there, and it will be ground to dust between Right and Left."[55] Salutsky himself doubted whether the JSF could survive long as an independent organization, but he believed it had no alternative at that moment. A "broad proletarian mass party" of the kind he desired did not exist.[56]

Between September and November 1921 the JSF attempted to rebuild. The JSF and like-minded groups, such as the Committee for the Third International and the Finnish Socialist Federation (which broke from the Socialist Party in December 1920), established the Workers' Council to keep alive the idea of a revolutionary but non-Communist political party. Council members hoped that the Communists would sober up and become "an open, aboveboard mass movement."[57] In addition, the JSF embarked on a campaign to transform *Di naye velt* into a daily newspaper. By the end of October the JSF had raised about fifteen thousand dollars and increased *Di naye velt*'s circulation to twenty thousand, four times higher than it was in September and double that of *Der emes.* Salutsky and his colleagues had reason to feel cautiously optimistic. They had the necessary journalistic talent; if they could just raise enough money, they would be able to challenge the *Forverts*'s "rule of vulgarity," to quote Salutsky. Before the JSF could complete its campaign, however, a new opportunity presented itself.[58]

In November the Communist Party reversed its position and decided to establish an aboveground party "to spread communism among the masses."[59] The decision came at the urging of the Third International, which had concluded during the previous summer that "world revolution" was no longer an immediate prospect (contrary to its claim in

1919) and that the Communist Party should engage in normal political activity. Toward that end, the Communist Party proposed a merger with the JSF (and the rest of the Workers' Council) to create a "broad proletarian mass party." The negotiations proved difficult from the beginning. What should the program of the new party be? How should power be distributed within it? Would the underground Communist Party continue to exist and, if so, what would its relationship be to the new, aboveground party? Eventually the two sides reached an agreement, which they scheduled to finalize during a convention between December 23 and 26. Yet as the convention approached, Salutsky, who with Olgin represented the JSF at the negotiating table, felt strong misgivings. He suspected the Communists were "intent on building a new vehicle to carry the old Communist ware," in the words of one contemporary, rather than establishing a truly independent, aboveground party.[60] By December 21 Salutsky wanted the JSF to withdraw from the proposed merger. "I know that it is humanly inexplicable," he confessed to his wife, Hannah, "after my performances during the last three months, the split, the daily, the unity, etc. . . . . Am sorry for all I have done lately. All I wish now is the strength to break up decisively. . . . Olgin is tempting, attempting to persuade, arguing, etc. He is right, I know, but I am right, too, and it is all just wrong."[61] After the first day of the convention, Salutsky called an emergency meeting of delegates affiliated with the Workers' Council in Olgin's apartment. He proposed a walkout, but the majority decided that it was too late to pull back. They elected to go forward with the merger with the hope of preventing the new party from being captured by the Communists. Salutsky reluctantly went along with the decision. On December 26 the convention established a new organization named the Workers' Party.[62] Its program omitted references to violent revolution and immediate seizure of power. Instead of dictatorship of the proletariat, the party's program spoke of a "workers' republic" to be achieved through political education, the union movement, elections, and, at some point in the future, democratically elected soviets. Thus, the Workers' Party promised to be genuinely independent, rather than a Communist Party by another name.[63]

Olgin touted the Workers' Party as an opportunity for the JSF to achieve long-standing goals. With backing from an authentic "proletarian party," Olgin claimed, the JSF could finally introduce a "pure, sustainable, serious spirit in the Jewish labor movement" and a "clear, principled position" on the Jewish Question.[64] Salutsky, by contrast, adopted a skeptical view of the Workers' Party and the place of the JSF—now renamed the Jewish Federation—within it. More politically savvy than Olgin, Salutsky recognized that the Jewish Federation's fate rested on a precarious balance of power between Communists and former members of the JSF, who were labeled centrists. Each side was allotted nine seats on the Jewish Federation's National Executive Committee, an arrangement that all but guaranteed a permanent stalemate.[65] Furthermore, Communists occupied twelve of seventeen seats on the Workers' Party's Central Executive Committee and therefore controlled the party as a whole. They also possessed direct ties to Moscow, which was a crucial source of political and financial support.[66] Finally, the status of the Communist Party and its relationship to the Workers' Party was left unresolved. The former JSF members expected the underground party ("the subway party," in Salutsky's words) to be dissolved, but the Communists did no such thing. They viewed the Workers' Party as the "transmission apparatus" of the underground Communist Party to the "less conscious and as yet non-revolutionary masses."[67] Communists referred to the underground party as number one and the Workers' Party as number two, suggesting an unmistakable chain of command. It is unclear why Salutsky and Olgin went ahead with the merger before clarifying the relationship between the two parties. Did they acquiesce to the continued existence of the underground Communist Party, as some historians claim? Had they been tricked? Was there a misunderstanding? Such questions cannot be answered definitively.[68] Whatever the case, the centrists did not enjoy a free hand in the Jewish Federation, contrary to Olgin's pronouncement. In the Jewish Federation they shared power equally with the Communists, who, in turn, dominated the Workers' Party as a whole.

By joining the Workers' Party, the JSF reunited with its former Left Wing. For two and a half years following the split of May 1919, the JSF had tried to push the Socialist Party leftward. Having failed, the JSF merged with its former adversaries located in the Communist Party to create a new party, one in which Bittelman would surely exercise more power than Salutsky. It was a risky move, given the JSF's weakened position. The communists had made some concessions, but it remained to be seen whether the deal struck by Salutsky and Olgin would bring the expected benefits. The outcome would be determined in 1922.

Consolidation

The Jewish Federation's first major undertaking was the publication of the daily *Di frayhayt*. Edited by Olgin and Shakhne Epshteyn, *Di frayhayt* brought together two avant gardes: the political and the cultural. The newspaper's premier editorial, on April 2, 1922, pledged "to bring about a revolution, not only in the economic, social, and political concepts of Jewish workers, but also in their outlook toward questions of culture." The upstart daily defined itself in opposition to the *Forverts*. Early editorials and articles inveighed against the *Forverts's* moderate socialism, lax literary standards, commercialism, and insufficient respect for Yiddish: "Instead of educating the masses in a truly cultural manner, in a truly revolutionary way, to awaken in them the most beautiful and best feelings and aspirations, it stooped to their level, to their crude instincts. . . . In the chase after material success, striving to become a man of substance with a ten-story brick-house, the *Forverts* did not become the organ of the conscious labor movement, but the street paper of the rabble, of the marketplace."[69]

Rather than indulge the "backward tastes" and "primitive inclinations" of the "rabble," *Di frayhayt* promised to offer "true revolutionary enlightenment, true education." "A true workers' newspaper," stated one editorial, "must be the intellectual leader and pathfinder of the workers; it must refine their tastes, make them into people with higher concepts and ideals, to awaken their fighting spirit."[70] *Di frayhayt*, Tsivion wrote, "must be particularly interested in enriching and refining Yiddish literature and art, as well as in developing the literary and artistic tastes of the Jewish masses."[71] The new daily should, according to Morris Vintshevsky, "give the Jewish worker a daily treasure of princi-

23. The Jewish Socialist Federation bids farewell to the *Forverts* following its September 1921 convention. The federation: "*I* have the principles!" *Forverts:* "But *I* have the biznes!" From *Der groyser kundes,* September 16, 1921.

pled articles . . . and true literature."[72] Members of the JSF had put forward identical goals since before the establishment of the organization in 1912, but, until 1922, the prohibitive cost of publishing a daily newspaper and unwillingness to rebel against the *Forverts* (which, for all its flaws, was accepted as the spokesman for the Jewish working class before September 1921) placed the goal of a "true workers' newspaper" beyond reach. Now, the Jewish Federation having broken with the *Forverts* and with backing from the Workers' Party, such a newspaper had become a reality.

Di frayhayt demonstrated its commitment to *yidishe kultur* in several ways. Regarding language, the editors used an updated orthography that discarded unnecessary silent letters used widely in Yiddish journalism to mimic German spelling.[73] The editors also favored a purer Yiddish than the *Forverts*'s "potato Yiddish," which employed numerous English words spoken by immigrants in daily life (such as *djob* [job] instead of *arbet,* or *vinde* [window] rather than *fenster*). Abraham Cahan staunchly defended his incorporation of English words on the ground that it reflected the actual speech of average immigrants.[74] *Di frayhayt*'s editors, however, considered excessive use of English words to be a kind of corruption, an imposition of "vulgar" street culture onto the printed page, where higher standards should prevail. While recognizing the need "to speak in an easy, understandable language," *Di frayhayt* refrained from using English words when perfectly intelligible Yiddish words were available. "We want to be popular," *Di frayhayt* explained in its first issue, "but not cheap and vulgar."[75]

In the literary sphere, *Di frayhayt* attracted the most impressive array of poets and fiction writers of any Yiddish newspaper. Regular contributors included Moyshe Leyb Halpern, Mani Leyb, Moyshe Nadir, Yoysef Opatoshu, H. Leyvik, Isaac Raboy, and Dovid Ignatov—experimental writers originally associated with the literary cohort Di Yunge. While these writers had socialist sympathies, their literary work was not primarily concerned with politics. What they perceived in *Di frayhayt,* as Ruth Wisse explains, was the intimacy and seriousness of a small literary journal combined with the wider readership and financial reward of a daily newspaper.[76] Olgin and Epshteyn allowed neither political ideology nor the dictates of the commercial marketplace to diminish *Di frayhayt*'s literary standards.[77] Writers thus felt they could publish in *Di frayhayt* (unlike the *Forverts*) without artistic compromise.[78]

Although successful from a literary standpoint, *Di frayhayt* was plagued by financial difficulties from the start. In its refusal to bend to "the marketplace" and "the rabble," *Di frayhayt* appealed to a relatively narrow segment of the public: extremely radical, intellectually inclined workers. Even readers sympathetic to *Di frayhayt*'s perspective found it difficult to read. "What do the masses know about 'initiative,' 'objective,' 'complicated,' 'situation,' 'sociology,' 'ideology,' and the like?" a Harlem man wrote. He recommended use of simpler language (though not necessarily like the *Forverts*'s potato Yiddish). "One should speak to a worker in his language, without stunts, about his muddled attitudes, to show him how he can liberate himself from his slavery, to live in a better, more beautiful world . . . through sketches, pictures, and short stories about workers' lives."[79] Whether the reader from Harlem expressed a common sentiment is difficult to know. In any case, *Di frayhayt*'s circulation dropped significantly during its first two months, from forty thousand to eighteen thousand, according to Salutsky. In a letter to his wife, Salutsky also mentioned that *Di frayhayt* was losing three thousand dollars per week. *Di frayhayt* raised some money from the sale of stock certificates and appeals to readers. Yet donations arrived "in a dribble" during the newspaper's early months, and *Di frayhayt* sold only 628 certificates (at ten dollars each) by the third week of May.[80] In September the Jewish Federation's Executive Committee warned that *Di frayhayt* faced bankruptcy.[81]

Di frayhayt probably could not have survived without financial assistance from Moscow. The Comintern (as the Third International had become commonly known) had pledged ten thousand dollars for a Yiddish daily in November 1921. Two months later, on January 12, the Communist Party's national office contacted its representative to the Comintern, Ludwig Katterfeld, with a request for an unspecified amount of money. Using a pseudonym and the coded language of a business transaction, the party's executive secretary, "G. Lewis," wrote: "We should like you to give special attention to our Jewish customers. They want to begin doing business at once daily, but cannot do so until you send the goods. Please dispatch it to them at once." On February 2 Lewis made a second, more urgent request, writing that "unless immediate aid is received" "our Jewish customers" might abandon "their plans for the joint daily advertising."[82] The day before *Di frayhayt*'s debut, the Communist Party's general secretary, Jay Lovestone, gave (without a request for a receipt) a crucial, last-minute infusion of fifteen hundred dollars.[83] In the summer Bittelman traveled to Moscow to procure more funds for *Di frayhayt* and the Jewish Federation. It does not appear that the Comintern lavished money on *Di frayhayt*, but it clearly provided enough to keep the newspaper afloat.[84]

While *Di frayhayt* struggled to survive, conflict raged between Communists and so-called centrists for control of the newspaper and the Jewish Federation as a whole. In January the two sides clashed over the name of the proposed daily newspaper. The Communists on the Jewish Federation's Executive Committee wanted to retain the name *Der emes*, in honor of the Moscow daily. But the former JSF leaders insisted on *Di frayhayt*: the name of the German Independent Socialist Party's newspaper, which stood between mainstream social democracy and Communism.[85] The Communists relented because they recognized that the success of *Di frayhayt* depended not only on Soviet money, but also on the talent and national reputations of people like Olgin, Salutsky, Tsivion, and Vintshevsky.[86] The Communists, however, refused to compromise on the selection of editors. The centrists wanted Salutsky, the former editor of *Di naye velt*, but the Communists, led by Bittelman and Epshteyn, insisted on Olgin, who was known to be more pliable and friendly. (Olgin had traveled to the Soviet Union in 1920 and had returned enamored.) By the time *Di frayhayt* appeared, Salutsky had grown estranged from the Jewish Federation and regretted the entire enterprise. He was not scheduled to speak at *Di frayhayt*'s debut celebration and did so only on the insistence of audience members after the meeting had formally ended.[87] Salutsky sounded the only dour note of the evening. He denounced the machinations taking place within the Jewish Federation and the Workers' Party. He also told audience members that while he would continue to oppose "Forvertsism," he would not write for *Di frayhayt*. "The whole time I spoke," Salutsky wrote to his wife, "the gathering stood in silence."[88] Salutsky left the celebration dejected and later recorded in his diary: "What culminated today in the F—t [*Frayhayt*] I started 10 years ago. No one believed it possible. I forced it to the front, cultivated the belief in the possibility to realize it, a daily challenge to the F—d's [*Forward*'s] rule of vulgarity. That paper is now a fact. If it is true that a new era in the movement starts . . . new leadership is the only hope. Unfortunately the caliber of people around the F—t is low, as bad as the F—d crowd. Not as corrupt in the material sense, but no less dishonest."[89] "Olgin's speech was shallow, soulless," Salutsky continued. "Zivion [sic] . . . hopelessly cheap-witty at its best. Bittelman stupid beyond measure." Salutsky remained a member of the Jewish Federation's National Executive Committee and the Workers' Party's Central Executive Committee, but he all but withdrew from the federation's day-to-day activities. "I cannot," he wrote, "fight one evil and tolerate another evil and [even] help it grow. . . . Rot is rot even if it pretends to be red."[90]

In the weeks and months following the debut of *Di frayhayt*, Jewish Federation members in cities throughout the United States wrote to Salutsky inquiring why he had absented himself from the newspaper. "What has happened to make you keep your distance?" asked a self-described "follower" of Salutsky in St. Paul. A comrade in New Haven wrote that he missed Salutsky's articles "very, very much." And in Los Angeles people were "asking from all sides why Salutsky isn't with *Di frayhayt*?"[91] Salutsky had become, in the words of his wife Hannah, "a fallen general."[92]

At the grassroots level, conflict between Communists and centrists consumed the Jewish Federation. At the direction of the underground party leadership, Communists in the Jewish Federation attempted to win control of the branches and the National Executive Committee. The committee's strategy was to propagate Communist ideas in the Jewish Federation until "we shall ourselves be in a position to successfully lead the fight of this organization against the reactionary and yellow gang in the Jewish labor movement." Given the dominant position of Communists in the Workers' Party, the Central Executive Committee felt confident that it would sooner or later win over recalcitrant centrists in the Jewish Federation and *Di frayhayt*. The Communist leadership considered this to be of utmost importance. Not only was the Jewish Federation one of the largest foreign-language federations in the Workers' Party (and one of the most resistant to Communist domination), but it also provided access to the larger Jewish labor movement, which, because of its size, power, and socialist orientation, served as the gateway to the American labor movement as a whole. In an unpublished report to the Comintern, probably written in October for its upcoming November 4 convention, the Communist Party's Central Executive Committee stated, "We consider winning this fight in the Jewish movement an absolute condition for the development of our influence among other sections of the organized working class; for to be beaten in this fight may mean complete extermination of our forces from the Jewish labor unions which will undoubtedly diminish our chances of progress in the other labor unions." The report also stated: "On account of the strong Jewish labor movement, the CEC [Central Executive Committee] of our party considers the Jewish work [of] the greatest importance and requests therefore the EC [Executive Committee] of the Communist International to pay very careful attention to the report of its special delegate on the Jewish press." When it wrote the report, the Communist Party did not believe the time was yet ripe for a "decisive battle" in the Jewish Federation. Its strategy was to abide by the power-sharing arrangement established in December 1921 "until such a time as when the Communist ideas have taken a stronger hold upon the advanced section of the Jewish workers."[93]

The Jewish Federation's centrists were well aware that Communists were following orders from the party's underground leadership, with the goal of taking over the organization. They demanded an end to the maneuvers and insisted that the Communist Party respect the Jewish Federation's autonomy. In October the conflict came to a head when three Communists on the Jewish Federation's National Executive Committee broke ranks and tipped the balance of power in favor of the centrists. The Communist faction, led by Bittelman, subsequently demanded an additional three seats in order to restore the "50–50" balance of power. But the Jewish Federation's new non-Communist majority refused. Bittelman and the remaining five Communists then resigned from the Executive Committee, declaring it illegal. They took the issue to the Workers' Party's Central Executive Committee, which scheduled a hearing on November 8. The Central Executive Committee, of course, sided with the Communists. It ruled that the 50–50 balance must be restored, and that 50 percent ownership of *Di frayhayt* be turned over to the Workers' Party. The Central Executive Committee added that if the Jewish Federation refused, it would "take charge of the affairs of the Federation."[94]

The Jewish Federation rejected the Central Executive Committee's decision, but the Central Executive Committee refrained from taking disciplinary action against the Jewish Federation, which it considered too important an asset to expel from the Workers' Party. Instead, the Central Executive Committee opted for negotiation, which dragged on through the fall. The Central Executive Committee offered minor concessions but stood by its basic position. As of November 23 negotiations between the Jewish Federation and the Central Executive Committee remained deadlocked. At that point the Central Executive Committee threatened, in the name of party unity, to take full possession of *Di frayhayt* and the Jewish Federation's administrative affairs. In response, a minority, led by Salutsky, wanted the Jewish Federation to break immediately from the Workers' Party. The majority, however, led by Olgin and George Vishnak, favored continuing negotiations but did not rule out the possibility of a split.

All the while, the Central Executive Committee campaigned against the Jewish Federation within the Workers' Party. On December 16, as the Jewish Federation's national convention opened in New York City, all of the Workers' Party's foreign-language federations (which represented upward of 80 to 90 percent of the Workers' Party's membership) condemned the Jewish Federation for "threatening to bring disruption" into the Workers' Party and violating party discipline.[95] The Jewish Federation found itself outnumbered and isolated.

By the end of the Jewish Federation's convention on December 19, however, something remarkable had happened. The conflict between the Jewish Federation and the Workers' Party's Central Executive Committee had been resolved, and on terms decisively favoring the Communist faction. Alexander Bittelman was appointed secretary of the Jewish Federation and Communists were granted a majority on its National Executive Committee. Most striking, the Jewish Federation agreed to transfer complete ownership of *Di frayhayt* to the Workers' Party and to issue a statement affirming its duty to submit to party discipline. "The Jewish Federation has passed through a crisis safely," the Workers' Party's Administrative Council declared on December 30. "The party has avoided a split in one of its units. Both the party and the federation will go forward in their work stronger than ever."[96] Even more surprising, the agreement between the Jewish Federation and the Workers' Party was reached before the federation's national convention opened on December 16; so revealed Charles Ruthenberg, the Executive Secretary of the Workers' Party's Administrative Council, in his December 30 declaration. Ruthenberg did not make known the details of the negotiations, but it seems that personal interests of the Jewish Federation's chief negotiators—Moyshe Olgin and George Vishnak—played an important role. Significantly, Olgin was appointed sole editor of Di frayhayt while Vishnak was appointed the newspaper's manager and perhaps offered a trip to the Soviet Union.[97] (Vishnak would travel to Moscow in the summer of 1923 on behalf of the Russian-American Industrial Corporation, founded by Sidney Hillman's Amalgamated Clothing Workers' of America to aid the development of the USSR's clothing industry.)[98] Having reached an agreement with the Workers' Party's leadership in advance of the Jewish Federation's national convention, Olgin and Vishnak went to the convention with the intention of persuading a majority of delegates (particularly the centrists) to accept the compromise already brokered (though it is not clear whether Olgin and Vishnak made that known to the delegates). In any case, enough delegates trusted their judgment and might have also believed that Olgin, as the chief editor of Di frayhayt, would possess sufficient power to prevent a full takeover by the Communist faction.[99]

Another factor had to do with an important change in Communist Party policy. Acting on a Comintern directive, leaders of the underground Communist Party had decided to liquidate itself, thus ending months of acrimonious debate about its status. The Jewish Federation's members may have viewed this as an important enough concession to warrant the sacrifice of the federation's autonomy. Furthermore, the Jewish Federation's members probably realized that they could not afford to publish Di frayhayt without financial assistance from the Soviet Union, something only the Communist faction could secure. Bittelman had exploited this advantage in previous weeks by promising to secure more money from Moscow if the Communist faction was permitted to exercise greater control over the newspaper.[100]

Finally, the Communists' constant appeals to party discipline in the name of unity probably had an effect on Jewish Federation members. Most (though not all) members of the federation wanted to avoid a split on principle: all thought of themselves as pro-Soviet revolutionaries and opponents of the "official socialists" who led the Jewish labor movement. Besides, where could the Jewish Federation go if it left the Workers' Party? No acceptable alternative existed.[101]

Whatever the reasons, the Jewish Federation's decision could only be considered a defeat in light of its earlier goals. The program adopted by the Workers' Party in early 1923 reflected a new reality in which the Communist faction gained greater control over the Jewish Federation and the Workers' Party as a whole. Unlike the December 1921 program, the new program used explicitly Communist terminology. Instead of calling for the "abolition of capitalism through the establishment of the Workers' Republic," the new program spoke of "supplanting the existing capitalist government with a Soviet Government" to be a "dictatorship of the workers." Whereas in 1921 the Workers' Party defined itself as a "sympathizing party" of the Comintern, the Workers' Party now officially accepted the "inspiration of the leadership of the Communist International." The Workers' Party had become Communist in all but name. On April 7, 1923, the Communist Party officially dissolved itself on the grounds that the Workers' Party "has developed into a Communist Party" and so the original party was no longer necessary. Two years later the Workers' Party would change its name to the Workers' (Communist) Party and again in 1929 to the Communist Party. Thus was the short history of the Workers' Party as an independent party.[102]

Factional conflict continued within the Jewish Federation through 1923, but the Workers' Party's leadership succeeded ultimately in quelling it. Late in the year the party's Central Executive Committee connived to depose Olgin, who had not yet gone over completely to the Communist side, as editor of *Di frayhayt*. The Workers' Party's leadership had for many months criticized *Di frayhayt* for being too concerned with Yiddish cultural issues at the expense of party propaganda. "The fight these Centrists have conducted against the yellow Socialist daily 'The Forward' has not been a Communist struggle but a Centrist fight for clean, literary journalism against dirty, vulgar journalism," the Workers' Party's Central Executive Committee declared in its party organ, *The Worker,* in December 1922.[103] In Bittelman's words, "The struggle against the *Forward* must be . . . on the basis of communist principles. We fight the *Forward* not merely and mainly because it is not a decent literary paper, but because it serves the reactionary and socially treacherous union bureaucracy."[104] In an interview conducted six decades later, Pesakh Novik, who was in 1923 still aligned with the centrists, recalled the hostility to *Di frayhayt.* "The communists said, 'It's . . . not a good communist paper. It's too literary. It's too busy with Jewish affairs, what's going on among Jews, the Jewish people. . . . They're not following the line completely. There's not enough agitation, propaganda. . . . Too much literature."[105] The party replaced Olgin with Benjamin Gitlow, who, according to the Communist Party leader James Cannon, "was not at home in the Yiddish language and had no qualification as a writer in this field." Gitlow later described his role at *Di frayhayt* as that of a commissar.[106] Gitlow's appointment signaled a new direction in *Di frayhayt* toward stricter adherence to party discipline. *Di frayhayt* was now expected to be the Yiddish mouthpiece of the Workers' Party, rather than the voice of the Jewish Federation.

During the course of 1923 the Jewish Federation and *Di frayhayt* lost a number of leading figures because of defections and expulsions.[107] Salutsky was expelled from the Workers' Party in July because, among other reasons, he refused to play his newly established journal, *American Labor Monthly,* under party control. He described his expulsion as a "glorious occasion." Salutsky would soon change his name to J. B. S. Hardman and become one of the foremost intellectuals in the American labor movement.[108] In June or July Tsivion was also expelled from the Workers' Party. In a sixty-three-page pamphlet entitled *Komunistn vos hobn oyfgegesn komunizm (Communists Who Have Devoured Communism,* 1923), Tsivion detailed the infighting and intrigue that had plagued the Jewish Federation and *Di frayhayt* from their beginnings. "We sought a home for our souls," Tsivion concluded, "but instead found a hell." In October Tsivion returned to the *Forverts* (after a long interview with Abraham Cahan and Baruch Charney Vladeck, and much debate within the Forverts Association), where he would remain an extremely popular columnist for the remainder of his career.[109] He concluded that the Jewish Socialist Federation's effort to build a revolutionary but non-Communist political organization wedded to *yidishe kultur* had ended in a terrible failure. The Communists had refused to allow it.

Others, such as Olgin and Novik, remained in the Jewish Federation and accommodated themselves to Communist control. They did so slowly, as Melech Epstein, a Communist in the 1920s, would later write, "like a man pushed in a certain direction, resisting every step, but taking it nonetheless."[110] In 1925 the Workers' Party, now known officially as the Workers' (Communist) Party, dissolved its foreign-language federations after adopting a policy of "Bolshevization" designed to create full, centralized control of the party. Subsequently, the Jewish Federation was reduced to the status of a "bureau."[111] Olgin would be reinstated as the editor of *Di frayhayt* in 1929, but without the same editorial latitude he had during his first tenure.

The search for a radical, pro-Yiddish alternative to the *Forverts* thus ended in failure. Leaders of the Jewish Socialist Federation had wagered in 1921 that an alliance with the Communist Party would enable them to create a rival center of power to the *Forverts* and advance the cause of *yidishe kultur*. For a brief period in 1922 these goals seemed possible. Backing by the Workers' Party, and in turn the Soviet Union, enabled the Jewish Federation to publish an experimental Yiddish daily linking revolution with *yidishe kultur*. Had the Yiddish newspaper market been able to support such a newspaper, perhaps an alliance with the Communists would have been unnecessary. As it turned out, however, *Di frayhayt* depended on Communists, who did not share the same goals as the Jewish Socialist Federation, for its existence. The Jewish Federation's eventual subordination to the Workers' Party did not signal the end of the Yiddish-speaking Communist movement. *Di frayhayt* survived and the Yiddish-speaking Communist movement, in fact, grew in size and scope as the 1920s progressed. Communist influence grew in the garment unions and the Arbeter Ring, touching off a series of civil wars and schisms in the second half of the decade. But the basic relations of power, in which Yiddish cultural work and Jewish group interests were made contingent on the prerogatives of the Communist Party and the USSR, would continue to shape the Yiddish-speaking Communist movement for the rest of its history.

Epilogue

An Ambiguous Legacy

In 1926, exactly four decades after the Great Upheaval gave birth to the Jewish labor movement, Abraham Cahan published the first three volumes of his five-volume autobiography, *Bleter fun mayn lebn (Pages from My Life)*. That same year Yisroel Kopelov came out with the first installment of his autobiographical trilogy, *Amol iz geven (Once upon a Time)*. Also in 1926 Shoel Yanovsky began writing his reminiscences for *Di fraye arbeter shtime,* the newspaper he edited throughout much of his adulthood. Cahan, Kopelov, and Yanovsky had followed similar trajectories. All three were born in the Russian Empire within six years of one another (Kopelov in 1858, Cahan in 1860, and Yanovsky in 1864), were raised in poor, religiously observant homes, studied Russian and secular subjects as teenagers, and aspired to become Russian revolutionary intellectuals. All three emigrated to New York City during or shortly after the pogroms of 1881–1882, reoriented themselves politically with the help of Kleindeutschland's German radicals, and were galvanized by the Great Upheaval of 1886. Over the next forty years, all three played important roles in the Jewish labor movement: Yanovsky as an anarchist, Kopelov as both an anarchist and a proponent of Chaim Zhitlovsky's Yiddish cultural nationalism, and Cahan as a Marxian social democrat. Despite differences of opinion, each imagined a "better, more beautiful world" without poverty or bigotry. As they approached old age, these three pioneers of the Jewish labor movement looked backward to take stock.

There is nothing unusual about intellectuals writing about themselves, but Cahan, Kopelov, and Yanovsky reflected a wide impulse among immigrant Jews to recount their lives and times. From the 1920s forward, hundreds and perhaps thousands of immigrant Jews—mostly men, but some women as well—wrote or relayed their life stories in Yiddish, English, and, to a lesser extent, German, Hebrew, and Russian. Their reminiscences can be found in books, newspapers, magazines, souvenir journals, unpublished manuscripts, and transcribed interviews sitting in archives.[1] In addition to the valuable information they contain, the preponderance of autobiographical accounts reflect something deeper about the authors: their self-perception as historical actors, participants in important events that had significance beyond their personal lives.[2] That awareness of having "made history" derived not from a traditional religious worldview, which accorded God the sole role in determining the destiny of the Jewish people, but rather from the dislocations and social struggles experienced by large numbers of immigrants, as filtered through the Jewish labor movement's socialist and socialist-nationalist ideologies. Indeed, socialist organizations like the Arbeter Ring actively encouraged their members to write their autobiographies.[3] Socialist ideologies of all kinds gave epochal meaning to the travails familiar to all immigrant Jews. They posited a process of rebirth in which working-class Jews would go from being submissive to assertive, ignorant to "enlightened," materialistic to idealistic, parochial to universal. Although autobiographical accounts did not usually follow such a predetermined script, they stressed common themes that permeated the intellectual world of immigrant Jews: hardship, awakening, self-betterment, and social justice. The desire to tell one's story, whether in five volumes or a few newspaper columns, grew out of a culture recast by socialism.

The Jewish labor movement began when a small number of Russian-speaking intellectuals decided to adopt Yiddish for the purpose of organizing and educating Jewish workers. It grew remarkably fast. Mounting class conflict and the leadership vacuum left by old elites made socialism attractive to a predominantly youthful immigrant Jewish population. The Jewish labor movement took organizational form in the mid-1880s, gained a large following in the 1890s, and by the 1910s became the leading force in immigrant Jewish life. By the end of World War I the movement's accomplishments surpassed anything Cahan, Kopelov, or Yanovsky would have imagined when they arrived in the United States. Socialists now dominated the Yiddish newspaper market, won the majority of votes in Jewish wards, created a vibrant, secular culture in Yiddish, and organized some of the largest, most innovative unions in the country.[4] Hundreds of thousands of people in New York (and other cities) came to understand themselves through the labor movement's ideas, institutions, and social-cultural milieu. It is true that many Jews remained hostile or indifferent to socialism, but socialists were the ones who defined the mainstream. They not only built a popular movement; they also molded the posture and character of the world's largest Jewish community in an era punctuated by upheavals and crises on both sides of the Atlantic.

From the start the Jewish labor movement—and the broader Yiddish culture it fostered—contained its own tensions and conflicts. How could it have been otherwise? Socialists espoused universal principles yet created a movement consisting entirely of Yiddish-speaking Jews. The Jewish labor movement's dual character—its universalism and particularity—wrestled with itself constantly. Some individuals viewed socialism as a process of cultural assimilation; others considered it essential for Jewish national revival. Some imagined a world without Jews or other national groups; others anticipated an international brotherhood of peoples that included Jews. Still others wavered in between. All the while, socialists disagreed about how to overturn capitalism and what kind of society should replace it. After the Bolshevik revolution forced preexisting divisions past the breaking point, the Jewish labor movement divided into left and right wings, which themselves contained Jewish nationalist and internationalist components. A century later one is struck by the persistence and ferocity of old arguments. As recent debate about the state of Israel attests, unresolved questions continue to burn even as the specific applications change.

During the Jewish labor movement's formative era between the 1880s and World War I, socialists of all persuasions looked forward to a bright future. All believed that capitalism would cease to exist in their lifetime and that Jews would, in some fashion, be redeemed in the coming society. Jewish socialists based their optimism, in large part, on the knowledge that hundreds of thousands of other immigrants and native-born Americans (not to mention millions of people abroad) shared a similar desire for radical change. Yet the First World War unleashed a wave of political repression, anti-Semitism, nativism, and anti-black racism that ushered in a decade of uncertainty and diminished prospects.[5] The Jewish labor movement remained more powerful than ever in many respects. Yet its members felt increasingly out of step with American society as it returned to "normalcy" in the 1920s. Pockets of radicalism continued to thrive among certain immigrant groups, such as the Germans of Milwaukee and the Finns of northern Michigan, but the Socialist Party lay in ruins (owing both to infighting and external repression) and organized labor was in retreat.[6] The abiding radicalism (in whichever political form) of immigrant Jews left them vulnerable and stigmatized. In addition to Henry Ford's infamous anti-Semitic screeds, there were many milder emanations from less malevolent types. In a series of interviews conducted by the researcher David Saposs in 1919 and 1920, for example, labor activists repeatedly assailed Jews as a "constant source of trouble," "non-compromising," given to "extreme action," "Bolsheviki," and "troublesome." American Federation of Labor officials faulted "Hebrews" for attempting to advance "the welfare of mankind," instead of looking after narrow, bread-and-butter interests like wage increases.[7] Thus, from the vantage point of 1920, one could not plausibly say that socialism served to ease the transition of immigrant Jews into American society, as historians would later claim. On the contrary, socialism had made Jews more conspicuous, so much so that many people viewed it as a specifically Jewish trait. Jews may not have been the only radicals in America, but, according to the AFL's New York director, they were among the "worst offenders." As they entered the 1920s, Jewish socialists felt anything but "at home in America."[8]

The 1920s was a decade of retrenchment for the Jewish labor movement. The country's prevailing conservatism and Congress's decision to curtail European immigration (thus halting further growth of the Jewish working class) chastened most socialists. J. B. S. Hardman (formerly Yankev Salutsky) lamented in 1928: "1919 seems to have happened ages ago. The language that was used then no longer sounds familiar to our ears. The emotions that overwhelmed people in those momentous days fail to excite us today. The world has grown not only older but old."[9] Socialists retained their ideals but slowly shed their militancy. The goal of transforming American society gave way to reforming it. The year 1936 marked a clear turning point. After thirty-five years of support for the Socialist Party, the *Forverts* endorsed Franklin Roosevelt for president and the garment unions established the American Labor Party to allow Left-Wingers to vote for Roosevelt while preserving their independence. According to Melvyn Dubofsky's description, the ALP functioned as a "halfway house between the Socialist Party and the regular Democratic organization." The ALP appealed to old-line Socialist Party members, independent voters, and even Communists (who were officially barred from the ALP but actually gained influence in it over the years). In 1937 approximately 40 percent of New York Jews voted for ALP candidates in municipal elections, effectively replacing the Socialist Party as the political voice of Jewish labor.[10]

Without doubt, accommodation to the established political order brought significant benefits. Between the 1930s and 1960s Jewish labor stood at the forefront of social reform in New York. One could literally see the influence of Jewish socialists in the city's urban landscape, particularly in the workers' housing cooperatives that began cropping up in Manhattan and the Bronx in the late 1920s. Finnish socialists in Brooklyn established the first cooperatives around the time of World War I, but Jews elaborated the concept. Starting in 1926, a group of Jewish workers affiliated with the Communist Party built the United Workers' Cooperative Colony ("the Coops") in the Bronx to serve as a self-contained, left-wing Yiddish cultural community. Soon after, disciples of Chaim Zhitlovsky established the Sholem Aleichem Houses (where the first Jewish Miss America, Bess Myerson, was raised), and socialist-Zionists established the Farband Houses. The Amalgamated Clothing

Workers followed suit with buildings in the Bronx and the Lower East Side. With the assistance of tax abatements from New York State, the Amalgamated and the ILGWU constructed housing cooperatives in every borough in New York, which totaled nearly forty thousand units occupied by roughly 120,000 people of all backgrounds by the end of the 1960s. The cooperative housing movement represented one example of how Jewish labor, because of its sheer size and left-wing orientation, took the lead in forging what Joshua Freeman has identified as New York's distinctive "social democratic polity": a diverse, working-class, political community committed to affordable housing, health care, education, access to the arts, and civil rights. It is not too much of an exaggeration to say that Jewish socialists, having transformed New York's Jewish community, proceeded to remake the city in their own image.[11]

Immigrant Jews did not abandon radicalism entirely during the interwar period. While most socialists veered toward the Democratic Party, a significant minority of radicals turned toward Communism in response to the Great Depression and the rising threat of fascism in the United States and Europe. It seemed to many Jews that the USSR, in addition to being home to the first successful socialist revolution, had solved the main problems of Jewish life in the Diaspora. The Communist government had outlawed anti-Semitism, granted official recognition to Jews as a nation, sponsored Yiddish schools, theater, scholarly institutions, and literary institutions, established Jewish agricultural colonies, and even created an autonomous region for Jews, Birobidzhan.[12] Of course, the new Soviet Jewish culture was built on extreme repression (and Stalin would later dismantle it), but that did not matter to the revolution's supporters. Not just Communists but sympathizers, such as Zhitlovsky, saw at least some of their goals fulfilled in the Soviet Union. The USSR was one of several countries to which American Jewish socialists could transfer their utopian aspirations after World War I. Bundists, for example, pinned their hopes on Poland, the center of independent Jewish politics and culture in the Diaspora between the two world wars. Though weak in the early 1920s, the Bund would emerge at the end of the next decade as the largest Jewish political party in Warsaw and Lodz.[13] Many socialists also evinced a new sympathy to the Zionist project in Palestine, where socialists achieved dominance in the emerging Jewish society and would remain in power after the establishment of the state of Israel until 1977. Abraham Cahan, for example, traveled to Palestine in 1925 and returned home inspired by the Yishuv's worker-owned enterprises and collective farms. The United Hebrew Trades purchased millions of dollars in bonds in the Histadrut, the socialist-Zionist movement's labor federation. After World War I New York no longer stood as the unofficial capital of Jewish socialism. New centers emerged in Palestine, Poland, and the Soviet Union that rivaled or eclipsed New York.[14]

During the interwar period the immigrant Jewish working class grayed and would eventually wane altogether. Jewish labor organizations survived (the Arbeter Ring and the *Forverts*, for example, exist to this very day), but by the 1950s the Jewish labor movement was no longer a movement. Nonetheless, radicalism continued to hold a strong attraction to the children and grandchildren of Yiddish-speaking Jews, though their connections to Yiddish were usually tenuous. During the 1930s and 1940s thousands of American-born Jews flocked to the Young People's Socialist League, the Communist Party and its affiliates, the party's Trotskyist offshoots, and various socialist-Zionist groups. Young Jewish leftists (who later became known as "Old Leftists") grew up in neighborhoods where "socialism was a way of life," as Alfred Kazin wrote of his native Brownsville. At the dinner table, on street corners, in Yiddish schools, and in socialist summer camps, second-generation Jews devoured radical ideas the way other American children did cookies and milk.[15] To be sure, generational tensions and conflicts persisted between Yiddish-speaking immigrants and their English-speaking children. Many American-born Jewish radicals wanted more than anything to escape the confines of home and neighborhood, just as their parents, in an earlier period, had rejected the parochialism of their religious upbringing. In their yearning for a wider world beyond the Jewish enclaves of Brooklyn, the Bronx, and Manhattan, American-born children often failed to realize that their European-born parents, too, were once rebels and not really "old world" at all. The common thread that connected immigrant and native-born Jewish radicals was a desire to break with the past in search of new horizons. But like immigrant Jewish radicals after World War I, American-born Jewish radicals confronted a wave of repression tinged with anti-Semitism following the Second World War. The Peekskill riots, HUAC's Hollywood hearings, and the Rosenberg trial once again focused accusations of subversion and disloyalty on "Communist kikes," to quote Congressman John Rankin. The taint of Communism prompted major Jewish organizations to purge leftists and embark on a public relations campaign to prove the patriotism of Jews. Radicalism had become something to be collectively disavowed by the organized Jewish community.[16]

The "tradition" of American Jewish radicalism and generational conflict continued into the 1960s. This time the conflict pitted student radicals against Old Leftists, many of whom, after the horrors of Nazism and Stalinism, had tempered their radicalism. Although rarely did student radicals identify themselves politically as Jews, many of them had been reared in a predominantly Jewish milieu as "red diaper babies" or in a less rigid left-liberal environment.[17] Some were descendants of the Jewish labor movement's leading figures. In the San Francisco Bay Area, a young Maoist named Chris Zhitlowsky Milton, Chaim's grandson, helped to found the Revolutionary Union in 1969, after his three-year stay in China during the Cultural Revolution.[18] Kathy Boudin, the great-niece of Louis Boudin, achieved national notoriety as a leader of the Weather Underground and, in 1981, an accomplice in an armed robbery that resulted in the death of a policeman. In the debates of the 1960s (over Vietnam, black power, women's liberation, the Eichmann trial, the Six-Day War, and a host of other issues) one can detect something of a family quarrel as New Leftists chastised their parents (both actual and metaphorical) for failing to live up to professed ideals. Disagreements were often wrenching, as each side accused the other of betrayal or simply talked past one another. Only after social unrest subsided in the 1970s did rifts begin to heal slowly.[19]

As it turned out, the 1960s witnessed the last great upsurge of radicalism among Jews. During the 1970s and 1980s, amid a conservative shift in the United States as a whole, radicalism's appeal to Jews dissipated, although no more (and probably less) than it did to other Americans.

Most former New Leftists settled into an amorphous "progressivism" or mainstream Democratic Party liberalism. Some disillusioned radicals broke ranks altogether and joined older ex-socialists in becoming "neo-conservatives." They would find a warm reception in influential Washington, D.C., think tanks and in the presidential administrations of Ronald Reagan and, more recently, George W. Bush. Rejection of the left, in other words, is also an important legacy of the Jewish labor movement. A thorough genealogy could trace a web of personal and organizational connections—from political parties and unions to schools and summer camps—that begins in New York's tenement slums and stretches all the way to the White House, branching out in many unexpected directions along the way.

The long encounter between Jews and socialism (and radicalism of all kinds) defies easy description. Socialism's battles, won and lost, shaped the larger arc of American Jewish experience and the great social struggles of modern America. More than a passing phase in the successful adaptation of immigrant Jews to a welcoming American society, the Jewish radical experience highlights how difficult and protracted that process of adaptation was. The Jewish labor movement did not serve to usher Jews into the respectable middle class. Rather, it forged a new collective identity, a new Jewish culture, a new way of being Jewish, that was internally conflicted and at odds with the American mainstream. "Jewish socialism (and Zionism also)," as Irving Howe has written, "transformed the posture of Jewish life, creating a new type of person: combative, worldly, spirited, and intent on sharing the future of industrial society with the rest of the world."[20] To be both a Jew and a socialist was never an easy endeavor, as Howe recognized. The two identities were locked in permanent tension with one another and the larger American society, tensions that were often fruitful but never resolved. If the Yiddish socialists and their descendants failed to achieve their largest goals and dreams, the questions they posed—Who are we? What is a just society? How might we achieve it?—remain forceful and relevant for Jews and all Americans.

Notes

Introduction

1. "Unzer 5ter yorefest," *Di arbeter tsaytung*, March 3, 1895, p. 1.

2. Ida Van Etten, "Russian Jews as Desirable Immigrants," *Forum* 15 (April 1893): 173; Reynolds quoted in Abraham Cahan, "The Russian Jews in America," *Atlantic Monthly*, July 1898, p. 263; R.F., "Jews as Radicals," *New Republic*, June 15, 1918, p. 209. Also see Archibald McClure, *Leadership of the New America: Racial and Religious* (New York: George H. Doran, 1916), p. 180.

3. David J. Saposs, "'Unionizing the Brain Worker,'" *Labor Age* 11, no. 3 (Dec. 1922): 2.

4. For a recent treatment of Russian Jewish revolutionaries between the 1860s and 1880s, see Erich E. Haberer, *Jews and Revolution in Nineteenth-Century Russia* (Cambridge: Cambridge University Press, 1995), p. 275. There were 63 Jews among the 1,054 revolutionaries identified by the Okhrana, the government secret police, between 1873 and 1877 and 579 Jews of 4,307 between 1884 and 1890. Jonathan Frankel, *Prophecy and Politics: Socialism, Nationalism, and the Russian Jews, 1862–1917* (Cambridge: Cambridge University Press, 1981), p. 119.

5. [Boris] Bogen, *Nedel'naia khronika voskhoda* 13, no. 39 (Sept. 1894): 1038–1039. Also see Jacob Panken's unpublished memoir, Jacob Panken Collection, Wisconsin State Historical Society, Madison, box 1, folder 5, pp. 4–5.

6. This theme, generally overlooked in immigration studies, is discussed at greater length in chapter 1. For a similar discussion, see James R. Barrett, "Americanization from the Bottom Up: Immigration and the Remaking of the

Working Class in the United States, 1880–1930," *Journal of American History* 78 (Dec. 1992): 996–1020.

7. Henry L. Feingold, *Zion in America: The Jewish Experience from Colonial Times to the Present* (New York: Twayne, 1974), p. 129. Referring to its role in the development of Yiddish literature, Chone Shmeruk refers to New York City as "no more than an admittedly very large offshoot of Eastern Europe." Shmeruk, "Aspects of the History of Warsaw as a Yiddish Literary Centre," *Polin* 3 (1988): 151.

8. Frankel, *Prophecy and Politics*, p. 194. Also see Sh. Epshteyn, "Di tsukunft, der Bund, un di yidishe literatur," *Di tsukunft* (Jan. 1912): 69–70; Frants Kursky, "Di 'Tsukunft' in untererdishe Rusland," in *Gezamlte shriftn* (New York: Der Veker, 1952), pp. 250–260; A. Litvak, "Di rol fu der revolutsyonerer lid in der arbeter-bavegung," in N. Oyslander et al., eds., *Yidishe literatur* (Kiev: Kultur Lige, 1928), p. 324; and A. Litvak, "Di krayzlekh," in Kh. Sh. Kazdan, ed., *Geklibene shriftn* (New York: Arbeter Ring, 1945), pp. 209–210.

9. L. Shpayzman, "Etapn in der geshikhte . . . ," in *Geshikhte fun der tsienistisher arbeter-bavegung in tsofen Amerike*, vol. 1 (New York: Farlag Yidisher Kemfer, 1955), p. 285; Dovid Shub, *Fun di amolike yorn: bletlekh zikhroynes*, vol. 1 (New York: TSIKO, 1970), pp. 471–476, 477–487; Louis Waldman, *Labor Lawyer* (New York: E. P. Dutton, 1944), pp. 63–64.

10. Frankel, *Prophecy and Politics*, pp. 39, 121; William J. Fishman, *East End Jewish Radicals, 1875–1914* (London: Duckworth, 1975), pp. 305–306; E. Tsherikover, "London un ir pionerishe role in der bavegung," in Eliyohu Tsherikover, ed., *Geshikhte fun der yidisher arbeter bavegung in di Fareynikte shtatn*, vol. 2 (New York: YIVO, 1945), pp. 76–137; Moshe Mishkinsky, "Regional Factors in the Formation of the Jewish Labor Movement," *YIVO Annual of Jewish Social Science* 14 (1969): 27–52; Ida Cohen Selavan, "Jewish Wage Earners in Pittsburgh, 1890–1930," *American Jewish Historical Quarterly* 65, no. 3 (March 1976): 272–285; Kenneth Waltzer, "Eastern European Jewish Detroit in the Early Twentieth Century," *Judaism* 49, no. 3 (Summer 2000): 298.

11. Ezra Mendelsohn, *On Modern Jewish Politics* (New York: Oxford University Press, 1993), pp. 93–103.

12. Piotr Wrobel, "Jewish Warsaw before the First World War," *Polin* 3 (1988): 165; Frederick W. Skinner, "Odessa and the Problem of Urban Modernization," in Michael F. Hamm, ed., *The City in Late Imperial Russia* (Bloomington: Indiana University Press, 1986), p. 215; Lloyd P. Gartner, *The Jewish Immigrant in England, 1870–1914* (Detroit: Wayne State University Press, 1960), p. 49; Gerald Sorin, *A Time for Building: The Third Migration, 1880–1920* (Baltimore: Johns Hopkins University Press, 1992), p. 137.

13. Simon Kuznets, "Immigration of Russian Jews to the United States: Structure and Background," *Perspectives in American History* 9 (1975): 100–112; Jacob Lestchinsky, "Economic and Social Development of American Jewry," in *The Jewish People: Past and Present*, vol. 4 (New York: Jewish Encyclopedic Handbooks, 1955), p. 83; Moses Rischin, *The Promised City: New York's Jews, 1870–1914* (Cambridge, Mass.: Harvard University Press, 1962), pp. 61, 94.

14. N. Goldberg, "Di yidishe sotsyalistishe bavegung in di 80er yorn," in Tsherikover, ed., *Geshikhte*, vol. 2, pp. 287–295; Paula E. Hyman, "Immigrant Women and Consumer Protest: The New York City Kosher Meat Boycott of 1902," *American Jewish History* 70 (Sept. 1980): 91–105; Hadassa Kossak, *Cultures of Opposition: Jewish Immigrant Workers, New York City, 1881–1905* (Albany: State University of New York Press, 2000), pp. 107–129; "Der beker strayk," *Forverts*, Jan. 7, 1901, p. 1; "Es kokht," *Forverts*, Jan. 10, 1901, p. 1; "Klok meker arestet," *Di yidishe gazetn*, Nov. 9, 1894, p. 13; "Vayber in a milkhome," *Di yidishe gazetn*, Nov. 16, 1894, p. 17.

15. Sergei Ingerman, "Ocherk razvitiia evreiskogo rabochego dvizheniia v Amerike," manuscript, Sergei Ingerman Collection, Tamiment Library, New York University, p. [1].

16. Raphael Mahler, "The Economic Background of Jewish Emigration from Galicia to the United States," *YIVO Annual of Jewish Social Science* 7 (1958): 258; Ezra Mendelsohn, *Class Struggle in the Pale: The Formative Years of the Jewish Workers' Movement in Tsarist Russia* (Cambridge: Cambridge University Press, 1970), p. 116. For a more positive assessment of the long-term impact of industrialization on Russian Jews, see Arcadius Kahan, *Essays in Jewish Social and Economic History*, ed. Roger Weiss (Chicago: University of Chicago Press, 1986), pp. 1–69.

17. Kahan [Abraham Cahan], "Bildung un sotsyalistishe propagande bay yidishe baley-melokhes in di litvishe shtet," *Forverts*, July 5, 1897, reprinted in *Historishe shriftn* 3 (1939): 397. The article, although written and signed by Cahan, is based entirely on his interview with Lesin, who had arrived in the United States one day earlier.

18. Youngsoo Bae, *Labor in Retreat: Class and Community among Men's Clothing Workers of Chicago, 1871–1929* (Albany: State University of New York Press, 2001), pp. 12–13; Melvyn Dubofsky, *When Workers Organize: New York City in the Progressive Era* (Amherst: University of Massachusetts Press, 1968), p. 5; Rischin, *The Promised City*, pp. 61, 67. On the role of garment unions in New York's social and political life during the mid-twentieth century, see Joshua B. Freeman, *Working-Class New York: Life and Labor since World War II* (New York: W. W. Norton, 2000), pp. 8–16, 55.

19. Kenneth T. Jackson, "100 Years of Being Really Big," *New York Times*, Dec. 28, 1997, sect. 4, p. 9.

20. For a description of New York's Russian Jewish intelligentsia, see Steven Cassedy, *To the Other Shore: The Russian Jewish Intellectuals Who Came to America* (Princeton, N.J.: Princeton University Press, 1997).

21. John H. M. Laslett, *Labor and the Left: A Study of Socialist and Radical Influences in the American Labor Movement, 1881–1924* (New York: Basic Books, 1970), pp. 100–101; Max Podell, "The Story of My Life," YIVO Institute of Jewish Research, New York City, RG 102, folder 178, p. 89. Similarly, Van Etten wrote in 1893: "The place which the Russian student holds among his own people is unique. . . . While American workingmen are prone to look with distrust upon educated men who take up their cause, the Jewish workingmen, with the great respect they have for learning, welcome the educated and acknowledge their leadership." Van Etten, "Russian Jews," p. 172. On relations between American intellectuals and labor, see Leon Fink, *Progressive Intellectuals and the Dilemmas of Democratic Commitment* (Cambridge, Mass.: Harvard University Press, 1997); Selig Perlman, *A Theory of the Labor Movement* (New York: Macmillan, 1928), pp. 176–182.

22. David E. Fishman, *Russia's First Modern Jews: The Jews of Shklov* (New York: New York University Press, 1995); Eli Lederhendler, *The Road to Modern Jewish Politics* (Oxford: Oxford University Press, 1989); Michael Stanislawski, *Tsar Nicholas I and the Jews: The Transformation of Jewish Society in Russia, 1825–1855* (Philadelphia: Jewish Publications Society, 1983); Steven J. Zipperstein, *The Jews of Odessa: A Cultural History, 1794–1881* (Stanford, Calif.: Stanford University Press, 1985).

23. Gershon C. Bacon, *The Politics of Tradition: Agudat Yisrael in Poland, 1916–1939* (Jerusalem: Magnes Press, Hebrew University, 1996); Isaac Levitats, *The Jewish Community in Russia, 1844–1917* (Jerusalem: Posner, 1981); Mendelsohn, *On Modern Jewish Politics*, pp. 23–27; Alexander Orbach, "The Development of the Russian Jewish Community, 1881–1902," in John D. Klier and Shlomo Lambroza, eds., *Pogroms: Anti-Jewish Violence in Modern Russian History* (Cambridge: Cambridge University Press, 1992), p. 159. On distinctions between tradition and orthodoxy, see Haym Soloveitchik, "Rupture and Reconstruction: The Transformation of Contemporary Orthodoxy," *Tradition* 28, no. 4 (1994): 64–130.

24. Arthur Hertzberg, "'Treifene Medina': Learned Opposition to Emigration to the United States," *Proceedings of the Eighth World Congress of Jewish Studies* (Jerusalem: World Congress of Jewish Studies, 1984), pp. 11–30. For a

more qualified view, see Ira Robinson, "The First Hassidic Rabbis in North America," *American Jewish Archives* 44, no. 2 (Fall–Winter 1992): 501–503.

25. Kuznets, "Immigration of Russian Jews to the United States," pp. 94–98.

26. Ella Wolff, transcribed interview, Dec. 27, 1963, YIVO, RG 113, box 3, pp. 1–2.

27. There were 326 permanent congregations on the Lower East Side as of 1907, mostly small *landsmanshaft* (hometown association) synagogues, which rarely had their own rabbis. Arthur Goren, *New York Jews and the Quest for Community: The Kehilla Experiment, 1908–1922* (New York: Columbia University Press, 1970), p. 20.

28. Ibid., pp. 88, 110–133; Jonathan D. Sarna, *American Judaism: A History* (New Haven, Conn.: Yale University Press, 2004), pp. 161–162; Jeffrey S. Gurock, *American Jewish Orthodoxy in Historical Perspective* (Hoboken, N.J.: KTAV Publishing House, 1996), pp. 1–26; Abraham J. Karp, "New York Chooses a Chief Rabbi," *Publications of the American Jewish Historical Society* 44 (1954): 129–135; Charles L. Liebman, "Religion, Class, and Culture in American Jewish History," *Jewish Journal of Sociology* 9, no. 2 (Dec. 1967): 227–242.

29. Thus the Alliance president, Rabbi Bernard Drachman, wrote to ILGWU president Benjamin Schlessinger in 1916: "Our society urgently appeals to you . . . to see to it that the unions in the new contracts make with the employers when the strike is over, insert a provision that Jewish workingmen, desiring to observe the Jewish Sabbath and holidays, shall have the full right to do so without molestation or danger of dismissal on that account. . . . In times past this point has always been overlooked despite its great importance, as if there was no such thing as a Jewish Sabbath." Drachman to Schlessinger, May 5, 1916, Benjamin Schlessinger Collection, Kheel Center, Cornell University, box 1, folder 12.

30. Leonard Bloom, "A Successful Jewish Boycott of the New York City Public Schools—Christmas 1906," *American Jewish History* 70, no. 2 (Dec. 1980): 180–188; Gurock, *American Jewish Orthodoxy;* Jonathan D. Sarna, "Editor's Introduction" to Jonathan D. Sarna, ed. and trans., *People Walk on Their Heads: Moses Weinberger's Jews and Judaism in New York* (New York: Holmes and Meier, 1982), p. 14.

31. Yisroel Faden, "Der ershter shtrayk fun der Agudes-hamorim in shikage," undated memoir published in *Forverts,* Dec. 15, 2000, p. 23; Saposs, "'Unionizing the Brain Worker,'" p. 2.

32. Jenna Weissman Joselit, *New York's Jewish Jews: The Orthodox Community in the Interwar Years* (Bloomington: Indiana University Press, 1990), p. xiv.

33. Daniel Blatman, "The Bund in Poland, 1935–1939," *Polin* 9 (1996): 58–82; Dan Horowitz and Moshe Lissak, *Origins of the Israeli Polity: Palestine under the Mandate* (Chicago: University of Chicago Press, 1978); Zvi Gitelman, *Jewish Nationality and Soviet Politics: The Jewish Sections of the CPSU, 1917–1930* (Princeton, N.J.: Princeton University Press, 1972).

34. Ezra Mendelsohn, "Editor's Introduction," *YIVO Annual of Jewish Social Science* 16 (1976): v; Feingold, *Zion in America*, p. 158.

35. Nan Enstad, *Ladies of Labor, Girls of Adventure* (New York: Columbia University Press, 1999), pp. 84–120; Susan Glenn, *Daughters of the Shtetl: Life and Labor in the Immigrant Generation* (Ithaca, N.Y.: Cornell University Press, 1990); Alice Kessler-Harris, "Organizing the Unorganizable: Three Jewish Women and Their Union," *Labor History* 17 (Winter 1976): 5–23; Carolyn Daniel McCreesh, *Women in the Campaign to Organize Garment Workers 1880–1917* (New York: Garland, 1985); Annelise Orleck, *Common Sense and a Little Fire: Women and Working-Class Politics in the United States, 1900–1965* (Chapel Hill: University of North Carolina Press, 1995); Maxine Schwartz Seller, "The Uprising of the Twenty Thousand: Sex, Class and Ethnicity in the Shirtwaist Makers' Strike of 1909," in Dirk Hoerder, ed., *"Struggle a Hard Battle": Essays on Working-Class Immigrants* (De Kalb: Northern Illinois University Press, 1986); Roger Waldinger, "Another Look at the International Ladies' Garment Workers' Union: Women, Industry Structure and Collective Action," in Ruth Milkman, ed., *Women, Work, and Protest: A Century of U.S. Women's Labor History* (Boston: Routledge and Kegan Paul, 1985).

36. On *World of Our Fathers* and its legacy, see the symposium in *American Jewish History* 88, no. 4 (Dec. 2000). Other popular works from the period are Nora Levin, *While Messiah Tarried: Jewish Socialist Movements, 1871–1917* (New York: Schocken Books, 1977), and Ronald Sanders, *The Downtown Jews: Portraits of an Immigrant Generation* (New York: Harper and Row, 1969).

37. See, for example, Frankel, *Prophecy and Politics*, pp. 453–551, and Ezra Mendelsohn, "The Russian Roots of the American Jewish Labor Movement," *YIVO Annual* 16 (1976): 150–201. Notably, both Frankel and Mendelsohn are specialists in Russian history.

38. Steven M. Cohen, *American Assimilation or Jewish Revival* (Bloomington: Indiana University Press, 1988), pp. 1–24; Alan M. Dershowitz, *The Vanishing American Jew: In Search of a Jewish Identity for the Next Century* (Boston: Little, Brown, 1997); Hillel Halkin, *Letters to an American Jewish Friend: A Zionist Polemic* (Philadelphia: Jewish Publication Society of America, 1977).

39. Todd Endelman, "Response," in Shaye J. D. Cohen and Edward L. Greenstein, eds., *The State of Jewish Studies* (Detroit: Wayne State University Press,

1990), p. 162; Hasia Diner, "American Jewish History," in Martin Goodman, ed., *The Oxford Handbook of Jewish Studies* (Oxford: Oxford University Press, 2003), pp. 471–490; Paula Hyman, "The Ideological Transformation of Modern Jewish Historiography," in Cohen and Greenstein, eds., *The State of Jewish Studies,* pp. 143–157; scholar quoted in Sarna, *American Judaism,* p. xviii.

40. Russell A. Kazal, "Revisiting Assimilation: The Rise, Fall, and Reappraisal of a Concept in American Ethnic History," *American Historical Review* 100 (April 1995): 437–471.

41. Jonathan D. Sarna, "Introduction" to Jonathan D. Sarna, ed., *The American Jewish Experience* (New York: Holmes and Meier, 1997), pp. xiii–xix.

42. See, for example, Hasia R. Diner, *A Time for Gathering: The Second Migration, 1820–1880* (Baltimore: Johns Hopkins University Press, 1992); Arthur A. Goren, *The Politics and Public Culture of American Jews* (Bloomington: Indiana University Press, 1999), pp. 1–10; Deborah Dash Moore, *At Home in America: Second Generation New York Jews* (New York: Columbia University Press, 1983) and *To the Golden Cities: Pursuing the American Jewish Dream in Miami and L.A.* (New York: Free Press, 1994); Jenna Weissman Joselit, *The Wonders of America: Reinventing Jewish Culture, 1880–1950* (New York: Hill and Wang, 1994); Gerald Sorin, *Tradition Transformed: The Jewish Experience in America* (Baltimore: Johns Hopkins University Press, 1997). One notable exception is Eli Lederhendler, *New York Jews and the Decline of Urban Ethnicity, 1950–1970* (Syracuse, N.Y.: Syracuse University Press, 2001). In "describing a downward curve in the [New York Jewish] community's historical trajectory," however, Lederhendler explains that he does not intend "to revise the established historical picture altogether, but merely to add a restraining note" (p. 11).

43. Joselit, *Wonders of America,* p. 103; William Toll, "The 'New Social History' and Recent Jewish Historical Writing," *American Jewish History* 69, no. 3 (March 1980): 325–341.

44. For example, Deborah Dash Moore writes of Jews in Los Angeles and Miami in the post–World War II period: "Nowhere did the possibilities to start afresh, unhampered by the mistakes and burdens of the past, appear as vividly as in the two American dream cities by the ocean. . . . The future lay ahead, filled with whatever one wanted to make of it. Here was the perfect setting for American Jewry's new age." Yet Moore's discussion of the civil rights movement in Miami and anti-Communism in Los Angeles shows that racism and anti-Semitism deprived civil rights activists, Communists, and fellow travelers of realizing "America's endless promise to reinvent themselves." Moore, *To the Golden Cities,* pp. 20, 263.

45. The lines between legitimate business practices and criminal activity

could be quite blurry. On this point, see Jay A. Gertzman, *Bookleggers and Smuthounds: The Trade in Erotica, 1920–1940* (Philadelphia: University of Pennsylvania Press, 1999), pp. 15–48. Three books that examine the economic life of middle-class and aspiring middle-class Jews in detail include Diner, *A Time for Gathering*, pp. 60–85; Eva Morawska, *Insecure Prosperity: Small-Town Jews in Industrial America, 1890–1940* (Princeton, N.J.: Princeton University Press, 1996), pp. 31–71; Beth S. Wenger, *New York Jews and the Great Depression: Uncertain Promise* (New Haven, Conn.: Yale University Press), pp. 10–32. All three complicate or partially question the standard narrative of economic success.

46. Tony Michels, "Socialism and the Writing of American Jewish History: *World of Our Fathers* Reconsidered," *American Jewish History* 88, no. 4 (Dec. 2000): 521–546.

47. Will Herberg, "The Jewish Labor Movement in the United States," *American Jewish Yearbook* 53 (1952): 65.

48. Marc Dollinger, *Quest for Inclusion: Jews and Liberalism in Modern America* (Princeton, N.J.: Princeton University Press, 2000), 7; Feingold, *Zion in America*, 169–172; Rischin, *The Promised City*, 168; Gerald Sorin, "Tradition and Change: American Jewish Socialists as Agents of Acculturation," *American Jewish History* 79 (Autumn 1989): 37–54. For a related discussion of "functionalist" and "intentionalist" interpretations of Jewish socialism, see Eli Lederhendler, *Jewish Responses to Modernity: New Voices in America and Eastern Europe* (New York: New York University Press, 1994), 129–132.

49. See the symposium in *American Jewish History* 77 (Dec. 1988).

50. Mitchell Cohen, "A Preface to the Study of Modern Jewish Political Thought," *Jewish Social Studies*, 9 (n.s.), no. 2 (Winter 2003): 1–27. For suggestive comparisons between blacks and Jews regarding this theme, see Mendelsohn, *On Modern Jewish Politics*, pp. 127–139; Robert Philipson, *The Identity Question: Blacks and Jews in Europe and America* (Jackson: University Press of Mississippi, 2000), pp. ix–29.

51. Jack Jacobs, *On Marxists and the Jewish Question after Marx* (New York: New York University Press, 1992); Enzo Traverso, *The Marxists and the Jewish Question: The History of a Debate, 1843–1943*, trans. Bernard Gibbons (Atlantic Highlands, N.J.: Humanities, 1994).

52. See, for example, Frankel, *Prophecy and Politics*, pp. 464–547; Annie Polland, "'May a Free Thinker Help a Pious Man?': The Shared World of the 'Religious' and the 'Secular'" (paper presented at the Association for Jewish Studies annual conference, Dec. 2001).

53. Cahan, "Tsu di yidishe arbeter fun di Fareynikte shtatn un kanade," *Di arbeter tsaytung*, Dec. 5, 1890, reprinted in Tsherikover, ed., *Geshikhte*, vol. 2,

p. 501. By contrast, German socialists viewed themselves as heirs to the finest in German-language literature, music, and scholarship, which they sought to perpetuate across future generations. Brigitte Emig, *Die Veredlung des Arbeiters* (Frankfurt: Campus-Verlag, 1980), pp. 9–18; Hartmut Keil, *German Workers' Culture in the United States, 1850–1920* (Washington, D.C.: Smithsonian Institution Press, 1988).

54. Miller, "Vos zol men ton?" p. 18; Randolph S. Bourne, "The Jew and Trans-National America," *The Menorah Journal* 2 (Dec. 1916): 277–284; Horace Kallen, "Democracy versus the Melting-Pot: A Study of American Nationality," *Nation*, Feb. 18 and 25, 1915, reprinted in Horace Kallen, *Culture and Democracy in the United States*, intro. Stephen J. Whitfield (New Brunswick, N.J.: Transaction, 1998), pp. 59–117.

55. S. K. Shneyfal, "Dos naye lebn," *Di tsukunft* (Jan. 1909): 54.

1. Coming to Shore

1. Shoel Yanovsky, *Ershte yorn fun yidishn frayhaytlekhn sotsyalizm* (New York: Fraye Arbeter Shtime, 1948), p. 91.

2. As used by Jews during the 1880s, the term "intellectual" referred to someone who had received some level of formal, secular education in Russia and had radical political sympathies. With the rise of the Jewish labor movement, the term "intellectual" also referred to people engaged in the production and dissemination of ideas (e.g., journalists, creative writers, lecturers), most but not all of whom were Russian-educated.

3. This estimate is based on the circulation of *Znamia*, New York's only Russian newspaper as of 1890, which was edited and read almost entirely by Jewish intellectuals. According to Robert A. Karlowich, *Znamia*'s circulation reached about eight hundred, but the actual number of readers was undoubtedly higher, since typically more than one person read a single issue of a newspaper. Karlowich, *We Fall and Rise: Russian-Language Newspapers in New York City, 1889–1914* (Metuchen, N.J.: Scarecrow Press, 1991), p. 64.

4. Ezra Mendelsohn, "The Russian Roots of the American Jewish Labor Movement," *YIVO Annual of Jewish Social Science* 16 (1976): 156.

5. Ibid., pp. 166–167.

6. George M. Price, "The Russian Jew in America," part 2 (trans. Leo Shpall), *Publication of the American Jewish Historical Society* 48, no. 2 (Dec. 1958): 130.

7. Steven Cassedy, *To the Other Shore: The Russian Jewish Intellectuals Who Came to America* (Princeton, N.J.: Princeton University Press, 1997), p. xxi.

Although Mendelsohn traces an evolution away from Russian influences, he minimizes the German socialist influence without explanation and ignores the Great Upheaval altogether. I disagree with Mendelsohn on those two important points, but I am indebted to his analysis in most other respects. Mendelsohn, "Russian Roots," p. 168.

8. In 1880 there were 7,004 Jewish boys enrolled in gymnasia and several thousand Jewish girls in technical schools and all-female gymnasia. Six years later the number of male Jews in gymnasia would climb to 9,225. Steven G. Rappaport, "Jewish Education and Jewish Culture in the Russian Empire, 1880–1914" (Ph.D. diss., Stanford University, 2000); Yehudah Salutski, "Tsmihatah shel ha-inteligentsia ha-yehudit ha-rusitit," in Emmanuel Etkes, ed., *Ha-dat veha-hayim: Tenuat ha-haskalah ha-yehudit be-mizrah eropah* (Jerusalem: Merkaz Zalman Shazar le-toldot Yisra'el, 1993), p. 287; Michael Stanislawski, "Russian Jewry, the Russian State, and the Dynamics of Jewish Emancipation," in Pierre Birnbaum and Ira Katznelson, eds., *Paths of Emancipation: Jews, States, Citizenship* (Princeton, N.J.: Princeton University Press, 1995), p. 263.

9. Gregory Weinstein, *The Ardent Eighties* (New York: International Press, 1928), p. 9. On the Jewish "student subculture," see Benjamin Nathans, *Beyond the Pale: The Jewish Encounter with Late Imperial Russia* (Berkeley: University of California Press, 2003), pp. 239–256.

10. E. Tsherikover, "Yidn-revolutsyonern in Rusland in di 60er yorn un 70er yorn," *Historishe shriftn* 3 (1939): 60–72.

11. Martin Malia, "What Is the Intelligentsia?" in Richard Pipes, ed., *The Russian Intelligentsia* (New York: Columbia University Press, 1961), p. 2; Philip Pomper, *The Russian Revolutionary Intelligentsia* (Wheeling, Ill.: H. Davidson, 1993), pp. 1–2.

12. Cassedy, *To the Other Shore*, pp. 3–48; Erich Haberer, *Jews and Revolution in Nineteenth-Century Russia* (Cambridge: Cambridge University Press, 1995), pp. 1–26; Mendelsohn, "Russian Roots," pp. 157–158.

13. Jonathan Frankel has made perhaps the most cogent case for the year 1881–1882 as a watershed. Frankel, *Prophecy and Politics: Socialism, Nationalism, and the Russian Jews, 1862–1917* (Cambridge: Cambridge University Press, 1981), and "The Crisis of 1881–82 as a Turning Point in Modern Jewish History," in David Berger, ed., *The Legacy of Jewish Migration: 1881 and Its Impact* (New York: Brooklyn College Press, 1983), pp. 9–22. Several Russian Jewish historians, however, have made important qualifications and, in at least one case, rejected the idea that the pogroms triggered a "revolution" in Russian Jewish life. Eli Lederhendler, *The Road to Modern Jewish Politics: Political Tradition and Political Reconstruction in the Jewish Community of Tsarist Russia* (New York:

Oxford University Press, 1989); Nathans, *Beyond the Pale,* pp. 7–10; Michael Stanislawski, *For Whom Do I Toil? Judah Leib Gordon and the Crisis of Russian Jewry* (New York: Oxford University Press, 1988). Even so, Frankel remains convincing in showing that the pogroms produced a profound (if not total) change in the politics of Russian Jewry by giving rise to autonomous Jewish socialist and nationalist movements. As Frankel points out, the medium-range political ramifications of the pogroms were more apparent in New York than in Russia, inasmuch as a distinct Jewish labor movement arose there first.

14. I. Michael Aronson, "The Pogroms of 1881–1884," in John D. Klier and Shlomo Lambroza, eds., *Pogroms: Anti-Jewish Violence in Modern Russian History* (Cambridge: Cambridge University Press, 1992), pp. 39–61; Alexander Orbach, "The Development of the Russian Jewish Community, 1881–1903" in Klier and Lambroza, eds., *Pogroms,* p. 143. Starting in the 1890s, female Jewish students began to be affected by restrictive quotas, though to a lesser extent than men.

15. Frankel, *Prophecy and Politics,* pp. 96–100; Haberer, *Jews and Revolution,* pp. 206–229. In contrast to Norodnaia Volia, the smaller revolutionary group Chernyi Peled condemned the pogroms. Moshe Mishkinsky, "'Black Repartition' and the Pogroms of 1881–1882," in Klier and Lambroza, eds., *Pogroms,* pp. 319–341.

16. Boris D. Bogen, *Born a Jew* (New York: Macmillan, 1930), p. 13; the Moscow student is quoted in Frankel, *Prophecy and Politics,* p. 92; "The Diary of Dr. George M. Price," in *Publication of the American Jewish Historical Society,* no. 40, part 2 (Dec. 1950): 174–175.

17. Frankel, *Prophecy and Politics,* p. 91; Bogen, *Born a Jew,* p. 13; Abraham Cahan, *The Education of Abraham Cahan,* trans. Leon Stein et al. (Philadelphia: Jewish Publication Society of America, 1969), p. 182. The long-term affects of the pogroms on Russian Jewish students, however, were more ambiguous. Many remained loyal to the revolutionary movement and more would join during the 1880s and 1890s. Haberer, *Jews and Revolution,* pp. 221–229; Nathans, *Beyond the Pale,* pp. 254–256.

18. Quoted in Frankel, *Prophecy and Politics,* p. 95; quoted in Abraham Menes, "Di 'Am Oylom' bavegung," in Eliyohu Tsherikover, ed., *Geshikhte fun der yidisher arbeter bavegung in di fareynikte shtatn,* vol. 2 (New York: YIVO, 1945), p. 212.

19. Cahan, *Education,* p. 182.

20. Menes, "Di 'Am Oylom' bavegung," pp. 226–238; Mendelsohn, "Russian Roots," p. 155.

21. Y. Lifshits and E. Tsherikover, "Di pionern-tkufe fun der yidisher

arbeter-bavegung," in Tsherikover, ed., *Geshikhte*, vol. 2, p. 267; Cahan, *Education*, p. 254.

22. Mendelsohn, "Russian Roots," p. 156; Kh. Spivak, "Erinerungen fun Kahan's grine tsaytn," in *Yubeleum-shrift tsu Ab. Kahan's 50stn geburtstog* (New York: Forverts, 1910), pp. 31–32; Cahan, *Education*, p. 255.

23. I. Kopelov, *Amol in Amerike: zikhroynes fun dem yidishn lebn in Amerike in di yorn 1883–1904* (Warsaw: Farlag Kh. Bzhoza, 1928), p. 130; Kalman Marmor, *Dovid Edelshtat* (New York: IKUF Farlag, 1952), pp. 25–26.

24. Kopelov, *Amol in Amerike*, pp. 138–139; Lifshits, "Di pionern-tkufe," pp. 269–272.

25. Yankev Gordin, "Der rusisher amerikanisher fareyn mit breyte idealn," in *Yankev Gordin's eyn-akters* (New York: Tog, 1917), p. 52. This version was translated from the Russian in 1916.

26. Kopelov, *Amol in Amerike*, pp. 140–141; Lifshits, "Di pionern-tkufe," pp. 270–272; Yanovsky, *Ershte yorn*, pp. 71–72.

27. Morris Hillquit, *Loose Leaves from a Busy Life* (New York: Rand School Press, 1934), p. 7.

28. M. Melamed, "Kinder yorn, dertsyung, un der ershter oystrit in der velt," in A. Frumkin and Khayim Faynman, eds., *Moyshe Kats zamlbukh* (Philadelphia: n.p., 1925), p. 16; Dr. Mikhl Kohn, "In Netter's keller," in B. Y. Bialostotsky, ed., *Dovid Edelshtat gedenk bukh* (New York: Dovid Edelshtat Komitetn, 1953), p. 184.

29. Spivak, "Erinerungen," p. 31.

30. Cahan, *Education*, pp. 228–229; Leon Kobrin, *Mayne fuftsik yor in Amerike* (New York: IKUF Farlag, 1966), pp. 191–200.

31. Hillquit, *Loose Leaves*, p. 7.

32. Cassedy, *To the Other Shore*, pp. 63–76, 109–145.

33. Cahan, *Education*, pp. 246–250; Kopelov, *Amol in Amerike*, p. 153; Spivak, "Erinerungen," p. 33.

34. Jacob Magidow, "Recollections of an Old Associate," in H. Lang and Morris C. Feinstone, eds., *Geverkshaftn* (New York: United Hebrew Trades, 1938), p. 29. On the German labor movement in New York, see Morris Hillquit, *History of Socialism in the United States* (New York: Funk and Wagnalls, 1910), pp. 177–278; Stanley Nadel, *Little Germany: Ethnicity, Religion, and Class in New York City, 1845–1880* (Urbana: University of Illinois Press, 1990), pp. 32, 41–42, 63; Dorothee Schneider, *Trade Unions and Community: The German Working Class in New York City, 1870–1900* (Urbana: University of Illinois Press, 1994), pp. 8, 15.

35. For an example of differing perceptions of Irish and Germans, see letter to the editor, *Di arbeter tsaytung*, Dec. 2, 1894, p. 6.

36. Eric Foner, "Class, Ethnicity, and Radicalism in the Gilded Age: The Land League and Irish America," in Eric Foner, ed., *Politics and Ideology in the Age of the Civil War* (New York: Oxford University Press, 1980), p. 187; David Brundage, "'In Time of Peace, Prepare for War': Key Themes in the Social Thought of New York's Irish Nationalists, 1890–1916," in Ronald H. Bayor and Timothy J. Meagher, eds., *The New York Irish* (Baltimore: Johns Hopkins University Press, 1996), pp. 321–334; John R. McKivigan and Thomas J. Robertson, "The Irish American Worker in Transition, 1877–1914: New York City as a Test Case," in Bayor and Meagher, eds., *The New York Irish*, pp. 301–320.

37. On German socialist attitudes toward German-language literature, music, and scholarship, see Brigitte Emig, *Die Veredlung des Arbeiters: Sozialdemokratie als Kulturbewegung* (Frankfurt: Campus-Verlag, 1980), pp. 9–18; Hartmut Keil, *German Workers' Culture in the United States, 1850–1920* (Washington, D.C.: Smithsonian Institution Press, 1988).

38. Samuel Gompers, *Seventy Years of Life and Labor: An Autobiography*, vol. 1 (New York: E. P. Dutton, 1925), pp. 99–100; advertisement quoted in Paul Avrich, *The Haymarket Tragedy* (Princeton, N.J.: Princeton University Press, 1984), p. 50; Yoysef Kahan, *Di yidish-anarkhistishe bavegung in Amerike* (Philadelphia: Workmen's Circle, 1945), pp. 112–113; Emma Goldman, *Living My Life*, vol. 1 (1931; rept., New York: Dover, 1970), p. 119; Cahan, *Education*, pp. 257–258; obituary for Schwab in *Forverts*, Dec. 18 and 19, 1900.

39. Schneider, *Trade Unions and Community*, p. 47.

40. Avrich, *The Haymarket Tragedy*, p. 55; Frederic Trautmann, *The Voice of Terror: A Biography of Johann Most* (Westport, Conn.: Greenwood Press, 1980), pp. 18–26, 115–116. On Most and the social revolutionaries and anarchists in the United States, see Hillquit, *History of Socialism in the United States*, p. 215; Bruce C. Nelson, *Beyond the Martyrs: A Social History of Chicago's Anarchists, 1870–1900* (New Brunswick, N.J.: Rutgers University Press, 1988); Raymond C. Sun, "Misguided Martyrdom: German Social Democratic Response to the Haymarket Incident, 1886–1887," *International Labor and Working Class History*, no. 29 (Spring 1986): 54–56.

41. Edelshtat's letter is reprinted (in Yiddish translation) in Marmor, *Dovid Edelshtat*, p. 190; Y. A. Benekvit, *Durkhgelebt un durkhgetrakht* (New York: Farlag Kultur Federatsye, 1934), p. 57; Goldman, *Living My Life*, vol. 1, pp. 42, 43; Weinstein, *The Ardent Eighties*, pp. 57–58.

42. Kopelov, *Amol in Amerike*, p. 114; Khayim Leyb Vaynberg, *Fertsik yor in*

kamf far sotsyaler bafrayung (Los Angeles: Los Angeles Vaynberg Book Committee, 1952), p. 26.

43. Yanovsky, *Ershte yorn*, p. 60; Goldman, *Living My Life*, vol. 1, p. 9. On the German American socialist press, see Elliott Shore et al., eds., *The German American Radical Press: The Shaping of a Left Political Culture, 1850–1940* (Urbana: University of Illinois Press, 1992).

44. The first Russian newspaper would not appear until 1889. Karlowich, *We Fall and Rise*, pp. 39–43.

45. Kopelov, *Amol in Amerike*, pp. 124–125. Cahan, *Education*, p. 227; Leon Koenig, "Die Volkszeitung und die jüdischen Arbeiter," Jan. 29, 1928, reprinted in Dirk Hoerder, ed., *Labor Newspaper Preservation Project* (Bremen, Germany: Universität Bremen, 1985), p. 116. For similar recollections of the German press, see Benekvit, *Durkhgelebt*, p. 51; Melamed, "Kinder-yorn," pp. 16–17; Simon Ritsh, "Tsu der forgeshikhte fun der 'Fraye arbeter shtime,'" *Di fraye arbeter shtime*, Jan. 29, 1943, p. 8; Weinstein, *The Ardent Eighties*, pp. 32, 30.

46. Trautmann, *The Voice of Terror*, p. 82; Max Pine, "Teg vos zaynen avek," in Lang and Feinstone, eds., *Geverkshaftn;* M. Vintshevsky, "25 yor sotsyalistishe arbet," in M. Terman, ed., *Dos yidishe yorbukh 1915* (New York: Jewish Socialist Federation, 1915), p. 32. See also "The Reminiscences of Joseph Schlossberg," Oral History Collection, Columbia University, pp. 7–10.

47. Cahan, *Education*, p. 228.

48. "The Red Flag," unidentified newspaper clipping, YIVO, RG 213, box 1, unnumbered folder.

49. Cahan, *Education*, p. 228; Yanovsky, *Ershte yorn*, p. 81.

50. It was originally called the Russian Workingmen's Party, but it changed its name to the Russian Jewish Workers' Association in February. Lifshits, "Di yidishe sotsyalistishe bavegung in di 80er yorn," p. 285.

51. Cahan, *Education*, p. 305; Frankel, *Prophecy and Politics*, p. 54; Lifshits, "Di pionern-tkufe," pp. 272–275, 485–486; obituary for Numia Gretsh, *Di arbeter tsaytung*, Dec. 16, 1894, p. 1.

52. N. Goldberg, "Leybor dey," *Di tsukunft* (Sept. 1944): 543–544; Lifshits, "Di pionern-tkufe," pp. 250–253, 493.

53. Jeremy Brecher, *Strike! The True History of Mass Insurgency in America* (San Francisco: Straight Arrow Books, 1972); Gerald N. Grob, *Workers and Utopia: A Study of Ideological Conflict in the American Labor Movement* (Evanston, Ill.: Northwestern University Press, 1961), pp. 73–76, 86, 108; Bruce Laurie, *Artisans into Workers: Labor in Late Nineteenth-Century America* (Urbana: University of Illinois Press, 1989), pp. 156–176; Selig Perlman, *History of Trade Unionism in the United States* (New York: Macmillan, 1937), pp. 81–105.

54. Leon Fink, *Workingmen's Democracy: The Knights of Labor in American Politics* (Urbana: University of Illinois Press, 1983); Grob, *Workers and Utopia*, pp. 86–87; Perlman, *History of Trade Unionism*, p. 93; Richard Schneirov, *Labor and Urban Politics: Class Conflict and the Origins of Modern Liberalism in Chicago, 1864–97* (Urbana: University of Illinois Press, 1998), pp. 211–235.

55. Bureau of Statistics of New York State, untitled report (New York, 1887); Michael A. Gordon, "The Labor Boycott in New York City, 1880–1886," *Labor History* 16, no. 2 (Spring 1975): 184–229; *New York Sun*, May 2, 1886, p. 1; Schneider, *Trade Unions and Community*.

56. Moses Rischin, *The Promised City: New York's Jews, 1870–1914* (Cambridge, Mass.: Harvard University Press, 1962), p. 224.

57. *New York Sun*, March 24 and 26, 1886, p. 3.

58. *New York Times*, March 25, 1886, p. 3; Bernard Vaynshteyn, *Yidishe yunyons in Amerike* (New York: United Hebrew Trades, 1929), pp. 315–317.

59. Cahan, *Education*, p. 326; Yanovsky, *Ershte yorn*, p. 9; M. Zametkin, "Unzer ershter kompromis," *Tsayt-gayst* (1907): 8. See also Kopelov, *Amol in Amerike*, p. 189.

60. Weinstein, *The Ardent Eighties*, p. 144.

61. In addition to weekly reports published in *Di nyu-yorker yidishe folkstsaytung*, see Herts Burgin, *Geshikhte fun der yidisher arbeter bavegung* (New York: United Hebrew Trades, 1915), pp. 106–109; Avrom Rozenberg, *Erinerungen fun di kloukmakher un zeyere yunyons* (New York: Klok Opereytors Yunyon Lokal 1, 1920), p. 8; Sh. Sheynfeld, *Fuftsik yor yidishe shriftzetser yunyon* (New York: YIVO, 1938), pp. 17–18; N. Goldberg, "Di yidishe sotsyalistishe bavegung in di 80er yorn," in Tsherikover, ed., *Geshikhte*, vol. 2, pp. 287–295; Vaynshteyn, *Yidishe yunyons*, pp. 125–127, 276.

62. A notable exception was the idiosyncratic figure Alexander Harkavy, who was a Yiddishist, Hebraist, proponent of Americanization, and anarchist all at the same time. In 1886 Harkavy published a philological treatise that set out to prove Yiddish's credentials as a legitimate language rather than an inferior dialect of German. Harkavy, *Shprakh-visnshaftlekhe biblyotek* (New York: Yidishe Gazeth, 1886). I thank Eric Goldstein for sharing this source with me. On Harkavy, see Dovid Katz, "Alexander Harkavy and His Trilingual Dictionary," introduction to the 1988 edition of Harkavy's *Yiddish-English-Hebrew Dictionary* (YIVO Institute for Jewish Research and Schocken Books, 1988), and Eliyohu Shulman, "Alexander Harkavy vi a redaktor," in *Portretn un etyuden* (New York: Bikher Farlag, 1979), p. 421.

63. On similarly negative attitudes toward Yiddish among *maskilim*, see

Dan Miron, *A Traveler Disguised: The Rise of Modern Yiddish Fiction in the Nineteenth Century* (Syracuse, N.Y.: Syracuse University Press, 1996), pp. 34–66.

64. Spivak, "Erinerungen," p. 35; Ab. Cahan, *Bleter fun mayn lebn* vol. 2 (New York: Forverts Association, 1926), p. 193. Yanovsky, *Ershte yorn*, p. 86.

65. Yanovsky, *Ershte yorn*, p. 87.

66. Cahan, *Education*, pp. 307–310; Kobrin, *Mayne fufstik yor*, pp. 178–181; Moyshe Shtarkman, "Tsum onhoyb fun der yidisher arbeter prese," in *Geklibene shriftn* (Tel Aviv: 1979), pp. 106–110.

67. See the following articles in the *Folkstsaytung*: "Di program," June 25, 1886, p. 1; "A por verter vegn unzer tsaytung," July 23, 1886, p. 2; "Unzer tsaytung," Oct. 8, 1886, p. 1; "Tsum geburtstog fun 'Shloyme yosl's organ,'" June 24, 1887, p. 1. On the *Folkstsaytung*, see Y. Lifshits, "Di nyu-yorker yidishe folkstsaytung," in Hyman Bass, ed., *Pinkes far der forshung far der yidisher literatur un prese*, vol. 3 (New York: Alveltlekher Yidisher Kultur Kongres, 1975).

68. Jonathan Sarna, ed. and trans., *People Walk on Their Heads: Moses Weinberger's Jews and Judaism in New York* (New York: Holmes and Meier, 1982), p. 70.

69. "Troubles of the Jewish Gazette," *American Hebrew*, Aug. 27, 1886, p. 40; "The Jewish Workingman's Union," *American Hebrew*, Oct. 1, 1886, p. 123; Sheynfeld, *Fuftsik yor yidishe shriftzetser yunyon*, pp. 17–18.

70. Rischin, *The Promised City*, pp. 172–173; Perlman, *Trade Unionism in America*, pp. 102–105; Schneider, *Trade Unions and Community*, pp. 119–129.

71. Zametkin, "Unzer ershter kompromis," p. 8.

72. *Folkstsaytung*, Oct. 13, 1886, p. 3; Goldberg, "Di yidishe sotsyalistishe bavegung," pp. 290–296; Weinstein, *The Ardent Eighties*, p. 34.

73. Rischin, *The Promised City*, pp. 119, 224.

74. Thomas J. Condon, "Political Reform and the New York City Election of 1886," *New York Historical Quarterly* 44, no. 4 (Oct. 1960): 391; Rischin, *The Promised City*, p. 173.

75. "Der groyser zig," *Folkstsaytung*, Nov. 12, 1886, p. 1.

76. Yanovsky, *Ershte yorn*, p. 90.

77. N. Goldberg, "Pionere der frayhayt," in Tsherikover, ed., *Geshikhte*, vol. 2, pp. 305–307.

78. Magidow, "Recollections of an Old Associate," p. 30; Herman Frank, "Di onheyb fun der treyd-yunyon-bavegung," in Tsherikover, ed., *Geshikhte*, vol. 2, pp. 346–394; Goldberg, "Di yidishe sotsyalistishe bavegung," pp. 291–294; Rischin, *The Promised City*, p. 174. On the structure of the garment industry, see Nancy Green, *Ready-to-Wear and Ready-to-Work: A Century of Industry and Im-*

migrants in New York and Paris (Durham, N.C.: Duke University Press, 1997), pp. 137–160.

79. Hartmut Kiel, "The Impact of Haymarket on German-American Radicalism," *International Labor and Working Class History* 29 (Spring 1986): 14–17; Laurie, *Artisans into Workers*, p. 177.

80. "My idea was to set up a copy of the German organization," recalls the UHT's first national secretary, Jacob Magidow. Magidow, "Recollections of an Old Associate," p. 29; Herman Frank, "Di Fareynikte yidishe geverkshaftn un di yidishe arbeter-federatsye, in Tsherikover, ed., *Geshikhte*, vol. 2, pp. 395–417; Morris U. Schappes, "The Political Origins of the United Hebrew Trades, 1888," *Journal of Ethnic Studies* 5, no. 1 (Spring 1977): pp. 13–44.

81. Goldberg, "Pionere der frayhayt," in Tsherikover, ed., *Geshikhte*, vol. 2, pp. 297–318. The roots of Yiddish socialism in other major cities have yet to be adequately researched, but evidence suggests that dynamics similar to those in New York were at work. See Abraham Bisno, *Abraham Bisno, Union Pioneer* (Madison: University of Wisconsin Press, 1967), pp. 75–77, and Kopelov, *Amol in Amerike*, pp. 107, 118–119.

82. [Boris] Bogen, "Mimokhdom: Prosvetiteli immigrantov," *Nedel'naia khronika voskhoda* 13, no. 23 (June 1894): 643.

83. Emmanuel Goldsmith, *Modern Yiddish Culture: The Story of the Modern Yiddish Language Movement* (New York: Fordham University Press, 1997), pp. 45–69; Miron, *A Traveler Disguised*, pp. 1–33.

84. For two points of contrast, see Gennady Estraikh, "From Yehupets Jargonists to Kiev Modernists: The Rise of a Yiddish Literary Center, 1880s–1914," *East European Jewish Affairs* 30 (2000): 17–28, and Chone Shmeruk, "Aspects of the History of Warsaw as a Yiddish Literary Centre," *Polin* 3 (1988): 142–155.

85. *Folkstaytung*, March 25, 1887, p. 3.

86. Cahan, "Tsu di yidishe arbeter fun di Fareynikte shtatn un Kanade," *Di arbeter tsaytung*, Dec. 5, 1890, reprinted in Tsherikover, ed., *Geshikhte*, vol. 2, p. 501.

87. See Kohn's letter in *Workmen's Advocate*, April 13, 1889, p. 3.

88. I. Krants, "Nastoiashchee pole deiatel'nosti. Pis'mo v redaktsiiu," *Znamia*, Feb. 15, 1890, pp. 1–2.

89. On the Hebrew press, see Arthur A. Goren, "The Jewish Press," in Sally M. Miller, ed., *The Ethnic Press in the United States: A Historical Analysis and Handbook* (Westport, Conn.: Greenwood Press, 1987), pp. 213–214; J. K. Miklizsanski, "Hebrew Literature in the United States," in *The Jewish People Past and Present*, vol. 4 (New York: Jewish Encyclopedic Handbooks, 1955), p. 308;

Khayim M. Rotblat, "Ha-itonut ha-ivrit be-shikago," in *Pinkas Shikago* (Chicago: College of Jewish Studies, 1951), pp. 36–40.

90. Cassedy, *To the Other Shore*, pp. 65–73; Karlowich, *We Fall and Rise*, pp. 24–25; Tony Michels, "Speaking to 'Moyshe': The Early Yiddish Press in the United States," *Jewish History* 14, no. 1 (2000): 40. Not until the second decade of the twentieth century would Russian newspapers achieve some stability.

91. Christine Stansell, *American Moderns: Bohemian New York and the Creation of a New Century* (New York: Metropolitan Books, 2000), pp. 64–65.

92. Konrad Bercovici, *It's the Gypsy in Me* (New York: Prentice-Hall, 1941), p. 51. I thank Yael Lifschutz for bringing this source to my attention.

93. See "Notitsn far an otobiografye," manuscript, YIVO, RG 251, folder 11, p. G. Edlin made this move against the advice of his close friend Anna Strunsky, who tried to convince Edlin that he was wasting his talents in the Jewish labor movement. See Anna Strunsky to Edlin, Jan. 24 and Nov. 10, 1897, YIVO, RG 251, folder 229. Strunsky moved to New York several years later and became a prominent figure in various radical and reform causes, eventually marrying the "millionaire socialist" William English Walling. On Strunsky, see James R. Boylan, *Revolutionary Lives: Anna Strunsky and William English Walling* (Amherst: University of Massachusetts Press, 1998).

94. Adolph Held, transcribed interview, YIVO, RG 113, box 2, pt. 3, p. 2; Hillel Rogoff, *Der gayst fun "Forverts"* (New York: Forverts, 1954), pp. 23–28.

95. Other émigrés from London during the 1890s included M. Baranov, Benyomen Faygnboym, Avrom Frumkin, Philip Krants, and Y. Yoffe.

96. Quoted in Frankel, *Prophecy and Politics*, p. 192.

97. E. Tsherikover, "Di onheyb fun der umlegaler literatur in Yidish," *Historishe shriftn* 3 (1939): 599–600. The government decree is reprinted on p. 801 of this volume.

98. Frankel, *Prophecy and Politics*, pp. 185–200; Ezra Mendelsohn, *Class Struggle in the Pale: The Formative Years of the Jewish Workers' Movement in Tsarist Russia* (Cambridge: Cambridge University Press, 1970), pp. 27–44; Joshua D. Zimmerman, *Poles, Jews, and the Politics of Nationality* (Madison: University of Wisconsin Press, 2004) pp. 36–68.

99. B. Faygnboym, "Di yidish-sotsyalistishe post fun Amerike (1886)," *Historishe shriftn* 3 (1939): 766; Sh. Epshteyn, "Di tsukunft, der Bund, un di yidishe literatur," *Di tsukunft* (Jan. 1912): 69–70; Frants Kursky, "Di 'Tsukunft' in untererdishe Rusland," in *Gezamlte shriftn* (New York: Veker, 1952), pp. 250–260; Sholem Levin, *Untererdishe kemfer* (New York: Sh. Levin Bukh-Komte, 1946), p. 106; A. Litvak, "Di rol fun der revolutsyonerer lid in der arbeter-bavegung," in N. Oyslander et al., eds., *Yidishe literatur* (Kiev: Kultur Lige, 1928), p. 324, and A.

Litvak, "Di krayzlekh," in *Geklibene shriftn* (New York: Arbeter Ring, 1945), pp. 209–210.

100. Quoted in Frankel, *Prophecy and Politics*, p. 194.

101. Cahan, *Education*, p. 337.

2. Speaking to "Moyshe"

1. Moses Rischin, *The Promised City: New York's Jews, 1870–1914* (Cambridge, Mass.: Harvard University Press, 1962), pp. 226–227.

2. Hubert Perrier, "The Socialists and the Working Class in New York: 1890–1896," *Labor History* 22, no. 4 (Fall 1981): 501; *Di arbeter tsaytung*, Oct. 28, 1892, p. 3; "Politik fun nuyorker sotsialistn," *Di yidishe gazetn*, Nov. 2, 1894, p. 17.

3. Jurgen Habermas, "The Public Sphere," *New German Critique* 1, no. 3 (Fall 1974): 49. Of course, Habermas originally formulated his idea of the public sphere in connection with the liberal bourgeoisie of early modern Europe, but it has since been elaborated and revised in a considerable body of scholarship. See Craig Calhoun, ed., *Habermas and the Public Sphere* (Cambridge, Mass.: MIT Press, 1992).

4. Moses Rischin, "Introduction" to Hutchins Hapgood, *The Spirit of the Ghetto*, ed. Moses Rischin (Cambridge, Mass.: Belknap Press of Harvard University Press, 1967), p. xxvi.

5. An exception is Ruth Gay, *Unfinished People: Eastern European Jews Encounter America* (New York: W. W. Norton, 1996), pp. 3–13. Gay pays little attention to socialism, however, and depicts this in-between generation not as self-assertive and confident, as I do, but generally weary of the larger society. Simon Kuznets, "Immigration of Russian Jews to the United States: Structure and Background," *Perspectives in American History* 9 (1975): 94–98.

6. Samuel Chotzinoff, *A Lost Paradise* (New York: Knopf, 1955), p. 82.

7. S. L. Blumenson, "Culture on Rutgers Square," *Commentary*, July 1950, p. 71.

8. Jacob Panken, manuscript, Jacob Panken Collection, Wisconsin State Historical Society, Madison, box 1, folder 5, section 1, pp. 4–5; "The Reminiscences of Joseph Schlossberg," Oral History Collection, Columbia University, pp. 6–7. Also see, Y. A. Benekvit, *Durkhgelebt un durkhgetrakht*, vol. 2 (New York: Farlag Kultur Federatsye, 1934), pp. 55, 118; Adolph Held, transcribed interview, May 9, 1964, YIVO, RG 570, box 2, p. 5.

9. Ab. Cahan, *Bleter fun mayn lebn*, vol. 2 (New York: Forverts, 1926), pp. 106–109; Y. Lifshits and E. Tsherikover, "Di pionern-tkufe fun der yidisher

arbeter-bavegung," in E. Tsherikover, ed., *Geshikhte fun der yidisher arbeter bavegung* in di Fareynikte shtatn, vol. 2 (New York: YIVO Institute for Jewish Research, 1945), pp. 263–265; Bernard Vaynshteyn, *Fertsik yor in der yidisher arbeter bavegung* (New York: Der Veker, 1924), p. 45.

10. Miller, "Vos zol men ton?" *Di tsukunft* (April 1892): 15–20; Herts Burgin, "Aynflus fun der yidisher sotsyalistisher inteligents af der yidisher arbeter bavegung in di Fareynikte shtatn," *Yidishe kultur* (Sept. 1946): 32; Morris Hillquit, *Loose Leaves from a Busy Life* (New York: Rand School Press, 1934), 35; Yankev Milkh, "Der tsushtayer fun der yidisher arbeter bavegung in Amerike tsu der yidisher shprakh un kultur," *Yidishe kultur* (June 1939): 29; Bernard Vaynshteyn, *Yidishe yunyons in Amerike* (New York: United Hebrew Trades, 1929), 155.

11. "Der arbeter un di visnshaft," *Folkstsaytung*, June 6, 1886, p. 3; Louis Miller, "Vos zol men ton?" *Di tsukunft* (April 1892): 15–20; Herts Burgin, "Aynflus fun der yidisher sotsyalistisher inteligents af der yidisher arbeter bavegung in di Fareynikte shtatn," *Yidishe kultur* (Sept. 1946): 32; Morris Hillquit, *Loose Leaves from a Busy Life* (New York: Macmillan, 1934), p. 35; Yankev Milkh, "Der tsushtayer fun der yidisher arbeter bavegung in Amerike tsu der yidisher shprakh un kultur," *Yidishe kultur* (June 1939): 29; Bernard Vaynshteyn, *Yidishe yunyons in Amerike* (New York: United Hebrew Trades, 1929), p. 155.

12. Rischin, *Promised City,* pp. 115–143; Cecile Kuznitz, "'Who Is to Guide the Destiny of the East Side Russian Masses?': The Educational Alliance, the Educational League, and the Struggle to Become 'Good Americans'" (unpublished paper in possession of author).

13. Sh. Niger, "Sotsyalistisher oyfklerungs-literatur," *Di tsukunft* (Oct. 1941): 41–42.

14. Shmuel Feiner, "Toward a Historical Definition of the Haskalah," in Shmuel Feiner and David Sorkin, eds., *New Perspectives on the Haskalah* (London: Littman Library of Jewish Civilization, 2001), pp. 184–219.

15. The *Haskalah* contained a range of attitudes toward religion, language, education, and politics. During the 1870s a politically radical wing of the *Haskalah* emerged. See Emmanuel Etkes, ed., *Ha-dat veha-hayim: Tenuat ha-haskalah ha-yehudit be-mizrakh eropah* (Jerusalem: Merkaz Zalman Shazar le-toldot Yisrael, 1993); Feiner, "Toward a Historical Definition of the Haskalah," pp. 200–202.

16. Der farvaltung's rat, "2100 zaytn visnshaft," *Di tsukunft* (Jan. 1897): n.p.; B. Gorin, "Di rikhtung in der hayntiker hebreyisher literatur in Rusland," *Di tsukunft* (Feb. 1895): 76–79, and "Di hayntike hebreyishe beletristik," *Di tsukunft* (March 1895): 22; Ab. Cahan, "Tsu vintshungen," *Di tsukunft* (Jan. 1897): 49.

17. Abraham Cahan, "Tsu di yidishe arbeter fun di Fareynikte shtatn un Kanade," *Di arbeter tsaytung,* Dec. 5, 1890, reprinted in Tsherikover, ed., *Geshikhte,* vol. 2, p. 501.

18. Hartmut Keil, "German Working-Class Immigration and the Social Democratic Tradition of Germany," in Hartmut Keil, ed., *German Workers' Culture in the United States, 1850–1920* (Washington, D.C.: Smithsonian Institution Press, 1988), pp. 14, 10.

19. Vaynshteyn, *Fertsik yor,* pp. 107, 75.

20. *Di arbeter tsaytung,* April 22, 1892, p. 5; Leon Kobrin, *Mayne fuftsik yor in Amerike* (New York: IKUF Farlag, 1966), pp. 42–52; Vaynshteyn, *Fertsik yor,* pp. 164–165, 187.

21. Adam Bellow, *The Educational Alliance: A Centennial Celebration* (New York: Educational Alliance, 1990), p. 36.

22. George Esdras Bevans, *How Workingmen Spend Their Spare Time* (Master's thesis, Columbia University, 1913), pp. 31, 33–39. See Pauline Newman and Ella Wolf, transcribed interviews, Jan. 26, 1965, and Dec. 27, 1963, respectively, YIVO, RG 113, box 3 and box 4, respectively.

23. An altyunger, "Di lektshurs in yidishn kvartl," *Forverts,* Oct. 25, 1904, p. 4.

24. Leon Kobrin, "Khayim Leyb Vaynberg, der anarkhistisher redner," in Herman Frank, ed., *Fertsik yor in kam far sotsyaler bafrayung* (Los Angeles and Philadelphia: Farlag Yid. Bukh, 1952), p. 160. Also see Y. Kopelov, *Amol in Amerike* (Warsaw: Farlag Kh. Bhoza, 1928), p. 326; Yankev Milkh, "Tsum 20-yorikn yubiley fun 'Tsukunft,'" in Shmuel Niger, ed., *Der pinkes* (Vilnius: B. Kletskin, 1912), pp. 218–219, and "Etlekhe verter vegn zikh aleyn," *Yidishe kultur* (Jan. 1942): 10.

25. M. E. Ravage, *An American in the Making* (New York: Harper and Brothers, 1917), p. 148; Bernard Fenster, transcribed interview, Dec. 6, 1963, YIVO, RG 113, box 4, p. 10; Held, interview, p. 9.

26. Yankev Magidov, *Der shpigl fun der Ist-sayd* (New York: Self-published, 1923), p. 18.

27. Cahan, *Bleter,* vol. 3, p. 198; Ab. Cahan, *Oylem haze un oylem habo fun der arbeter bavegung* (n.p., n.d.) (YIVO, RG 1139, folder 7a), p. 8; Magidov, *Der shpigl,* pp. 28–29.

28. Cahan, *Oylem haze,* pp. 18–19.

29. Cahan, *Bleter,* vol. 3, pp. 217–221.

30. Kobrin, *Mayne fuftsik yor in Amerike,* pp. 276–277.

31. Panken, manuscript, section 1, pp. 4–5; reports of the tour are in *Di arbeter tsaytung,* May 11 and May 18, 1894.

32. Yankev Milkh, *Di anshteyung fun "Forverts"* (New York: Yankev Milkh, 1936), p. 36; Y. B. Beylin, "Filip Krants—Der ershter redaktor fun a sotsyalistisher tsaytung in yidish," *Di morgn frayhayt,* Feb. 5, 1956, p. 15.

33. Robert Karlowich, *We Fall and Rise: Russian Language Newspapers in New York City, 1889–1914* (Metuchen, N.J.: Scarecrow Press, 1991), p. 107; Magidov, *Der shpigl,* p. 69; Milkh, *Di anshteyung fun "Forverts,"* pp. 22, 25.

34. Cahan, *Bleter,* vol. 3, pp. 229–230; Kobrin, *Mayne fuftsik yor in Amerike,* p. 66; Milkh, *Di anshteyung fun "Forverts,"* pp. 24, 36; Dovid Shub, *Fun di amolike yorn,* vol. 1 (New York: TSIKO Bikher Farlag, 1970), pp. 61–62; Borukh Tsukerman, *Zikhroynes* (New York: Idisher Kemfer, 1962), pp. 170–171. The view that Faygnboym's use of religious texts reflected an abiding attachment to Judaism is entirely unfounded. Gerald Sorin, *A Time for Building* (Baltimore: Johns Hopkins University Press, 1992), pp. 119–121.

35. Hapgood, *The Spirit of the Ghetto,* p. 85.

36. *Leksikon fun der nayer yidisher literatur,* vol. 8 (New York: Alveltlekhn Yidishen Kultur-Kongres, 1981), p. 191, and Kean Zametkin's obituaries in *Forverts,* May 21, 1931, p. 6, and *Di tsukunft* (July 1931): 489.

37. Mari Jo Buhle, *Women and American Socialism, 1870–1920* (Urbana: University of Illinois Press, 1981), p. 126; Anna Ingerman's obituaries in *Forverts, New Leader,* and *Volkszeitung* are located in the Sergei Ingerman Papers, Tamiment Library, New York University. On the Ingermans' participation in the GEL, see Abraham Ascher, *Pavel Axelrod and the Development of Menshevism* (Cambridge, Mass.: Harvard University Press, 1972), p. 96.

38. Blumenson, "Culture on Rutgers Square," p. 65; J. R. Schwartz, *Orchard Street* (New York: Comet Press Books, 1960), pp. 160–161; Max Podell, "The Story of My Life," YIVO, RG 102, folder 178, p. 88. Also see Chotzinoff, *A Lost Paradise,* pp. 80–92.

39. Held, interview, pp. 27, 34; Oscar Feuer, "Mayne 50 yor in der peynters yunyon," typescript, YIVO, RG 102, folder 270, p. 2.

40. Chotzinoff, *A Lost Paradise,* pp. 137, 139.

41. Tsvi Hirsh Masliansky, *Masliansky's zikhroynes: firtsik yor lebn un kemfn* (New York: Farlag Zerubavel, 1924), p. 205.

42. Zevi Hirsch [Tsvi Hirsh] Masliansky, *Sermons,* trans. Edward Herbert (New York: Hebrew Publishing Co., 1960), p. 198.

43. Maks Payn [Max Pine], "Teg vos zaynen lang avek," in H. Lang and Moris Faynston, eds., *Geverkshaftn* (New York: United Hebrew Trades, 1938), p. mt (Hebrew numerals).

44. The only two Yiddish newspapers to appear in the Russian Empire before 1899 were the weeklies *Kol mevaser* (1862–1871), published as the Yid-

dish supplement to *Ha-melits*, and *Dos yidishes folksblat* (1881–1890). David Fishman, "The Politics of Yiddish in Tsarist Russia," in Jacob Neusner, Ernest S. Frerichs, and Nahum M. Sarna, eds., *From Ancient Israel to Modern Judaism: Intellect in Quest of Understanding: Essays in Honor of Marvin Fox*, vol. 4, *The Modern Age: Theology, Literature, History* (Atlanta: Scholars Press, 1989), pp. 159–163.

45. A.G., "Mayn otobiografye," manuscript, YIVO, RG 102, folder 117, p. 18. For a similar recollection, see Y. Goldbaum, "Epizodn fun lebn mit finf tsendlik yor tsurik," *Di fraye arbeter shtime*, Jan. 29, 1943, p. 8.

46. Arthur Goren, "The Jewish Press," in Sally M. Miller, ed., *The Ethnic Press in the United States* (Westport, Conn.: Greenwood Press, 1987), p. 206; Michael Taub, "Yiddish Newspapers in America: A Selective Overview," *Yiddish* 13, nos. 2–3 (2003): 112.

47. B. Bogen, "Mimokhodom. Prosvetiteli immigrantov," *Nedel'naia khronika voskhoda* 13, no. 23 (June 1894): 641; Bevans, *How Workingmen Spend Their Spare Time*, pp. 37–91.

48. B. Gorin, "Der yidisher vanderer," *Der fraynd*, Dec. 27, 1904, p. 1.

49. Hapgood, *The Spirit of the Ghetto*, p. 178; Robert E. Park, *The Immigrant Press and Its Control* (New York: Harper and Brothers, 1922), p. 89; Edward A. Steiner, "The Russian and Polish Jew in New York," *Outlook* 72, no. 9 (Nov. 1, 1902): 536. Also see Maurice Fishberg, "The Russian Jews in America," *American Monthly Review of Reviews* (Sept. 1902): 318; Mordecai Soltes, *The Yiddish Press: An Americanizing Agency* (New York: Teachers' College, Columbia University, 1924), pp. 14–29.

50. Victor R. Greene, *American Immigrant Leaders, 1890–1910: Marginality and Identity* (Baltimore: Johns Hopkins University Press, 1987), pp. 89–95; Y. Khaykin, *Yidishe bleter in Amerike* (New York: M. Sh. Shklarski, 1946), pp. 100, 110; Kalman Marmor, *Der onheyb fun der yidisher literatur in Amerike* (New York: IKUF, 1944), pp. 114–117; Samuel Niger, "Yiddish Culture," in *The Jewish People: Past and Present*, vol. 4 (New York: Jewish Encyclopedic Handbooks, 1955), pp. 282–293.

51. Milkh, *Di anshteyung fun "Forverts,"* pp. 117–119; Zeifert, "Mimokhod. Zhargonnaia pressa v N′iu-Iorke," *Nedel′naia khronika voskhoda* 5, no. 22 (June 1886): 627–631.

52. Y. Lifshits, "Di nyu yorker yidishe folkstsaytung," in *Pinkes far der forshung fun der yidisher literatur un prese*, vol. 3, ed. Hyman Bass (New York: Alveltlekhn Yidishen Kultur-Kongres, 1975), pp. 251–318; Moyshe Shtarkman, "Tsu der geshikhte fun der sotsyalistisher yidisher prese in di Fareynikte shtatn," *YIVO Bleter* (Dec. 1932): 356, and "Tsum onheyb fun der yidisher arbeter prese,"

in Mordekhai Halamish and Itzhak Yanasowicz, eds., *Geklibene shriftn* (New York: n.p., 1979), pp. 103–106.

53. Eliyohu Shulman, "Di varhayt," in Yankev Shatski, ed., *Zamlbukh lekoved dem tsvey hundert un fuftsikstn yoyvl fun der yidisher prese, 1686–1936* (New York: Amopteyl fun YIVO, 1936), pp. 197–211.

54. Goldberg, "Di yidishe sotsyalistishe bavegung sof di 80er yorn," in Tsherikover, ed., *Geshikhte,* vol. 2, pp. 340–345.

55. "Di konstitutsye fun der 'Arbeter tsaytung,'" in A. Mukdoyni and Yankev Shatski, eds., *Yorbukh fun Amopteyl,* vol. 1 (New York: YIVO, 1938), pp. 341–342, 346. I do not know how many people joined the publishing association in 1890. It appears that it reached its peak membership of more than one hundred in 1897, at the height of the factional struggle that resulted in its collapse. Though tendentious, Milkh's *Di anshteyung fun "Forverts"* provides the most detailed account of the publishing association's inner life. On the German socialist press, see Elliot Shore et al., eds., *The German-American Radical Press: The Shaping of a Left Political Culture, 1850–1940* (Urbana: University of Illinois Press, 1992).

56. Cahan, *Bleter,* vol. 3, p. 25; Eliyohu Shulman, "Di arbeter tsaytung," in Yankev Shatski, ed., *Zamlbukh tsu der geshikhte fun der yidisher prese in Amerike* (New York: Yidisher Kultur Gezelshaft, 1934), p. 30; Vaynshteyn, *Fertsik yor,* pp. 126–128.

57. Philip Krants, "Mit 25 yor tsurik," *Di fraye gezelshaft* (Aug. 1910): 678, 680–681; Yankev Milkh, "Philip Krants," *Di tsukunft* (July 1906): 19–20; M. Vintshevsky, "Der 'Arbeter fraynd,'" *Dos naye lebn* (July 1910): 37.

58. Haberer, *Jews and Revolution,* p. 306 n. 15, p. 312 n. 66; P. Krants, "Mayne erinerungen vegn Grinevtski," *Di arbeter tsaytung,* July 11, 1890, p. 2. For a biographical summary of Krants, see *Leksikon fun der nayer yidisher literatur,* vol. 8 (New York: TSIKO, 1984), pp. 243–249.

59. I. Krants, "Nastoiashchee pole deiatel'nosti," *Znamia,* Feb. 15, 1890, pp. 1–2; Philip Krants, "Di yidishe shprakh, ir literatur, ire shrayber, un lezer," *Literatur un lebn* (Feb. 1914): 37; Y. B. Beylin, "Philip Krants—der ershter redaktor fun a sotsyalistisher tsaytung in Yidish," *Di morgn frayhayt,* Feb. 5, 1956, p. 7; Cahan, *Bleter,* vol. 3, pp. 27, 96; Kobrin, *Mayne fuftsik yor in Amerike,* pp. 90–102; Magidov, *Der shpigl,* p. 32; Milkh, *Di anshteyung fun "Forverts,"* pp. 37, 42; Vaynshteyn, *Fertsik yor,* p. 128.

60. "Dos program fun di Arbeter tsaytung publishing asotsyatsyon," *Di arbeter tsaytung,* March 7, 1890, p. 1.

61. Ida Van Etten, "Russian Jews as Desirable Immigrants," *Forum* 15 (April 1893): 178; Bogen, "Mimokhodom. Prosvetiteli immigrantov," pp. 641–644.

62. Krants, "Dos program fun der sotsyal demokratye," *Di arbeter tsaytung,* March 28, 1890, p. 2.

63. Der proletarishker magid [Abraham Cahan], "Di sedre," *Di arbeter tsaytung,* March 14, 1890, p. 2.

64. Cahan, *Bleter,* vol. 3, pp. 20–21, 32; M. Baranov, "Philip Krants—vos er iz yo geven un vos er iz nit geven," *Di tsukunft* (Feb. 1923): 93.

65. Hillquit, *Loose Leaves,* pp. 35–37; "The Jewish Paper," *The Workingman's Advocate,* March 1, 1890, p. 3; The following recollection is from one of *Di arbeter tsaytung's* early readers. "One Friday, going home from work and considering what paper to buy, I noticed a Yiddish paper with the name 'Arbeiter Zeitung.' I bought it and began to read it, and remarkable, this was the thing I wanted. It was the first Yiddish, socialist newspaper. Although till then I had never heard about socialism and its doctrine, still I understood it without any interpretation. I liked it because its ideas were hidden in my heart and in my soul long ago; only I could not express them clearly" (Ephraim Morris Wagner, "The Village Boy," YIVO, RG 102, folder 45, p. 161).

66. In a report to the Socialist International in mid-1891 Cahan reported a circulation of eight thousand. For similar estimates, see Hillquit, *Loose Leaves,* p. 36; Milkh, *Di anshteyung fun "Forverts,"* p. 17; George Price, "The Russian Jews in America," trans. and repr. in *Publication of the American Jewish Historical Society* (Dec. 1958): 133. On the basis of a later study, Mordecai Soltes found that the readership of Yiddish newspapers could be as much as 75 percent greater than their reported circulations, because more than one individual read a single copy. Soltes, *The Yiddish Press,* pp. 38–39.

67. Cahan, *Bleter,* vol. 3, p. 41.

68. P. Krants, "1890: A kurtser iberblik af dem fargangenem yor," *Di arbeter tsaytung,* Jan. 2, 1891, p. 4. Vaynshteyn, *Yidishe yunyons,* pp. 147, 154; Y. M. Budish, *Geshikhte fun der klot, het, kep, un milineri arbeter* (New York: Cloth Hat, Cap, and Millinery Workers International Union, 1925), p. 53.

69. Vaynshteyn, *Yidishe yunyons,* pp. 147, 154; Payn, "Teg vos zaynen lang avek," p. mt.

70. P. Krants, "Tsum yors-fest fun di 'Arbeter tsaytung,'" *Di arbeter tsaytung,* March 6, 1891, p. 1.

71. Yoysef Kahan, *Di yidish-anarkhistishe bavegung* (Philadelphia: Workman's Circle, 1945), pp. 60–69; Kopelov, *Amol in Amerike,* p. 257. *Di arbeter tsaytung's* typesetters struck twice in 1890, but the UHT helped the newspaper to resolve the disputes quickly. Sh. Sheynfeld, *Fuftsik yor Yidishe shriftzetser yunyon* (New York: YIVO, 1938), pp. 25–29.

72. *Di arbeter tsaytung,* Sept. 28, 1894, p. 1.

73. *Di arbeter tsaytung,* Feb. 24, 1895, p. 3; Sergei Ingerman, "Ocherk razvitiia evreiskogo rabochego dvizheniia v Amerike," manuscript, Sergei Ingerman Collection, Tamiment Library, New York University, p. 14.

74. Held, interview, p. 2; A.G., "Mayn otobiografye," p. 18; Milkh, *Di anshteyung fun "Forverts,"* pp. 72–73n.

75. Cahan, *Bleter,* vol. 3, pp. 294–295; Krants to "comrade," Dec. 11, 1896, YIVO, RG 204, folder 671.

76. Burgin, *Di geshikhte,* pp. 372–416, Frankel, *Prophecy and Politics,* pp. 466–467. For detailed but conflicting partisan accounts, see Cahan, *Bleter,* vol. 3, pp. 378–458, and Milkh, *Di anshteyung fun "Forverts,"* pp. 16–101.

77. Handbill for the *"Geshprokhene tsaytung"* and other documents pertaining to the founding of the *Forverts* are located in YIVO, RG 205, folder 768; Bernard Lilienblum, transcribed interview, Dec. 6, 1963, YIVO, RG 113, box 3, p. 19; Hillel Rogoff, "Di geshikhte fun Forverts," *Forverts* (yubeleum oysgabe), April 22, 1917, p. 7.

78. Irving Howe, *World of Our Fathers* (New York: Harcourt Brace Jovanovich, 1976), p. 545. According to Frankel, the *Forverts*'s annual profits were fifty thousand dollars by World War I. Frankel, *Prophecy and Politics,* p. 456.

79. For a discussion of a different kind of Yiddish "newspaper culture," see Sarah Abrevaya Stein, *Making Jews Modern: The Yiddish and Ladino Press in the Russian and Ottoman Empires* (Bloomington: Indiana University Press, 2004), pp. 23–54.

80. Yekhezkl Sarasohn, "A blik tsurik," *Tageblat,* March 20, 1910, reprinted in Mukdoyni and Shatski, eds., *Yorbukh fun Amopteyl,* p. 287.

81. *Di arbeter tsaytung,* Feb. 9, 1894, p. 6; April 18, 1890, p. 7; Oct. 24, 1890, p. 6; Dec. 6, 1895.

82. *Di arbeter tsaytung,* July 25, 1890, and June 27, 1895; handbill for an 1898 *Forverts* excursion, YIVO, RG 205, folder 8.

83. N. Goldberg, "Di antireligyeze bavegung," in Tsherikover, ed., *Geshikhte,* vol. 2, pp. 418–457.

84. "Unzer boll," *Forverts,* Jan. 21, 1898, p. 2; "A masken revolutsyon," *Forverts,* Jan. 31, 1898, p. 1.

85. "A masken revolutsyon," *Forverts,* Jan. 31, 1898, p. 1.

86. "2te oysgabe fun 29tn," *Forverts,* Feb. 1, 1898, p. 1; "Der 19ter," *Forverts,* Feb. 21, 1898, p. 2.

87. Held, interview, pp. 8, 29; Rogoff, "Di geshikhte fun Forverts," pp. 11, 26; Frankel, *Prophecy and Politics,* p. 456.

88. Kuznets, "Immigration of Russian Jews to the United States," pp. 80–81.

89. Iris Parush, "Readers in Cameo: Women Readers in Jewish Society of Nineteenth-Century Eastern Europe," *Prooftexts* 14 (1993): 12–23; Steven G. Rappaport, "Jewish Education and Jewish Culture in the Russian Empire, 1880–1914" (Ph.D. diss., Stanford University, 2000), p. 32; David Roskies, "The Medium and Message of the Maskilic Chapbook," *Jewish Social Studies* 41 (Summer–Fall 1979): 275–290; Shaul Stampfer, "Gender Differentiation and Education of the Jewish Woman in Nineteenth-Century Eastern Europe," *Polin* 7 (1992): 63–87, and "What Did 'Knowing Hebrew' Mean in Eastern Europe?" in Lewis Glinert, ed., *Hebrew in Ashkenaz: A Language in Exile* (New York: Oxford University Press, 1993), pp. 129–140.

90. Arcadius Kahan, *Essays in Jewish Social and Economic History*, ed. Roger Weiss (Chicago: University of Chicago Press, 1986), pp. 45–46; B. Rosen, "Far vos bin ikh avek fun der alter heym un vos hob ikh dergreykht in Amerike," manuscript, YIVO, RG 102, folder 215, pp. 36–37. Also see Cahan, *Bleter*, vol. 3, p. 198.

91. Quoted in Kalman Marmor, *Der onhoyb fun der yidisher literatur in Amerike* (New York: Shrayber-Sektsye, 1944), p. 126.

92. L. Markuz, "A bisele historye," *Yidishe tageblat*, March 20, 1910, reprinted in Shatski, ed., *Zamlbukh tsu der geshikhte*, p. 47; M. Zeyfert, "Zhargonnaia pressa v N´iu-Iorke," *Nedel'naia khronika voskhoda* 22 (June 1886): 629. See also Goldbaum, "Epizodn fun lebn mit finf tsendlik yor tsurik," p. 8.

93. Cahan, *Bleter*, vol. 3, p. 18. Similarly, Hillquit described his Yiddish as "German in Hebrew characters." Hillquit, *Loose Leaves*, pp. 17, 37.

94. Christopher Hutton, "Normativism and the Notion of Authenticity in Yiddish Linguistics," in David Goldberg, ed., *The Field of Yiddish* (Evanston, Ill.: Northwestern University Press, 1993), pp. 14–28; Kobrin, *Mayne fuftsik yor in Amerike*, pp. 263–277; Kalman Marmor, "Vos di amerikaner yidishe prese hot amol gedenkt vegn Yidish," *Di morgn frayhayt*, April 16, 1928, p. 5; Sh. Niger, "Afn shvel fun der yidisher literatur in Amerike," *Di tsukunft* (Jan. 1940): 9–13, and (Feb. 1940): 99–101.

95. *Di nyu yorker yidishe ilustrirte tsaytung*, Dec. 28, 1887, Jan. 27, 1888, Feb. 15 and 29, 1888; Maks Vaynraykh [Max Weinreich], "Di ershte yidishe tsaytungen in Amerike un zeyer aynflus af der yidisher shprakh," *Forverts*, Aug. 22, 1937, p. 2.

96. In later decades, however, *khaver* would come to replace *genosse* as the standard word for comrade.

97. B. Gorin, "Der yidisher vanderer," *Der fraynd*, Dec. 20, 1904, p. 1. Also see A.G., "Mayn otobiografye," p. 20.

98. Leon Kobrin, *Mayne fufstik yor in Amerike* (Buenos Aires: Farlag Yidish Bukh, 1955), pp. 80, 84, 62; Shloyme Geltner, *Mayne yunge un grine yorn* (Armada, Mich.: n.p., 1956), p. 137; A. Litvak, "Di krayzlekh," in Kh. Sh. Kazdan, ed., *Gezamlte shriftn* (New York: Arbeter Ring, 1945), p. 210.

99. *Di arbeter tsaytung,* Jan. 9, 1894, p. 6.

100. Abraham Bisno, *Abraham Bisno, Union Pioneer* (Madison: University of Wisconsin Press, 1967), pp. 84–85, 105; S. S. Garson, manuscript, YIVO, 102, folder 1, pp. 5–6, 10; Lilienblum, interview, pp. 13–14, 20–21; Pauline Newman, interview, p. 13.

101. Shoel Yanovsky, *Ershte yorn fun yidishn frayhaytlekhn sotsyalizm* (New York: Fraye Arbeter Shtime, 1948), pp. 110–111. Also see Burgin, *Geshikhte,* p. 140.

102. This estimate is based on my count of announcements printed in *Di arbeter tsaytung, Di fraye arbeter shtime,* and *Forverts* between 1890 and 1900. I counted not every issue of these newspapers but issues over selected periods. Ingerman, "Ocherk razvitiia," p. 14.

103. Daniel Soyer, *Jewish Immigrant Associations and American Identity in New York, 1880–1939* (Cambridge, Mass.: Harvard University Press, 1997), pp. 49–80.

104. An altyunger, "Di lektshurs in yidishn kvartl," p. 4.

105. "Shtimen oys dem folk," *Di arbeter tsaytung,* Dec. 1, 1893, p. 5.

106. The earliest title I have located is Dr. Ab. Kaspe, *Mekhanike: di hoypt mekhanishe gezetse fun Sir Ayzik Newton* (New York: n.p., 1899). On Yiddish book publishing see Niger, "Yiddish Culture in America," pp. 275–278, 282–286; Moyshe Shtarkman, "Fun popular-visnshaft biz visnshaft (1882–1942)," *Jewish Book Week Annual* (Yiddish section) 1 (1942): 41–51.

107. Sh. Niger, "Kharakter-shtrikhtn fun der radikaler oyfklerungs-literatur," *Di tsukunft* (Nov. 1941): 120. A short-lived "scientific" magazine entitled *Di yidishe visnshaftlekhe biblyotek* appeared in 1899, but I have found little information about it.

108. "'Di tsukunft' gehert aykh!" *Di arbeter tsaytung,* July 31, 1891, p. 5.

109. Ibid.; "Unzer 'Tsukunft,'" *Di tsukunft* (Jan. 1892): 1. A translation of the editorial appears in Steven Cassedy, ed., *Building the Future: Jewish Immigrant Intellectuals and the Making of Tsukunft* (New York: Holmes and Meier, 1999), pp. 26–28.

110. "2100 zaytn visnshaft," *Di tsukunft* (Dec. 1897): 1.

111. Ingerman, "Ocherk razvitiia," p. 15.

112. Ravage, *An American in the Making,* pp. 179–183; Dr. A. Ortman, "A bletl geshikhte," *Di tsukunft* (Jan. 1892): 60. Also see Fenster, interview, p. 10;

Held, interview, pp. 20–21, 37; Lilienblum, interview, p. 21; "Gubernator," manuscript, YIVO, RG 102, folder 191, p. 87; Max Podell, "The Story of My Life," p. 88; Hyman Rogoff, transcribed interview, Nov. 17, 1963, YIVO, RG 102, box 5, p. 11; Schwartz, *Orchard Street,* 131–132; Wolff, interview, p. 18.

113. "Tsukunft," *Di yidishe gazetn,* June 8, 1894, p. 9; Masliansky, *Masliansky's zikhroynes,* pp. 208–209.

114. *Di arbeter tsaytung,* Dec. 15, 1893, p. 3; *Di arbeter tsaytung,* Nov. 7, 1894, p. 3; "Ershter may in Nyu york," *Di yidishe gazetn,* May 4, 1894, p. 1.

115. B. Gorin, "Der yidisher vanderer," *Der fraynd,* Dec. 20, 1904, p. 1.

116. Steiner, "The Russian and Polish Jew in New York," p. 543.

117. Miller, "Vos zol men ton?" p. 18.

118. Sh. Peskin, "Di yudn-frage," *Di tsukunft* (Jan. 1897): 14.

119. Philip Krants, "A blik af di [*sic*] yidishe prese in Amerike," *Yidishes tageblat,* March 20, 1910, p. 9.

3. The Politics of *Yidishe Kultur*

1. Emma Goldman, *Living My Life,* vol. 1 (1931; rept., New York: Dover, 1970), p. 360.

2. Abraham Cahan, *Bleter fun mayn lebn,* vol. 4 (Vilnius: B. Kletskin, 1928), pp. 424–426; Jane E. Good and David R. Jones, *Babushka: The Life of the Russian Revolutionary E. K. Breshko-Breshkovskaia* (Newtonville, Mass.: Oriental Research Partners, 1991), pp. 78–90; Y. Kopelov, *Amol un shpeter* (Vilnius: Altney, 1932), pp. 31–36; Dovid Shub, *Fun di amolike yorn,* vol. 1 (New York: TSIKO, 1970), pp. 80–81; Christine Stansell, *American Moderns: Bohemian New York and the Creation of a New Century* (New York: Metropolitan Books, 2000), p. 65.

3. In 1892 or 1893, for example, Abraham Cahan met Zhitlovsky during the Socialist International's conference in Zurich. Cahan, *Bleter,* vol. 3, p. 337. Anski to Zhitlovsky, Sept. 9, 1893, reprinted with Yiddish translation by M. Krutikov, "Briv fun Sh. Anski tsu Khayim Zhitlovsky," *YIVO Bleter* 2 (n.s.) (1994): 304.

4. Leon Kobrin, *Mayne fuftsik yor in Amerike* (New York: IKUF, 1966), p. 252.

5. Sh. Ellsberg, "Dr. Zhitlovsky's tetikeyt in Amerike (a kurtser iberblik)," in *Zhitlovsky-zamlbukh* (Warsaw: Kh. Bzshoza, 1929), pp. 172–189.

6. On socialist reactions to Kishinev, see Jonathan Frankel, *Prophecy and Politics: Socialism, Nationalism and the Russian Jews, 1862–1917* (Cambridge: Cambridge University Press, 1981), pp. 473–484; A. Lesin, "Mit 25 yor tsurik," *Der veker,* Dec. 27, 1930, p. 6.

7. Frankel, *Prophecy and Politics*, pp. 258–287.

8. Zhitlovsky published a Russian translation in 1904 and a Yiddish translation in 1908. My discussion is based on the Yiddish version, which originally appeared in pamphlet form and contained no substantial revisions of the earlier two editions. Dr. Kh. Zhitlovsky, *Der sotsyalizm un di natsyonale frage* (New York: A. M. Evelenko, 1908).

9. Ibid., pp. 5, 6.

10. Ibid., pp. 82–83.

11. Ibid., p. 9.

12. Ibid., p. 73.

13. Emmanuel Goldsmith states that Zhitlovsky based his understanding of nationalism in part on Karl Renner's and Otto Bauer's writings. Goldsmith, *Modern Yiddish Culture: The Story of the Yiddish Language Movement* (New York: Fordham University Press, 1997), p. 170. Bauer published his major work on the national question in 1907, however, eight years after Zhitlovsky's article in *Deutsche Worte*. Renner published his work almost at the same time as Zhitlovsky's 1899 treatise. No doubt Zhitlovsky read Renner and Bauer (who, likewise, probably read Zhitlovsky), but Zhitlovsky had been working up his ideas independently since the late 1880s.

14. Enzo Traverso, *The Marxists and the Jewish Question: The History of a Debate, 1843–1943*, trans. Bernard Gibbons, (Atlantic Highlands, N.J.: Humanities Press, 1994), p. 78. Also see Jack Jacobs, *On Socialists and "The Jewish Question" after Marx* (New York: New York University Press, 1992), pp. 86–117.

15. Chaim Zhitlovsky, "Tsvey forlezungen vegn yid un mentsh," in *Gezamlte shriftn*, vol. 2 (New York: Yubuleum Oysgabe, 1912), pp. 111, 186.

16. David H. Weinberg, *Between Tradition and Modernity: Haim Zhitlowski, Simon Dubnow, Ahad Ha-am, and the Shaping of Modern Jewish Identity* (New York: Holmes and Meier, 1996), pp. 133–134.

17. Chaim Zhitlovsky, "Tsienizm oder sotsyalizm," in *Gezamlte shriftn*, vol. 5 (New York: Yubuleum Oysgabe, 1917), pp. 72–73.

18. John Klier, "'Exit, Pursued by a Bear': The Ban on Yiddish Theatre in Imperial Russia," in Joel Berkowitz, ed., *Yiddish Theatre: New Approaches* (Oxford: Littman Library of Jewish Civilization, 2003), pp. 159–174; Dan Miron, *A Traveler Disguised: The Rise of Modern Yiddish Fiction in the Nineteenth Century* (1973; rept., Syracuse: Syracuse University Press, 1996), pp. 22–33.

19. Frankel, *Prophecy and Politics*, p. 217–227.

20. Ibid., p. 171.

21. Ibid., pp. 274, 278–286.

22. Ibid., pp. 279–280; M. Zilbefarb, "Di grupe 'Vozrozhdenie,'" *Royter pinkes*, vol. 1 (Warsaw: Kultur-Lige, 1921), pp. 124–125.

23. Jacobs, *On Socialists and "The Jewish Question" after Marx*, pp. 118–124.

24. *Forverts*, Nov. 14, 1904, p. 1.

25. Yankev Milkh, "Farvos shenden zey kvorim?" in *Kegn di onfaler af Dr. Khayim Zhitlovsky* (New York: Dr. Hayyim Zshitlovski Folks-Komitet, 1944), p. 33; Shub, *Fun di amolike yorn*, p. 85. Also see Kobrin, *Mayne fuftsik yor in Amerike*, p. 257.

26. I. Krants, "Nastoiashchee pole deiatel'nosti. Pis'mo v redaktsiiu," *Znamia*, Feb. 15, 1890, pp. 1–2; Cahan, "Kritishe studyen iber zhargonishe mayster-verk," *Di tsukunft* (Jan. 1896): 56. On literary criticism in *Di tsukunft*, see Steven Cassedy, "Radical Literary Criticism in Yiddish: The Example of *Di tsukunft*, 1892–1918," *YIVO Annual* 23 (1996): 181–208.

27. P. Viernik, "Vi lang vet unzer literatur blien?" *Der nayer gayst* (March 1898): 356.

28. Simon Solomon, *Derinerungen fun der yidisher arbeter bavegung* (New York: n.p., 1952), p. 143; Kopelov, *Amol un shpeter*, p. 56; Kobrin, *Mayne fuftsik yor in Amerike*, p. 257. Also see H. Erenraykh, "Di virkung fun Dr. Khayim Zhitlovsky's optimizm af der yidisher yugnt," *Dos naye lebn* (Dec. 1912): 31–35.

29. Yudl Mark, "Vegn Dr. Zhitlovsky's sintaks un stil," *Yidishe shprakh* 5, no. 2 (March–April 1945): 33, and "Vegn Dr. Zhitlovsky's shprakh," *Yidishe shprakh* 5, no. 1 (Jan.–Feb. 1945): 8–21. See Yehoash to Zhitlovsky, Sept. 20, 1905, YIVO, RG 208, folder 464.

30. Kopelov, *Amol un shpeter*, p. 39.

31. Ibid., p. 40.

32. Kopelov to Zhitlovsky, Oct. 5, 1913, YIVO, RG 208, folder 830.

33. Cahan, *Bleter*, p. 428; Y. Perlman to Zhitlovsky, March 21, 1914, YIVO, RG 208, folder 733.

34. See the following reminiscences in *M. Kats zamlbukh* (Philadelphia: n.p., 1925): Y. Kopelov, "M. Kats' tetikyet in der anarkhistisher un sots. revolutsyonerer bavegung," pp. 21–29; Kh. Slutski, "M. Kats—der sotsyalist revolutsyoner," pp. 43–49; Leon Elbe, "Der teritorialistisher farzukh," pp. 61–62.

35. The controversy surrounding Kobrin's sketch is discussed in Kobrin, *Mayne fuftsik yor in Amerike*, pp. 191–200.

36. Lesin, "Mit 25 yor tsurik," p. 6.

37. Kh. A. [Khayim Aleksandrov], "Der yidisher literatur fareyn in Nyu-York," *Dos lebn* (May 1905): 125–128.

38. Goldman, *Living My Life*, p. 370; Shoel Yanovsky, "Di ershte 20 yor 'Fraye arbeter shtime,'" *Di fraye arbeter shtime*, April 19, 1929, pp. 3, 5.

39. Y. Gordin, "Natsyonalismus un asimilatsyon (shlus)," *Di tsukunft* (Nov. 1905): 602, 603, 604.

40. Milkh, "Farvos shenden zey kvorim?" p. 37; Shub, *Fun di amolike yorn*, p. 88.

41. "*Di tsukunft* fun di felker in Amerike," in *Gezamlte shriftn*, vol. 2 (New York: Yubuleum Oysgabe, 1912), pp. 198, 204, 217, 239–241, 258, 263–264, 278–280, 285.

42. Dr. Kh. Zhitlovsky, *Dos program un di tsiln fun der monatshrift "Dos naye lebn"* (New York: Fareyn "Dos Naye Lebn," 1908), pp. 3–5.

43. Kenneth Moss, "Jewish Culture between Renaissance and Decadence: *Di Literarishe Monatshriftn* and Its Critical Reception," *Jewish Social Studies* 8, no. 1 (Fall 2001): 153–198; Ruth R. Wisse, *A Little Love in Big Manhattan: Two Yiddish Poets* (Cambridge, Mass.: Harvard University Press, 1988), pp. 10–20.

44. Ab. Cahan, "Unzer inteligents," *Di tsukunft* (Feb. 1910): 112–113.

45. Kh. Zhitlovsky, "A por verter vegn inteligents un amaratses," *Dos naye lebn* (May 1910): 8.

46. Management of *Dos naye lebn*, Nov. 1909, YIVO, RG 208, folder 1138; H. Salutski to Zhitlovsky, Dec. 13, 1913, YIVO, RG 208, folder 671, p. 2.

47. Jacob Kranzer to Zhitlovsky, Feb. 27, 1911, YIVO, RG 208, folder 865; N. Mishkovski to Zhitlovsky, Dec. 16, 1912, YIVO, RG 208, folder 599; L. Luleff to Zhitlovsky, Jan. 15, 1913, YIVO, RG 208, folder 502; "Oyfruf," *Dos naye lebn* (Jan. 1912): 54; "Derklerung," *Dos naye lebn* (April 1913): n.p.

48. "Notitsn," *Dos naye lebn* (Dec. 1908): 64; "Miteylungen," *Dos naye lebn* (April 1914): 35. On Waterbury, see Solomon, *Derinerungen fun der yidisher arbeter bavegung*, pp. 156–183; Moyshe Vaysman, *A halber yorhundert in Amerike* (Tel Aviv: Farlag Y. L. Perets, 1960), pp. 70–72.

49. Circular from the Organizatsyons Komitet, July 10, 1911, YIVO, RG 204, folder 60; "Der yidisher literatn klob," *Dos naye land*, Oct. 20, 1911, p. 1; "Der obend fun yidishn literatn klob," *Dos naye land*, Dec. 1, 1911, p. 31; also see club correspondence in YIVO, RG 701, folder 267.

50. "Di statutn fun der Kropotkin literatur gezelshaft," reprinted in Ferdinand Lassalle, *Geklibene shriftn* (New York: Yubuleum Oysgabe, 1916), n.p.; Maryson to Strunsky, Jan. 23, 1917, Anna Strunsky Collection, Yale University, reel 8, folder 18; D. Izakovits, "Vos 'Kropotkin literatur gezelshaft' hot oyfgeton," *Di fraye arbeter shtime*, April 2, 1943, pp. 9–10. Also see M. Terman, "Di 'Kropotkin literatur gezelshaft' un ir letste oysgabn," *Di tsukunft* (June 1917): 369–371.

51. N. L. Horeker et al., "Liova Fradkin–L. M. Shteyn," in Y. Kh. Pomerants and A. Pravatiner, eds., *Yoyvl bukh tsu L. M. Shteyns finf un tsvantsik yorikn yubiley fun kultur-gezelshaftlekhe tetikeyt* (Chicago: Sholem Aleykhem Folk Institut, 1938), pp. 32–33, 36; Sarah Abrevaya Stein, "Illustrating Chicago's Jewish

Left: The Cultural Aesthetics of Todros Geller and the L. M. Shteyn Farlag," *Jewish Social Studies* 3 (n.s.), no. 3 (Spring–Summer 1997): 74–77, 104–106.

52. "Fun der redaktsyon," *Di naye velt* (Oct. 1909): 4; Bagrisung," *Di yidishe vokhnshrift*, Jan. 19, 1912, pp. 1–2; "Unzer tsvekn," *Literatur un lebn* (Jan. 1914): 3. Dr. Eliyohu Shulman, "Di tsaytshrift 'Di yidishe velt,'" in Shloyme Bikl, ed., *Pinkes far der forshung fun der yidisher literatur un prese* (New York: Congress for Jewish Culture, 1965), pp. 166–169.

53. On the conflict between *Di tsukunft* and the *Forverts*, see the following articles, which represent both sides: Di redaktsyon, "An entfer af der 'Erklerung' fun 'Forverts Assosyeyshon,'" *Di tsukunft* (Jan. 1912): 1–8; Tsivion, "A perzenlekhe erklerung fun genose Tsivion," *Di tsukunft* (Jan. 1912): 6; Av. Kaspe, "A perzenlekhe erklerung Dr. Av. Kaspe," *Di tsukunft* (Jan. 1912): 7–8; Av. Kaspe, "Unzer 'Tsukunft' un unzer 'Forverts,'" *Di tsukunft* (Jan. 1912): 46–48, and (Feb. 1912): 151–156; Di redaktsyon, "Ver zaynen unzere kritiker?" *Di tsukunft* (Feb. 1912): 182–187; report from the Tsukunft Press Federation, *Di tsukunft* (Feb. 1912): 192; F. Rozenblat (Ben-Yakir), "Di 'Tsukunft' un ir historiker," *Di tsukunft* (August 1914); 869–874; and F. Rozenblat, "Vider di 'Tsukunft' un ir historiker," *Di tsukunft* (Dec. 1914): 1284–1288.

54. Sh. Niger, "Di 'Tsukunft' un di yidishe literatur in Amerike," *Di tsukunft* (May–June 1942): 314–323; Hillel Rogoff, "Finf un tsvantsik yor 'Tsukunft' unter Lesin's redaktsye," *Di tsukunft* (May–June 1942): 289–296.

55. Marmor to Lesin, Feb. 9, 1923, YIVO, RG 201, folder 741; A. Lesin, "An entfer tsu der redaktsyon fun 'Forverts,'" *Di tsukunft* (Feb. 1914): 214.

56. "Dr. Zhitlovsky's yubileum a groyser derfolg," *Di varhayt*, Dec. 30, 1912, p. 2. Sholem Aleichem's letter is reprinted in *Dos naye lebn* (May 1913): 59. The members of Zhitlovsky's anniversary committee are listed on the committee's letterhead. See Zhitlovsky to Dovid Pinsky, July 8, 1912, YIVO, RG 208, folder 724.

57. Magnes to Dr. [Paul] Kaplan, June 21, 1906, YIVO, RG 208, folder 545.

58. It should be recalled that the original post-1881 wave of Jewish radicals experienced a similar sense of dissatisfaction with life in the United States. Ezra Mendelsohn, "The Russian Roots of the American Jewish Labor Movement," *YIVO Annual of Jewish Social Science* 16 (1976): 158–165.

59. Lena Sh. Vaynberger, "Lebnsgeshikhte," American Autobiographies, YIVO, RG 102, folder 160, p. 12.

60. Dr. Knapnogel, "Di yidishe agitatsyons byuro," *Di yidishe arbeter velt*, Aug. 14, 1908, p. 2. See also Baruch Charney Vladeck, "Grine un gele," *Di yidishe arbeter velt*, Feb. 16, 1909, p. 5; Simon, *Derinerungen fun der yidisher arbeter bavegung* (New York: n.p., 1952), p. 139.

61. Y. Sh. Herts, *Di yidishe sotsyalistishe bavegung in Amerike* (New York: Der Veker, 1954), p. 106; Herts, *50 yor Arbeter-ring in yidishn lebn* (New York: Arbeter Ring, 1950), pp. 65–69; M. Ivenski, "Di role fun bundistishe landsmanshaftn in dem oyfboy fun Arbeter-ring," in S. Volos, ed., *Zamlbukh aroysgegebn tsum finf-un-tsvantsikstn yoresfest fun dem Dvinsker bundistisher brentsh 75 Arbeter-ring* (New York: n.p., 1929), pp. 74–76 (Workman's Circle, Bund Archives, folder 101).

62. Frankel, *Prophecy and Politics*, p. 456.

63. As of 1904 the Socialist Party in New York claimed only 922 members, two-thirds of whom were German-born. Charles Leinenweber, "The Class and Ethnic Bases of New York City Socialism, 1904–1915," *Labor History* 22 (Winter 1981), p. 31. On the state of the Socialist Party's Yiddish-speaking branches during the early 1900s, see Herts Burgin, *Di geshikhte fun der yidisher arbeter bavegung* (New York: United Hebrew Trades, 1915), pp. 612–613, 616–617. By contrast, the Arbeter Ring grew from 4,358 members to almost 39,000 between 1904 and 1910. Yefim Yeshurin, ed., *Arbeter-ring boyer un tuer* (New York: Arbeter Ring Boyer un Tuer Komitet, 1962), p. 426.

64. J. B. S. Hardman, "The Jewish Labor Movement in the United States: Jewish and Non-Jewish Influences," *Publication of the American Jewish Historical Society* 52 (Sept. 1962–June 1963): 105.

65. On the evolution of the Bund's "national" program, see Frankel, *Prophecy and Politics*, pp. 171–257; Jacobs, *On Socialists and "The Jewish Question" after Marx*, pp. 118–141; Henry J. Tobias, *The Jewish Bund in Russia: From Its Origins to 1905* (Stanford: Stanford University Press, 1972), pp. 105–220; and Traverso, *The Marxists and the Jewish Question*, pp. 92–122.

66. Quoted in Maks Koyfman [Max Kaufman], "Di yidishe sotsyalistishe agitatsyons byuro," *Der veker*, Dec. 27, 1930, p. 4.

67. Herts, *Di yidishe sotsyalistishe bavegung in Amerike*, p. 99. Koyfman to Isaac Hourwich, Dec. 24, 1905, YIVO, RG 587, folder 77.

68. Quoted in Herts, *Di yidishe sotsyalistishe bavegung in Amerike*, p. 100; Maks Koyfman, "Di yidishe sotsyalistishe agitatsyons byuro," p. 5.

69. M. Zametkin, "Yidishe opgezundertkeyt," *Tsayt-gayst*, Jan. 18, 1907, p. 8.

70. M. Zametkin, "Opgezundertkeyt in di arbeter bavegung," *Tsayt-gayst*, Feb. 1, 1907, p. 7. See also Herts Burgin, "Vegn a yidisher sotsyalistisher partey," *Tsayt-gayst*, Jan. 18, 1907, p. 4.

71. Maks Koyfman, "Tsi iz noytik a yidishe sotsyalistishe partey," *Tsayt-gayst*, Feb. 8, 1907, p. 17. See also V. Tsukerman, "Iz a yidishe sotsyal-demokratishe partey noytvendik?" *Tsayt-gayst*, Feb. 1, 1907, p. 14.

72. Herts, *Di yidishe sotsyalistishe bavegung in Amerike*, p. 106; Tsivion, "Der

'Bund' af der konvenshon fun der yidisher agitatsyons byuro," *Di yidishe arbeter velt,* Sept. 3, 1909, p. 5.

73. Herts, *Di yidishe sotsyalistishe bavegung in Amerike,* p. 106; Yankev Salutsky, "Unzer arbeter-bavegung un di sotsyalistishe organizatsyonen," *Di tsukunft* (October 1911): 557.

74. A facsimile of the letter is printed in Herman Frank, *A. S. Zaks: Kemfer far folks-oyflebung* (New York: A. S. Zaks Gezelshaft, 1945), p. 86.

75. Ibid., pp. 43, 72–100, 104–110; Moyshe Shtarkman, "Bio-bibliografye fun A. S. Zaks," in B. Ts. Goldberg, ed., *Shtudies in sotsyaler visnshaft: lekoved dem fuftsikstn geburtstog fun A. S. Zaks* (New York: Yidisher Lerer-Seminar, 1930), pp. 184–187.

76. "Vegn Dr. Ben Tsion Hofman," *Dos vort bibliotek,* Jan.–Feb. 1955, pp. 8–9 (Bund Archives, ME-40, folder 39); Kh. Sh. Kazdan, "Dos lebn un shafn fun B. Tsivion" in Tsivion, *Far 50 yor: geklibene shriftn* (New York: A. Laub, 1948), pp. xviii–xxv; M. Osherovitsh, "B. Tsivion (Dr. B. Hofman)," *Di tsukunft* (July 1944): 427–428.

77. "Yid. agitats. byuro," *Di yidishe arbeter velt,* Dec. 11, 1908, p. 2; Herts, *Di sotsyalistishe bavegung in Amerike,* p. 112.

78. Executive of the Jewish Socialist Agitation Bureau, "An entfer tsum 'Forverts,'" *Di yidishe arbeter velt,* March 5, 1909, p. 5.

79. "Yid. agitats. byuro," p. 2; "Der agitatsyons byuro nemt on vikhtike bashlise," *Di yidishe arbeter velt,* Sept. 11, 1908, p. 1.

80. "Fun unzer post," *Forverts,* Feb. 16, 1909, p. 5. See also M. Baranov, "Der griner reformer," *Forverts,* Jan. 15, 1909, p. 4.

81. "Lok-out fun 'Forverts' shrayber," *Der arbeter,* Feb. 27, 1909, p. 1; "Der trobel in *Forverts,*" *Di yidishe arbeter velt,* March 12, 1909, p. 1; "Der 'Forverts' lok-out," *Der arbeter,* March 6, 1909, p. 1; "Unzer entfer," *Der arbeter,* March 13, 1909, p. 1; "Der entfer fun di shrayber," *Der arbeter,* March 20, 1909, p. 1; "Der 'Forverts' lok-out nokh nit geendikt," *Der arbeter,* March 20, 1909, p. 1; "Der shrayber lok-out," *Der arbeter,* March 27, 1909, p. 1; "Der 'Forverts' lok-out kamf," *Der arbeter,* April 10, 1909; "'Forverts' terror," *Der arbeter,* April 17, 1909, p. 1; "Der shrayber lok-out," *Der arbeter,* May 8, 1909, p. 1; "Der shrayber kamf," *Der arbeter,* May 15, 1909, p. 1. Also see A. S. Zaks, *In kamf far a beserer velt: geklibene ksovim vegn sotsyale problemen un revolutsyonere perzenlekhkeytn* (New York: Aroysgegebn fun der A. S. Zaks Gezelshaft: Farlag Idisher Lerer Seminar, 1938), p. 144.

82. Tsivion, "Tsayt-fragn," *Di yidishe arbeter velt,* June 11, 1909, p. 4. See also Tsivion's column under the same rubric in the June 4, 1909, issue.

83. Quoted in Frank, *A. S. Zaks: Kemfer far folks-oyflebung,* p. 119.

84. Ibid., p. 4.

85. Editor [A. S. Zaks], "Di konvenshon fun der Yidisher agitatsyons byuro," *Di yidishe arbeter velt*, July 9, 1909, p. 4.

86. David E. Fishman, "The Politics of Yiddish in Tsarist Russia," in Jacob Neusner, Ernest S. Frerichs, and Nahum M. Sarna, eds., *From Ancient Israel to Modern Judaism*, vol. 4, *The Modern Age: Theology, Literature, History* (Atlanta: Scholars Press, 1989), pp. 159–163.

87. Y. B. Salutsky, "Der yidisher zhurnal," *Di tsukunft* (Jan. 1912): 73.

88. Editor, "Redaktsyonele notitsn," *Di tsukunft* (June 1909): 373–374; *Di tsukunft* (July 1909): 437.

89. "Barikht fun der 'Agitatsyons byuro' konvenshon," *Di yidishe arbeter velt*, Sept. 10, 1909, p. 1.

90. Ibid.

91. It is worth noting that Tsivion was prevented from attending the convention on technical grounds, which raises the question of whether the decision might have gone another way had the anti-*Forverts* bloc been better represented. Zaks, *In kamf far a beserer velt*, pp. 145–148.

92. "Berikht fun der 'Agitatsyons byuro' konvenshon," *Di yidishe arbeter velt*, Sept. 24, 1909, p. 5. See also Herts, *Di yidishe sotsyalistishe bavegung in Amerike*, pp. 113–115, and Zaks, *In kamf far a beserer velt*, pp. 145–148.

93. Jonas Franklin, "The Early Life and Career of B. Charney Vladeck" (Ph.D. diss., New York University, 1972), pp. 30–31; Vladeck, "Grine un gele," p. 5. In fact, Vladeck had been on good terms with the *Forverts* since his arrival in 1908, an event the newspaper celebrated with a front-page announcement and a reception in his honor. Franklin, "The Early Life and Career of B. Charney Vladeck," pp. 64–65, 67–68.

94. A. Sh. [Shiplacoff] to Levinson, Aug. 25, 1910, Bund Archives, M-13, folder 129; Frank, *A. S. Zaks: Kemfer far folks-oyflebung*, p. 131; Zaks to "genosse," Sept. 1 [1910], Bund Archives, M-2, folder 48.

95. M. Vintshevsky, "A yidish-amerikanisher sotsyalistn-bund," *Di tsukunft* (Nov. 1911): 601; A. Y. Shiplacoff, "Di yidishe agitatsyons byuro, ire noytn, un ir konvenshon," *Di yidishe arbeter velt*, April 21, 1911, p. 2; Y. Salutsky, "Di oyfgabn fun der Yidisher sotsyalistisher agitatsyons-byuro," *Di yidishe arbeter velt*, May 20, 1910, p. 4. Also see Tsivion, "Di yidishe velt," *Di tsukunft* (Feb. 1911): 108.

96. Frankel, *Prophecy and Politics*, p. 456.

97. Yeshurin, *Arbeter-ring boyer un tuer*, p. 426.

98. Shakhne Epshteyn, "Di oyfgabn fun der yidisher sotsyalistisher arbeter-bavegung in Amerike," *Di tsukunft* (May 1912): 332.

99. Tsivion, "Tsayt-fragn," *Di yidishe arbeter velt*, Dec. 4, 1908, p. 4, and "Di yidishe agitatsyons byuro," *Di tsukunft* (May 1909): 274–281.

100. Editor [Zaks], "Redaktsyonele notitsn," pp. 297, 298.

101. Epshteyn, "Di oyfgabn fun der yidisher sotsyalistisher arbeter-bavegung in Amerike," pp. 334–336.

102. This summary is based on the following articles: Dr. K. Fornberg, "Di yidishe masn un di yidishe interesn," *Di yidishe arbeter velt*, May 6, 1910, p. 5; Salutsky, "Di oyfgabn fun der yidisher sotsyalistisher agitatsyons-byuro," p. 4; M. Vintshevsky, "Der filadefyer tsuzamenfor," *Di tsukunft* (Sept. 1909): 501–505, and "A yidish-amerikanisher sotsyalistn-bund," pp. 599–603; Editor [Zaks], "Redaktsyonele notistn," pp. 296–298.

103. Shakhne Epshetyn, "Yidishkeyt in der sotsyalistisher organizatsyon," *Di yidishe arbeter velt*, Sept. 27, 1912, p. 2.

104. Ibid.

105. Tsivion, "Yidishkeyt," *Di tsukunft* (July 1911): 390.

106. B. Faygnboym, "Yidishkeyt in der sotsyalistisher bavegung fun Amerike," *Di tsukunft* (June 1912): 393. See also B. Faygnboym, "Alts heyst asimilatsyon," *Di tsukunft* (July 1912): 444–452.

107. Ibid.

108. K. Frumin, "Natsyonaler oder natsyonalistish," *Di tsukunft* (Feb. 1904): 46. Also see A. S. Zaks's five-part series "Natsyonen un natsyonalizm" in *Di yidishe arbeter velt* between Jan. 22, 1909, and Feb. 19, 1909.

109. Tsivion, "Yidishkeyt," *Di tsukunft* (August 1911): 437.

110. Jacobs, *On Socialists and "The Jewish Question" after Marx*, chaps. 1, 5; Traverso, *The Marxists and the Jewish Question*, chap. 4.

111. Epshteyn, "Di oyfgabn fun der yidisher sotsyalistisher arbeter-bavegung in Amerike," p. 333.

112. Tsivion, "Di yidishe agitatsyons byuro," p. 275.

113. David Shannon, *The Socialist Party of America* (New York: Macmillan, 1955), p. 44; John Spargo, ed., *Proceedings: National Convention of the Socialist Party* (Chicago: M. A. Donahue, 1912), p. 244.

114. Ira Kipnis, *The American Socialist Movement, 1897–1912* (New York: Columbia University Press, 1952), p. 275; James Weinstein, *The Decline of American Socialism, 1912–1925* (New York: Monthly Review Press, 1967).

115. "Yidishe sotsyalistishe federatsyon gegrindet," *Di yidishe arbeter velt*, June 7, 1912, p. 4.

116. *Partey buletin*, June 1, 1919, pp. 3, 4, Bund Archives, M-13, folder 60.

117. Y. B. Salutsky, circular to JSF members, July 1, 1915, Bund Archives, M-13, folder 55, p. 2.

118. Y. B. Beylin, "Di natsyonale sotsyalistishe federatsyonen fun der partey," in M. Terman, ed., *Dos yidishe yorbukh* (New York: Yidishe Sotsyalistishe Federatsye, 1915), p. 51; Dr. Max Goldfarb, "Di yidishe sotsyalistishe federatsye

in Amerike," *Di tsukunft* (Aug. 1914): 799. See also Solomon, *Derinerungen fun der yidisher sotsyalistisher bavegung*, p. 188.

119. Membership, budget, and branches for 1917 are listed in Y. B. Salutsky, ed., *Dos yidishe yorbukh* (New York: Yidishe Sotsyalistishe Federatsye in Amerike, 1918), pp. 112–116.

120. Frank F. Rosenblatt, "The Jewish Socialist Federation," in *The Jewish Communal Register* (New York: Kehillah of New York City, 1918), pp. 1262–1263.

121. Dr. Max Goldfarb, "Di yidishe sotsyalistishe federatsye in Amerike," *Di tsukunft* (August 1914): 799.

122. Herts, *Di yidishe sotsyalistishe bavegung in Amerike*, pp. 144, 154–155.

123. Both publications were edited by a three-man editorial committee, of which Salutsky was the only constant member. Salutsky's wife, Hannah, was also active in the JSF's National Executive Committee. Herts, *Di yidishe sotsyalistishe bavegung in Amerike*, pp. 154–155.

124. Salutsky eased himself into writing in Yiddish by composing his articles in Russian, then using his speaking knowledge of Yiddish to translate them. J. B. S. Hardman [Salutsky], transcribed interview, J. B. S. Hardman Collection, Tamiment Institute, box 38, folder F-399, p. 45.

125. Abraham Shiplacoff described Salutsky as "an outstanding young man [who] understands socialism in its many-sided phases." Shiplacoff to Levinson, n.d. (1910 or 1911), Bund Archives, M-13, folder 129. Pesakh Novik, who was for a time Salutsky's assistant, concurs with Shiplacoff about Salutsky's poor oratorical skills. P. A. N., "Tog-ayn tog-oys," Bund Archives, M-17, folder 153. Simon, *Derinerungen fun der yidisher sotsyalistisher bavegung*, p. 188.

126. Nokhum Khanin, "Di grindung fun Yidishn sotsyalistishn farband," in *Tsen yor sotsyalistishe arbet* (New York: Farlag Veker, 1931), p. 13.

127. N. Kh., "Unzer tsvey yorike tetikeyt," 2 ter yerlikher yubileum harlemer brentsh S.P. fun Yid. sots. fed. fun Amerike (New York, n.p., 1914), pp. 5–6 (Bund Archives, M-13, folder 58); Y. A. Hurvitsh, "Di grindung un tetikeyt fun unzer brentsh," in *Yubileum oysgabe fun finf yerikn yubileum fun Harlemer yidishn brentsh sotsyalistishe partey* (New York: n.p., 1918), pp. 6–8 (Bund Archives, M-13, folder 60).

128. Hurvitsh, "Di grindung un tetikeyt fun unzer brentsh, pp. 6–8.

129. Y. B. Salutsky, "1917," in Salutsky, ed., *Dos yidishe yorbukh*, p. 61; the titles of JSF publications are listed on p. 113.

130. Epshteyn, "Yidishkeyt in der sotsyalistisher organizatsyon," p. 2. His series ran between August 9 and September 27.

131. Tsivion, "20 yor Bund un 5 yor Federatsye," *Di tsukunft* (Nov. 1917): 629.

132. Jonathan Frankel, "The Jewish Socialists and the American Jewish Congress Movement," *YIVO Annual of Jewish Social Science* 16 (1976): 211–216. The following account is based on Frankel's study.

133. Quoted ibid., p. 291.

134. Quoted ibid., p. 292.

4. Purely Secular, Thoroughly Jewish

1. Yankev Levin, "Di veltlekhe yidishkeyt," *Der fraynd* (Oct. 1918): 15–16.

2. Judah L. Shapiro, *The Friendly Society: A History of the Workmen's Circle* (New York: Media Judaica, 1970), pp. 38, 128–133; Yefim Yeshurin, ed., *Arbeterring boyer un tuer* (New York: Arbeter Ring, 1962), p. 426.

3. Daniel Soyer, *Jewish Immigrant Associations and American Identity in New York, 1880–1939* (Cambridge, Mass.: Harvard University Press, 1997), pp. 61–70.

4. On workers' education, see "Workers' Education Enterprises in the United States," in *Workers Education Year Book 1924* (New York: Workers Education Bureau of America, 1924), pp. 184–190; Marius Hansome, "The Development of Workers' Education in the United States," in Theodore Brameld, ed., *Workers Education in the United States* (New York: Harper and Brothers, 1941), pp. 48–66; Susan Stone Wong, "From Soul to Strawberries: The International Ladies' Garment Workers' Union and Workers' Education, 1914–1950," in Joyce L. Kornbluh and Mary Frederickson, eds., *Sisterhood and Solidarity: Workers' Education for Women, 1914–1984* (Philadelphia: Temple University Press, 1984), pp. 39–74.

5. Y. Baskin, "Der shmid, der mashinist un der kirzhner vos hobn gegrindet dem Arbeter-ring," in *Y. Baskin: Tsu zayn 70-yorikn yubiley* (New York: Arbeter Ring, 1951), pp. 151–158; A. S. Zaks, *Di geshikhte fun der Arbeter-ring*, vol. 1 (New York: Natsyonale Ekzekutiv Komite fun Arbeter Ring, 1925), pp. 76, 80–81.

6. Abraham Cahan, *Bleter fun mayn lebn*, vol. 3 (New York: Forverts Asosyeyshon, 1926), p. 422; Zaks, *Di geshikhte*, vol. 1, pp. 74–84, 95–99, 102–106, 123–129.

7. Bernard Lilienblum, transcribed interview, Dec. 6, 1963, YIVO, RG 113, box 3, p. 5; A. Lesin, "Der yubileum fun dem dvinsker bundistishn brentsh Arbeter-ring," in A. Lesin et al., eds., *Zamlbukh: Aroysgegebn tsum tsentn yoresfest fun dem dvinsker bundistisher brentsh 75 Arbeter-ring* (New York: n.p., 1914), p. 4; Zaks, *Di geshikhte*, vol. 1, pp. 190–209.

8. Zaks, *Di geshikhte*, vol. 1, p. 214.

9. Ibid., p. 137. See also Y. A. Benekvit, *Durkhgelebt un durkhgetrakht:*

erinerungen, epizodn un bilder fun der alter haym (New York: Farlag Kultur Federatsye, 1934), pp. 193–194.

10. Zaks, *Di geshikhte*, pp. 135, 134. Faygnboym attributed the Arbeter Ring's inclusiveness to the rank-and-file composition of its membership, which, he claimed, was uninterested in doctrinal debates conducted by intellectuals and was, therefore, more tolerant. This is a dubious explanation, however, in light of the Arbeter Ring's highly ideological admissions policy during the 1890s, when its members were all working class.

11. Letters quoted in Annie Polland, "The Sacredness of the Family: New York's Immigrant Jews and Their Religion, 1890–1930" (Ph.D. diss., Columbia University, 2004), pp. 32, 36. On Rozentsvayg's role in the Arbeter Ring, see Zaks, *Di geshikhte*, vol. 1, pp. 290–293.

12. Anon., *Der Arbeter-ring* (New York: Arbeter Ring, 1906), p. 2.

13. Quoted in Zaks, *Di geshikhte*, vol. 1, p. 215.

14. Y. Rozenberg, "Di tetikeyt fun b. 286, A.R.," in souvenir journal Brisker Branch 286 (New York: Arbeter Ring, p. 3); "Bagrisung fun dem froyen klub," in Y. H. Grinberg, ed., *Suvenir zhurnal: A zhurnal vos dershaynt tsu unzer yetstn banket* (New York: Branch 33, Arbeter Ring, 1937), n.p.; Feni [Fanny] Katsman, "Bagrisung fun der Ekzekutiv fun froyen-klub, br. 498, A.R.," in D. Polishtshok, ed., *Finf un tsvantsik yorikn yubileum fayerung* (New York: Novoselitser besarabier prog. br. 498, 1938); Dr. H. Yudkuf, "Meyvuder tipn," in *Yubileum-oysgabe Meyvud br. 319 A.R.* (Maywood, Ill.: Meyvud Brentsh 319 Arbeter Ring, 1919); p. 15; *Di froyen klubn fun Arbeter-ring* (New York: Arbeter Ring, 1929).

15. Zaks, *Di geshikhte*, vol. 1, pp. 132, 138–140, 155. Information about individual branches can be found in the "Almanac of Branches," Zaks, *Di geshikhte*, vol. 2.

16. Y. Sh. Herts, *50-yor Arbeter-ring in yidishn lebn* (New York: Arbeter Ring, 1950), p. 78.

17. Zeydl Khabotski, "Draysik yor geshikhte fun Brentsh 88," *Bialistoker fraynt* (March 1935): 18; Herts, *50-yor Arbeter-ring in yidishn lebn*, pp. 66, 67, 158.

18. Sam Siegel, "History of Branch 208," typescript, YIVO, RG 1123, box 1, folder 8, p. 1; S. Valas, "Di geshikhte fun br. 75 A.R.," in Lesin et al., eds., *Zamlbukh*, p. 14.

19. Ewa Morawska, *Insecure Prosperity: Small-Town Jews in Industrial America, 1880–1940* (Princeton, N.J.: Princeton University Press, 1996), p. 138.

20. Polland, "The Sacredness of the Family," pp. 34, 44; B. Vladeck, "Der Arbeter-ring in kontri," in *Der Arbeter-ring zamlbukh* (New York: Tsentn Yehrlikhn Konvenshon Konferents, 1910), pp. 17–18. On the country branches, see Herts, *50-yor Arbeter-ring in yidishn lebn*, pp. 81–93.

21. Zaks, *Di geshikhte,* vol. 1, pp. 124, 117–119, 198, and "Almanac," vol. 2, p. i; A. Lesin, "Der Arbeter-ring, zayn vuks, un zayne oyfgabn," in *Der Arbeter-ring zamlbukh,* p. 7.

22. A. S. Zaks, "Tsum 10-yerlekhn yubeleum fun Arbeter ring," in *Der Arbeter-ring zamlbukh,* p. 127.

23. Dr. N. Syrkin, "Der Arbeter-ring un zayne oyfgabn," *Der fraynd* (Feb. 1911): 57.

24. *Report fun Arbeter ring fun dem 1tn yanuar biz dem 31tn detsember 1908 tsu der naynter yerlekher konvenshon* (May 6–9, 1909): 71; Zaks, *Di geshikhte,* vol. 2, p. 505.

25. Moyshe Terman to Moyshe Vinakur, Feb. 17, 1910, Bund Archives, ME-17, folder 227; Moyshe Terman to M. Stern, Jan. 22, 1912, YIVO, RG 231, box 2.

26. Tsivion, "Der Arbeter-ring un zayne kultur-oyfgabn," in *Der Arbeter-ring zamlbukh,* p. 172; B. Vladeck, "Der Arbeter ring in kontri," p. 19.

27. Zaks, *Di Geshikhte,* vol. 2, pp. 481–482.

28. *Arbeter-ring steyt komite ov Nyu york: Report far 1908* (April 1909): 2; *Tsveyter yerlikher report fun der nyu yorker steyt komite Arbeter-ring* (1910): 5; *Driter yerlikher report fun der nyu yorker steyt komite Arbeter-ring* (June 1911): 8. All three reports are located in the Arbeter Ring collection, Bund Archives, RG 1400.

29. The first Educational Committee was composed of two subcommittees: one in charge of "oral propaganda" and the other of "written propaganda." The latter was responsible for publishing *Der fraynd;* in 1911 it was renamed the Press Committee and made independent of the Educational Committee.

30. The lines separating Di Yunge from Di Alte were actually quite fluid: on certain issues, those affiliated with Di Yunge sided with Di Alte, and vice versa. These were not hard factions but shifting alliances. Yitzchak Yankel Doroshkin, "From Zhitkovitch throughout the World: Episodes from My Life," American Jewish Autobiography Collection, YIVO, RG 102, pp. 114–115; Zaks, *Di geshikhte,* vol. 1, pp. 579, 580, 583.

31. By 1918 citywide educational committees operated in Albany, Baltimore, Buffalo, Chicago, Detroit, Hartford, Milwaukee, New York, Newark, Philadelphia, Providence, Rochester, Toronto, and perhaps other cities.

32. These tours were much more economical than single trips: an average of twelve dollars for each lecture rather than thirty to thirty-five dollars. The EC paid five dollars per lecture and branches paid the remainder.

33. Moyshe Terman, ed., *Di velt un di mentsheyt* (New York: Edyukeyshonal Komite fun Arbeter Ring, 1913), p. xv.

34. "Berikht fun der Edyukeyshonal komite," *Der fraynd* (March 1913): 179.

35. Z. Sher, transcribed interview, Oct. 1, 1965, YIVO, RG 113, box 6, pp. 13–14. "Fun der Edyukeyshonal komite," *Der fraynd* (Aug. 1913): 254–255; "Fun der Edyukeyshonal komite," *Der fraynd* (Dec. 1913): 353.

36. "Report fun der Edyukeyshonal komite, *Der fraynd* (May 1914): 42.

37. Zaks, *Di Geshikhte,* vol. 1, p. 211; see advertisement in *Dos naye lebn* (June 1909): n.p.; Abraham Cahan, *Bleter,* vol. 4, pp. 581–588.

38. F.K. [Philip Krants], "Naye bikher," *Der fraynd* (Jan. 1914): 14. Also see A. Koyre, "Fun der yidisher literatur," *Literatur un lebn* (Feb. 1914): 51–53; Dr. Ab. Kaspe, "Ekhte visnshaft un ekhte Yidish," *Literatur un lebn* (May 1914): 435; Dovid Shub, "Vos an arbeter darf lezn," *Der fraynd* (Nov. 1910): 67.

39. M. Baranov, "'Di velt un di mentsheyt,'" *Forverts,* Feb. 22, 1914, p. 4. Also see Av. Epshteyn, "A nayer proyekt far di Edyukeyshonal komite," *Der fraynd* (Nov. 1912): 322.

40. "Velkhe bikher darf men hobn far di members fun Arbeter ring?" *Forverts,* March 9, 1914, p. 7; "Velkhe bikher darf men hobn far di members fun Arbeter ring?" *Forverts,* March 2, 1914, p. 7; "Shlus der debate," *Forverts,* April 1, 1914, p. 5. Also see Ab. Cahan, "Velkhe sortn visnshaftlekhe bikher darfn mir hobn af Yidish," *Forverts,* April 14, 15, and 16, 1914.

41. Miller quoted in Cahan, "Velkhe sortn visnshaftlekhe bikher darfn mir hobn af Yidish," April 14, p. 5; "Velkhe bikher darf men hobn far di members fun Arbeter ring?" *Forverts,* March 19, 1914, p. 7.

42. M. Terman, "Vos iz bilkher?" *Forverts,* March 1, 1914, p. 4.

43. Philip Krants, *Gants Amerike: Di geshikhte fun ale lender in der nayer velt,* 2 vols. (New York: Edyukeyshonal Komite fun Arbeter Ring, 1915).

44. M. Faynston, *Khemye* (New York: Edyukeyshonal Komite fun Arbeter Ring, 1920); Dr. Av. Kaspe, *Fizik* (New York: Edyukeyshonal Komite fun Arbeter Ring, 1917), and *Geologye* (New York: Edyukeyshonal Komite fun Arbeter Ring, 1918); Dr. Y. Levin, *Der treyd-yunyonizm* (New York: Edyukeyshonal Komite fun Arbeter Ring, 1916); Dr. Y. Merison, *Higenye* (New York: Edyukeyshonal Komite fun Arbeter Ring, 1916) and *Fiziologye* (New York: Edyukeyshonal Komite fun Arbeter Ring, 1918); Khane Salutsky, *Dos kind: fizishe dertsiung* (New York: Edyukeyshonal Komite fun Arbeter Ring, 1920); Arn Stolinski, *Di kooperative bavegung* (New York: Edyukeyshonal Komite fun Arbeter Ring, 1920); Tsivion, *Astronomye* (Edyukeyshonal Komite fun Arbeter Ring, 1918); A. S. Zaks, *Botanik: Dos lebn fun flantsn* (New York: Edyukeyshonal Komite fun Arbeter Ring, 1916), and *Politishe ekonomye,* 3 vols. (New York: Edyukeyshonal Komite fun Arbeter Ring, 1918–1920); Dr. Khayim Zhitlovsky, *Der sotsyalizm fun sotsyalistish-revolutsyonern shtandpunkt* (New York: Edyukeyshonal Komite fun Arbeter Ring, 1916).

45. See advertisement in *Der fraynd* (April 1916): inside front cover; Dr. Herman Frank, *A. S. Zaks: Kemfer far folks-oyflebung* (New York: A. S. Zaks Gezelshaft, 1945), pp. 193–194; Z. Reyzen, "Avrom-Simkhe Zaks: 1878–1931," *YIVO Bleter* 2 (Sept. 1931): n.p.

46. Zaks, *Di Geshikhte*, vol. 2, pp. 503–504. For a list of Arbeter Ring publications, see Yeshurin, ed., *Arbeter-ring boyer un tuer*, pp. 451–462.

47. Dr. Kh. Zhitlovsky, "Vegn di 'fertsik protsent,'" *Der fraynd* (June 1913): 200–201.

48. Report in *Der fraynd* (May 1914): 134.

49. S. Yellin, "Di klasn far yidish-shraybn un arifmetik," *Der fraynd* (May 1916): 28.

50. Zaks, *Di Geshikhte*, vol. 2, pp. 499–500.

51. List of lectures in *Der fraynd* (Jan. 1913): 20–21.

52. By comparison, 19,639 people attended the board's Italian lectures. Stephen F. Brumberg, *Going to America, Going to School: The Jewish Immigrant Public School Encounter in Turn-of-the-Century New York City* (New York: Praeger, 1986), p. 170.

53. Nelson R. Beck, "The Use of Library and Educational Facilities by Russian-Jewish Immigrants in New York City, 1880–1914: The Impact of Culture," *Journal of Library History* 12, no. 2 (Spring 1977): 128–149.

54. "Report fun der Edyukeyshonal komite" *Der fraynd* (May 1916): 132; "Barikht fun der Edyukeyshonal komite," *Der fraynd* (May 1917): 59.

55. Dr. D. Veyksel, "Yidishe arbeter un yidishe kintsler," *Di tsukunft* (Sept. 1915): 862.

56. I. Pirozhnikov, "Estetik in dem yidishn lebn," *Der fraynd* (Sept. 1917): 7–9. On Russian Jewish *maskilim* and the "esthetics of ugliness," see Dan Miron, *A Traveler Disguised: The Rise of Modern Yiddish Fiction in the Nineteenth Century* (1973; rept., Syracuse, N.Y.: Syracuse University Press, 1996), pp. 34–66.

57. Saul Raskin, "A shpatsir ibern brookliner museum," *Di tsukunft* (May 1914): 532–538; A. Faynman, "Iber filedelfier lektshurs fun A.R. un lektshurs in algemeyn," *Der fraynd* (March 1916): 15.

58. Sher [Shereshevski], transcribed interview, p. 10.

59. "Berikht fun der Edyukeyshonal komite," *Der fraynd* (Oct. 1914): 25. The committee actually organized two "singing choirs" in 1914, but the one based on the Lower East Side soon disbanded.

60. Ester Feldman, "Brav mit tener," in Ester Feldman, ed., *Finf-un-draysik yoriker yoyvl-bukh* (New York: Arbeter Ring Khor, 1951), n.p.; "Report fun der Edyukeyshonal komite" (1916): 135. See also Mordkhe Yardeyni, ed., *50 yor yidish gezang in Amerike* (New York: Yidish Muzik Farband, 1964).

61. *Suvenir-zhurnal aroysgegebn tsum Arbeter-ring karnaval un maskerad bal* (Dec. 1922): 16.

62. In 1912, about a year after it joined, the Progressive Dramatic Club withdrew from the Hebrew Dramatic League. Yankev Fishman, "Di onheyb yorn fun der Folksbine," in Yankev Fishman et al., eds., *Fertsik yor Folksbine* (New York: Brentsh 555, A.R., 1955), p. 32.

63. "Report fun der edyukeyshonal komite" (1916): 19; *Suvenir-zhurnal aroysgegebn tsum arbeter-ring karnaval un maskarad bal*, p. 19.

64. Quoted in Fishman, "Di onheyb yorn fun der Folksbine," p. 56.

65. Nahma Sandrow, *Vagabond Stars: A World History of Yiddish Theater* (Syracuse, N.Y.: Syracuse University Press, 1977), pp. 254–278.

66. Y. Vayntroyb, "Der 'Arbeter ring' un di sotsyalistishe zuntiks shuln," in B. Fingerhud, ed., *Zamlbukh: Tsum 5-yerikn yoresfest fun dvinsker brentsh 75* (New York: n.p., 1909), p. 12; M.Z. [Mikhail Zametkin?], "Der kamf far di sondey-skools," *Di yidishe arbeter velt*, July 1, 1911, p. 3. Also see M. Bakal, "Kinder dertsyung un kinder-shuln," *Der fraynd* (March 1917): 5.

67. "Sunday Schools That Teach Children Anarchy," *New York Times*, May 8, 1910, p. SM8.

68. "Driter report yerlikher fun der nyu yorker steyt komite Arbeter-ring," *Der fraynd* (June 1911), pp. 6–7.

69. Kenneth Teitelbaum, *Schooling for "Good Rebels": Socialist Education for Children in the United States, 1900–1920* (Philadelphia: Temple University Press, 1993), pp. 61, 155.

70. Ibid., p. 128; Konrad Bercovici, "Sotsyalistishe sondey skuls," *Der fraynd* (Oct. 1911): 531.

71. Teitelbaum, *Schooling for "Good Rebels,"* pp. 145–146.

72. "Driter report yerlikher fun der Nyu yorker steyt komite Arbeter-ring," pp. 6–7.

73. H. Novak, "Dr. Chaim Zhitlovsky un zayn badayt far der yidisher shul bavegung," in Shloyme Berkovitsh et al., eds., *Shul-pinkes* (Chicago: Sholem Aleichem Folk Institute, 1946), pp. 151–154.

74. Harry Garfinkle, "Ideological Elements in the Development of the American Yiddish School Movement" (Ph.D. diss., Columbia University, 1954), pp. 65, 70, 58.

75. A. Glants-Leyeles, "Zikhroynes vegn der yidisher shul-bavegung in Amerike," in Berkovitsch et al., *Shul-pinkes*, pp. 200–215.

76. Quoted in Garfinkle, "Ideological Elements in the Development of the American Yiddish School Movement," p. 72.

77. Tsivion, "Vegn yidishe sotsyalistishe zuntogs-shuln," *Di yidishe arbeter velt*, Aug. 5, 1910, p. 5.

78. Garfinkle, "Ideological Elements in the Development of the American Yiddish School Movement," pp. 101–102.

79. Sh. Niger, *In kamf far a nayer dertsyung* (New York: Arbeter Ring Education Committee, 1940), pp. 39–40; Rakhel Rozhanski, *Zehuiot nifgashot: Poale tsion bitsafon Amerika, 1903–1951* (Sde Boker, Israel: Ben-Gurion University of the Negev Press, 2004), pp. 119–122.

80. Doroshkin, "From Zhitkovitch Throughout the World," p. 115.

81. Krants, editorial note attached to A. Glants, "Der A.R. un di yidishe dertsyung," *Der fraynd* (April 1917): 13; Niger, *In kamf far a nayer dertsyung*, pp. 55–56.

82. Quoted in Niger, *In kamf far a nayer dertsyung*, p. 54.

83. Yoel Entin, "Di naye yidishe dertsyung," in *Yidisher natsyonaler arbeter farband, 1910–1946* (New York: Jewish National Workers Alliance, 1946), pp. 191–194; Niger, *In kamf far a nayer dertsyung*, pp. 50–51.

84. Quoted in Y. Sh. Herts, *Di yidishe sotsyalistishe bavegung in Amerike* (New York: Der Veker, 1954), p. 154.

85. Isaiah Trunk, "The Cultural Dimension of the American Jewish Labor Movement," *YIVO Annual of Jewish Social Science* 16 (1976): 362, 372.

86. L. Bekin, "Di ershte trit tsu efenen a shul," *Der fraynd* (Dec. 1919): 25–26; Y. Levin, "Vi tsu efenen a moderne yidishe shul," *Der fraynd* (Jan. 1918): 11–13.

87. "Fun der Arbeter ring shul bavegung," *Der fraynd* (June–July 1920): 56; *Harlemer yidishe Arbeter-ring shul suvenir-zhurnal* (1921), YIVO, RG 1400, folder 277, p. 20; *Yubileum zhurnal fun 5 yorikn shul-ekzistents* (1924), YIVO, RG 1400, folder 277, p. 1.

88. Of these 61 percent were boys, 39 percent girls; the gap would narrow by five percentage points three years later.

89. "Harlemer yidishe Arbeter ring shul," *Der fraynd* (May 1919): 83; "Fun der Arbeter ring shul bavegung," *Der fraynd* (March–April–May 1920): 82; *Harlemer yidishe Arbeter-ring shul suvenir-zhurnal*, pp. 5, 7–9, 19.

90. Yudl Mark, "Di lernbikher far der yidisher shul in Amerike," in Berkovitsh et al., eds., *Shul-pinkes*, pp. 270–280. Also see Niger, *In kamf far nayer dertsyung*, pp. 184–191.

91. Yankev Levin, "Mentshlekhkeyt," in *Suvenir-zhurnal aroysgegebn tsum Arbeter-ring karnaval un maskarad bal*, pp. 1–4.

92. Ibid., p. 9.

93. *Yubileum zhurnal*, pp. 16–19.

94. Ibid., p. 6.

95. Trunk, "The Cultural Dimension of the American Jewish Labor Movement," p. 372.

5. "We Sought a Home for Our Souls"

1. Quoted in Zosa Szajkowski, *Jews, Wars, and Communism*, vol. 1 (New York: KTAV, 1972), pp. 119, 120, 123–124, 120.

2. Shakhne Epshteyn, *Inem land fun der sotsyaler revolutsye* (New York: Farlag Frayhayt, 1928), pp. 21–42; Dovid Shub, *Fun di amolike yorn*, vol. 1 (New York: TSIKO, 1970), pp. 500–501.

3. Vladeck quoted in Szajkowski, *Jews, Wars, and Communism*, vol. 1, pp. 285, 288; Y. Sh. Herts, ed., *Doyres bundistn*, vol. 1 (New York: Der Veker, 1956), pp. 225–227; A. Lesin, "Moyshe Terman—afn frishn keyver," *Di tsukunft* (Jan. 1918): 1–2.

4. Melvyn Dubovsky, "Success and Failure of Socialism in New York City, 1900–1918: A Case Study," *Labor History* 9 (Fall 1968): 370.

5. Christopher M. Sterba, *Good Americans: Italian and Jewish Immigrants during the First World War* (New York: Oxford University Press, 2003), pp. 160–161.

6. August Claessens, *Didn't We Have Fun!* (New York: Rand School Press, 1953), pp. 88–89; Morris Rosenfeld, "Tsum yidishn arbeter," *Di tsukunft* (Dec. 1917): 676. Dana Frank, "Housewives, Socialists, and the Politics of Food: The 1917 New York Cost-of-Living Protests," *Feminist Studies* 11, no. 2 (Summer 1985): 255–285.

7. "Editoryele notitsn," *Di naye velt*, Aug. 23, 1918, p. 1; Cahan is quoted in Theodore Draper, *The Roots of American Communism* (New York: Viking, 1957), p. 110.

8. Dana Frank, *Purchasing Power: Consumer Organizing, Gender, and the Seattle Labor Movement, 1919–1929* (Cambridge: Cambridge University Press, 1994); David Montgomery, *The Fall of the House of Labor: The Workplace, the State, and American Labor Activism, 1865–1925* (Cambridge: Cambridge University Press, 1987), pp. 370–464.

9. Robert Justin Goldstein, *Political Repression in Modern America: From 1870 to the Present* (Cambridge, Mass.: Schenkman, 1978), pp. 139–163; Robert K. Murray, *Red Scare: A Study in National Hysteria, 1919–1920* (New York: McGraw-Hill, 1955), pp. 210–222.

10. Quoted in Zosa Szajkowski, *Jews, Wars, and Communism*, vol. 2 (New York: KTAV, 1974), p. 8. A Lusk Committee agent, evidently a Yiddish-speaking Jew, described the *Forverts* as "extremely radical. Ardent supporter of Bolshevist and Soviet Russia. Appeals to prejudices and emotions of its readers by presenting news items in a manner that transforms news into propaganda and agitation." Joint Legislative Committee to Investigate Seditious Activities, New York State Archives, L0038, box 2, folder 9.

11. Szajkowski, *Jews, Wars, and Communism*, vol. 2, pp. 11, 16–36; "The Albany Trial—A Digest," *Socialist Review* (April 1920): p. 306.

12. Melech Epstein, *The Jew and Communism 1919–1941* (New York: Trade Union Sponsoring Committee, 1959); Alexander Bittelman, "Things I Have Learned—An Autobiography," manuscript, Alexander Bittelman Collection, Tamiment Institute, New York University, box 1, folder 12, p. 306.

13. James Weinstein, *The Decline of Socialism in America, 1912–1925* (New York: Monthly Review Press, 1967), p. 192.

14. Ira Kipnis, *The American Socialist Movement, 1897–1912* (New York: Columbia University Press, 1952), p. 275; Weinstein, *The Decline of Socialism in America*, p. 194.

15. Dos Passos is quoted in Weinstein, *The Decline of Socialism in America*, pp. 200–201.

16. Ibid., p. 209.

17. Epstein, *The Jew and Communism*, p. 68.

18. Louis Hendin, a Left-Winger, is quoted in Epstein, *The Jew and Communism*, pp. 81–82.

19. Bittelman, "Things I Have Learned," p. 313; Epstein, *The Jew and Communism*, pp. 70–72; Y. Sh. Herts, *Di yidishe sotsyalistishe bavegung in Amerike* (New York: Der Veker, 1954), pp. 190–193.

20. Editor [Yankev Salutsky], "Far a linker partey—kegn a 'linker fligl,'" *Di naye velt*, March 21, 1919, p. 3. See also "Der linker fligl in der sotsyalistisher partey," *Di naye velt*, March 14, 1919, p. 3.

21. Olgin, "An oysgetrakhte velt," *Forverts*, June 7, 1919, p. 3.

22. Tsivion, "Di hoypt oyfgabe fun der bostoner konvenshon," *Di naye velt*, May 30, 1919, p. 5; "Rezolutsyes fun dem 4tn tsuzamenfor fun der yidisher sotsyalistisher partey," *Di naye velt*, June 13, 1919, p. 3. For the Left Wing's response, see its declaration "Far vos mir hobn farlozn di konvenshon," n.d., in the Jewish Socialist Federation Collection, Bund Archives, folder 55.

23. Epstein, *The Jew and Communism*, p. 67. Also see Draper, *The Roots of American Communism*, p. 332; Irving Howe, *The World of Our Fathers* (New York: Harcourt Brace Jovanovich, 1976), p. 327.

24. Draper, *The Roots of American Communism*, p. 138; Weinstein, *The Decline of Socialism in America*, p. 183.

25. Auvo Kostiainin, *The Forging of Finnish-American Communism, 1917–1924: A Study in Ethnic Radicalism* (Turku, Finland: Turin Yliopisto, 1978), pp. 69–96.

26. See Zvi Gitelman, *Jewish Nationality and Soviet Politics: The Jewish Sections of the CPSU, 1917–1930* (Princeton, N.J.: Princeton University Press, 1972), pp. 151–230.

27. Jonathan Frankel, *Prophecy and Politics: Socialism, Nationalism, and the Russian Jews, 1862–1917* (Cambridge: Cambridge University Press, 1981), pp. 184–185.

28. Ibid., p. 185.

29. Draper, *The Roots of American Communism*, p. 206; *Barikht fun der tsveyter konvenshon fun der Yidisher federatsye fun der Komunistisher partey* (1920), American Communist Collection, Bund Archives, folder 62, pp. 5–6; David Prudzon, "Ha-komumizm ve-tenuat ha-poalim ha-yehudit be-Artsot ha-Brit, 1919–1929," Ph.D. diss., Tel Aviv University, 1984, pp. 18–19.

30. Bittelman, "Things I Have Learned," p. 315; Epstein, *The Jew and Communism*, p. 398.

31. Epstein, *The Jew and Communism*, p. 79.

32. *Barikht fun der tsveyter konvenshon fun der Yidisher federatsye fun der Komunistisher partey*, p. 61.

33. Epstein, *The Jew and Communism*, p. 73.

34. *Barikht fun der tsveyter konvenshon fun der Yidisher federatsye fun der Komunistisher partey*, p. 62.

35. Draper, *The Roots of American Communism*, pp. 272, 303.

36. Gitelman, *Jewish Nationality and Soviet Politics*, pp. 261–262, 278 n. 130; Shub, *Fun di amolike yorn*, vol. 2, pp. 571–573; A *Forverts*ist [Dovid Shub?], "Vi azoy Shakhne hot zikh ibergekuliet," *Der veker*, July 1, 1922, pp. 11–12.

37. Arkadieff [Shakhne Epshteyn] to C.E.C of the C.P.A., Oct. 30, 1922, Records of the Communist Party of the United States in the COMINTERN Archives (Fond 515), microfilm edition compiled by the Library of Congress and the Russian State Archive of Social and Political History (Tamiment Library copy), reel 6, delo 100.

38. Kalman Marmor, "Fun der 'Emes' tsu der 'Frayhayt,'" *Di morgnfrayhayt*, April 12, 1922, n.p. (YIVO, RG 295, folder 378).

39. See the following articles by Salutsky: "Zol di Federatsye farblaybn in der Sotsyalistisher partey?" *Di naye velt*, June 4, 1920, pp. 6–8; "Der krizis in der Sotsyalistisher partey," *Di naye velt*, Jan. 21, 1921, pp. 6–8; "For the Third International," *Socialist Review* (April–May 1921): 64–68.

40. "Tsum tsuzamenfor," *Di naye velt*, Sept. 2, 1921, p. 4.

41. Quoted in "Der 'Forverts' bakemft di 'Federatsye,'" *Di naye velt*, Aug. 12, 1921, p. 6; A. Gorelik, "Ver bakemft unz?" *Di naye velt*, Aug. 19, 1921, p. 5.

42. "Der 'Forverts' bakemft di 'Federatsye,'" p. 5. Also see "Tsum tsuzamenfor," p. 4.

43. "Tsum tsuzamenfor," p. 4.

44. "Konvenshon fun Yid. sots. federatsye efent zikh mit redes kegn aroystretn fun der partey," *Forverts*, Sept. 4, 1921, p. 1.

45. "Tsum tsuzamenfor," p. 4.

46. A. Lesin, "Di komunistishe Esho un der yidisher arbeter," *Di tsukunft* (Oct. 1921): 554, 553. Lesin, "Der kundes ha-katan," *Di tsukunft* (Oct. 1921): 608.

47. Epstein, *The Jew and Communism,* p. 94.

48. Nokhum Khanin, "Di grindung fun Yidishn sotsyalistishn farband," in Nokhum Khanin, ed., *Tsen yor sotsyalistishe arbet* (New York: Farlag Veker, 1934), p. 14.

49. Di tsentrale ekzekutive fun der Yidisher sotsyalistisher federatsye in Amerike, *Manifest: tsu di yidishe arbeter in Amerike* (printed in early September 1921 by the Jewish Socialist Federation, but no date given), p. 1 (Jewish Socialist Federation Collection, Bund Archives, folder 55).

50. Ibid., p. 2.

51. Ibid., p. 3.

52. "A rezolutsye fun der *Forverts* Asotsyatsye," *Forverts,* Sept. 19, 1921, p. 4; "Fun vokh tsu vokh," *Di naye velt,* Sept. 16, 1921, p. 2; "A pasiringl," *Di naye velt,* Sept. 23, 1921, p. 3.

53. J. Carr [Ludwig Katterfeld] to Salutsky, Aug. 1, 1921, J. B. S. Hardman Collection, Tamiment Institute, box 38, folder F399.

54. "Tsum tsuzamenfor," p. 6.

55. Yoysef Berson [Shakhne Epshteyn], "Di sibe fun an erfolg," *Der emes,* Sept. 30, 1921, p. 18.

56. "Tsum tsuzamenfor," p. 6; P. Novik, "Tsu a partey—durkh a federatsye!" *Di naye velt,* Aug. 26, 1921, p. 7.

57. Draper, *The Roots of American Communism,* pp. 333–334.

58. Advertisement, *Der groyser kundes,* Oct. 21, 1921, n.p.; Salutsky to Hannah Salutsky, Oct. 26, 1921, J. B. S. Hardman Collection, Tamiment Institute, box 3, folder 15.

59. Quoted in Draper, *The Roots of American Communism,* p. 275; Weinstein, *The Decline of Socialism in America,* chap. 6.

60. Epstein, *The Jew and Communism,* p. 99.

61. Salutsky to Hannah Salutsky, Dec. 21, 1921, J. B. S. Hardman Collection, Tamiment Institute, box 3, folder 15.

62. J. B. S. Hardman [Salutsky], transcribed interview, June 23, 1962, J. B. S. Hardman Collection, Tamiment Institute, box 6, folder 474, p. 57; Alexander Bittelman, "Things I Have Learned," pp. 351–355.

63. J. Louis Engdahl, "The Workers' Party Is Launched," *Labor Age* 11 (Feb. 1922): 14; Weinstein, *The Decline of Socialism in America,* pp. 258–259.

64. M. Olgin, *A proletarishe partey in Amerike* (New York: Yidisher Sotsyalistisher Federatsye, 1922), pp. 37–41 (Bund Archives, M-13, folder 55).

65. Bittelman, "Things I Have Learned," p. 355. For additional assessments of Salutsky as a political leader, see Khanin, "Di grindung fun Yidishn sotsyalistishn farband," p. 13.

66. Draper, *Roots of American Communism*, p. 342; J. B. S. Hardman [Salutsky], interview, June 23, 1962, p. 55. Salutsky was one of the seven non-Communists on the National Executive Committee.

67. Draper, *The Roots of American Communism*, p. 343.

68. According to Theodore Draper, Salutsky, Olgin, and other JSF members were well aware that the Communist Party would retain its underground status. He bases this conclusion on the fact that the Communist Party had repeatedly stated its position in the press and that Communist negotiators were not given the authority to promise a different policy. Communist Party leaders Alexander Bittelman and James Cannon concur in their recollections. Bittelman, "Things I Have Learned," p. 355; James Cannon, *The First Ten Years of American Communism: Report of a Participant* (New York: L. Stuart, 1962), pp. 105–107; Draper, *The Roots of American Communism*, p. 449 n. 23. Melech Epstein offers a different explanation; he notes that even if the Communists had made clear their intentions to maintain the underground party, it does not necessarily follow that the JSF officially consented to the underground party's control of the Workers' Party. Second, Epstein suggests that certain JSF members (such as Olgin) may have consented to Communist control but did so secretly and in an unofficial capacity. Epstein, *The Jew and Communism*, pp. 101, 410–411 n. 23. There are other reasons to question Draper's interpretation. First, while the Communist position may have been stated in the Communist press, other accounts of the Workers' Party did not make this clear. See Engdahl, "The Workers' Party Is Launched." Second, both Salutsky and Tsivion denied they acquiesced to the Communist position in December 1921. Their denials are certainly consistent with the JSF's unwavering opposition to the Communist Party on this issue from 1920 to 1921. A plausible scenario was that certain Communist leaders, who themselves favored liquidating the underground party apparatus, had unofficially stated or hinted that liquidation would take place after the creation of the Workers' Party. If so, then some JSF leaders might have been led to believe that the underground party would be dismantled shortly. That was perhaps a naive hope or an unwise approach to political negotiations, but it does not mean that JSF leaders knew in advance that the Communists intended to maintain their underground party and use it to control the Workers' Party.

69. "Unzer 'Frayhayt' yontev in Leksington Opera Hoyz," *Di frayhayt*, April 3, 1922, p. 6.

70. "Der 25-yoriker yubileum fun 'Forverts,'" *Di frayhayt*, April 23, 1922, p. 4.

71. B. Rozman [Tsivion], "Unzere yidishe oyfgabn," *Di frayhayt,* April 2, 1922, p. 6.

72. "A bagrisung fun M. Vintshevsky," *Di frayhayt,* April 2, 1922, p. 1.

73. Mordkhe Schaechter, *Fun folkshprakh tsu kulturshprakh: an iberblik af der historye funem eynheytlekhn yidishn oysleyg* (New York: YIVO, 1999), p. 36.

74. Howe, *World of Our Fathers,* pp. 529–530.

75. "Unzer 'Frayhayt,'" p. 6.

76. Ruth Wisse, *A Little Love in Big Manhattan: Two Yiddish Poets* (Cambridge, Mass.: Harvard University Press, 1988), pp. 105–141.

77. "Unzer 'Frayhayt,'" p. 6.

78. Efrayim Shedletsky, "Moyshe Nadir in der amerikaner yidisher prese," *Gesher* 6 (Nov. 1989): 102–103; Wisse, *A Little Love in Big Manhattan,* p. 13.

79. H. Alshansky, "Rekomendirt oysbeserungen far der 'Frayhayt,'" *Di frayhayt,* Oct. 4, 1922, p. 5; "Lezer fregn," *Di frayhayt,* Oct. 3, 1922, p. 6.

80. Certificate no. 628, dated the third week in May, is located in the Yiddish Press Collection, YIVO, folder 27.

81. Salutsky to Hannah Salutsky, May 28, 1922, J. B. S. Hardman Collection, Tamiment Institute, box 3, folder 15; reports by the Jewish Federation's Executive Committee dated August 8, 1922 (American Communism Collection, Bund Archives, folder 1) and September 6, 1922 (Kalman Marmor Collection, YIVO, folder 455).

82. G. Lewis to Carr (Katterfeld), Jan. 12, 1922, Communist Party Records (Tamiment Library copy), reel 6, delo 100, p. 7; G. Lewis to "Friend," Feb. 2, 1922, Communist Party Records (Tamiment Library copy), reel 6, delo 100, p. 10.

83. Epstein, *The Jew and Communism,* p. 111.

84. Ibid., p. 411 n. 26.

85. Ibid., p. 103.

86. Bittelman, "Things I Have Learned," p. 357.

87. "Unzer 'Frayhayt,'" pp. 1–2; Peysakh Novik, "Tog-ayn tog-oys," Bund Archives, ME-17, folder 153.

88. Salutsky to Hannah Salutsky, April 2, 1922, J. B. S. Hardman Collection, Tamiment Institute, box 3, folder 16.

89. Salutsky, diary entry, April 1, 1922, J. B. S. Hardman Collection, Tamiment Institute, box 7, folder 50.

90. Ibid., April 2, 1922.

91. L. Levi to Salutsky, April 7, 1922; Y. Spektor to Salutsky, April 13, 1922; Rozenshteyn to Salutsky, June 6, 1922, all in J. B. S. Hardman Collection, Tamiment Institute, box 60, folder 40.

92. Hannah Salutsky to Salutsky, Feb. 3, 1922, J. B. S. Hardman Collection, Tamiment Institute, box 3, folder 15.

93. "Report on the United States of America," Communist Party Records (Tamiment Library copy), reel 10, delo 162, p. 107.

94. Minutes of a meeting of the Administrative Council, Nov. 8, 1922, Communist Party Records (Tamiment Library copy), reel 8, delo 144, pp. 8–10.

95. "Statement by the Central Executive Committee of the Workers Party," *The Worker,* Dec. 9, 1922, pp. 1–5; "All Party Federations Condemn Breach of Discipline by Jewish Federation Bureau," *The Worker,* Dec. 16, 1922, p. 7 (photocopies in Noah London Collection, Tamiment Institute, box 1, folder 2).

96. Administrative Council, Workers' Party of America, "Jewish Federation United," *The Worker,* Dec. 30, 1922, p. 10 (photocopy in Noah London Collection, Tamiment Institute, box 1, folder 2).

97. Editor, "Di Yidishe federatsye fun der Vorkers partey nemt zikh tsu der arbet," *Di frayhayt,* Dec. 31, 1922, p. 4.

98. Epstein, *The Jew and Communism,* p. 168.

99. Relevant in this regard is Olgin's conciliatory speech on the opening day of the Jewish Federation's convention. The speech is reprinted under the title "Khaver Olgin's referat vegn der taktisher linye fun der 'Vorkers parti,'" *Di frayhayt,* Dec. 21, 1922, p. 4.

100. P. Yuditsh, "Vos dertseyln di faktn?" *Di frayhayt,* Dec. 10, 1922, p. 4.

101. J. B. S. Hardman [Salutsky], interview, June 23, 1962, p. 58. On this point, see Rafoel Abramovitsh, *In tsvey revolutsyes: Di geshikhte fun a dor,* vol. 2 (New York: Arbeter Ring, 1944), p. 348, and Danyel Tsharni, *A yortsendlik aza* (New York: TSIKO Bikher Farlag, 1943), pp. 290–293.

102. Draper, *The Roots of American Communism,* pp. 389–390; Epstein, *The Jew and Communism,* p. 101.

103. Statement by the Central Executive Committee of the Workers' Party, *The Worker,* Dec. 9, 1922 (Noah London Collection, Tamiment Institute, box 1, folder 2).

104. Bittelman quoted in Epstein, *The Jew and Communism,* 108.

105. Peysakh Novik, transcribed interview by Joel Saxe, June 1987, in possession of author.

106. Cannon, *The First Ten Years of American Communism,* p. 108. Also see Epstein, *The Jew and Communism,* p. 111; Benjamin Gitlow, *I Confess: The Truth about American Communism* (New York: E. P. Dutton, 1940), pp. 160–162; Paul [Pesakh] Novik, transcribed interview, May 26, 1988, Noah London Collection, Tamiment Institute, box 1, no folder number, p. 5.

107. Y. Khaykin, *Yidishe bleter in Amerike* (New York: M. Sh. Shklarski, 1946), p. 270.

108. Salutsky to George Wishniak [Vishnak], Sept. 18, 1923, J. B. S. Hardman

Collection, Tamiment Institute, box 38, folder 399; Nelson Lichtenstein, "The New Men of Power," *Dissent* (Fall 2001): 123–124.

109. Dr. B. Hofman [Tsivion], *Komunistn vos hobn oyfgegesn komunizm* (New York: Levant Press, 1923), p. 5. On Tsivion's resignation from *Di frayhayt* and return to the *Forverts*, see Tsivion to Olgin, n.d., Bund Archives, ME-40, Tsivion folder, and Cahan to Tsivion, Oct. 29, 1923, Bund Archives, ME-40, folder 40.

110. Epstein, *The Jew and Communism*, p. 110.

111. Nathan Glazer, *The Social Basis of American Communism* (New York: Harcourt, Brace, 1961), pp. 46–89; Mark Solomon, *The Cry Was Unity: Communists and African Americans, 1917–1936* (Jackson: University Press of Mississippi, 1998), pp. 22–37.

Epilogue

1. E. Lifschutz, ed., *Bibliography of American and Canadian Jewish Memoirs and Autobiographies in Yiddish, Hebrew, and English* (New York: YIVO, 1970).

2. Jocelyn Cohen and Daniel Soyer, "'To Unburden My Heart': Autobiographies of Eastern European Jewish Immigrants," manuscript in author's possession, pp. 8–41; Virginia Yans-McLaughlin, "Metaphors of Self in History: Subjectivity, Oral Narrative, and Immigration Studies," in Virginia Yans-McLaughlin, ed., *Immigration Reconsidered: History, Sociology, and Politics* (New York: Oxford University Press, 1990), pp. 275–276. Also see Marcus Moseley, "Jewish Autobiography: The Elusive Subject," *Jewish Quarterly Review* 95, no. 1 (Winter 2005): 16–59; Jeffrey Shandler, *Awakening Lives: Autobiographies of Jewish Youth in Poland before the Holocaust* (New Haven, Conn.: Yale University Press, 2002).

3. See David G. Roskies, *The Jewish Search for a Usable Past* (Bloomington: Indiana University Press, 1999); Yosef H. Yerulshalmi, *Zakhor: Jewish History and Jewish Memory* (Seattle: University of Washington Press, 1982).

4. J. B. S. Hardman, "The Needle-Trades Unions: A Labor Movement at Fifty," *Social Research* 27, no. 3 (Autumn 1960): 321–358.

5. Roger Daniels, *Not Like Us: Immigrants and Minorities in America, 1890–1924* (Chicago: Ivan R. Dee, 1997), pp. 101–121; Leonard Dinnerstein, *Antisemitism in America* (New York: Oxford University Press, 1994), pp. 78–104.

6. On Germans in Milwaukee, see Sally M. Miller, "Milwaukee: Of Ethnicity and Labor," in Bruce M. Stave, ed., *Socialism and the Cities* (Port Washington, N.Y.: Kennikat Press, 1975), pp. 41–71. On Finns, see Auvo Kostiainin, *The Forging of Finnish-American Communism, 1917–1924: A Study in Ethnic Radicalism* (Turku, Finland: Turin Yliopisto, 1978); Paul Mishler, "Red Finns, Red Jews:

Ethnic Variation in Communist Political Culture during the 1920s and 1930s,"
YIVO Annual 22 (1995): 131–154.

7. E. Roach, interview, Feb. 17, 1919, David Saposs Papers, Wisconsin State Historical Society, box 21, folder 15; John Frey to Benjamin Schlessinger, July 26, 1920, Benjamin Schlessinger Collection, Kheel Center, Cornell University, box 1, folder 8.

8. Carl Andelin (Jan. 2, 1919), Frank X. Hoschong (Jan. 21, 1919), Michael B. Newman (March 17, 1919), Geo. W. Perkins (Dec. 23, 1918), and R. L. Reeves (Dec. 17, 1918), interviews, David Saposs Papers, Wisconsin State Historical Society, box 21, folder 15; Robert Asher, "Jewish Unions and the American Federation of Labor Power Structure," *American Jewish Historical Quarterly* 65, no. 3 (March 1976): 215–227; John H. M. Laslett, *Labor and the Left* (New York: Basic Books, 1970), pp. 104, 119, 124; Irwin Yellowitz, "Jewish Immigrants and the American Labor Movement, 1900–1920," *American Jewish History* 71, no. 4 (Dec. 1981): 188–217.

9. J. B. S. Hardman, *American Labor Dynamics in the Light of Post-War Developments* (New York: Harcourt, Brace, 1928), p. 10.

10. Melvyn Dubofsky, *When Workers Organize: New York City in the Progressive Era* (Amherst: University of Massachusetts Press, 1968), p. 156; Deborah Dash Moore, *At Home in America: Second Generation New York Jews* (New York: Columbia University Press, 1981), p. 221.

11. Joshua B. Freeman, *Working-Class New York: Life and Labor since World War II* (New York: New Press, 2000), pp. 55–71, 105–142. Freeman does not explicitly credit Jews to the same extent I do, but his evidence justifies that conclusion. For a discussion of how Jews influenced the character of New York, see Eli Lederhendler, *New York Jews and the Decline of Urban Ethnicity, 1950–1970* (Syracuse, N.Y.: Syracuse University Press, 2001), pp. 1–35; Moses Rischin, *The Promised City: New York's Jews, 1870–1914* (Cambridge, Mass.: Harvard University Press, 1962): pp. 236–267.

12. Zvi Gitelman, *Jewish Nationality and Soviet Politics: The Jewish Sections of the CPSU, 1917–1930* (Princeton, N.J.: Princeton University Press, 1972); David Shneer, *Yiddish and the Creation of Soviet Jewish Culture, 1918–1930* (Cambridge: Cambridge University Press, 2004); Robert Weinberg, *Stalin's Forgotten Zion: Birobidzhan and the Making of a Soviet Jewish Homeland* (Berkeley: University of California Press: Judah L. Magnes Museum, 1998).

13. Ezra Mendelsohn, *The Jews of East Central Europe between the World Wars* (Bloomington: Indiana University Press, 1983), pp. 63, 77.

14. Daniel Soyer, "Abraham Cahan's Travels in Jewish Homelands: Palestine in 1925 and the Soviet Union in 1927," in Gennady Estraikh and Mikhail

Krutikov, eds., *Yiddish and the Left: Papers of the Third Mendel Friedman International Conference on Yiddish* (Oxford: Legenda, 2001), pp. 56–79.

15. Alfred Kazin, *Starting Out in the Thirties* (Boston: Little, Brown, 1965), p. 4. Also see Melvyn Dubofsky, *Hard Work: The Making of Labor History* (Urbana: University of Illinois Press, 2000), p. 7; Nathan Glazer, *The Social Basis of American Communism* (New York: Harcourt, Brace, 1961), p. 221 n. 1; Irving Howe, *World of Our Fathers* (New York: Harcourt Brace Jovanovich, 1976), p. 307; Beth Wenger, *New York Jews and the Great Depression: Uncertain Promise* (New Haven, Conn.: Yale University Press, 1996), pp. 105–107. On Jewish working-class life in Brownsville, see Wendell Pritchett, *Brownsville, Brooklyn: Blacks, Jews, and the Changing Face of the Ghetto* (Chicago: University of Chicago Press, 2002), pp. 9–49.

16. Deborah Dash Moore, *To the Golden Cities: Pursuing the American Jewish Dream in Miami and L.A.* (New York: Free Press, 1994), pp. 189–226; Victor Navasky, *Naming Names* (New York: Viking, 1980), pp. 368–369, 408–410; Stuart Svonkin, *Jews against Prejudice: American Jews and the Fight for Civil Liberties* (New York: Columbia University Press, 1997).

17. Judith Kaplan and Linn Shapiro, eds., *Red Diapers: Growing Up in the Communist Left* (Urbana: University of Illinois Press, 1998); Arthur Liebman, "The Ties That Bind: Jewish Support for the Left in the United States," *American Jewish History* 66, no. 2 (Dec. 1976): 285–321. A self-defined Jewish radical student movement arose in the late 1960s, which was often very critical of the New Left's treatment of Israel and anti-Semitism; see Jack Nusan Porter and Peter Dreier, eds., *Jewish Radicalism* (New York: Grove Press, 1973).

18. Report by the Committee on Internal Security, U.S. House of Representatives, *America's Maoists* (Washington, D.C.: U.S. Government Printing Office, 1972), pp. 2–3, 13, 86–87, 148.

19. On connections, interactions, and tensions between old and new Jewish leftists, see Paul Breines, "Germans, Journals, and Jews/Madison, Men, Marxism and Mosse: A Tale of Jewish-Leftist Identity Confusion in America," *New German Critique* 1, no. 20, special issue 2 (Spring–Summer 1980): 81–103; Mordecai S. Chertoff, ed., *The New Left and the Jews* (New York: Pitman, 1971); Irving Howe, *A Margin of Hope: An Intellectual Biography* (San Diego: Harcourt Brace Jovanovich, 1982), pp. 283–327; Maurice Isserman, *If I Had a Hammer . . . The Death of the Old Left and the Birth of the New Left* (New York: Basic Books, 1987), pp. 202–219.

20. Howe, *World of Our Fathers*, p. 323.

Index